D1221426

INTRODUCTION TO PARALLEL COMPUTING

Ted G. Lewis and Hesham El-Rewini
with In-Kyu Kim

PRENTICE HALL, *Englewood Cliffs, New Jersey 07632*

WITHDRAWN
ITHACA COLLEGE LIBRARY

Library of Congress Cataloging-in-Publication Data

Lewis, T. G. (Theodore Gyle)
    Introduction to parallel computing / by Ted G. Lewis & Hesham El-Rewini.
        p.   cm.
    Includes index.
    ISBN 0-13-498924-4
    1. Parallel processing (Electronic computers)   I. El-Rewini,
Hesham.   II. Title.
QA76,58.L48 1992
004'.35--dc20   91-39589
                                                           CIP

This book was acquired, developed, and produced by Manning Publications Co.

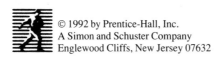

© 1992 by Prentice-Hall, Inc.
A Simon and Schuster Company
Englewood Cliffs, New Jersey 07632

All rights reserved. No part of this book may be
reproduced, in any form or by any means,
without permission in writing from the publisher.

The author and publisher of this book have used their best efforts in preparing this book. These efforts include the development, research, and testing of the theories and programs to determine their effectiveness. The author and publisher make no warranty of any kind, expressed or implied, with regrad to these programs or the documentation contained in this book. The author and publisher shall not be liable in any event for incidental or consequential damages in connection with, or arising out of, the furnishing, performance, or use of these programs.

Printed in the United States of America

10   9   8   7   6   5   4   3   2   1

ISBN 0-13-498924-4

Prentice-Hall International (UK) Limited, *London*

Prentice-Hall of Australia Pty. Limited, *Sydney*

Prentice-Hall Canada Inc., *Toronto*

Prentice-Hall Hispanoamericana, S. A., *Mexico*

Prentice-Hall of India Private Limited, *New Delhi*

Prentice-Hall of Japan, Inc., *Tokyo*

Simon & Schuster Asia Pte. Ltd., *Singapore*

Editora Prentice-Hall do Brasil, Ltda., *Rio de Janeiro*

To Molly, Woofer, and Fuji
Ted Lewis

To my mother, who taught me to give!
Hesham El-Rewini

Contents

12   Parallel Programming Support Environments 347

Preface

Parallel computing is one of the most exciting technologies to achieve prominence since the invention of electronic computers in the 1940s. The shift toward multiple processing units per computer takes its place alongside other major shifts in computing since the Dawning Age of the 1950s; the Age of Mainframes in the 1960s; the Age of Minis in the 1970s; the Age of Personal Computers in the 1980s; and finally, the Age of Parallel Computers in the 1990s. With such a profound influence on all of computing, it is important to understand the fundamentals of parallel computing, and how it changes the way we think about computers. Fundamentals is what this book is about.

New technologies go through several distinct stages on their way to mainstream acceptance. First, there is the experimental stage, when researchers study ways to best apply technology to certain problems. Then, there quickly follows an entrepreneurial stage, when products are manufactured and sold to "early adopters." In stage three, a rapid climb up the logistics growth curve is experienced, while the new technology moves into the mainstream. At the time of this writing, we are at the base of this logistics curve. By the mid-1990s, we will reach its mid-point, and by the year 2000, parallel computing will be as mainstream as personal computers were in 1989.

Information dissemination plays an important role in moving a new idea into the mainstream. Research articles in journals are quickly followed by research monographs, of keen interest to a limited number of researchers. But, for the technology to begin its climb along the logistics growth curve, readable explanations of the new ideas must find their way into the hands of non-experts. Hopefully, this book will serve that purpose.

This book is appropriate for a one-semester first course on parallel computing. Each of the 12 chapters covers a different portion of parallel computing in approximately one week of class meetings. Exercises are given at the end of each chapter to stimulate discussion, and a number of references are listed so the student can dig deeper into each subject. In most American universities, this course will precede other, more detailed courses on parallel processing, parallel programming, and applications of parallel computers.

This book is also appropriate for an introduction to parallel computing for practitioners—experts in the field of computing who are curious to learn more about parallelism, but who do not want to plow through large volumes of research to extract the basic ideas. In other words, this book is also written for the knowledgeable computer engineer, scientist, and student who has not participated in the parallel computing revolution. For this group of people, we have tried to relate the ideas to specific products and techniques that existed in 1990. We have also attempted to survey the emerging techniques and products that we think will become pivotal by the mid-1990s. (As in any crystal ball exercise, we may be totally wrong in our estimation of where parallel computing is headed.)

Our first goal in writing this book has been to provide a survey of all available technologies for parallel computing and to relate them to applications. Therefore, in Chapter 1, we cover the entire field of parallel computing at a very introductory level. In the most succinct manner possible, we describe the different styles or paradigms of parallel computing using several analogies. This establishes a common terminology that we rely on throughout the book.

Parallelism has been touted as a solution to the problem of making computers faster and faster. Indeed, it would seem that there is no limit to the performance of electronic devices as we hear about increases in speed on a daily basis. But, in fact, there are physical limits to switching speeds of components. Sooner or later, these limits will be reached, and parallelism will be the only recourse. However, even before the speed limit is reached, there is an economic motivation to use parallel processing in place of faster and more expensive single-processor systems. Indeed, the economic advantage of low-cost, multiple processing systems was realized in the mid-1980s. Hence, the 1990s were poised for the decade of parallelism simply due to economic forces. But, what do we mean by "performance"? Chapter 2 develops both theoretical and practical measures of performance and shows that there is more to measured performance than raw MFLOPS (million floating point operations per second).

This book is not about parallel processing hardware—the application of parallel hardware to construct parallel computers—but instead, on the essence of parallel computing: hardware plus software plus applications. To gain a solid understanding of the hardware devices used in parallel computing, we provide an overview of parallel processors in Chapter 3. This survey describes the many ways to connect multiple processors together, and shows how each might be used to solve certain problems.

We are especially concerned with the paradigm shift that takes place in software when the target machine is a parallel processor. The traditional programming style and way of thinking about a problem no longer works when the solution can be computed by a collection of parallel parts all cooperating to achieve a final result. Parallel computing is an opportunity to rethink programming from an entirely fresh perspective. Such "new perspectives" are called paradigms. In Chapters 4 through 8, we elaborate on a number of paradigms and show how parallelism is employed in a variety of programming styles. The shared-memory paradigm is perhaps most like traditional programming; the distributed-memory paradigm introduces the concept of message passing; the object-oriented paradigm introduces the concept of a server; the data parallel paradigm relies on the single-instruction-multiple-data (SIMD) model; and the functional dataflow paradigm introduces the concept of a side-effect-free MIMD (multiple-instruction-multiple-data) model.

One of the major differences between serial computing and parallel computing is the notion of optimal resource allocation. In a parallel computer, multiple processors are resources to be carefully allocated and used to advantage. A poorly designed parallel computer application may run slower in parallel than on a serial machine! Thus, careful planning and design are needed to utilize the processors in the most efficient and "optimal" manner. Chapter 9 develops the theory of optimal processor utilization more fully. This is the general problem of scheduling parts of a parallel program onto the processors in such a pattern that the application runs as fast as possible. Chapter 10 continues along this line of reasoning by concentrating on perhaps the greatest opportunity for parallelism—loops. Loops consume much time in serial processing, so they naturally become targets for parallelization.

Facing the prospect of converting billions of lines of serial program code into parallel code has deterred many from using parallel computing technology. Unfortunately, it is not possible to gain the maximal benefit of parallelism without major restructuring of existing software. Chapter 11 describes the technology of program restructuring and parallelization. This difficult problem remains stuck in the world of research, but some progress has been made. Chapter 11 discusses both theory and practical tools for conversion of serial programs into parallel equivalents.

Finally, we would like to combine all that we know about parallelism into one "dream environment" that makes application development simple and easy. Such a parallel programming environment does not exist, but progress is being made along several fronts. Chapter 12 surveys what has been done, what is available, and what is still needed in this vital area.

We have attempted to provide a complete reference to the field of parallel computing without overly burdening the reader with details. Large pieces of parallel program code, benchmarks, and other details are placed in the appendices.

We owe much to the people who have contributed to this work. In particular, to Inkyu Kim, who wrote Chapter 11 and provided many suggestions for other chapters. Youfeng Wu, Shala Arshi, Gary Graunke, Mike Quinn, and others provided sample programs. Norris Smith, Marjan Bace, Mike Evangelist, Bruce Shriver, David Padua, Doug DeGroot, Janice Cuny, John Gustafson, Bruce Boghosian, Shreekant Thakkar, Gregory Riccardi, and Marilynn Livingston all contributed to many improvements in the original manuscript. We are indebted to them for many suggestions and insightful conversations. Responsibility for errors and inconsistencies rests with us.

Ted Lewis, lewis@cs.orst.edu
Hesham El-Rewini, rewini@unocss.unomaha.edu

Chapter 1

What Is Parallel Computing?

In the first computing wave, scientific and business computers were more or less identical—big and slow. This was the "prehistory of computing," where computing had to be employed at any cost. And, even if early electronic computers were not very fast, they achieved speeds that easily exceeded human computers.

The second and third waves brought on mainframes, minis, and finally micros. This diversity of computing caused a number of niches to develop which broadened and deepened the computer industry. Scientific and business computing went their separate ways, and there seemed to be a computer in just about everyone's price range.

But the original power users who pioneered computing continued to emphasize speed above all else. Single-processor supercomputers achieved unheard of speeds beyond 100 million instructions per second, and pushed hardware technology to the physical limits of chip building. But soon this trend will come to an end, because there are physical and architectural bounds which limit the computational power that can be achieved with a single-processor system.

We are now enjoying the Parallel Wave of computing, where performance is enhanced by using multiple processors. What is parallel computing and how does it work? In this chapter we survey the (somewhat overlapping) paradigms of parallel computing, touching on synchronous versus asynchronous, SIMD, MIMD, SPMD, vector/array, systolic array, and dataflow. In each case, a fundamental parallel computing paradigm is illustrated using a hypothetical bank as an analogy with a parallel computer (tellers are parallel processors and customer transactions are tasks to be performed).

Finally, we show that MIMD is the most general form of parallel computing, but that there are certain performance advantages to each of the other forms. As a consequence, it is important to know when and why to apply each one. SIMD and SPMD forms of parallelism appear to be very good at scientific problem solving where speed can be achieved because the data are regular and the calculations are uniform and repetitious. MIMD appears to be appropriate for medium-grained parallelism where communication overhead is not too great. While some scientific computing may benefit from the MIMD style of parallelism, medium-grain problems are typical of business transaction processing applications.

1.1   THE NEXT REVOLUTION IN COMPUTING

Modern society is particularly susceptible to changes in computer technology. The insurance and banking industries were forever changed by the mainframe data processing computer; science and engineering will never be the same after the impact of minicomputers and workstations; and our personal lives have been enriched by personal computers. Computers, and the advances they make, affect everyone. So revolutions in computing make front-page news.

To determine the next step in computing, we must look to the past, because, like most progress in technology, computing evolves through time in an orderly fashion. Once we understand the pattern, we can extrapolate to surmise what will most likely happen in the future.

1.1.1   Modern Prehistory

The Alwac 3E computer was typical of the state of computing in 1963. It could store 32,000 numbers, each with 32 bits, and read punched paper tape at an unheard of 100 frames per second. The Alwac was less powerful than a 1980 personal computer, but it was operated by one person at a time much like a personal computer.

Early computers such as the Alwac had one major disadvantage compared with personal computers: they were expensive. Because of high hardware costs, the first generation of computers had to be shared by a lot of users to justify their cost. It would take 20 years before these simple, easy-to-use machines were to reappear as inexpensive alternatives to centralized computing.

1.1.2   The Age of Dinosaurs

By 1965 the Alwac "personal computer" and its contemporaries had been pushed aside by the radically new IBM System/360 mainframe. Mainframes boosted IBM from medium-sized office equipment manufacturer to global master of the computing industry, and established large centralized computers as the standard form of computing for decades.

The IBM System/360 was the right computer in the right place at the right time. It was in harmony with the instincts of most programmers of the mid-1960s and early 1970s. It had a real operating system, multiple programming languages, and incredibly large disks capable of 10 megabytes of storage! This was the first wave of modern computing, and the world quickly jumped on the mainframe bandwagon (see Figure 1.1).

The System/360 filled a room with boxes and people to run them. Its transistor circuits were reasonably fast. Power users could order magnetic core memories with up to one megabyte of 32-bit words. This machine was large enough and expensive enough to support many programs in memory at the same time, even though the central processing unit had to switch from program to program as if it were juggling balls in a circus. It quickly became the workhorse of business and made "IBM" a household word for "computer."

1.1.3 The Second Wave

The mainframes of the first wave were firmly established by the late 1960s when advances in semiconductor technology made the solid state memory and integrated circuit feasible. These advances in hardware technology spawned the minicomputer era. They were small, fast, and inexpensive enough to distribute throughout the company. Minicomputers made by DEC, Prime, and Data General led the way in defining a new kind of computing: departmental.

By the 1970s it was clear that there existed two kinds of commercial or business computing: (1) centralized data processing mainframes, and (2) decentralized transaction processing minicomputers. The minis expanded the usefulness of computing into engineering, scientific, and non-data processing applications. Computing got broader, and in the process, touched more people's lives (see Figure 1.2).

1.1.4 The Third Wave

When personal computers were introduced in 1977 by Altair, Processor Technology, North Star, Tandy, Commodore, Apple, and many others, they were largely ignored. But then a strange program called VisiCalc suddenly catapulted the original "personal" computing idea of the 1960s into orbit. By 1981, personal computing was becoming so pervasive that IBM entered the "billion dollar baby" market.

Personal computers enhanced the productivity of individuals, and in turn departments. Because big companies are made up of individuals, the productivity improvements of individuals using stand-alone computers was too compelling to ignore. PCs soon became pervasive (see Figure 1.3).

Networks of powerful personal computers and workstations began to replace mainframes and minis by 1990. The power of the most capable "big" machine could be had in a desktop model for one-tenth the cost. But, these individual desktop computers were soon to be connected into larger complexes of computing by networking.

One of the clear trends in computing is the gradual substitution of networks in place of central computers. These networks connect inexpensive, powerful desktop machines to one another to form unequaled computing power. Networks are an early form of parallel computing.

Clearly, there is a limit to the power of a single computer. Even networking has limitations. Within the decade of the 1990s, the maximum switching speed of silicon will be reached and the rapid progress in achieving greater computing speed will level off.

1.2 THE PARALLEL WAVE

What is the next wave of computing? How can machines continue to operate faster and faster in the face of fundamental limits to the hardware? Parallel computing is the answer to both of these questions. The 1990 decade is to parallel computing what the

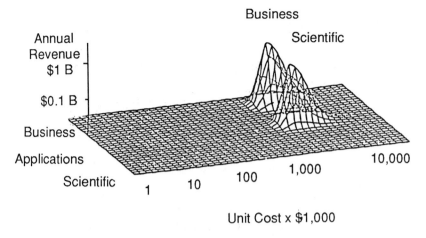

Figure 1.1   Profile of computing circa 1960. Annual revenues vs. unit cost, application type

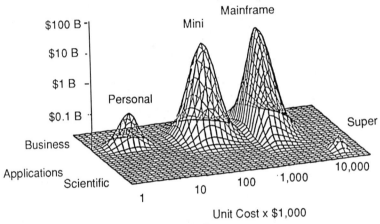

Figure 1.2   Profile of computing circa 1977

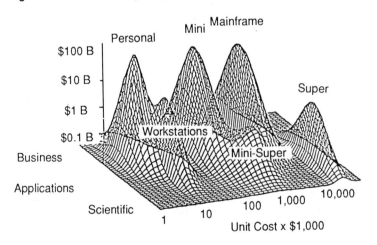

Figure 1.3   Profile of computing circa 1987

1980 decade was to personal computing. But we must first define parallel computing and explore its capabilities.

Parallelism is the process of performing tasks concurrently. To get a better feel for parallel computing, we need to study a number of parallel paradigms. Then we can classify these paradigms in some reasonable way, and use the classification as a basis for an informal theory. This informal theory will be of immense value in determining what approach is best to use in each application we want to put on a parallel computer.

1.2.1 Paradigms of Parallelism

The definition of paradigm has taken on a specific meaning among computer experts. A *paradigm* is a model of the world that is used to formulate a computer solution to some problem. Paradigms give us a context in which to understand and then solve a real-world problem. Because a paradigm is a model, it abstracts the details of the problem from the reality, and in doing so, makes it easier to solve. However, like all abstractions, the model may be inaccurate because it is only an approximation to the real world.

Paradigms are especially important in parallel computing, because we need something to anchor our thoughts when thinking about concurrent processing. In particular, we need a clear way to think about parallelism so we can control the complexity of details that tends to overwhelm parallel programmers.

Some of the more popular paradigms for thinking about parallel computing are shown in Figure 1.4. This is not a complete classification system, but one that includes the major approaches taken by scientists, engineers, and researchers in a variety of fields, who apply parallel computing.

To understand Figure 1.4, we fabricate a purposely contrived example to illustrate the unique and similar features of each paradigm. To the author's knowledge, no real bank operates this way.

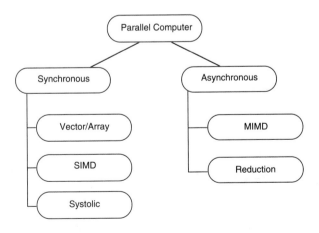

Figure 1.4 Taxonomy of parallel computing paradigms

A banking analogy

We make an analogy between a bank and a parallel computing system (see Figure 1.5). The bank tellers are like computer processors, and customers play the role of program tasks that need to be executed. Having only $n = 1$ teller to help customers is analogous to a uniprocessor system where program tasks are executed serially, one after another. When the number of available tellers is greater than one, the bank operates somewhat like a multiprocessor system.

Suppose there are m customers each waiting to perform a transaction that takes t_i units of time for a single teller to process. If there is only one teller, the customers are served sequentially so the time to serve all customers is $\sum_{i=1}^{m} t_i$.

Now suppose additional tellers return from their break and begin serving more than one customer at a time. If the number of working tellers is equal to the number of customers, $n = m$, then each teller can serve exactly one customer. In this case, the time for serving all customers is $t_{max} = \text{Max}(t_1, t_2, ...t_m)$.

Of course this is the best case because all customers are served concurrently. We call this form of parallelism *trivially parallel*, because it is trivial to find and use the parallelism intrinsic to the problem. In general, parallelism is much more difficult to exploit than we have indicated in this simple example.

If the number of tellers happens to be less than the number of customers, n < m, then some customers end up waiting on others to finish. Suppose for simplicity that there are twice as many customers as there are tellers. Each teller would, on the average, serve two customers. In general, it may be necessary for one teller to do more work than the others. Clearly, if all tellers work at the same rate, then it is best to spread the work evenly across all tellers. Sharing the burden equally is a form of *load balancing*—one of the goals of a well-tuned parallel processor system.

Figure 1.5 The bank analogy: Tellers are like parallel processors, customers are like tasks, transactions are like operations, and accounts are like data in a parallel computer

Even if the load is spread evenly across all tellers, it may be necessary for each teller to serve more than one customer. That is, each processor may be required to do several tasks because there are more tasks than processors. *Grain size* is a measure of computation used to indicate how much work each processor does compared to elementary instruction execution time. Grain size is equal to the number of serial instructions done within a task by one processor.

When there are twice as many customers as tellers, $m = 2n$, the grain size is two because each teller must process two customers. The grain size of each teller might also be increased when a customer requests more than one transaction to be performed by the teller, or when one transaction takes longer to perform than another.

Let the amount of work performed by each teller be the sum total of the time to process k transactions, W_k, where k is approximated by $k = m/n = $ number of customers divided by number of tellers. The time to perform all m transactions in parallel is approximately W_k because we have assumed all tellers work simultaneously. Thus, the elapsed time to process all m customers is the largest W_k over all n tellers.

1.2.2 Synchronous versus Asynchronous Computing

Now consider the following scenario. Customer A, who is using teller #1, wants to deposit $1,000 in a joint account AB with an initial balance of zero. Customer B, who is using teller #2, wants to withdraw $500 from the joint account AB immediately after customer A has finished the deposit transaction. Even though customers A and B are using two different tellers, they cannot be served completely simultaneously. And, because a withdrawal before the deposit would cause an overdraft of the account, coordination is needed to make sure that the deposit takes place before the withdrawal. The two transactions appear to be independent and parallel, but in fact the tellers must coordinate their actions to retain the integrity of the account.

Coordination is required in parallel programs when a task is dependent on others. There are two general methods of coordinating parallel computers: (1) asynchronous and (2) synchronous (see Figure 1.4).

The first approach is to build synchronous or lockstep coordination into the hardware by forcing all operations to be performed at the same time and in a manner that removes the dependency of one task on another. The second form, called asynchronous because there is no lockstep coordination, relies on coordination mechanisms called *locks* to coordinate processors.

Figure 1.4 lists three of the major forms of synchronous parallel computing that we will illustrate, once again using the bank example.

Vector/array paradigm

Suppose the bank tellers organize themselves into a coordinated assembly line of workers (see Figure 1.6). Each teller would be given a very fine-grained task to perform rather than a whole transaction. For example, suppose each transaction is divided into four stages: (1) get the customer's account number, (2) use the account

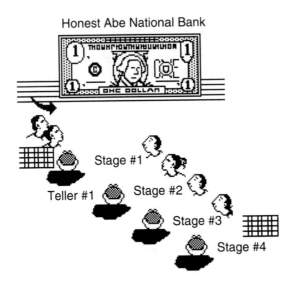

Honest Abe National Bank

Stage #1
Teller #1
Stage #2
Stage #3
Stage #4

Figure 1.6 Vector/array paradigm: The banking analogy with tellers working on one transaction at a time, but as an assembly line of workers

number to validate the customer and his or her balance, (3) update the account by posting the transaction, and (4) take or return cash or checks to or from the customer. The first teller is responsible for repeatedly performing stage 1, teller #2 does stage two, and so forth.

The key to gaining speed with this method is to overlap these fine-grained tasks in time. Teller #1 passes the results of stage #1 on to teller #2, who performs stage #2, passes the results on to teller #3, and so forth. When the pipeline is full, all four tellers are working in parallel, but on different stages. In this scenario, we can process all customers four times as fast with four tellers working on fine-grained tasks.

This form of parallelism has nearly the same effect on transaction processing time as the previous example. The difference is subtle and important. In the previous case, we used large-grained parallelism to achieve a performance improvement. In this case, we use fine-grained parallelism to achieve total processing time of approximately $\sum_{i=1}^{m} \frac{t_i}{n}$. Once again, n is the number of tellers (stages), and we have assumed the simplicity of $n = m$.

This analysis ignores overhead in communicating among the processors, a subject we turn to later. But, the point is that there is more than one way to achieve performance improvement.

From the perspective of a single customer, the response time is still the same once a transaction is started. But, once the processing stages are in full use, four customers are served at the same time, so the total elapsed time to get served is decreased for all customers. Thus, pipelined parallelism is good for handling batches of data when

What Is Parallel Computing? Chapter 1

the operations can be broken down into fine-grained stages. This is what happens in most numerical problems involving matrix and vector calculations. For this reason, the pipeline paradigm is often called *vector/array* processing.

SIMD paradigm

Another form of synchronous parallelism is called SIMD (Single-Instruction-Multiple-Data). In the SIMD paradigm, all processors do the same thing at the same time or else they remain idle. But, control of processors is not the point of SIMD. The data are the important thing in the SIMD paradigm.

Suppose the accounts (data) are physical folders containing the information on each customer which the tellers update during each transaction. For example, when the teller learns what account is to be modified, he or she goes to the bank's vault and reads the balance, updates the total, and replaces the folder. (We exaggerate to make a point.) If each teller does this for each folder, he or she would spend most of the time retrieving the data, and little time actually processing the transactions.

Now, suppose the calculations are driven by the availability of data instead of steps to be carried out by each teller. In other words, we move the data to the tellers

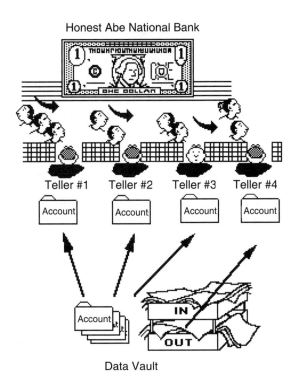

Figure 1.7 SIMD paradigm: The banking analogy in two phases. Phase 1—Partition and distribute account folders. Phase 2—Perform transactions on multiple folders in parallel

so they can efficiently process the transactions. SIMD solves this management problem using two *phases* over and over:

Phase 1. Partition and distribute the data, e.g., identify and distribute the accounts to be updated to each teller, and then,

Phase 2. Process the data in parallel, e.g., perform the transactions in parallel.

These two phases are called *data partitioning* and *distribution*, and *data-parallel processing*, respectively. In fact, the SIMD paradigm is often called *data-parallel programming*.

The SIMD solution is shown in Figure 1.7. First, we partition the account files into two groups based on the type of task that is to be done on the data, one group that is to be updated and all other accounts. Next, the update accounts are distributed to the tellers. Assuming we have enough tellers, we distribute one account folder to each teller. Phase one is now complete, so we move on to the data parallel processing phase.

Each teller holds only one set of data and each customer is directed to the teller holding the customer's folder. All tellers simultaneously perform their data parallel update, or else they remain idle during the update. Still, updates must be synchronized because customers A and B might otherwise overdraft account AB. This added synchronization is provided by a supervisor who determines what everyone does, and when they do it. In this particular case, making all deposits before any withdrawals solves the timing problem between customers A and B.

The efficiency of SIMD depends on how many accounts are processed in parallel. If there is only one deposit, and millions of withdrawals, then there are problems at two extremes. First, SIMD would not be very effective at updating only one deposit folder, and second, it is impractical to hire a million tellers to stand by while waiting for a million simultaneous withdrawals to occur, unless the bank is very large, indeed!

Assume the problem is balanced so that $m/2$ customers want to make deposits, and $m/2$ customers want to make withdrawals. Further, assume there are at least m tellers, and that it takes C time units to partition and distribute the account folders to the m tellers, and another C time units to put the folders back after updates. Under these tight restrictions, the estimated time for the SIMD solution is $2(C + t_{max})$ where t_{max} is the time taken to perform the longest transaction (either a withdrawal or deposit).

Notice how the time to complete all transactions depends on the number of tellers rather than the sum of the transaction times. This is a key ingredient in the SIMD paradigm. The best way to use SIMD is to match the size of the problem with the size of the parallel processor. Here, *size of problem* means how many pieces of data we might want to update, and size of the parallel processor means the number of processors it contains. Clearly, if the problem matches the parallel computer, great speed can be attained.

This form of data parallelism should not be confused with SPMD (Single-Program-Multiple-Data), which is a form of asynchronous parallelism. The sublety lies in noting that SPMD permits simultaneous processing of different data, but without lockstep coordination. In SPMD, processors may execute different instructions at the same time, e.g., different branches of an if-then-else statement.

SIMD is often identified with trivially parallel problems, but this is not the true value of SIMD, because as we have shown, this paradigm is most useful for solving problems that have lots of data that needs to be updated on a wholesale basis. SIMD is an especially powerful paradigm for many numerical calculations that are regular, such as vector and matrix computations. The Thinking Machines Connection Machine and the MasPar parallel computer are examples of SIMD computers. The 1989 Gordon Bell Prize was won by a Thinking Machines CM-1 with 64K parallel processors operating in lockstep synchronization.

The systolic paradigm

The final form of synchronous parallelism is called systolic, because of the even tighter coordination of processors. Invented in the early 1980s by H. T. Kung of Carnegie Mellon University, a systolic parallel computer is a pipelined multiprocessor in which data are distributed and pulsed from memory to an array of processors before returning to memory. A macroscopic view of systolic computing is that of a two-dimensional array of processors with memory at the boundary of the array. It incorporates features of both pipeline and SIMD paradigms.

The major contribution of this mode of parallel computing is that it achieves very high speeds by avoiding input/output bottlenecks. This is usually achieved by circulating data among the processors as much as possible before returning it to memory.

To carry our bank analogy into the systolic array paradigm, we must reorganize the bank tellers as a two-dimensional array and circulate account folders from teller to teller with a minimum number of accesses to memory. Only tellers nearest to the data vault access the account folders, thus limiting the amount of time spent in the bottleneck.

Like the vector/array paradigm, systolic arrays are best suited to fine-grained parallelism, because communication time delays can be kept to a minimum. Even though a systolic computation may require movement of large amounts of data, the transfer is usually masked by concurrent processing steps. However, the efficiency of this approach depends largely on the regularity of the data and/or processing steps.

To realize fine-grained processing in the hypothetical bank, we decompose each transaction into four small steps as shown in Figure 1.6. Then we connect the pipelines to the data vault so that the folders flow from data vault to the first teller in each pipeline, then through additional tellers, and finally back to the vault (see Figure 1.8). This will reduce communication delays caused by excessive memory accesses.

The overall effect of the systolic array organization is to reduce the delay due to input/output and memory references. While new folders are being taken out of the

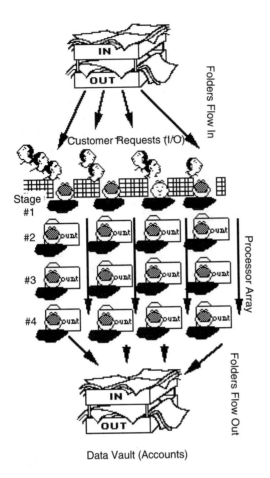

Figure 1.8 Systolic array paradigm: The banking analogy as a combination of pipeline and SIMD parallelism

vault, completed folders can be returned, thus eliminating C time units. Similarly, the overall time to complete a transaction is cut by a factor of 4 because of the 4 pipelined tellers working at the same time on different steps of the transaction. The combined effect is to reduce the time as before: $t_{max} / 4$, where t_{max} is the longest time to perform a transaction.

The synchronization problem between customers A and B can be solved in a variety of ways, but the simplest is to process all deposits before withdrawals as in the SIMD example.

There are limitations to this approach, however. First, the systolic array of tellers are utilized only if they have something to do. This may not always be the case, especially if there are decisions to be made, and the operations to be performed differ, depending on which branch is taken in the decision tree. Secondly, what happens

What Is Parallel Computing?   Chapter 1

when we need only to process a few of the accounts, rather than all of them? How do we partition and distribute the data?

The best utilization of this paradigm is realized when we update all accounts *en masse*. This might occur in a bank, for example, when the interest earned on each account is added to each account balance.

1.2.3 Asynchronous Parallelism

Figure 1.4 contains another family of parallel computing paradigms under the asynchronous heading. *Asynchronous* parallelism is the most general form of parallelism, whereby processors operate freely on tasks, without regard for global synchronization. In place of the lockstep rhythm of the various forms of synchronized parallelism, the asynchronous method relies on locks and explicit control flow.

Once again, we use the bank analogy to illustrate two forms of asynchronous parallelism. Keep in mind that the tellers are processors, customers and their transactions are tasks to perform, and the accounts to be updated are the data to be processed.

The MIMD paradigm

MIMD (Multiple-Instruction-Multiple-Data) means that many processors can be simultaneously executing different instructions on different data. Furthermore, these processors operate in a largely autonomous manner as if they are separate computers. They have no central controller, and they typically do not operate in lockstep fashion.

Most real-world banks run this way. Tellers do not consult with one another, nor do they perform each step of every transaction at the same time. Instead, they work on their own, until a data access conflict arises.

For example, in Figure 1.8, the tellers operate in MIMD mode. Processing of transactions occurs in parallel without concern for timing or customer order. But, customers A and B must be explicitly prevented from simultaneously accessing the AB account balance. In MIMD, such synchronization is enforced by a *synchronization mechanism*.

Suppose the bank uses the simple synchronization mechanism called *mutual exclusion*. This mechanism is usually implemented by a *lock* which prevents all but one access to the data at any instant in time. All other accesses must wait until the mutual exclusion lock is removed by the teller who originally placed the lock on the account.

A simple mutual exclusion lock can be implemented by physically moving each account folder from teller to teller. The contents of the folder cannot be changed by more than one teller at a time, because there is only one copy. However, this can be very inefficient because many accesses are typically benign. Suppose three tellers want to simultaneously read the balance from a folder without making any changes. The time taken to merely look at a balance would increase linearly with the number of tellers wishing to look.

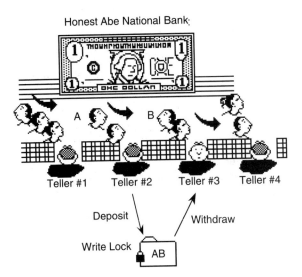

Honest Abe National Bank:

Figure 1.9 MIMD paradigm with locks: The banking analogy when customers A and B both access Account AB. A lock is used to synchronize the two tellers

A second approach might be to keep all folders in the data vault and place one of two possible locks on the folders at any instant in time. A *write lock* is exclusive, and so allows only one writer to change the contents of a write-locked folder. A *read lock* permits any number of readers to look at the folder at the same time, but locks out writers. All other tellers must wait for a write-lock to be removed, and only reading tellers are permitted to simultaneously look at an account. This is called *shared-memory* MIMD, and is the method employed by simple bus-organized multiprocessors.

A third choice is possible which tries to reduce the amount of work needed to fetch the folders from the data vault. This approach uses copies of the folders at each teller's desk. All folders originate from the vault and are returned there at the end of the day. When a teller needs a folder, a copy is made and placed at the teller's desk. The teller can conveniently make references to this folder all day long until another teller attempts to make a change.

There are two ways to change the contents of a folder when one of the tellers wants to update an account balance. The simplest method is to retrieve the folder and all of its copies, in effect destroying all copies and reverting to the original. The original is updated, and then the process starts over again with one original in the data vault. The next time anyone wants to reference the folder, it is once again copied, unless the update is a modification. This method is similar to the methods used in sophisticated shared-memory multiprocessors such as the Sequent Symmetry, and Encore Multimax.

The second major method is to send a message to all tellers to inform them that their copies are out of date, and that they should update each copy to reflect the new balance. This method can be employed in shared-memory systems with very sophisticated *cache memories*, or it can be employed by *message-passing* in distributed-memory machines such as the Intel iPSC/2. In effect, a cache memory is a local memory along with circuitry to automatically implement one of the update mechanisms described above.

The observant reader will still be unsatisfied with this analogy. Locks do not prevent an overdraft of account AB. Even with mutual exclusion, customers A and B can enter the bank in the wrong order, and attempt to withdraw money from a zero balance account. This discrepancy is the responsibility of the parallel programmer, and must be explicitly checked by the application.

MIMD parallelism is best suited to large-grained problems because of the overhead in passing data and control from task to task. For example, MIMD processing in the bank analogy works best when each teller has lots of transactions to perform per customer because there is less time wasted starting and stopping each session (humans are notorious for overhead such as being pleasant, asking about family members, and following a costly termination protocol when saying good-bye—none of which is aimed at completing the transactions at hand).

MIMD is often confused with *dataflow* parallelism, because the dataflow paradigm is frequently employed on MIMD machines. In dataflow computing, tasks are processed in the order dictated by the arrival or availability of their input data. This is a simple model that can frequently be used to provide the appropriate locks on the appropriate data in order to synchronize MIMD tasks, but MIMD is less restricted than dataflow and as a result, leads to more problems.

There are a number of rather interesting control issues that arise in this paradigm, which illustrate why MIMD is not pure dataflow parallelism. For example, suppose at the end of each day, all bank tellers are required to tally the amount of money that was deposited, and the amount that was withdrawn. These totals are then reported to the bank vice president, who must check the grand totals to see if debits equal credits. Under the MIMD paradigm, each teller can operate at his or her own speed, which means they will all finish totaling the day's transactions at different times. Without an explicit control mechanism, tellers might leave for home before the grand total is checked. If debits do not equal credits, then all tellers must return to their desks to find the error.

We can prevent some tellers from going home before other tellers with a barrier. A *barrier* is a synchronization mechanism for coordinating tasks even when data accesses are not involved. The barrier is removed only after the vice president obtains a satisfactory grand total.

The reduction paradigm

Another general parallel paradigm is based on the graph reduction model. Graph reduction achieves synchronized parallelism by a method called *demand-driven dataflow*. A task is enabled for execution by a processor when its results are required by another task which is also enabled. A reduction program consists of reducible expressions which are replaced by their computed values as the computation progresses through time. Most of the time, the reductions are done in parallel. In fact, nothing prevents parallel reductions except the availability of data from previous reductions.

Once again, the bank example serves to illustrate this concept. We have two competing transactions pending in the banking example: a withdrawal and a deposit. Suppose we disable all transaction processing in the bank until a desired result is demanded (hence the name!). Next, suppose customer B arrives at the bank first, and requests that $500 be withdrawn from account AB. This causes the teller to search for an expression to enable and then reduce in order to obtain the desired withdrawal. Finding that customer A is waiting in line to deposit $1,000 in account AB, the bank assigns a teller to customer A before any other waiting customers, and enables the transaction.

After customer A deposits $1,000, the value of this transaction enables the pending transaction on the part of customer B. This allows customer B's withdrawal transaction to be completed, thus concluding the parallel tasks. All other tasks continue to wait until there is a demand for their values. When a demand is either created, or derived from a reduction of some other transaction, the waiting and enabled customers are processed by one or more tellers.

The name *reduction* is derived from the fact that most reduction programs are expressed as dataflow graphs. The computation is carried out by successively reducing the graph to a smaller and smaller graph. The program terminates when the graph is reduced to a single node.

This may seem strange to the reader, so an additional example is offered. This is taken from the world of mathematics. The problem is to compute the familiar formula for the roots of the quadratic equation, $AX^2 + BX + C = 0$:

$$X = \frac{-B \pm \sqrt{B^2 - 4AC}}{2A}$$

This equation is enabled by supplying values to the graph of Figure 1.10, and then successively reducing the graph to a single node. The final graph contains the result of the calculation (see Figure 1.10(g)).

The graph reduction calculation is done in parallel whenever possible. For example, all inputs can be made at once. Then, Figure 1.10(b) is obtained by doing three operations in parallel. One operation is done in Figure 1.10(c), and so forth.

How much parallelism is realized by this method? There are nine operations to be performed in the whole formula, and it took seven reductions to compute the final graph. This yields an improvement of 9/7 = 1.28 times over a purely sequential solution. The question is, does this result in an improvement in speed?

Reduction machines have not been commercialized because of the high overhead in processing graphs. Perhaps someday this elegant solution will become more practical, and therefore widespread. For now, this method provides a theoretical basis for

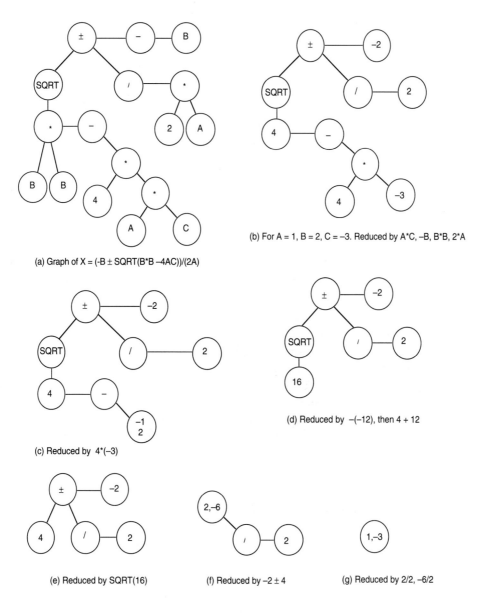

(a) Graph of X = (-B ± SQRT(B*B −4AC))/(2A)

(b) For A = 1, B = 2, C = −3. Reduced by A*C, −B, B*B, 2*A

(c) Reduced by 4*(−3)

(d) Reduced by −(−12), then 4 + 12

(e) Reduced by SQRT(16)

(f) Reduced by −2 ± 4

(g) Reduced by 2/2, −6/2

Figure 1.10   Reduction paradigm: Solution to the quadratic equation as a graph reduction problem

the dataflow paradigm. Given a large-grained problem, and a MIMD paradigm, we can often borrow from the reduction paradigm to guide the implementation of real parallel programs.

1.3 FLYNN'S HARDWARE TAXONOMY

The discussion above is by no means a complete description of all parallel programming paradigms. We have not, for example, covered the object-oriented, declarative/functional, and applicative paradigms. These are mainly based on programming languages, which we will cover in greater detail later.

No book on parallel computing is complete without a historical note on Flynn's taxonomy, which was originally proposed to classify hardware as SISD, SIMD, or MIMD.

In the following summary sections, we describe hardware as SISD, SIMD, or MIMD and relate each to the broader classification scheme presented in Figure 1.4. In general, even software-based paradigms are rooted in Flynn's well-known taxonomy.

1.3.1 SISD

SISD (Single-Instruction-Single-Data) computing is the traditional single-processor model. An application is run on a single processor under control of a single instruction stream (one instruction is taken from the program at a time), and each instruction operates on a single datum at a time.

SISD machines are often given the appearance of parallelism through operating system features for supporting multitasking. Multitasking works much like an FM stereo radio station, which alternates between two signals so quickly that it is impossible for the human ear to detect the switch between left and right speakers. When equipped with time-multiplexing of tasks, a fast SISD machine can support a form of concurrency, but true parallelism is not supportable. Therefore, SISD hardware is incapable of parallel computing.

1.3.2 SIMD

SIMD (Single-Instruction-Multiple-Data) seems restrictive at first, but is perhaps the most useful paradigm for massively parallel scientific computing.

In a SIMD computer, a single instruction stream is acted upon by many processing elements, in lockstep sequence. That is, one instruction counter is used to sequence through a single copy of the program. The data that is processed by each processing element differs from processor-to-processor. Therefore, a single program and a single control unit simultaneously act on many different collections of data.

Many scientific and engineering applications naturally fall into the SIMD paradigm, e.g., image processing, particle simulation, and finite element methods.

To be specific, suppose we want to compute the temperature gradient within a flat, elongated plate with constant temperatures at each end. The standard approach uses finite differences to numerically solve Laplace's partial differential equation in two dimensions. Figure 1.11 shows how we might model the plate as a 3×4 grid of elements where each element represents a temperature region within the plate.

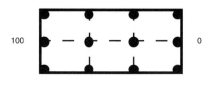

$$T = (N + E + W + S)/4$$

Figure 1.11   Simple finite difference model of a plate with temperature of 100 on one end and 0 on the other end

The finite difference technique applied to the Laplace equation results in NEWS averaging (North + East + West + South) to approximate the temperature at the center point. The NEWS approach is simple enough, and we might wonder how SIMD hardware is useful in this case.

When the NEWS average is applied to every interior point of the plate, we get a system of simultaneous equations. For example, the two interior points in Figure 1.11 can be averaged using the NEWS formula to yield a 2×2 system of equations in the classical form $Ax = b$. Here, x is the unknown temperature at each grid point, A is the matrix of coefficients obtained by averaging, and b is the right-hand side of the resultant equations. In a realistic application, there may be thousands of interior points to average, resulting in a vector, x, of thousands of elements. Solving for x means inverting matrix A, which involves many identical calculations on different data. Thus, SIMD appears to be a good paradigm for this problem.

Each solution to $Ax = b$ is only an approximation to the final temperature within the plate. Repeated application of $Ax = b$ will (under certain conditions) converge to a solution. Thus, in realistic problems involving thousands of points, we not only must process a large number of vector operations, but we must repeat these calculations a great many times.

SPMD

SIMD is an example of *synchronous* data parallel computing. A related *asynchronous* version of data parallel computing is called SPMD (Single-Program-Multiple-Data). SPMD is not part of Flynn's taxonomy. In fact, SPMD is not a hardware paradigm at all; rather, it is the software equivalent of SIMD.

SPMD means running the same *program* but with different data. Because an entire program is executed on separate data, it is possible that different branches are taken, leading to asynchronous parallelism. The processors are no longer doing exactly the same thing, or nothing, in lockstep. Rather, they are busy executing different instructions within the same program. SIMD involves one instruction counter, whereas SPMD involves multiple instruction counters.

The SPMD variation on SIMD is important enough to illustrate with an example where the data are not regular as in a matrix. The lack of regularity in the data can cause each copy of the program to execute a different branch, thus leading to a form of data parallelism that does not require synchronized or lockstep sequencing.

Suppose a consumer wants to know the monthly payment and total cost of a $5,000 loan. But, the payments depend on the interest rate and the term of the loan. The consumer is given these options:

10% for 60 months

9% for 48 months

11% for 36 months

Three monthly payments and three total costs can be computed in parallel by running the same calculations on three different processors at the same time, and comparing the answers. Even for this simple problem, it is not immediately obvious that the least expensive loan is the one at 11% for 36 months. (We can guess that the 10% loan for 60 months yields the lowest monthly payments.)

This is a simple problem so the time taken to compute the three pairs of numbers is insignificant, even on a single-processor personal computer. But suppose the problem involves thousands of options, or the calculations are enormous.

SPMD applications are admittedly trivially parallel, but they abound in real life. SPMD is different than SIMD, because processors are not tightly synchronized; rather, they are synchronized only at the beginning and end of a procedure or section of code that is duplicated on all processors. The processors execute asynchronously within each procedure or identical section of code, to yield a form of pseudo-SIMD operation.

1.3.3 MIMD

MIMD is the most general model of parallelism. Synchronization is achieved explicitly and locally rather than through a global synchronization mechanism. This is flexible, but it also means the software is more difficult to control because more details must be tracked.

Because of the flexibility of MIMD, a variety of programming paradigms may be used, as we illustrated. However, the overriding question is, "when should the MIMD paradigm be employed?" As a generalization, MIMD is useful when the problem allows multiple, heterogeneous tasks to be performed at the same time. This is most likely to occur when either the number of tasks to be performed is not known ahead of time, the tasks perform different operations from one another, or both. Let us examine a simple application to illustrate this idea.

Suppose the problem is to find the largest element of a vector, $V = (12, 5, 21, 25, 34, 2, 8, 16, 10)$. The MAX function might be implemented on a serial computer by sequentially scanning the vector comparing each element with the largest known element. If a larger element is found, then it is designated the largest and the scan continues. This takes approximately N comparisons, where N is the length of the vector.

Now, suppose we divide the job among several MIMD processors. The parallel version of MAX is carried out in two phases as shown in Figure 1.12. In the first phase,

What Is Parallel Computing?   Chapter 1

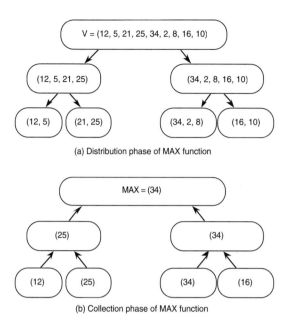

(a) Distribution phase of MAX function

(b) Collection phase of MAX function

Figure 1.12 MIMD implementation of MAX function. Note varying grain size of tasks and two phases of the algorithm

the first processor divides the vector into two (roughly) equal subvectors, and passes them on to two other processors. Each of the two other processors do the same: they divide the vector into roughly equal subvectors and pass them on to other processors. This continues until the final processors receive a vector of length one or two, or we run out of processors.

In phase two, processors (except the leaves in the tree) wait for a local MAX to be handed them, they select the largest element, and pass it back to the processor that gave them the short vector. Repeating this at each processor ultimately yields the desired MAX.

Why is this a MIMD paradigm? First, note how each processor operates independently except for an occasional synchronization (waiting). Processors running short tasks such as the ones evaluating single-element vectors finish before processors running longer tasks. Indeed, the processors may at any instant in time be doing different things, such as waiting, comparing, and sending data.

Second, note that the solution involves an unknown number of tasks when the parallel program starts, and therefore uses an unknown number of processors. We do not know how many levels there will be in the tree until the vector is subdivided a number of times. Of course, we could have computed the number of levels from N, but in general we may not know the value of N until the program begins to run.

This example illustrates two fundamental features of MIMD: (1) the lack of a centralized or global synchronization mechanism, and (2) the generality of heterogeneous tasks operating simultaneously, even though they are performing different operations on different data in different spans of time.

MIMD is general enough to encompass the reduction/dataflow paradigm. In fact, it is general enough to encompass SIMD, because we can emulate SIMD behavior by restricting MIMD through careful programming. However, there may be severe performance penalties inherent in simulation of one form on a machine of a different form.

To complicate matters even more, MIMD machines are typically composed of SISD processors, and each processor is capable of supporting many tasks from different applications at the "same" time. Indeed, most shared-memory multiprocessor systems such as the Sequent and Encore support multiple Unix tasks on each processor, giving rise to a class of machines not covered by Flynn's taxonomy. Such hybrids of the concurrent and parallel processing worlds make very cost-effective transaction processing systems because they are able to dramatically improve response time in a multitasking operating system.

1.4   GRAND CHALLENGES

The grand challenges of the 1990s, as suggested by the High Performance Computing Initiative of the United States Government, are shown in Figure 1.13. Solving these very large scientific and engineering problems will enable technological progress to more rapidly take place. But it is clear that they cannot be solved without parallel computers. Hence, one of the major computational challenges of the 1990s is to increase both memories and speeds of parallel computers to the teraflop (TFLOPS) level. This is one million times the performance of 1989 technology.

These challenging scientific problems are matched by correspondingly challenging business data processing problems characterized by database and transaction processing demands of the airline reservations system, telecommunications processing, and the like. These applications will demand very high processing rates exceeding 100,000 TPS (Transactions Per Second). Clearly, the demands on computing from both scientific and commercial worlds will be present into the next century.

The top end of parallel computing will be driven by the performance requirements of the grand challenges. Current estimates are that the 10 GW (GigaWord) × 1 TFLOPS (Teraflops) goal will be reached around the year 2000. We predict that this form of computing will be dominated by SIMD and SPMD machines.

The mid-level portion of parallel computing will be dominated by transaction processing machines with roughly 100 processors. These machines will be capable of rapid response in the range of 10,000 transactions per second. We predict that this form of computing will be dominated by MIMD machines, probably employing multitasking on each processor.

The low end of parallel computing will encroach on personal computers and deliver roughly 1990 supercomputer performance for 1990 personal workstation

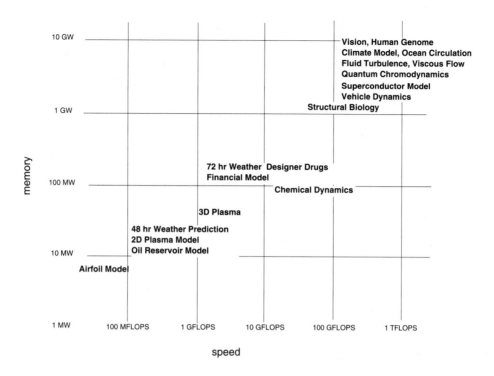

Figure 1.13   Some grand challenges of science and technology, and the computational storage and processing speeds required

prices. These machines will incorporate from 4 to 32 processors and be able to perform high-speed graphics and network multiprocessing. We predict that this form will be marked by special-purpose processors rather than homogenous processing units, e.g., special-purpose graphics, file access, network management, and number crunching processing elements. Limited forms of SIMD, SPMD, and MIMD may be employed to achieve high performance while at the same time maintaining a degree of "general purpose" computing.

1.4.1   Design of Parallel Algorithms

More than three decades have been spent designing serial algorithms for sequential machines. The challenging problems of the future will rely on algorithms appropriate to parallelism. Thus, it is no surprise that much of what we know about algorithms will have to be revisited in the context of parallelism. In the chapters to follow, we develop algorithm design techniques appropriate to each paradigm.

Trivial parallelism is generally exploited by one of two general approaches: 1) supervisor/worker algorithms, or 2) divide-and-conquer algorithms. Supervisor/worker algorithms simply divide the total computational work to be done into equal parts and subtask each part to a different worker. This structure was illustrated in the simple bank example, where tellers are under the direction of a single supervisor.

Divide-and-conquer algorithms work in a treelike fashion, where the root task is divided into two or more parts, and each part is subdivided further into subparts, and so forth until the leaves of the tree are reached. When their work is done, each leaf task passes its results back to its parent, and so forth, until the final result reaches the root task. This approach was illustrated in the MIMD example shown in Figure 1.12.

More elaborate parallelism requires more elaborate algorithms. In general, the goal of parallel algorithm design is to reduce the time complexity of a serial algorithm by a factor of N, where N is the number of processors in the parallel computer. For example, an algorithm that processes N data points in time proportional to N^2 might be reduced to an algorithm that runs in time proportional to N, or more realistically to $N (\log_2 N)$, using a parallel divide-and-conquer algorithm.

In the following chapters, we explore the "how to" questions that surround the design of parallel algorithms on a variety of parallel computers. In most cases, the value of parallel algorithm design is in reducing time complexity by a factor of N, where N is the number of processors in the parallel computer.

PROBLEMS FOR DISCUSSION AND SOLUTION

1 What has been the trend in computing from the following points of view?
(a) physical size of computer,
(b) cost of the hardware,
(c) speed of the hardware,
(d) size of memory and,
(e) number of processors per computer system.

2 Characterize the following applications according to the parallel paradigms described in the chapter:
(a) Large mathematical model, requiring 10 billion matrix calculations to arrive at an answer,
(b) Managing the records of a large insurance company with many inquiries such as client address, amount insured, etc.,
(c) Controlling a factory with an assemblyline of different machines, all working at the same time,
(d) Simulating a physical system such as the traffic at an airport, blood flow through a human body, or circuits in a computer system,
(e) Searching a disk volume for a matching string of characters.

3 Assume that a switching component such as a transistor can switch in zero time. We propose to construct a disk-shaped computer chip with such a component. The only limitation is the time it takes to send electronic signals from one edge of the chip to the other. Make the simplifying assumption that electronic signals travel

300,000 kilometers per second. What must be the diameter of a round chip so that it can switch 10^9 times per second? What would the diameter be if the switching requirements were 10^{12} times per second? Is such a chip feasible?

4 Modify the bank analogy to include consideration of "overhead" incurred while switching from one customer to the next. What feature of a parallel computer does the overhead represent? Repeat the same consideration for the time taken to communicate between customer and teller, and among the tellers themselves.

5 Explain the most important differences between SIMD and systolic array computing, when the systolic array is one-dimensional.

6 Make a list of the unique features of SISD, SIMD, and MIMD. Your list should contain only those features of one paradigm that are not found in any other paradigm.

7 Compare the differences between the following code executed on a SIMD machine versus executed on a SPMD system:

```
gcd (X, Y) :   {Calculate the Greatest-Common-Divisor of X and Y}
while X <> Y Do
  if X > Y then X := X - Y else Y := Y - X
```

Suppose different values of X and Y are spread across 100 processors, and the result of this calculation is 100 greatest-common-divisors of (X, Y). [Try this with two processors, and $X = (52, 24)$, $Y = (12, 64)$.]

8 What is the difference between multitasking and multiprocessing? Concurrency and simultaneity? Synchronous and asynchronous?

9 What is the difference between a lock and a barrier?

10. Give a reduction paradigm solution to the following calculation of A. Show the steps in the reduction in a manner similar to Figure 1.10.

$$A = (1 + i)^k / (1 - V), \text{ for } i = 0.1, k = 2, \text{ and } V = 0.5.$$

References

Duncan, R., "A Survey of Parallel Computer Architectures," *Computer*, 23, 2, pp. 5 – 16, February 1990

Flynn, M. J., "Very High Speed Computing Systems," *Proc. IEEE*, 54, pp. 1901 – 1909, 1966

Kung, H. T., "Why Systolic Architectures?" *Computer*, 15, 1, pp. 37 – 46, January 1982

Chapter 2

Measures of Performance

Parallel computing has always had its skeptics. First, *Grosch's Law* had to be overturned by making computers four times as fast in order to sell them for two times as much. Grosch's Law was repealed by large-scale integration of electronics.

Then, v*on Neumann's bottleneck* had to be dealt with. A von Neumann computer is limited in performance by the narrow connection between the processor and its memory. The most obvious route around von Neumann's bottleneck is to use parallel processors. But, *Amdahl's Law* predicted very limited improvement in performance because the speed of a computer was limited by its slowest (sequential) part. Regardless of the number of parallel processors, the problem could never be solved faster than the naturally occurring serial part would permit.

Amdahl's Law was shown to be invalid in certain very interesting cases—cases where the problem size could be increased and the regularity of the problem could be used to feed as many parallel processors as the problem needed. Thus, large matrix calculations could grow even larger without sacrificing speed, if more and more processors were "thrown at the problem." The *Gustafson-Barsis Law* stimulated great interest once again in parallelism.

This brings up the issue of performance measurement. How should we characterize the performance of a parallel computer when in effect, parallel computing redefines traditional measures such as *MIPS* (Million Instructions Per Second) and *MFLOPS* (Million Floating Point Operations Per Second)? A new measure of performance is needed to relate parallel computing to performance.

The most often quoted measure of parallel performance is the *speedup curve*. This is computed by dividing the time to compute a solution to a certain problem using one processor by the solution time using *N* processors in parallel. While this is a popular measure, it is also a controversial one. In this chapter, we examine several versions of speedup as well as other measures of parallel computer performance.

In the final analysis we can classify or characterize applications according to the kind of parallel computing that best suits the application. For example, *trivially parallel* problems usually can be run on thousands of processors by increasing their size. *Divide-and-conquer* problems can use parallel computers, but in a more restricted manner. And, *communication-bound* problems employ parallelism in an even more restricted manner. Parallelism is also useful for improving response times in transaction processing systems, where absolute speed is not as important as reliability and short response times.

When cost-effective computing is the measure rather than speedup, we learn that parallel processors can be used effectively to increase response time in *transaction processing* applications, and to extend system *throughput* beyond the limits of a single-processor system. Cost-effective computing may not mean supercomputing, but rather, a major return in performance for a low cost. In particular, multitasking multiprocessor systems such as the Sequent Symmetry yield a very cost-effective solution to applications where the number of transactions per second are very high even though the amount of calculation is very low.

Finally, we conclude this chapter with a survey of *benchmarks* or programs designed to measure the performance of a computer in more or less real situations. Benchmarks tell a lot about the actual performance of a computer system, but lack a theoretical basis.

2.1 FASTER THAN THE SPEED OF LIGHT

In the previous chapter we claimed that circuit switching speeds would reach a physical limit in the 1990s that cannot be exceeded by a single processor. Shrinking the size of the processor helps by reducing the time taken by a signal to flow from one part of the circuit to another. If electrons flow at the speed of light, then switching speeds depend on the size of the computer as well as the fundamental characteristics of the chip.

Aside from the limitations of packaging, heat dissipation, and switching speed of semiconductors, fundamentals such as speed of light and size of circuit would seem to be surmountable by adding parallel processors. This, of course, is the ploy behind parallel computing. Is this really the solution? Some skeptics have claimed that there are even more fundamental barriers to speed, which will prohibit increased performance at any cost. In the following, we examine the reasoning behind this skepticism.

2.1.1 Grosch's Law

An often quoted maxim of the 1960s was a "law" credited to Herb Grosch, "To sell a computer for twice as much, it must be four times as fast." Grosch reasoned that the rapid advancement of technology combined with the reluctance of buyers to consume new hardware forced buyer and seller to place a value on performance according to his rule of thumb. Buyers of expensive mainframes, he conjectured, were not impressed by marginal performance improvements. They preferred to wait for a fourfold improvement to upgrade the old machine to a new one. On the other hand, sellers placed a premium on speed, and doubling the price of a machine that ran four times as fast seemed like a fair price.

Grosch's law defied the Keynesian economics of the mainframe world. When twice as much hardware actually cost twice as much, computer hardware designers had to be extremely clever to coax four times the performance out of twice as many transistors. Few designers were up to the task.

2.1.2 Smaller Is Faster

Seymour Cray outsmarted Grosch's Law (for a time) by being uniquely clever. The Cray 1, announced in 1976, was capable of 80 million operations per second (MIPS) and literally defined the word *supercomputer*. Supercomputers hold the enviable reputation of being the fastest computers on earth.

By 1988, the Cray Y-MP had crept through the *gigaflop barrier* (1 gigaflop equals one billion floating point operations per second). To computer engineers, crashing through the gigaflop barrier was psychologically the equivalent of Chuck Yeager breaking the sound barrier.

This speed was largely achieved by using fast circuits and pipelined parallelism. (Heat dissipation and packaging also played a major role in making Cray Y-MPs run fast.) But to be even faster, circuits must be as small as possible, because shrinking reduces the distance information must travel, and hence its transit time. It is no surprise then, that the successors of the Cray 1 have become smaller and smaller.

Even with reduced dimensions, supercomputers must use the fastest possible circuits, e.g., gallium arsenide (which switches three times as fast as silicon) and clock at nanosecond rates. (A ray of light can travel about one meter in three nanoseconds.)

With large-scale integration we can construct small, fast computers that are also less expensive to mass produce. The economic law of Grosch is repealed, and it is possible to construct faster and less expensive computers over time.

Ultimately, switching speeds reach a limit and the size of the circuits cannot be reduced so they are limited by the speed of light. Barring unexpected breakthroughs in biotechnical computing at the molecular level, we will reach the practical limit to the performance of a single computer in the 1990s. Parallel computing will be a necessary design alternative, so we must determine the limits to the parallel approach.

2.1.3 Von Neumann's Bottleneck

The serial computers of the past were created in the image of the so-called *von Neumann machine*. John von Neumann, the great mathematician of the 1940–50 era, made certain assumptions about the structure of computers that may not hold for machines that employ parallelism. These assumptions have been the basis of most single-processor computers of the past several decades. (To be fair to von Neumann, he recognized the value of parallel hardware, but compromised his own designs for practical considerations such as cost and reliability.)

A von Neumann machine consists of a single control unit connecting a memory to a processing unit (see Figure 2.1). Instructions and data are fetched one at a time from

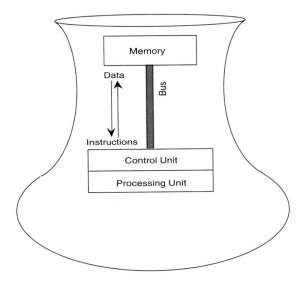

Figure 2.1 von Neumann design for a computer. Connection between processor and memory forms a bottleneck

the memory and fed to the processing unit under control of the control unit. The processing speed of the entire machine is limited by the rate at which instructions and data can be transferred from memory to processing unit. This "narrow" connection between instructions and data held in memory and the single processing unit forms von Neumann's bottleneck.

The bottleneck can be avoided by removing the assumptions implicit in a von Neumann design. First, we can employ many processing units and many memories. We might also increase the number of control units so that many instruction and data streams are active at once. Finally, we could connect these memories and processors together by some sort of *interconnection network* (see Figure 2.2). Such machines are called *non-von*, because they do not follow the von Neumann design.

It is not entirely obvious how to arrange multiple processors into a cooperative non-von system in a way that increases the overall speed of calculation, or reduces the overall cost of processing. But, if such a feat can be achieved, it means that a team of N processors, each computing at some peak rate of T instructions per second, can together compute at $(N*T - V)$ instructions per second, where V is some overhead cost associated with the processor architecture and application being run. Even if the processing speed P of individual processors is relatively low, the effective peak speed of the team might rival that of a supercomputer. Economically speaking, this means a relatively low-cost parallel computer might deliver supercomputer performance at much lower cost than a very expensive single-processor supercomputer. In this sense, a *parallel computer* is a collection of multiple processors that work on a single prob-

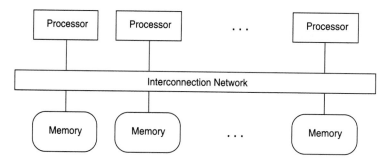

Figure 2.2 General structure of a non-von computer

lem. Such a computer system is capable of achieving tremendous cost/performance benefits.

2.1.4 Amdahl's Law

With such an economic incentive, why haven't non-von machines been built long ago? From the earliest days of computing, designers have been skeptical of the multiplying effect of parallel processors working in harmony on a single problem. In 1967, Gene Amdahl, an IBM designer said:

> For over a decade prophets have voiced the contention that the organization of a single computer has reached its limits and that truly significant advances can be made only by interconnection of a multiplicity of computers in such a manner as to permit cooperative solution...The nature of this overhead (in parallelism) appears to be sequential so that it is unlikely to be amenable to parallel processing techniques. Overhead alone would then place an upper limit on throughput of five to seven times the sequential processing rate, even if the housekeeping were done in a separate processor...At any point in time it is difficult to foresee how the previous bottlenecks in a sequential computer will be effectively overcome.

Known as *Amdahl's Law*, this advice has been quantified into a formula by a number of people who have used it as the major reason why parallel computing cannot defy Grosch's Law. The following is one such derivation.

Suppose we construct a parallel computer from N processors interconnected by some as yet unknown scheme (see Figure 2.2). The purpose of this non-von machine is to run a program consisting of naturally occurring parallel and serial parts. In fact, suppose β is the fraction of the program that is "naturally serial," and $(1-\beta)$ is the fraction of the program that is "naturally parallel." The definition of "naturally serial and parallel" will remain purposely vague for the moment. We want to know how much of an improvement is theoretically possible in the best case, ignoring overhead and communication costs.

Let S be the *speedup* achieved by using N processors instead of one processor to solve the problem. We define S as follows:

$$S = T(1) / T(N)$$

where $T(j)$ is the time taken to solve the problem using j processors.

The serial part of the program can be computed in time equal to $\beta T(1)$, and the parallel part of the program in time $(1-\beta) T(1)/N$, because we assume the ideal case of "N workers can do the job in fraction $1/N$ of the time of one worker." That is, $(1-\beta)$th of the program can be done by N processors in less time than one processor. Then,

$$T(N) = T(1)\beta + \frac{T(1)(1-\beta)}{N}$$

and by substitution into the equation for S,

$$S = \frac{1}{\beta + \frac{(1-\beta)}{N}} = \frac{N}{\beta N + (1-\beta)}$$

(Amdahl's Law)

Example

Suppose a program consists of $\beta = 0.67$ fractional parts of serial code, and 0.33 fractional parts of parallel code. What is the expected speedup for this program when it is run on $N = 10$ parallel processors?

$S = 1/[0.67 + (0.33/10)] = 1.42$

Amdahl's Law is very pessimistic because it predicts at best a 50% improvement over a single processor using 10 processors. The economic payoff is simply not there for this problem.

Amdahl's Law prevented designers from exploiting parallelism for many years because even the most trivially parallel programs contain a small amount of natural serial code. At $\beta = 10\%$, for example, Amdahl's Law predicts at best a tenfold speedup. This is hardly good news for designers.

2.1.5 The Gustafson-Barsis Law

Amdahl's Law became such a nuisance to vendors of parallel computers that Gordon Bell offered a $1,000 cash prize to anyone who could successfully apply parallel computing to real-world problems. Bell was particularly interested in running "production programs" on parallel computers to demonstrate that they could be used by everyday people on everyday problems.

In 1988 a team of researchers at Sandia Labs won the *Gordon Bell Prize* for parallel processing with a 1,024 processor nCUBE/10. Seemingly, they overthrew Amdahl's Law by achieving a thousandfold speedup on a problem with β in the range of 0.004 to 0.008. Amdahl's Law predicts speedups ranging from 125 to 250 instead of 1,000.

While Sandia researchers are not quite everyday people, the Gordon Bell Prize was won in subsequent years by a number of people who solved a number of extremely practical and real-world problems. It seemed as if Amdahl's Law had finally been repealed. What did these pioneers do?

John Gustafson and Ed Barsis, two of the Sandia researchers who shared in the award-winning breakthrough, derived an alternate to Amdahl's Law to explain how they had won. The key is in observing that β and N are not independent of one another. Gustafson states:

> The expression and graph (for Amdahl's Law) both contain the implicit assumption that $(1 - β)$ is independent of N, which is *virtually never the case.*

Again, starting with the speedup formula, $S = T(1)/T(N)$, Gustafson-Barsis interpreted this law to mean that parallelism can be used to increase the (parallel) size of the problem. That is, if one processor is used, it must compute both the serial part and the parallel part

$$T(1) = β + (1 - β)N$$

But, if N parallel processors are used, the problem can be scaled up so all N parallel processors execute the serial and parallel part of the program, one followed by the other. Adding the serial and parallel part yields unity as shown below.

$$T(N) = β + (1 - β) = 1$$

Substituting into the speedup formula gives the Gustafson-Barsis Law:

$$S = N - (N - 1)β \qquad \text{(Gustafson-Barsis Law)}$$

This formula was derived in exactly the same way as Amdahl's Law, except $T(N)$ is set to one, meaning the problem is scaled up to fit the parallel computer. Contrary to Amdahl's derivation, $T(1)$ is the time to compute both serial and parallel fractional parts of the program on a single processor.

Keep in mind that these formulas ignore communication costs and overhead associated with operating system functions such as process creation, memory management, and message buffering.

In its most elementary form, this law says that a certain kind of parallelism can defeat Amdahl's Law, and therefore, economical supercomputing gains can be realized by parallel processors. In particular, SIMD and SPMD parallelism fit this model.

Example.

Calculate the expected speedup for the previous problem using the Gustafson-Barsis Law. Recall $N = 10$ and $β = 0.67$.

$$S = 10 - (9)(0.67) = 3.97$$

Thus, Gustafson-Barsis predicts over twice the speedup of Amdahl's Law. Does this make sense? A fourfold increase in speed is achieved using 10 processors. Given that 67% of the program contained naturally serial code, this is an encouraging result.

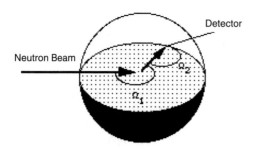

Figure 2.3 Simulated neutron scattering experiment. A beam of neutrons collides with atoms and deflects according to some cross section. How many collisions before each neutron is detected?

2.2 CHARACTERIZING PARALLEL PROGRAMS

Clearly there is a difference between Amdahl's view of parallelism and Gustafson-Barsis's view. How can we characterize these two views of parallelism? To answer this question, and to set the stage for much of what is to come, consider the following simple example taken from experimental physics.

Computational physics is an alternative to theoretical and experimental physics. In the computational approach, experiments are performed only within the memory of a computer. Consider the following such experiment.

Figure 2.3 shows a simulated neutron scattering experiment. A stream of neutrons bombards a substance placed in a vacuum. As neutrons collide with the atoms of the substance, they are deflected at some angle Ω_1. The deflected neutron strikes another atom and is deflected again, and so forth, until being detected at angle Ω_2. We want to count the number of collisions that occur before the detector picks up the neutron. The approach will be to simulate the experiment by "throwing random numbers."

The simulated experiment is carried out by sampling random points from the spherical surface, rejecting the subsequent solid angles according to the scatter cross section curve $s(\Omega)$, and using a suitable solid angle to direct the beam toward a second atom, and so forth.

The simulation program must generate two samples: (1) a solid scattering angle selected by sampling from a distribution uniform over the surface of the unit sphere, $x^2 + y^2 + z^2 = 1$, and (2) angles rejected according to the cross-sectional curve $s(\Omega)$. An empirical curve is obtained by running this simulation for 36 subdivisions of Ω at 5 degrees each. The count of numbers in each subdivision is compared with the expected count for N angles using a chi-square test.

The sampling is done by generating two uniformly random numbers $0 \leq R_1$, $R_2 < 1$, and applying the following transformations to obtain the solid angles on the surface of the sphere:

$$z = 2R_1 - 1$$

$$\Omega = \pi(2R_2 - 1)$$

$$y = \sqrt{1 - z^2}\cos\Omega$$

$$x = \sqrt{1 - z^2}\sin\Omega$$

For this experiment, $s(\Omega) = \pi(1 - \Omega/\pi)$, $0 \leq \Omega \leq \pi$.

This is an ideal computational problem for a parallel computer because of the high degree of parallelism. First, there is fine-grained parallelism in the mathematics, because the two random numbers R_1 and R_2 can be computed in parallel and then z and Ω can be simultaneously calculated, followed by parallel computation of y and x.

The fine-grained parallelism is not likely to gain much in performance, however. A greater gain can be obtained by simultaneously working on the 36 subdivisions separated by 5 degrees. Even greater concurrent operation is possible if we assign each neutron to one processor and let many experiments run at the same time. This is a classic example of the supervisor/worker paradigm of parallel programming.

Many problems in computing fall into the *worker* or *supervisor/worker* characterization. That is, the problem can be solved by a supervisor who delegates pieces of the problem to many workers who each work on a subproblem and then return the result after some time. The supervisor collects the results of each worker's labor and composes an overall result.

The scattering experiment can be solved in parallel by assigning one or more neutrons to each worker who works independently until obtaining a result. Each worker might be further divided into fine-grained parallelism, but we will simplify the simulation by using a large-grain approach. One supervisor is needed to collect the results and output the answer.

We can show the parallel program as a *task graph*, where each bubble corresponds to a task, and each arc corresponds to synchronization and/or communication between tasks (see Figure 2.4). The start and stop tasks are performed by the supervisor, and each subtask is performed by a worker. A task begins as soon as it gets all of its inputs from its incoming arcs, and each task sends its results to other tasks along outgoing arcs. Once started, a task cannot be preempted or halted. Each task runs to completion.

The supervisor/worker model describes a program independent of the computer it is going to run on. We could, for example, perform all of the tasks on a single processor, in which case the result might look like the Gantt chart of Figure 2.5(a).

A *Gantt chart* simply shows which tasks run on which processor, and at what times. A Gantt chart schedule of tasks can be constructed by various means, but once it is

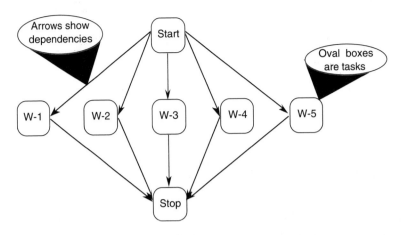

Figure 2.4 Task graph for supervisor/worker program. Tasks W-1,..., W-5 may all start after task "start." "Stop" task must wait for all tasks to complete

obtained, we can analyze the goodness of the parallel processor for a certain program. Matching the tasks to the parallel computer is one of the major challenges of parallel programming which we return to in a later chapter.

The Gantt chart of Figure 2.5(b) illustrates a schedule for the same supervisor/worker program, but running on five processors. Notice that in this chart, some of the tasks are performed in parallel. Hence, the total time to complete all tasks is reduced. How does this chart compare with the predictions of Amdahl's Law and the formula given by Gustafson-Barsis?

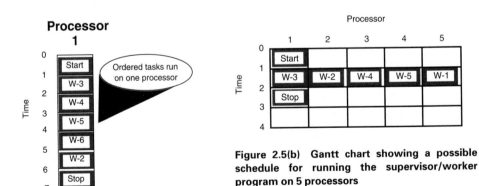

Figure 2.5(b) Gantt chart showing a possible schedule for running the supervisor/worker program on 5 processors

Figure 2.5(a) Gantt chart showing a possible schedule for running the supervisor/worker program on one processor

Measures of Performance   Chapter 2

Example.

What is the speedup realized by the schedule in Figure 2.5(b)? The time scale in Figure 2.5(a) shows one unit of time for all tasks in the supervisor/worker program. Therefore, the serial schedule takes 7 units of time, $T(1) = 7$, and the 5-processor schedule takes 3 units of time, $T(5) = 3$.

$$S = T(1)/T(5) = 7/3 = 2.33$$

Using Amdahl's Law, and noting that the sequential part of the program is only 2 parts out of the total of 7 parts:

$$S = N/(\beta N + 1 - \beta) = 5/[0.2857\,(5) + 0.7143] = 2.33$$

Using the Gustafson-Barsis Law we first claim that β equals 2/7 as before:

$$S = N - (N - 1)\beta = 5 - (4)(0.2857) = 3.86$$

The reader could argue that β is incorrectly calculated by each of these formulas. Instead, β might be computed as the average processor utilization in Figure 2.5(b). That is, processor 1 is used 100% of the 3 time units, while processors 2 through 5 are utilized only 33% of the time. If we use this interpretation, and average over all 5 processors, we obtain an estimate of

$$\beta = [1.0 + 4\,(0.33)]/\,5 = 7/15 = 0.467$$

Computing Amdahl's Law for $\beta = 0.467$ yields a speedup of 1.7, and using the Gustafson-Barsis formula yields 3.13! Indeed, the difference between Amdahl's Law and Gustafson-Barsis' Law will grow as the size of the problem grows because the latter is scalable with problem size. Clearly, there is much disagreement over the meaning of speedup in parallel computers.

2.2.1 Limits to Parallelism

We have made several sound arguments to justify various estimates of speedup for the simple supervisor/worker program, yet the results range from 1.42 to 3.97! Gelenbe analyzed Amdahl's Law and a number of other laws in an effort to understand speedup in more precise terms. His results are merely summarized here.

An extreme-case analysis made by Gelenbe places bounds on the potential improvement in performance obtained by "throwing processors at the problem." The upper bound assumes perfection, while the lower bound assumes diminishing processor utilization as the number of processors increases. Both bounds assume an Amdahl's Law rather than a scalable law such as Gustafson-Barsis have proposed.

$$N/\log_2 N \leq S \leq N$$

The lower bound can be obtained by assuming a problem can be solved in time proportional to N on a single processor, and time proportional to $\log_2 N$ on a parallel processor.

For example, using $N = 5$ as before, the bounds given by Gelenbe's formulas suggest yet another range of possibilities!

$$2.16 \leq S \leq 5$$

Such simple assumptions are unrealistic for real applications on real machines. Even so, why are there so many interpretations of "speedup"? Differences in measuring speedup stem from assumptions that may be valid in one parallel program, but invalid in another. The most obvious source is the imbalance of processor utilization as illustrated by Figure 2.5(b). Processor one is doing most of the work, while the others stand idle 67% of the time.

A second source of inefficiency is in communication among processors. The models proposed thus far have not considered the time taken to move data from one processor to another. This will be a major obstacle to gaining speedup in many problems, yet the formulas examined thus far do not consider communication delays.

Gelenbe suggests a speedup formula for communication intensive applications where communication time delays dominate the total elapsed time. Given some expression for communication time as a function of number of processors, N, the anticipated speedup:

$$S \approx 1/C(N)$$

where $C(N)$ is some function of communication overhead among N processors

Example

Suppose $C(N)$ is given by a linear relation, $C = 0.1N + 0.9$ and as before, $N = 5$. A five-processor solution is worse than a single-processor solution. This illustrates how communication delays may cause parallel programs to run slower than serial equivalents.

Furthermore, rapid communication of data may not be enough, as we consider contention for physical links among processors. What happens when two or more tasks on processor j attempt to communicate with two or more tasks on processor $k \neq j$? This is an important issue in the design of parallel hardware and software.

Finally, process creation time may be relatively large in comparison to the work to be done by the process. In this case, communication delays may not be significant when compared with starting up a new process.

Can it be that the von Neumann bottleneck which plagues serial computers also plagues parallel computers in the form of a communication bottleneck? We examine interconnection network topology in greater detail in the next chapter.

2.2.2 Speedup Curves

We have shown that speedup may not imply faster executions of programs. Rather, *speedup* is merely a measure of the application software's utilization of multiple processors. Speedup, as we have defined it here, has become the most straightforward and easily recognized measure of parallel computer utility. But, the original purpose of speedup was to compare the time of the fastest serial program, T^1, with the time of the parallel equivalent of the same program, $T(N)$. This "pure" definition of speedup yields a different meaning, e.g., $S = T^1/T(N)$. But the pure definition is

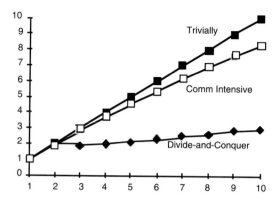

Figure 2.6 Speedup curves measure the utility of parallel computing—not speed. Trivially parallel is shown as a 45-degree line

rarely used in practice due to the difficulty in measuring T^1. Instead, $T(1)$ is used as an approximation, thus adding to the controversy. Practically speaking, speedup is estimated from measurements for $T(1)$ and $T(N)$.

Figure 2.6 illustrates some typical speedup graphs. Each line in Figure 2.6 can be obtained by scheduling and running the same parallel program on j = 1, 2, 3,... 10 processors. At each point in the graph, $S = T(1)/T(j)$ is computed and plotted as shown. In Figure 2.6, $S = N$ for trivially parallel; $S = N/\log_2 N$ for divide-and-conquer parallel; and $S = 1/[0.02 + (1.0/N)]$ for communication intensive programs.

Clearly, the straight line with slope of 45-degrees is from a trivially parallel application, which is ideal. We say the speedup is *linear* if the parallel program falls on this line. If T^1 is actually used instead of the estimate $T(1)$, a plot of speedup may exceed the slope of the 45 degree line! This is called *super-linear* speedup and means the parallel algorithm is superior to the best serial algorithm to the extent that even the parallel algorithm runs faster on one processor.

Until a more elegant measure of the utility of parallel computing is generally accepted, the speedup curve will be employed. Indeed, in the remainder of this book, we often use the approximation $T(1)/T(N)$ to compute speedup.

2.2.3 The Character of Parallel Programs

The speedup measure should be used with caution, but in general, we can place parallel programs into categories based on expected speedups. The following are very general, and should be used as a first-order approximation only.

Trivially parallel

$S = N$. This is rare, and assumes complete parallelism with no overhead due to communication, contention, or serial nature of the application. Examples of trivially parallel programs are: compiling independent procedures of a high-level language program; matrix multiplication; and simple ray-tracing applications in computer graphics.

The Gustafson-Barsis Law illustrates how one might trick a parallel computer into running a serial program much faster on a parallel computer by increasing the size of the problem to fit the parallel computer. Size of problem can be increased in these cases by *data-parallel programming*. For example, a matrix multiply program can be parallelized by computing all row-by-column inner products at the same time (see Chapter 1). Increasing the size of the matrix has little effect as long as we can increase the number of processors to handle the additional inner products.

Divide-and-conquer parallelism

$S \approx N/\log_2 N$. The task graph of divide-and-conquer problems tends to look like a binary tree because of the divide-and-conquer nature of many algorithms. There are many leaves of the tree representing tasks which can be run in parallel. But, as the calculations move up the tree, the number of parallel tasks decreases until only one task, the root task, can be performed. Thus, the speedup tends to be bounded by the logarithm of the number of processors. Examples of this kind of problem abound: merge sorting, summation of a list, searching, and computing the maximum of a list of numbers (see Chapter 1).

Communication-bound parallelism

$S \approx 1/C(N)$; typically, we can estimate $C(N)$ as an inverse relation, e.g., $A + B/N$, or a logarithmic function, e.g., $C(N) = A + B\log_2 N$, where A, B are constants determined by the communication mechanism between processors. If A and B are large relative to N, then it is possible for a parallel program to run slower than an equivalent serial program! Examples of communication-bound programs are large matrix calculations where entire matrices must be constantly passed around to most processors, parallel programs running on local area networks (where A and B are large due to the low bandwidth of the network hardware), and applications where the data is "global" to all processors, and it is being constantly updated by all processors.

Example

Consider a simple divide-and-conquer program like the one shown as a task graph in Figure 2.7(a). The parallel program might be merge sorting, adding up a list of numbers in parallel, or the MAX function. Instead of a supervisor task with many worker tasks as in the supervisor/worker program, this parallel program uses a *hierarchy* of workers and subworkers. Thus, the task graph is a tree.

Each node of the modified task graph is labeled with an identifier number (top portion of node), and an estimated execution time (bottom portion of node). In addition, each arc is labeled with a number representing the delay caused by communication when tasks are located on separate processors. The delays are assumed to be zero in Figure 2.7(a).

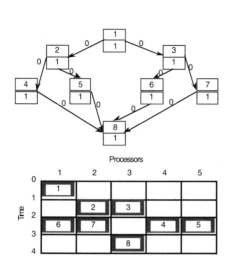

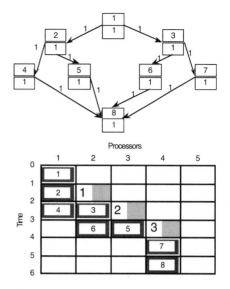

Figure 2.7(a) Divide-and-conquer task graph along with schedule on 5 processors. Note the speedup of 8/4 = 2.0

Figure 2.7(b) Divide-and-conquer task graph along with its schedule on 5 processors. Communication delays are shown as shaded blocks. This schedule yields a speedup of 8/6

The ideal schedule shown in the Gantt chart of Figure 2.7(a) yields a speedup of 2.00. This makes good sense because there are two levels in the hierarchy. Using the divide-and-conquer formula, $S = N/\log_2 N = 2.3$ is a close approximation to this ideal case.

Figure 2.7(b) shows a more realistic model of the divide-and-conquer program. Each arc on this task graph is labeled with a "1" to indicate that it takes one unit of time to communicate between tasks whenever they are located on distinct processors. Clearly, if we put all tasks on one processor, the communication time goes to zero, but the fraction of parallelism also goes to zero! Conversely, if we put all tasks on as many processors as we can run in parallel, the communication time dominates. This paradoxical situation is known as the *minimax problem* of parallel programming, because as we try to minimize communication, we limit parallelism, and as we try to maximize parallelism, we increase delays due to communication overhead.

Figures 2.7(a) and 2.7(b) are identical in every respect except for the communication delays on the arcs. The best schedule for Figure 2.7(b) is a compromise between maximum parallelism and minimum communication overhead. The Gantt chart of Figure 2.7(b) provides a speedup of 1.33. Had we used the communication-bound speedup curve to estimate this value, we might have chosen $C(N) = \log_2 K/N$, where K is the number of tasks. Given $K = 8$ and $N = 5$, we get $S = 5/3 = 1.67$. Again, this seems to be a reasonable approximation for this kind of problem.

2.3   OTHER PERFORMANCE MEASURES

Parallel computers are rated by their speedup, but what about raw speed? Also, the speedup measures described thus far assume a single problem is being solved on a dedicated parallel computer. What about time-shared parallel computing? There are other reasons to employ parallel processors besides running speedup tests!

2.3.1   Single Program Performance

Figure 2.8 lists additional measures of performance. The most obvious is the elapsed time to compute the solution to a single problem as shown in Figure 2.8(a). As the number of processors M is increased, the *elapsed time* should decrease according to the inverse relation 1/M. But of course this does not happen unless the program is trivially parallel and there is no communication overhead.

The problem size graph in Figure 2.8(b) illuminates the Gustafson-Barsis measure in a slightly different manner. Instead of increasing processors, we increase the size of the problem and let the problem determine how many processors to use. For example, suppose the problem is to multiply matrix *A* times matrix *B* to produce matrix *C* using the SIMD paradigm. Furthermore, suppose *A* and *B* are 10 × 10

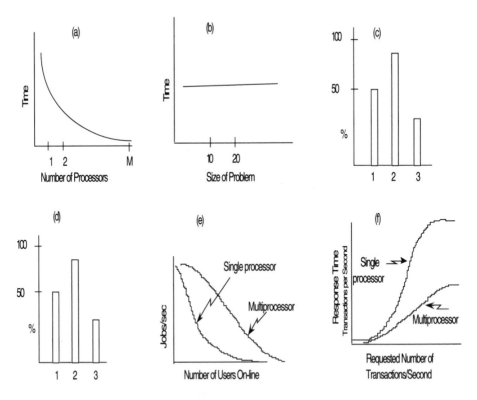

Figure 2.8   (a) Execution time vs. number of processors; (b) Processing time vs. size of problem; (c) Processor utilization; (d) Processor efficiency; (e) Throughput; (f) Processing rate

matrices. The most trivially parallel algorithm would assign each processor the task of computing one element of $C = A*B$. That is, 100 processors might be used to solve the problem in parallel in say 10 units of time.

Now, suppose the problem is increased in size by increasing A, B, and C to 20×20 matrices. This multiplication can be performed in about the same time by 400 processors. Thus, perhaps 11 units of time are required to do 4 times as much processing! (The additional 1 unit of time was needed to move the larger matrices to all 400 processors.)

Figures 2.8(c)–(d) illustrate another view of performance. *Processor utilization* is a measure of the utility of each processor for solving a certain problem. Let ComputeTime (j) be the amount of time processor j spends computing, and IdleTime (j) the amount of time processor j remains idle during the solution when N processors are employed.

$$U(j) = \text{ComputeTime}(j)/[\text{ComputeTime}(j) + \text{IdleTime}(j)], \quad j = 1, 2,..., N$$

In this formulation, it is not clear why a certain processor is idle. Perhaps it has no work to do, or perhaps it is waiting for data to process. This measure does not explain why utilization may be less than 100%, only that it is.

Processor efficiency measures the contribution of each processor to the parallel solution when i processors are employed. That is, $E(i)$ equals the average efficiency per processor when the problem is run with i parallel processors. This is slightly different than the utilization formula $U(j)$, which is computed for each processor when the problem is run on all N processors. Don't confuse these two measures.

$$E(i) = \text{Speedup}(i)/i, \quad i = 1, 2,..., N$$

Clearly, an efficiency rating of 100% means the problem runs in linear speedup time. An efficiency of 0% means the processor is of no use in solving the problem in parallel.

2.3.2 Multiple Program Performance

Up to this point, we have considered a restricted form of parallel computing where the entire parallel computer is dedicated to solving one problem. This ignores time-sharing, for example. What happens to performance when the parallel computer is shared by a number of users?

Performance can mean different things to different users. One user might seek to solve the largest possible problem in the shortest possible time; another user might want rapid response to short inquiries; while a third user might want low-cost computing. Parallel computers can be used to increase a number of performance measures which are unrelated to raw speed.

For example, Figure 2.8(e) shows the effect of multiple processor parallelism on system throughput. *Throughput* is measured by the number of jobs completed per unit of time. Some jobs are short, others are long, thus the number of completed jobs per unit of time are averages taken over some period of time.

This sort of parallel processing can be compared to waiting lines or queues in a bank with several tellers. As the number of customers increases, the time taken to go through a single line rapidly increases. If multiple tellers are employed, the long line is spread across several servers with the net effect of reducing the wait. Banks with multiple tellers achieve a higher rate of throughput than single-line banks as shown in Chapter 1.

How can multiple-processor computers be cost-effective? The answer lies in economics. The overall cost of a computer system is dominated by disk storage and other peripherals. The cost of the processors is such a small fraction of the overall system cost that adding processors has a high return. If we add 10% to the overall cost of the system, and get 400% return in terms of throughput, then we can use parallel computing to reduce costs rather than reduce the elapsed time to compute a solution to a single problem. Vendors of parallel and multiple processor computers have established a number of niche markets based on price points established by careful balance between number of processors and ancillary devices such as disks.

Some problems are *transaction oriented.* That is, the amount of computing is very small and occurs in short bursts. For example, getting a stock market quotation, returning the balance of a bank account, or controlling a factory machine are all examples of transaction-oriented computing. In such applications, the important point is to meet a brief deadline rather than perform a billion operations.

Figure 2.8(f) shows the impact of parallel computing on transaction processing applications. Transaction processing performance is measured by counting the number of transactions per unit of time. Transactions may originate from a single or many different users. For example, the stock market problem must accommodate a large number of inquiries from thousands of users. On the other hand, a factory machine might require thousands of small adjustments per unit of time. In any case, the ability to respond in a timely fashion is the important performance feature of the computer system.

2.4 BENCHMARK PERFORMANCE

A *benchmark* is a program whose purpose is to measure a performance characteristic of a computer system. Benchmarks often measure only one characteristic such as floating point speed, I/O speed, or speedup for a restricted class of problems. When a collection of special-characteristic benchmarks are combined into a set, we call this a *benchmark suite.*

Typical benchmarks are small applications designed to focus on a characteristic while at the same time introduce some reality into the computation. The Linpack, Livermore Loops, and Perfect Club benchmarks are small applications extracted from full applications. As such, they are *kernels* of actual applications, containing the most challenging sections of code. They are frequently used to measure raw computing speed.

These programs are usually written in a high-level language such as Fortran, and made as real-world as possible. For example, the Perfect Club suite is a collection of small applications in fluid mechanics, chemistry, physics, design, and signal processing.

Sometimes it is more important for a benchmark program to be portable and easy to run on a variety of computers than to accurately represent a real-world problem. A *synthetic benchmark* is a simple, relatively small program which approximates the behavior of a typical application. Its goal is to mimic both the relative frequencies of the statements and data structures found in a real application program. The Whetstone benchmark suggested in 1976 by Curnow and Wichmann is an example of a synthetic benchmark.

2.4.1 Other Benchmarks

Other benchmarks not described fully below are listed here for convenience. The curious reader can find a complete survey in the 1990 paper by Weicker.

TP1 and Debit-Credit Benchmarks were proposed in a 1985 Datamation article. TP1 is a widely accepted benchmark for gauging relational database performance. Throughput is measured in transactions/second, rather than MIPS, MFLOPS, or other measures of raw speed. This is an example of a benchmark for measuring responsiveness.

UNIX Today! Workstation Benchmark includes floating point, integer, disk I/O, memory and cache, and software development performance of UNIX systems. It attempts to measure the speed of the UNIX operating system, compilers, C Libraries, X-windows, and network (TCP/IP, ethernet, and NFS) subsystems of UNIX.

Ghrafstone Benchmark Rating is a set of 122 tests for measuring the graphics performance of computer systems developed by Workstation Laboratories (an independent hardware testing lab headed up by Egil Juliussen in Irving, Texas).

Picture Level Benchmark is a suite proposed by a consortium of 12 companies (the Graphics Performance Characterization group—Alliant, DEC, DuPont Pixel Systems, Evans & Sutherland, Hewlett-Packard, IBM, Intergraph, Megatek, Prime, Silicon Graphics, Sun, and Tektronix) attempting to agree on a meaningful set of benchmarks for graphics workstations. The Graphics Performance Characterization group has selected SimGraphics Engineering of Pasadena, California to develop Picture Level Benchmark software and benchmark test files.

SPEC (System Performance Evaluation Cooperative Effort) benchmarks, principally devised for workstations, were created by a consortium of computer vendors: Hewlett-Packard, MIPS, Sun, AT&T, Bull, CDC, Compaq, Data General, DEC, Dupont, Fujitsu, IBM, Intel, Intergraph, Motorola, NCR, Siemens, Silicon Graphics, Solbourne, Stardent, and Unisys. SPECmark was released in 1989, and consisted of 10 applications:

gcc: GNU C compiler

espresso: Program Logic Array simulator

spice 2g6: Analog circuit simulator

doduc: Monte Carlo simulation

nasa6: NASA/Ames Suite from Ames Research Center

li: Lisp Interpreter

eqntott: Switching function minimization involving sorts

matrix300: Various matrix multiplication algorithms

fpppp: Solution to Maxwell's equations

tomcatv: Highly vectorizable mesh generation

This suite consists of over 150,000 lines of code and requires that a license be signed before a tape can be obtained.

In the following sections, we survey the more widely used synthetic and real-world benchmark suites. A detailed explanation of each suite can be found in the references.

2.4.2 Classical Benchmarks

Serial computer benchmarks have been around since the classical sieve and Whetstone programs were described. Indeed, the National Institute for Standards and Technology collects benchmarks for all sorts of computers, and can be accessed by e-mail at nbslib@icmr.icst.nbs.gov. For further information, send a one-line message to NIST that says, "send index."

The Whetstone is a synthetic benchmark which reflects mostly numerical computing. Originally developed in ALGOL-60 to exercise 42 basic statements, it is composed of 11 modules for testing elementary mathematical operations, array processing, conditional jumps, integer arithmetic, trigonometry functions, procedure calls, and floating point calculations. A piece of this benchmark is shown below in C, for testing conditional jumps:

```
j = 1;
for (i = 1; i <= N4; i += 1) {
    if (j = 1)
        j = 2;
    else j = 3;
    if (j > 2)
        j = 0;
    else j = 1;
    if (j < 1)
        j = 1;
    else   j = 0;
}
```

The Dhrystone is another synthetic benchmark created by Weicker in 1984 to test performance of Ada statements, operations, and data access. It has been converted to other languages such as C with the following mix of statements:

53%: Assignment statements

32%: Control statements

15%: Procedure/function calls

The Sieve of Eratosthenes was proposed in 1981 by Gilbreath to measure the ability to do memory references, control statements, and simple I/O operations. It computes the first 100 prime numbers using the ancient algorithm.

The Linpack benchmarks have become perhaps the most widely referenced benchmarks for numerical computing. Linpack is a collection of linear algebra subroutines that are used to solve a system of linear equations as well as solve other kinds of linear algebra problems. The Linpack benchmark, however, is a very small section of the overall code, called a kernel, containing the innermost loops.

The Linpack benchmark is far from a real application. It does factoring and back solving on nonsymmetric, 100×100 dense matrices containing randomly generated 64-bit elements.

There are $2n^3/3 + 2n^2$ operations to be performed in the benchmark, where n is the order of the matrix. For example, when $n = 100$, a solution takes $2(1,000,000)/3 + 2(10,000) = 686,666$ operations. We can convert this into MFLOPS (million floating point operations per second), by dividing by the time in microseconds taken to solve a 100×100 system. So, if a certain computer solves a 100×100 system in 10 seconds, we get a rating of 0.0686666 MFLOPS.

Computer	Linpack MFLOPS	Theoretical MFLOPS
Cray Y-MP/832	200	2,667
Cray 2S	82	1,951
IBM 3090/180S VF	16	133
Alliant FX/80	9.5	165
Sequent Balance 8000		
	0.059	–
IBM PC w/8087	0.0069	–
Sun 2/50	0.0055	
Macintosh	0.0038	

Table 2.1   Linpack benchmarks reported by Dongarra

Table 2.1 contains a partial list of the 100×100 Linpack benchmarks for a selection of computers. The "Theoretical MFLOPS" rating is obtained by formula. Most of the code was written in Fortran, but some Fortran compilers are capable of optimizations that use vector parallelism.

This table should give the reader an idea of the magnitude of MFLOPS! Even with a math accelerator chip, a personal computer is many orders of magnitude away from a supercomputer.

2.4.3 Parallel Benchmarks

The NIST held a workshop in 1985 to discuss techniques for measuring and evaluating parallel computers. The conclusions of this meeting are reported by Martin and Riganati [1988], and the NIST has published a number of benchmarks for parallel computers:

Linpack: solution of a system of linear equations by LU decomposition. This benchmark is widely used and circulated by Oak Ridge National Labs.

Stones: the Whetstone and Dhrystone suite

Livermore Loops: a collection of Fortran code segments extracted from a number of scientific applications.

Fermi: codes used in equipment procurement at Fermi National Accelerator Lab

JRR: numerical problem set for parallel and vector machines created by John Rice

Mendez: Raul Mendez's benchmarks used on Japanese machines

NAS Kernel: the NASA/Ames benchmark of 12 subroutines in Fortran

In 1987, Levitan proposed a suite of synthetic benchmarks designed to evaluate the interconnection architecture of parallel computers. His suite has not been as widely used, but it provides perhaps the best synthetic suite for parallel computers:

Broadcasting: a processor sends a message to all other processors

Reporting: a processor gathers information about the state of the entire network

Extreme Finding: find the largest or smallest value from a set of values distributed one to a processor in the network

Packing: move data from a higher numbered processor to lower numbered processors

Saturating: each processor sends a message to all other processors

MST: compute the minimum spanning tree of a graph spread across the network

Sun, Shen, and Lewis report results for these synthetic benchmarks on shared-memory and distributed-memory computers, in addition to results for the following:

Parallel matrix multiply: classical matrix multiply across parallel processors

Disk file I/O: all processors issue I/O to one disk file to measure contention

Memory transfer: move data from one memory location to another

Math functions: test the performance of built-in math functions

The source code and results of these benchmarks can be obtained from their technical report.

2.4.4 PERFECT Benchmarks

The PERFECT (PERFormance Evaluation for Cost-effective Transformations) benchmarks and the Gordon Bell PERFECT Awards are collected by CSRL (see reference to Pointer). These are significant measures of performance because they are complete applications, except that I/O has been removed from most of the code. Started in 1987, the suite currently consists of 13 Fortran codes spanning four application areas: fluid dynamics, signal processing, physical and chemical modeling, and engineering design.

ADM: a 3-D fluid flow code that simulates pollutant concentration patterns in lakeshores. It solves a set of hydrodynamic equations.

ARC3D: a finite-difference code for 3-D fluid flow. It solves Euler and Navier-Stokes equations.

FLO52: 2-D transonic inviscid fluid flow past an airfoil. It solves Euler equations.

OCEAN: solves the dynamical equations of a 2-D fluid layer

SPEC77: a global model for simulating atmospheric flow to predict weather patterns

BDNA: simulations of molecular dynamics of biomolecules in water

MDG: a molecular dynamics model of 343 water molecules used to predict a variety of static and dynamic properties of liquid water

QCD: Monte-Carlo simulation to update the complex 3×3 matrices that represent the action of gluons

TRFD: simulation for the computational aspects of a 2-electron integral transformation

DYFESM: a 2-D finite element code for the analysis of symmetric anisotropic structures

SPICE: a general-purpose circuit simulation program for nonlinear DC, nonlinear transient, and linear AC analysis

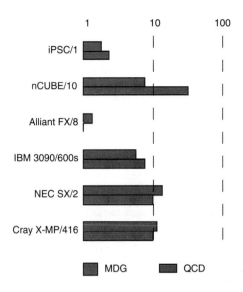

Figure 2.9 Relative performance vs. different computers for the MDG and QCD Perfect Club Benchmarks

MG3D: a seismic migration code used to study geological structure

TRACK: a missile tracking code used to determine the course of a set of unknown number of targets, such as missiles

Clearly, each benchmark will result in a different performance rate because the amount of parallelism varies among the benchmarks. Also, the performance for a given benchmark will vary across different machines because of their ability to utilize parallelism in the benchmark. Figure 2.9 illustrates these differences for two benchmarks run on different supercomputers.

The horizontal axis in Figure 2.9 is a relative number obtained by dividing the number of floating point operations performed by one CPU of a Cray X-MP/416 by the elapsed execution time of each machine. The benchmarks were run on as many processors as possible in each case: 4 Cray X-MP/416 processors; 256 nCUBE processors; 8 Alliant FX/8 processors; 6 IBM 3090 processors, etc.

2.4.5 NAS Kernel

The NAS (NASA/Ames Suite) Kernel Benchmark suite is a collection of seven FORTRAN subroutines that are typical of computational fluid dynamics calculations done at NASA Ames Research Center. The subroutines are:

MXM: Matrix multiply

CFFT2D: Two-dimensional Fast Fourier Transform

CHOLSKY: Cholesky decomposition

BTRIX: Block tri-diagonal linear system solver

GMTRY: Gaussian elimination

EMIT: Pressure calculation in aerodynamic flow

VPENTA: Invert 3 penta-diagonals

These benchmarks all have the following characteristics: (1) they share a common block of memory, (2) they use small amounts of memory because they solve relatively small problems, (3) they use 64-bit floating point operations, and (4) the code can easily be vectorized because it has been tuned for a Cray.

A total value for the seven routines is computed by running all seven subroutines within the NAS Kernel, which calls up these routines in turn. The total for a 32-node iPSC/860 is 16.73 MFLOPS. A single Cray Y-MP/832-1 achieves a value of 161 MFLOPS; and a Convex C-220 achieves 32 MFLOPS total performance on this benchmark. Obviously, the vector machines (Cray and Convex) achieve superior performance when the problem is small, as is the case here.

Figure 2.10 shows the effect on performance as the number of iPSC/860 processors is increased from 1 to 32 nodes. Speedup is very low because of the fixed, small size of the problem. That is, Amdahl's Law applies instead of Gustafson-Barsis' Law.

2.4.6 The SLALOM

SLALOM Benchmark (Scalable, Language-independent, Ames Laboratory, One-minute Measurement) is a scalable, fixed-time benchmark focused on general scientific computing, proposed by John Gustafson. This is perhaps the only meaningful benchmark for data-parallel computing because it is designed to measure the performance of a parallel computer as a function of problem size.

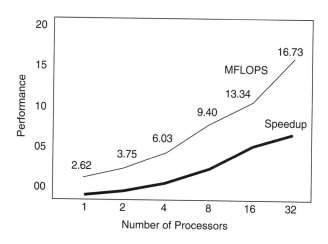

Figure 12.10   Speed and speedup of the NAS Kernel when run on an iPSC/860 parallel processor. The numbers are for total values

This benchmark program always runs in one minute. How much computation can be performed in one minute determines the speed of the system under test.

The SLALOM application is a simple radiosity calculation taken from computer graphics (see Goral et al. and Appendix A). The problem is to find the equilibrium radiation inside a box made of diffuse colored surfaces. The faces of the box are divided into finite elements called patches, and equations are solved in each patch for red, green, and blue components.

The system under test solves these equations for as many patches as possible within 60 seconds. Thus, a fast computer will solve more patches than a slower one. In addition, this problem involves real-world processing steps such as I/O, set-up costs, and solving a nearly dense system of equations.

Excerpts from a few SLALOM runs are listed below. At the time of this writing, the benchmark was only a few months old; hence the limited results.

Machine/Environment   # Processors# PatchesDate

Cray Y-MP8, 167 MHz
Fortran + tuned LAPACK85120September 90

nCUBE 2, 20MHz
Fortran + Asm10243736September 90

Intel iPSC/860, 40 MHz
Fortran + Asm BLAS642167January 91

MasPar MP-1, 12.5 MHz
Plural C (mpl)63842047November 90

Alliant FX/2800
Fortran (-Ogc, KAI Libs)141736January 91

Silicon Graphics
4D/380S, 33 MHz
Fortran + block Solver81352April 91

IBM RS/6000 540, 30 MHz
Fortran +ESSL calls,
XLF V2, –O11304January 91

SUN 4/370, 25 MHz

C (ucc –O4 -dalign)1419October 90

2.4.7 The Gordon Bell Prize

In an interview with *IEEE Software* in 1986, Gordon Bell offered two prizes of $1,000 each (for 10 years from 1987 to 1997) to anyone contributing significant advances to practical parallel computing. Subsequently, Editor-in-Chief of Software magazine *T. G. Lewis* organized a panel of judges to evaluate and recommend annual winners of the prestigious prize. The prize has become an activity of the Computer Society, which recognizes winners at its annual CompCon meetings each spring and/or the annual Supercomputing Conference held in the fall of each year.

The rules for this prize changed in subsequent years. In 1988, three categories of performance were established:

1   Raw Performance: The application must run faster than any comparable engineering or scientific application, as measured by MFLOPS. Comparisons with known machines such as the Cray X-MP should be used to evaluate the raw performance on a new machine.

2   Price/Performance: The performance divided by the cost of the system is better than any other entry. Cost should be the list price of the processors and memory, but not peripherals.

3   Compiler Optimization: The compiler that generates the most speedup will be the winner. Speedup is to be measured by dividing the execution time of the program compiled without automatic parallelization by the execution time with automatic parallelization.

The first annual prize for performance was given in 1987 to Robert Benner, John Gustafson, and Gary Montry of Sandia National Laboratories in Albuquerque, New Mexico. They ran three applications: (1) beam stress analysis, (2) surface wave simulation, and (3) unstable fluid flow, on a 1,024 processor nCUBE/10. Each processor had only 512KB of local memory, and was capable of approximately 80 KFLOPS.

The Gordon Bell Prize judges anticipated a fiftyfold speedup in the first year. Surprisingly, the Sandia team turned in an amazing 400- to 600-fold Amdahl (thousandfold Gustafson-Barsis) speedup on these real-world applications. This startling result was made possible by data-parallel programming techniques.

The beam stress analysis program computed the deflection in a two-dimensional beam fixed at one end, and loaded along its upper edge. The Sandia program used a finite element formulation where one rectangular section of the beam is assigned to a processor, and the collection of rectangles representing the entire beam are distributed across the entire parallel computer. The beam is divided into 2,048 bilinear elements—the largest number of elements that would fit in the machine's memory. At each boundary between adjacent rectangles, messages must be sent to convey the boundary values to the next rectangle. Mathematically, the stress in the finite-element model is computed by a conjugate-gradient algorithm.

The first Gordon Bell Prize winners have established a benchmark of sorts. Subsequent entrants must exceed the achievement of prior winners to be considered. The speedups and price/performance ratios are enviable goals for the parallel computing industry as a whole.

2.4.8 Supercomputer Performance in the Year 2000

There is little doubt that the performance of very fast computers will depend heavily on parallelism in the year 2000. Combined with increases in electronic packaging densities, and sheer speed increases in components, the computer of year 2000 will be both fast and small even though it will contain 100 to 1,000 processors.

One prediction given by James Key estimates that each 1M gate processor will be capable of supporting 256 MB of 30 ns access time RAM yielding a single processor peak performance 1,000 times that of a 1990 Cray. When combined with 1,000 processors, the theoretical speed will be expected to exceed one million times the MFLOPs of current technology. Assuming the results given here by various benchmarks, we can expect Teraflop (1,000,000 MFLOPS) speeds within the next ten years.

PROBLEMS FOR DISCUSSION AND SOLUTION

1 Devise a Gantt chart schedule for the task graph in Figure 2.7(b) when the communication time delays on all arcs is 5. Draw the Gantt chart to show the schedule. What is the schedule when only 3 processors are used? When 8 processors are used?

2 Compute the theoretical speedup of a program with $\beta = 1\%$ on $N = 100$ processors. Use both Amdahl's and Gustafson-Barsis Laws.

3 What is the value of β for a problem that runs 25 times faster on 100 processors than it does on 1 processor? Give your answer for both Amdahl's and Gustafson-Barsis Laws.

4 How many processors does it take to speed up a problem by a factor of 10 when using SIMD data-parallel techniques yielding $\beta = 10\%$?

5 Assume the communication delays grow according to the formula :

$C(N) = (0.01)N + 0.5$. How many processors should be used to gain the greatest amount of speedup? What is the speedup if one-half as many processors are used?

6 Compare Amdahl's Law with the Gustafson-Barsis Law when $\beta = 0$. When $\beta = 1$. What interpretation can you place on these results?

7 Give a Gantt chart schedule for the supervisor/worker task graph in Figure 2.4 when all arcs are labeled with a delay of one.

8 What is the number of operations performed in a $1,000 \times 1,000$ Linpack benchmark? Use this to compute the MFLOPS ratings in Table 2.1.

9 Apply the Gustafson-Barsis Law to the following situation posed by the Sandia winners of the first Gordon Bell Prize. Solving the beam stress analysis problem with a 64×32 grid on a single processor takes 1,614 seconds. A problem with 64×32 finite elements per processor, but running on 1,024 processors, is expected to take how long? (This means that 2 million elements are solved over 1,024 processors.

Also, it helps to know that the time increases as the square root of the number of processors.) The answer can be found on pp. 109 of the *IEEE Software* article by Dongarra, Karp, and Kennedy.

References

Amdahl, G. M., "Validity of the Single-Processor Approach to Achieving Large-Scale Computing Capabilities," *AFIPS Conference Proceedings 30*, AFIPS Press, pp. 483 – 485, 1967.

Bokhari, S. H., "Multiprocessing the Sieve of Eratosthenes," *Computer*, pp. 50 – 58, April 1987.

Curnow, J. P., and Wichmann, B. A., "A Synthetic Benchmark," *Computer Journal*, pp. 43 – 49, February 1976.

Dongarra, J. J., "Performance of Various Computers Using Standard Linear Equations Software," CS–89–85, Computer Science Department, University Tennessee, Knoxville, TN 37996-1301, October 1989. E-mail: dongarra@cs.utk.edu.

Dongarra, J., Karp, A., and Kennedy, K., "First Gordon Bell Awards Winners Achieve Speedup of 400," *IEEE Software*, Volume 5, 3, pp. 108 – 112, May 1988.

Gelenbe, E., *Multiprocessor Performance*, Wiley Series in Parallel Computing, John Wiley and Sons, 1989.

Gilbreath, J., "A High-Level Language Benchmark," *Byte*, pp. 180, September 1981.

Goral, C. M., Torrance, K. E., Greenberg, D. P., and Battaile, B., "Modeling the Interaction of Light Between Diffuse Surfaces," *Computer Graphics*, 18, 3, July 1984.

Grumman, G., "Parallel Distributed Processing Lead NSF Software Research Directions," *IEEE Software*, 4, 4, pp. 102 – 104, July 1987.

Gustafson, J. L., "Reevaluating Amdahl's Law," *Comm. ACM*, 31, 5, pp. 532 – 533, 1988.

Gustafson, J., Rover, D., Elbert, S., and Carter, M., "SLALOM: The First Scalable Supercomputing Benchmark," *Supercomputing Review*, November 1990, pp. 56 – 61. E-mail: slalom@tantalus.al.iastate.edu.

Gustafson, J., Rover, D., Elbert, S., and Carter, M., "The Design of a Scalable, Fixed-Time Computer Benchmark," Ames Laboratory, Ames, IA 50011-3020.

Key, J., "Supercomputer Performance in the Year 2000," *Supercomputing Review*, pp. 40 – 43, November 1990.

Levitan, S. P., "Measuring Communications Structures in Parallel Architectures and Algorithms," in *Characteristics of Parallel Programming*, MIT Press, 1987.

Martin, J. L, and Mueller-Wichards, D., "Supercomputer Performance Evaluation: Status and Directions," *J. Supercomputing*, Volume 1, No. 1, pp. 87 – 104, 1987.

Pointer, L., (ed). Perfect Report 1, Center for Supercomputing Research & Development, Univ. Illinois, Champaign-Urbana, IL., July 1989. E-mail for documentation and code: waltz@uicsrd.csrd.uiuc.edu.

Riganati, J. P., and Schneck, P. B., "Supercomputing," *Computer*, Volume 13, 10, pp. 97 – 103, October 1984.

Salazar, S., and Smith, C., Workshop on Performance Evaluation of Parallel Computers, NIST, NBSIR-86-3395, July 1986.

Sun, T-J, Shen, J., and Lewis, T. G., *A Benchmark Suite for Parallel Processors: Part I, and Part II*, TR-89-70-3, TR-89-60-6, Computer Science Dept., Oregon State University, Corvallis, OR 97331-3902, 1989.

Weicker, R. P., "An Overview of Common Benchmarks," *Computer*, 23, 12, pp. 65 – 75, (December 1990).

Weicker, R. P., "Dhrystone: A Synthetic Systems Programming Benchmark," *Comm. ACM*, pp. 1013 – 1030, October 1984.

Chapter 3

Parallel Processors

A *parallel processor* is a computer consisting of two or more processing units connected via some interconnection network. There are two major features of a parallel processor: (1) the processing units themselves, and (2) the interconnection network that ties together the collection of processors. We argue that the interconnection network is the more important of the two, and so concentrate on the *topology* of networks before examining specific commercial parallel processors.

Parallel processors can be categorized by their interconnection network (IN) topologies. Also, we classify parallel processors as either shared-memory or distributed-memory machines. Within each of these categories we further divide machines into vector versus MIMD within the shared-memory category, and static versus dynamic within the distributed-memory category. Dynamic INs create links between processors and/or memories on the fly, as the parallel program executes. Static INs are fixed by design.

The simplest IN is a bus connecting many processors to a single shared memory. The classic problem of designing a bus-connected shared-memory multiprocessor is that of cache memory design. Without cache memory, a bus-structured parallel processor would quickly saturate the bus and become rather useless. But with a carefully designed cache, 98% of the bus requests can frequently be avoided because the cache contains the desired data and instructions. Such systems as commercially available from Sequent Computer Corporation and are low cost and capable of supporting 20 to 30 processors.

Distributed-memory designs offer higher levels of parallelism through the interconnection of thousands of processors, but they require programmers to adopt a message-passing paradigm. (There is no global memory, hence no global program data space.) The design of a distributed-memory parallel processor places great demands on communication speed, routing, and data partitioning. We illustrate these difficulties with an extended example.

Hypercube INs are the most popular form of a static IN for constructing a distributed-memory machine. The Intel iPSC and nCUBE families are commercial examples. Hypercube INs are popular because of mathematical simplicity, and the fact that the number of links grows slowly as the number of processors is increased. Hypercubes can time-share many user programs by partitioning a large hypercube into smaller hyper-

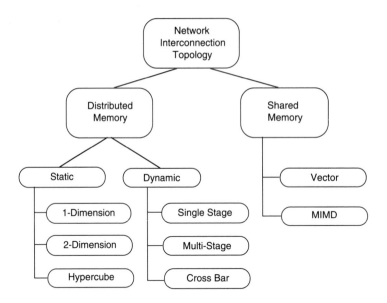

Figure 3.1   A brief (hardware) taxonomy of interconnection network topologies

cubes. A 64-processor hypercube might be partitioned into one 32-node subcube, and two 16-node subcubes, for example.

In this chapter we give a hardware taxonomy based on the IN of parallel computers. Then we describe the major classifications in our taxonomy beginning with the simplest (shared-memory) classification, followed by the more elaborate distributed-memory classification (static INs), and finally the most difficult category (dynamic INs). In addition, we illustrate each type of architecture with a simple back substitution program to solve $Ux = b$.

3.1   A TAXONOMY OF TOPOLOGIES

An *interconnection network topology* is a mapping function from the set of processors and memories onto the same set of processors and memories. In other words, the topology describes how to connect processors and memories to other processors and memories. A fully connected topology, for example, is a mapping in which each processor is connected to all other processors in the computer. A ring topology is a mapping that connects processor k to its neighbors, processors $(k - 1)$ and $(k + 1)$.

Nearly all parallel processors can be distinguished by their IN topology. While the speed and capacity may vary, the most significant difference between parallel processors is their IN topology. Therefore, we devote the majority of this chapter to an introduction of these topologies and how they are used in constructing a certain parallel computer.

Figure 3.1 gives a brief taxonomy of IN topologies showing the types of parallel processor architectures they lead to. This is a high-level classification because it does not distinguish between the different kinds of network communication protocols such as circuit-switched versus packet-switched. For a discussion of the lower level details of these protocols, see Feng.

Product	Type	Topology
nCUBE	distributed-memory	hypercube
iPSC/2	distributed-memory	hypercube
Wavetracer	distributed-memory	3-D mesh
MultiMax	shared-memory	bus
Symmetry	shared-memory	bus
FX/8	shared-memory	bus
Cray Y-MP	shared-memory	multiport memory

Table 3.1   Some examples of commercial systems and their IN topologies

3.1.1   Shared versus Distributed Architectures

INs belong to one of two important groups: (1) distributed-memory, and (2) shared-memory. A *distributed-memory architecture* typically combines local memory and processor at each node of the IN. Message-passing is used to communicate between any two processors, and there is no global, shared memory. Commercial examples of distributed-memory architectures circa 1990 are the nCUBE, iPSC/2, Wavetracer, and various Transputer-based systems (see Table 3.1).

A *shared-memory architecture* typically accomplishes interprocessor coordination through a global memory shared by all processors. Commercial examples of shared-memory multiprocessors are Encore Computer's Multimax, Sequent Computer's Balance and Symmetry, Alliant FX/8, and multiprocessor Cray computers (see Table 3.1).

Figure 3.2 illustrates the topology of two general groups. Processors exchange information through their central shared memory in one architecture, and exchange information through their interconnection network in the other. Typically, shared-memory systems employ a single bus, while distributed-memory systems employ true networks. The bus architecture alleviates the need for expensive multiported memories and interface circuitry as well as the need to adopt a message-passing paradigm when developing application software.

Figure 3.2(b) is different from Figure 3.2(a), largely because memory is spread throughout the collection of processors. In place of a shared memory, each processor has a local memory where program and data reside.

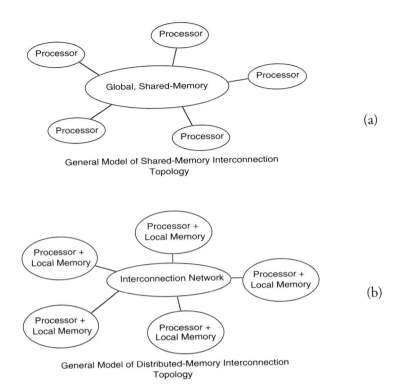

(a)

General Model of Shared-Memory Interconnection
Topology

(b)

General Model of Distributed-Memory Interconnection
Topology

Figure 3.2 Comparison of shared-memory and distributed-memory interconnection topologies

The distributed-memory approach is in principle scalable to massive proportions, e.g., 10^6 processors within a single parallel computer. By scalable, we mean that the number of processors can be increased without significant decrease in efficiency of operation. Therefore, it is technically feasible to increase a distributed-memory machine from 1,000 processors to 1,000,000 processors without major alteration in its basic design. Machines in this class are called *massively parallel* computers because of the large number of processors they contain. Whether or not such machines are actually constructed is an economic question instead of a technical hurdle.

If software developers are willing to adopt a programming model based on message-passing or data parallelism, then the scalability of a distributed memory computer becomes very attractive. Indeed, some very large scale scientific problems may easily require millions of processors in order to obtain a timely solution. Programming massively parallel computers is no easy task, as we will see later.

The model of Figure 3.2 is a simplification because some distributed-memory machines distribute both processors and memories throughout the parallel computer. This allows any processor to equally access any memory or other processor. Systolic computers would also diverge from the simple view of parallel computer architecture given in Figure 3.2.

Parallel Processors   Chapter 3

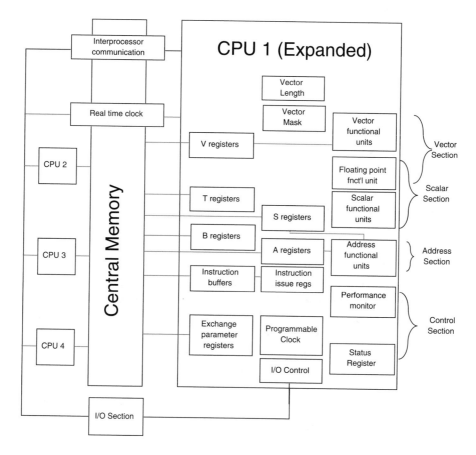

Figure 3.3(a)   Architecture of a vector parallel shared-memory computer, the Cray Y-MP

3.1.2   Vector versus MIMD

Henry Ford's company produced 15,007,033 Model *T* automobiles between 1913 and 1927; a record that was not exceeded until 1972 by Volkswagen. To do this, his Highland Park factory in Detroit had to employ a form of parallelism called the *assembly line* by Ford, and pipeline or vector parallelism by computer designers.

In Chapter 1 we learned that *pipelined parallelism* can achieve a limited form of parallelism by overlapping fine-grained stages of a computation. The pipeline of such machines must be kept full to realize high degrees of parallelism, and this usually means the pipelines are very tightly coupled to the source of the data.

Vector parallel computers can be interconnected by shared-memory to yield even higher processing rates. The pipelined processors share access to the central memory (see Figure 3.3(a)). The Cray Y-MP is a classic vector parallel computer, but when multiple vector processors are combined together as shown in Figure 3.3(a), the result is a very powerful shared-memory parallel computer (see Figure 3.3(b)). In general, gain-

# of Processors	1,2,4, or 8
Peak Performance	167 MIPS
Floating Point Arithmetic	2,667 MFLOPS
Memory	32/64/128/256 64-bit MWords
Disk Capacity	60 GB - 500 GB

Figure 3.3(b)   Cray Y-MP performance summary

ing performance benefits from shared-memory INs is a challenging problem of cache design, as we will see in the next section.

3.1.3   Cache Memory Design

Chapter 1 illustrated the shared-memory MIMD paradigm using an analogy of a bank, tellers, and customer account folders. We proposed several methods of sharing multiple-teller access to the same folder. One method was to make copies of the popular account folders and place them at each teller's work counter. The copies at each counter are equivalent to cache memory. Cache memories are the key to understanding the IN found in the shared-memory MIMD machines manufactured by Sequent and Encore.

A *cache memory* is a special-purpose random access memory designed to reduce a number of contention problems which arise from a bus-structured shared-memory IN topology (see Figure 3.4). A typical bus-structured parallel computer as shown in Figure 3.4 attempts to reduce contention for the bus by fetching instructions and data directly from each individual cache, as much as possible. In the extreme, the bus con-

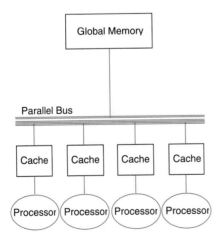

Figure 3.4   General interconnection network of a bus-structured multiprocessor. Cache memories are necessary to reduce contention for the single bus

tention might be reduced to zero after the cache memories are loaded from the global memory, because all instructions and data might be contained within the cache.

High-speed caches connected to each processor on one side, and the bus on another side, maintain local copies of global memory instructions and data and supply these to the local processors at the highest possible rate. If the local processor finds all of its instructions and data in the local cache, we say the *hit rate* is 100%. The *miss rate* of a cache is the fraction of the references that cannot be satisfied by the cache, and so must be copied from the global memory, across the bus, into the cache, and then passed on to the local processor. One of the goals of the cache is to maintain a high hit rate, or low miss rate under high processor loads. A high hit rate means the processors are not using the bus.

Hit rates are determined by a number of factors, ranging from the application programs being run to the manner in which cache hardware is implemented. Engineers at several vendors of bus-connected computers claim that it takes about 0.5 MB of cache memory per processor for each MIPS of processor speed to maintain acceptable cache hit rates. In the following, we look at this problem in great detail, which the casual reader may want to skip.

A processor goes through a *duty cycle*, where it executes instructions a certain number of times per clock cycle. Typically, individual processors execute less than one instruction per cycle, thus reducing the number of times it needs to access memory. *Subscalar* processors execute less than one instruction per cycle, and *superscalar* processors execute more than one instruction per cycle. In any case, we want to minimize the number of times each local processor tries to use the central bus. Otherwise, processor speed will be limited by bus bandwidth.

To quantify the importance of good cache memory design, define the variables for hit rate, number of processors, processor speed, bus speed, and processor duty cycle rates as follows:

N = Number of processors

h = hit rate of each cache, assumed to be the same for all caches

$(1 - h)$ = miss rate of all caches

B = Bandwidth of the bus, measured in cycles/second

I = Processor duty cycle, assumed to be identical for all processors, in fetches/cycle

V = Peak processor speed, in fetches/second

The effective bandwidth of the bus is BI fetches/second. If each processor is running at a speed of V, then misses are being generated at a speed of $V(1 - h)$. For an N-processor system, misses are simultaneously being generated at a speed of $N(1 - h)V$. This leads to saturation of the bus when N processors simultaneously try to access the bus. That is, $N(1 - h)V \leq BI$. The maximum number of processors with cache memories that the bus can support is given by the relation, $N \leq BI/(1 - h)V$.

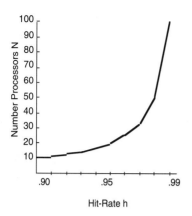

Figure 3.5 Number of processors supported as a function of cache hit rate

For a derivation of the performance of interconnection networks that considers the stochastic behavior of random accesses, consult Strecker, who presents original derivations, and Bhuyan, who presents various surveys.

Example

Suppose a shared-memory parallel computer is constructed from processors that can execute 10^7 instructions/second and the processor duty cycle $I = 1$. The caches are designed to support a hit rate of 97%, and the bus supports a peak bandwidth of $B = 10^6$ cycles/second. Then, $(1 - h) = 0.3$, and the maximum number of processors N is $N \le 10^6/0.3 \times 10^7 = 3.33$. Thus, the parallel computer we have in mind can support only 3 processors!

We might ask what hit rate is needed to support a 30-processor system. In this case, $h = 1 - BI/NV$, so for the parallel computer we have in mind, $h = 0.9967$.

A graph of N versus cache hit rate for a parallel system with $BI = V$ is shown in Figure 3.5. Note the great sensitivity to the number of processors that a bus can support versus very small increases in hit rate near 99.99%. This sensitivity comes at a price, however, as the hit rate increases only by dramatically increasing the size of the cache memory.

The Sequent Symmetry shown in Figure 3.6 is representative of the class of bus-structured, shared-memory IN architectures we have discussed in this section. Its bus can accommodate up to 30 processors as well as memory modules, network and disk controllers, and other peripherals such as tape, modem, and remote terminals. In Figure 3.6, processors are shown as CPUs and caches, shared global memory is shown as an expandable collection of modules, disks and tapes are shown under control of peripheral device controllers MBUS and DCC, and the heart of the system is shown as a bus under control of SCED, a bus scheduler and arbitrator.

The hit rate of cache is such a powerful factor in determining the peak performance of a shared-memory IN system that it often inspires the name of the computer. For

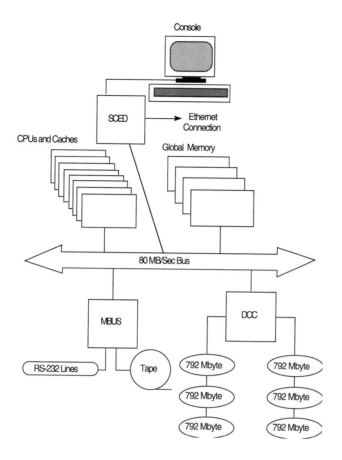

Figure 3.6 Sequent Symmetry shared-memory multiprocessor with bus arbitrator SCED, disk controller DCC, and serial device controller MBUS

example, the Sequent S27 and S81 were named after the hit rates of their caches as follows. In the S27, each processor was rated at 1 MIPS, and the cache hit rates permit 30 processors to be interconnected via the bus. Thus, the theoretical peak processing rate is 30 MIPS. But, the designers of the S27 wanted to be conservative, so they subtracted 10% to obtain a rating of 27 MIPS, hence the name Symmetry 27000, or S27 for short. Similarly, the Symmetry 81000 is theoretically a 90 MIPS machine because each of its processors is rated at 3 MIPS, but to be conservative, it is rated at 90% of peak, i.e., 81 MIPS. Later models dropped this designation.

Cache Coherency

Multiple copies of data, spread throughout the caches, lead to a *coherence problem* among the caches. The copies in the caches are *coherent* if they are all equal in value. But, if one of the processors writes over the value of one of the copies, then the copies become *inconsistent*. If data are allowed to become inconsistent (incoherent), incorrect results will be propagated through the system, leading to incorrect results.

Cache coherence algorithms are needed to maintain a level of consistency throughout the parallel computer. There are a number of algorithms that can be used to maintain cache coherency [Dubois and Thakkar], but we look at only the algorithms that have been implemented in real parallel computers. We use the hardware designer's term *coherency* when describing hardware design issues, and the equivalent software term *consistency* when describing software issues. For our purposes, the two terms are identical.

When a task running on processor *P* requests the data in global memory location *A*, for example, the contents of *A* are copied to processor *P*'s local cache, where it is passed on to *P*. Now, suppose *A* is also accessed by processor *Q*, only *Q* wants to write a new value over the old value of *A*.

There are two fundamental *cache coherence policies* that we can use at this point: (1) write-invalidate, and (2) write-update. Write-invalidate maintains consistency by reading from local caches until a write occurs. When any processor updates the value of *A* through a write, all copies are invalidated by posting a *dirty bit* for *A*. Processor *Q* will invalidate all other copies of *A* when it writes a new value into its cache. This sets the dirty bit for *A*. *Q* can continue to change *A* without further notifications to other caches because *Q* has the only valid copy of *A*. However, when processor *P* wants to read *A*, it must wait until *A* is updated and the dirty bit is cleared.

Write-update maintains consistency by immediately updating all copies in all caches. All dirty bits are set during each write operation. After all copies have been updated, all dirty bits are cleared. This is a form of *write-through*, because the new value of *A* is written to all caches.

If we permitted a write-through directly on global memory location *A*, the bus would start to get busy and ultimately all processors would be idle while waiting for writes to complete. On the contrary, if the write is limited to the copy of *A* in cache *Q*, the caches become inconsistent on *A*. Setting the dirty bit prevents the spread of inconsistent values of *A*, but at some point, the inconsistent copies must be updated. We can get a better idea of how these two policies might affect the performance of a shared-memory computer by examining two applications.

3.1.4 Applications on Cache Memory Machines

Cache coherency algorithms are typically implemented in hardware to make them fast, but they incur delays when misses and data "invalidates" force accesses across the bus. In some cases, a separate dirty bit bus is provided in hardware to supplement the data bus. Even so, it is desirable to reduce the number of times that data are accessed, misses are registered, and dirty bits are set if we want to obtain maximum speed from a bus-structured IN.

In the next two sections we examine two applications in some detail to illustrate the two cache coherency algorithms. The first application is based on the Producer-Consumer problem which occurs whenever two tasks must communicate through a shared-memory buffer. The second problem is a classic application in numerical methods. We study a section of code taken from an application that solves a system of linear equations by the famous iterative method.

Bounded Buffer Applications

Consider the classic producer-consumer problem sometimes called the *bounded-buffer problem* in books on operating systems. Task *P* produces a stream of items to be sent to task *Q*, which stores them in a buffer of length *B*. For simplicity, we assume task *P* runs on processor *P* and task *Q* runs on processor *Q*. This problem is frequently found in applications where data are being sent between two or more tasks, each of which wants to use the data and pass it on to others. How do the cache schemes described above work in this important case?

The shared data are *count, in, out,* and *buffer. Count* is the number of items in *buffer* at any instant in time, and *in* and *out* are used to index into *buffer*. Initially, *count* = 0, *in* = 0, *out* = 0, and *B* > 0. Pseudocode for each task is shown below:

```
P:Producer (item)                    Q:Consumer (item)
    if count ≤ B then begin              if count ≠ 0 then begin
       LOCK (mutual)                         LOCK (mutual)
       buffer [in] = item                    item = buffer [out]
       in = (in + 1) mod B                   out = (out + 1) mod B
       count = count + 1                     count = count - 1
       UNLOCK (mutual)                       UNLOCK (mutual)
    endif                                endif
endProducer                          endConsumer
```

When task *P* executes LOCK (mutual), task *Q* must wait until *P* executes UNLOCK (mutual), and conversely, when task *Q* executes LOCK (mutual), *P* must wait until *Q* executes UNLOCK (mutual). The LOCK/UNLOCK pair enforce mutual exclusion for the benefit of the application, but they do not solve the cache coherency problem.

The shared data, *buffer, in, out,* and *count,* begin life in global memory, but soon find themselves bouncing between caches (see Figure 3.7). As soon as *P* begins to execute, a *cache fault* occurs because of a miss when *P* tries to access *count* and it is not in cache *P*. We continue to get misses until all shared values have been copied into cache *P* (see Figures 3.7(a)–(b)).

Similar actions take place when *Q* executes. The result of *P* executing followed by *Q* executing is shown in Figure 3.7(c). The inconsistency between *P* and *Q* caches grows as shown in Figures 3.7(c)–(e).

In Figure 3.7 it quickly becomes apparent that *in* is local to *P* and *out* is local to *Q*. The major difficulty is in keeping *count* up to date as it is changed by both tasks.

The write-update policy would ping-pong the updated values of *count* between caches *P* and *Q*. It may also update the master copy in global memory, but whether it does this is an implementation decision. There seems to be little benefit from the write-update policy in the Producer-Consumer application.

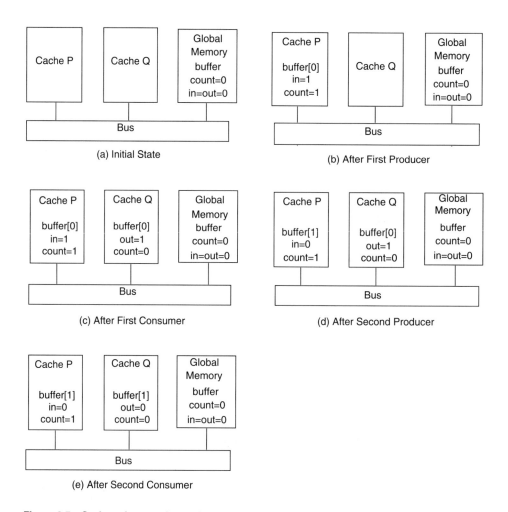

Figure 3.7   Cache coherency in producer-consumer application

The write-invalidate policy would behave no better unless P and Q repeatedly produce or consume in batches. Suppose, for example, P produces an entire buffer full of data in sequence. That is, let P produce B outputs, followed by B inputs by Q. This reduces the ping-ponging to once per batch of B items. In other words, the write-invalidate policy reduces thrashing between caches by a factor of B in this case. The write-invalidate policy is superior in this application.

There appears to be little difference between the write-update and write-invalidate policies, but in most real machines the write-update policy will run faster because of lower communication overhead. There is no need, for example, to watch the bus and intercept dirty bits. Even so, both policies must use some form of *snoopy cache protocol* to watch the bus and carry out the appropriate coherency command when necessary.

The first snoopy cache protocol was proposed by Goodman and surveyed by Stenstrom [Dubois and Thakkar]. It is called the *write-once protocol* and uses a copy-back *update policy* which means that data are written back to memory when it is updated. Global memory is moved in blocks, and each block has a state associated with it which determines what happens to the entire contents of the block. Block states are:

Invalid: The copy is inconsistent.

Valid: The copy is consistent with global memory.

Reserved: Data has been written exactly once and the copy is consistent with global memory. There is only one copy of the global memory block in one local cache.

Dirty: Data has been updated more than once and there is only one copy in one local cache. When a copy is dirty, it must be written back to global memory.

The write-once protocol works as follows:

Read Hit: Use the local copy from the cache.

Read Miss: If no dirty copy exists, then supply a copy from global memory. Set the state of this copy to VALID. If a dirty copy exists, make a copy from the cache that set the state to DIRTY, update global memory and local cache with the copy. Set the state to VALID in both caches.

Write Hit: If the copy is DIRTY or RESERVED, perform the write locally, and set the DIRTY bit. If the state is VALID, then broadcast an INVALID to all caches. Update the global memory and set the state to RESERVED.

Write Miss: Get a copy from either a cache with a DIRTY copy which updates global memory, or from global memory itself. Broadcast an INVALID command to all caches. Update the local copy and set its state to DIRTY.

Many other policies have been proposed in the literature, but these policies are among the few that have been implemented in commercially available parallel computers. For example, the write-invalidate policy has been implemented on the Sequent Symmetry and Alliant FX. The Digital Equipment Corporation Firefly uses the write-update policy.

3.1.5 Parallel Solution to $Ux = b$

The previous examples illustrate the impact of shared data on cache memory and give a general idea of how to program a shared-memory computer. In this section we make the ideas more specific and concrete by giving the actual code for solving $Ux = b$ on the Sequent Symmetry multiprocessor system. This code is written in Fortran, which has been extended by Sequent to accommodate parallel activation of loops.

Perhaps the most elementary operation performed in a number of applications is the familiar back substitution to obtain the solution to a system of n linear equations.

Assuming an upper block matrix U, and a right-hand-side vector b, the problem is to solve for vector x:

$$Ux = b$$

$$U = \begin{bmatrix} U_{11} & U_{12} & U_{13} & \cdots & U_{1n} \\ 0 & U_{22} & U_{23} & \cdots & U_{2n} \\ 0 & 0 & U_{33} & \cdots & U_{3n} \\ \cdots & \cdots & \cdots & \cdots & \cdots \\ 0 & 0 & \cdots & \cdots & U_{nn} \end{bmatrix}$$

U is an $n \times n$ upper block matrix with all elements below the diagonal set to zero, x and b are n-length vectors, b is known, and x is unknown. We use $U_{i,j}$ or simply U_{ij} to designate the (i,j)-th element of U, x_j to designate a single element of X, and b_j to designate a single element of b.

The back substitution equations are simply

$$x_n = \frac{b_n}{U_{nn}}$$

$$x_i = b_i - \frac{\displaystyle\sum_{j=n}^{i+1} U_{jj} X_j}{U_{ii}}, \quad i = (n-1), (n-2), \ldots 1$$

This succinct form of the equation hides the potential parallelism we might get if we looked more closely at the full set of formulas for $n = 5$.

$$x_5 = b_5 / U_{5,5}$$

$$x_4 = (b_4 - x_5 U_{4,5}) / U_{4,4}$$

$$x_3 = (b_3 - x_5 U_{3,5} - x_4 U_{3,4}) / U_{3,3}$$

$$x_2 = (b_2 - x_5 U_{2,5} - x_4 U_{2,4} - x_3 U_{2,3}) / U_{2,2}$$

$$x_1 = (b_1 - x_5 U_{1,5} - x_4 U_{1,4} - x_3 U_{1,3} - x_2 U_{1,2}) / U_{1,1}$$

Note that x_5 must be computed first, followed by x_4, x_3,... x_1. If we wait until x_5 is available, then x_4 can be computed. After x_4 is solved, x_3 can be computed, and so forth. On the surface, it appears that there is little parallelism in the problem. The parallelism is in the summations, and not the simultaneous calculation of each element of vector x.

We can expose the parallel summation operations by writing the same equations in an iterative form as follows, where $x(t)$ is used to designate the t-th partial sum of x. Starting with $t = 0$, we get initial values:

$x_5(0) = b_5/U_{5,5}$ which is a solution for x_5

$x_i(0) = b_i;$ $i = (n-1), (n-2),...\ 1$

For subsequent steps, $t = 1, 2,...\ (n-1) = 4$, we get partial sums from the previous solution element, the diagonal block $U_{i,i}$, and the last-to-first columns of U:

$t = 1$:

$x_4(1) = (x_4(0) - x_5(0)\, U_{4,5})\ /\ U_{4,4}$

which is a solution for x_4

$x_i(1) = x_i(0) - x_5(0)\, U_{i,5}\ ;\ i = (n-2), (n-3),...1$

$t = 2$:

$x_3(2) = (x_3(1) - x_4(1)\, U_{3,4})\ /\ U_{3,3}$

which is a solution for x_3

$x_i(2) = x_i(1) - x_4(1)\, U_{i,4};\ \ i = 2,...\ 1$

$t = 3$:

$x_2(3) = (x_2(2) - x_3(2)\, U_{2,3})\ /\ U_{2,2}$

which is a solution for x_2

$x_i(3) = x_i(2) - x_3(2)\, U_{i,3};\ \ i = 1$

$t = 4$:

$x_1(4) = (x_1(3) - x_2(3)\, U_{1,2})\ /\ U_{1,1}$

which is a solution for x_1

The solutions are obtained piece-meal, one for each t as follows:

$x_i = x_i(n-i);\ \ i = n, (n-1),...\ 1$

This example can be generalized into an algorithm that works for any n as shown below.

1. Initialize.

   $x_n(0) = b_n/U_{n,n}$

   $x_i(0) = b_i;\ i = 1,...\ (n-1)$

2. Sequentially, for $t = 1$ to $(n-1)$ do

   $x_i(t) = x_i(t-1) - x_{n-t+1}(t-1)\, U_{i,n-t+1};\ i = 1,...\ (n-t)$

   $x_{n-t}(t) = x_{n-t}(t)\ /\ U_{n-t,n-t}$

3. Output. $x_i(n-i);\ i = 1,...\ n$

The core of this algorithm is step 2, where the partial sums are computed because we can exploit the parallelism in the inner loop. In each *t*-step, a partial column of *U* is multiplied by the most recently calculated solution to obtain the incremental value added to each partial sum.

The sequential Fortran code for this version of back substitution is as follows, where we have dropped the data declarations and input/output statements for simplicity.

```
c Initialize all X
  DO 10 I = 1, N-1
10 X(I) = B(I)
c Compute first solution
  X(N) = B(N) / U(N,N)
c Iterate backward -- X(N-1), X(N-2), ...X(1)
  DO 30 T = 1,N-1
  DO 20 I = 1,N-T
20 X(I) = X(I) - X(N-T+1) * U(I,N-T+1)
c Divide by diagonal element
30 X(N-T) = X(N-T) / U(N-T,N-T)
```

Now, the Sequent Symmetry Fortran compiler reads comments to obtain compiler directives which it uses to parallelize loops. One of these compiler hints is the *DOACROSS* comment. Placing a DOACROSS in a comment immediately before a loop tells the compiler what variables are shared and what variable is the loop counter. This information is used to fork each iteration of the loop into a separate task which is run in parallel with all other loop iteration tasks.

The DOACROSS only works when there are no loop-carried dependencies. A *loop-carried dependency* is one in which the value of variables in loop iteration j depend on the values in loop iteration $j - k$, for some $k \neq 0$.

There are two loops in the Fortran code above that have no loop-carried dependencies. The first is DO 10 $I = 1$, $N - 1$, but it has very little to do, so it is probably less efficient to parallelize this initialization loop than to execute it serially on one processor. Why? UNIX based shared-memory machines use costly task instantiation techniques. When a UNIX task is instantiated on the Sequent Symmetry, the entire program image is copied to disk, and two or more images are copied back into memory at some later time. Each image supports one parallel task. When the images are copied back into memory, they must set up page tables and so forth. This is costly.

When tasks are spawned in such systems, we call them *heavy-duty tasks*, because of the high overhead associated with creating the task. A *light-weight task*, on the other hand, is one in which very little overhead is required to start a new task. One significant difference between MACH and UNIX is the ability for MACH to support light-weight tasks.

So, we pass up the chance to parallelize the initialization loop. The second opportunity is found in the inner loop, DO 20 $I = 1$, $N - T$, because $N - T + 1$ remains constant throughout all iterations. The following program, written by Youfeng Wu of Sequent Computer, illustrates the DOACROSS solution to $Ux = b$.

```
      c  Initialize all X
         DO 10 I = 1, N-1
10       X(I) = B(I)
      c  Compute first solution
         X(N) = B(N) / U(N,N)
      c  Iterate backward -- X(N-1), X(N-2), ...X(1)
         DO 30 T = 1,N-1
      c$ DOACROSS LOCAL(I) SHARED (N, T, X, U)
         DO 20 I = 1,N-T
20       X(I) = X(I) - X(N-T+1) * U(I,N-T+1)
      c  Divide by diagonal element
30       X(N-T) = X(N-T) / U(N-T,N-T)
```

The DOACROSS LOCAL comment tells the compiler to make loop counter I a local variable so each copy of the loop body can have its own I. The SHARED comment informs the compiler to treat N, T, X, and U as shared variables within each task. But, since N, T, and U are read-only throughout the loop, there is no possible synchronization problem with sharing these variables. Variable X is both read and write, so there may be a synchronization problem. However, since there is no loop-carried dependency due to $X(I)$, there is no synchronization problem with X either.

What speedup should we expect from this version? The bulk of computing is done in the nested loops. In fact, the nested loops in the serial version compute in time proportional to N^2, while the serial version executes in $O(N)$ time if we ignore task creation overhead. Thus, the speedup is expected to be $O(N)$. How does this compare with Amdahl's Law? The Gustafson-Barsis Law? The answers to these questions are left to the reader.

3.2 DISTRIBUTED-MEMORY NETWORKS

A distributed-memory IN consists of processors and their local memories connected by communication links. There is no global memory so it is necessary to move data from one local memory to another by means of *message-passing*. This is typically done by a SEND/RECEIVE pair of commands which must be written into the application software by a programmer. Thus, programmers must learn the message-passing paradigm, and cope with the details of data copying and the attendant consistency issues.

A *node* in such a network consists of a processor and its local memory. Nodes are typically able to store messages in buffers (temporary memory locations where messages wait until they can be sent or received), and perform send/receive operations at the same time as processing. Simultaneous message processing and problem calculating are handled by the underlying operating system.

WITHDRAWN
ITHACA COLLEGE LIBRARY

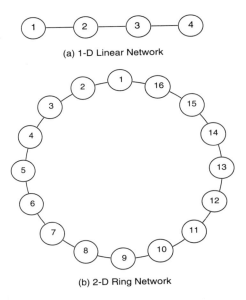

(a) 1-D Linear Network

(b) 2-D Ring Network

Figure 3.8   Simple networks: (a) linear, and (b) two-dimensional ring

According to Figure 3.1, distributed memory INs can be divided into static and dynamic INs. Dynamic INs establish a connection between two or more nodes on the fly as messages are routed along the links.

Static networks form all connections when the machine is designed rather than when the connection is needed. In a static network, messages must be routed along established links. This often means a single message must *hop* through intermediate processors on its way to its destination.

In the following, we will limit discussion to the most popular INs and concentrate mainly on commercially available INs. However, the reader should be aware that many promising INs have been proposed that have yet to be used in building a real parallel computer. Some of these experimental INs provide better performance than existing INs. As always, there are cost and performance trade-offs to be considered.

3.2.1   Static Networks

The simplest network we can imagine is a linear IN, where each node contains a processor and local memory (see Figure 3.8(a)). It takes $N-1$ links to construct a linear network, and on the average, it takes approximately $N/3$ hops to send a message from a source processor to a destination processor. The *number of hops* in a path from source to destination node is equal to the number of point-to-point links a message must traverse to reach its destination.

We can reduce the average number of hops from source to destination node by increasing the dimensionality of the IN as shown in Figure 3.8(b). A ring network reduces the average number of hops from approximately $N/3$ to approximately $N/6$

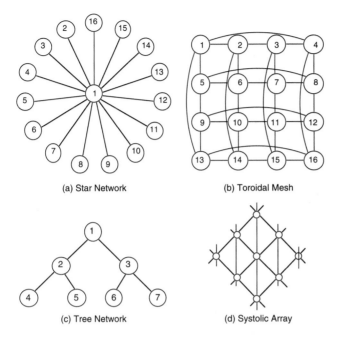

(a) Star Network   (b) Toroidal Mesh

(c) Tree Network   (d) Systolic Array

Figure 3.9   **Some proposed two-dimensional INs**

because the message can be routed along the shortest path, effectively cutting the distance in half. For a modest increase of one link, the ring doubles the number of paths from any node to any other node.

The goal of IN design is to reduce hardware costs by reducing links, and at the same time, minimize the time taken to send a message by reducing the number of hops. The linear IN is an example of a one-dimensional IN, and the ring an example of a two-dimensional IN (see Figure 3.1). A number of other two-dimensional INs have been proposed (see Figure 3.9). What is the average number of hops from source to destination in each of these INs? What is the cost of these INs in terms of the number of links?

3.2.2   Hypercubes

When it is impossible to connect nodes without crossing point-to-point links, we must resort to higher dimensions so that links do not cross one another. But, higher dimensioned INs usually mean a geometric growth in links. For example, Figure 3.10(a) contains $N(N + 1)/2$ links to fully connect N processor nodes in three-dimensional space. For $N = 16$, this means 136 connections. Even large-scale-integration is insufficient to accommodate over 500,000 links to fully connect 1,024 processors.

A compromise between rapid growth in links versus small number of hops is to project the IN topology into higher dimensions and connect only adjacent nodes in the same dimension. That is, we connect nodes along one axis of the hyperspace. Figure

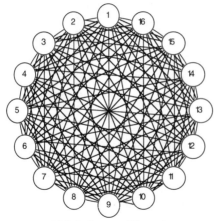

(a) Fully Connected Network

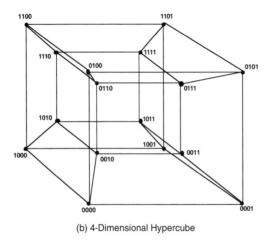

(b) 4-Dimensional Hypercube

Figure 3.10 (a) 16 fully connected processors with 136 links, (b) 16 hypercube connected processors with 32 links

3.10(b) illustrates this idea for four-dimensional hyperspace. The number of links in hyperspace grows linearly with N, thus 16 processors can be connected together using only 31 links. (Of course, the number of hops is increased because it is no longer possible for all processor pairs to directly communicate with one another.)

Think of each axis of a 4-D hyperspace as a perpendicular line emanating from the origin marked as point 0000 in Figure 3.10(b). The so-called x-axis is drawn to the right to point 0001; the y-axis fades into the page to point 0010; the z-axis is drawn straight up to point 0100; and finally, the v-axis is drawn in the fourth dimension and connects to point 1000. Notice that each position of the binary number corresponds to a dimension. That is, the x-axis defines the first dimension, and so it is designated in bit

Parallel Processors Chapter 3

position one (from right to left); the y-axis defines the second dimension so it is designated in bit position two; z-direction is designated in position three; and v-direction in bit position four. Each bit position designates a direction along a dimension of the hyperspace.

We have used binary digits to indicate a distance along an axis. Such a hyperspace is called binary, because it is based on binary digits. In a *binary hypercube*, processors are embedded in a binary hyperspace. In the 4-D binary hyperspace shown in Figure 3.10(b), one processor is placed at each coordinate in the binary hyperspace. The processors are connected along each axis in 4-D hyperspace, thus there are four connections in the IN.

In general, an n-dimensional hypercube contains $2^n = N$ processors connected by a link along each of axis. There are $n = \log_2 N$ links at each processor. The observant reader may have noticed that the binary encoding of processor locations in the hypercube forms a simple gray code, where each neighboring processor is just one bit away. Thus, changing a single bit in the coordinate corresponds to moving along one axis in binary hyperspace.

Designers of binary hypercube INs typically use a binary *Hamming code* to number the nodes. This simplifies the circuits needed to perform routing. Recall that the *Hamming distance* between binary numbers A and B equals the number of bits in which A and B differ. Thus, the distance between $A = 0101$ and $B = 0110$ is two because the third and fourth bits from left-to-right differ.

Starting at node 0000 in the four-dimensional hypercube shown in Figure 3.10(b), we can move in any direction by changing one bit at a time. Hence, the nearest neighbors of node 0000 are 1000, 0100, 0010, 0001. Moving along any axis in binary hyperspace corresponds to a change in only one bit at a time. This simple scheme can be used to advantage in routing a message from node A to B.

Example

Suppose source node $A = 1010$ and destination node $B = 1100$. We can compute a route from A to B by taking the Hamming difference between A and B, moving in the dimension which reduces the difference one dimension at a time, and stopping when the difference reduces to 0000. The difference between two Hamming codes is obtained by writing a 1 in each dimension where the bits of A and B differ, and writing a 0 in places where they are the same. In other words, $A - B$ is the exclusive-or of A and B. (The Hamming distance is the number of "1" bits in (A ex-or B).)

$$A = 1010 \qquad B = 1100 \qquad A - B = 0110$$

The difference is shown as two 1s in dimensions 1 and 2. So, we can move in either of these dimensions to get closer to the destination. Suppose we move in the direction of the high-order bits first. This is the same as moving to (1010 ex-or 0100) = 1110. The next move is in the direction of 0010, so (1110 ex-or 0010) = 1100.

	iPSC/2	iPSC/2 SX	iPSC/2 VX	iPSC/860 Series
Number of Nodes (Processors)	16 – 128	16-128	8-128	8-128
Processor Performance	64 – 512 MIPS	64 – 512 MIPS	32 – 512 MIPS	40 – 60 MFlops
Floating Point Performance	MFlops	MFlops	MFlops	MFlops
Single Precision	4 – 32	18 – 141	160 – 1280	640 – 10240
Double Precision	3.4 – 27	10 – 81	53 – 424	480 – 7680
Memory Capacity	1 – 16 MBytes	1 – 16 MBytes	1 – 8 MBytes	128 – 2048
Disk Capacity (Formatted)	1.1 – 510 GBytes	1.1 – 510 GBytes	1.1 – 510 GBytes	9.1 – 165.1
I/O Nodes	1 – 127	1 – 127	1 – 127	1,2,4,8
I/O Bandwidth (Aggregate)	← 2.8 – 711.2 MBytes/sec →			9.1 – 355.6 MBytes/sec

	nCUBE 3200 Series	nCUBE 6400 Series
Processor	4 – 1,024	64 – 8,192
Processor Performance	8 – 2000 MIPS	490 – 60,000 MIPS
Floating Point Performance	2 – 500 MFlops	210 – 27,000 MFlops
Memory Capacity	2MBytes – 0.5 GBytes	64 MBytes – 512 GBytes
Disk Capacity (Formatted)	800 MBytes – 4.TBytes	800 MBytes – 400 TBytes
Bus Bandwidth (Sustained)	160 MBytes – 8 GBytes/sec	52 MBytes – 640 GBytes/sec
I/O Bandwidth	1.4 GBytes/sec	36 GBytes/sec

Figure 3.11   Intel iPSC and nCUBE family capabilities

The simplicity of binary numbers can be used to imbed other INs into a hypercube. A hypercube of dimension $k < n$ is said to be imbedded in hypercube of dimension n if and only if the k-dimensional hypercube is a proper subcube of the n-dimensional hypercube. That is, the smaller hypercube forms a true hypercube from the unaltered components of the larger hypercube. This idea can be used to imbed other structures in hypercubes as well. For example, a ring structure might be imbedded in a hypercube of sufficient dimension. Thus, in general, an imbedding is a mapping from one structure to another that preserves both topological structures.

For example, a ring is imbedded in a 4-D binary hypercube by simply traversing all nodes from 0000 to 0001, 0011, 0010,... 1111, and back to 0000. Each step changes only one bit at a time, preserves the topology of both structures, and maps the processors of one IN into the processors of another IN.

A tree can be imbedded in a hypercube in similar fashion, where two paths are spawned at each stage. For example, if the root node is 0000, then the left descendant is 0001 and the right descendant is 0010. Similar mappings are possible for other lower-dimensional INs.

The maximum distance from an arbitrary processor node to any other node in an IN is called its *diameter*. This is a measure of the efficiency of the IN as a message-passing mechanism, because the maximum number of hops is equal to the IN's diameter. For a binary hypercube, this is $n = \log_2 N$. Thus, the diameter of a hypercube increases linearly as the number of processors increases exponentially. This is a very desirable property.

N = number of processors = 2^n

Diameter = n

Chapter 5 develops the binary hypercube concept in greater detail and illustrates a number of more sophisticated imbeddings. The key concept here is that hypercubes can be partitioned into smaller structures that conform to the application's requirements. This concept is very useful for single application performance and time-sharing of the larger hypercube.

Commercial Hypercubes

The Intel iPSC and nCUBE families of parallel computers are two of the leading MIMD parallel computers that use the hypercube IN (see Figure 3.11).

These machines have optimized the hypercube IN for scientific calculations in applications of VLSI design (circuit simulation), particle simulation (N-body interactions such as found in crystals), fluid flow modeling (Navier-Stokes equations), computer vision (object recognition), protein-sequence matching, document retrieval in large databases, neural network simulations, and computer graphics. In addition, the nCUBE machines are being developed to perform very high transaction processing rates in database applications. In both machines, the mapping of such applications onto the hypercube IN is no simple exercise, even for the most trivial problems, because of the message-passing form of communication required of all parallel applications.

MIMD Solution to Ux = b

Once again we use the solution to $Ux = b$ as a vehicle to illustrate elementary programming issues for MIMD programming, and to compare the MIMD solution with the previous approaches.

This problem suggests data-parallel programming. Recall from Chapter 1, the two steps involved in the data-parallel paradigm: (1) partition and distribute the data, and (2) process the data in parallel. In addition, we must map these phases onto a particular target machine. In this section we examine how we might map data-parallel tasks onto a hypercube IN.

Assuming $n = 5$ as before suggests 5-way parallelism, so we begin by assuming there are $n = 5$ virtual processors. A *virtual processor* is a task that exists only in the software sense. In fact, there may be fewer physical processors than virtual processors. This complicates the mapping of the problem onto the machine because we must try to minimize the communication costs incurred from matching the topology of the problem to the topology of the machine. Specifically, we will try to map a ring of 5 virtual processors onto 4 physical processors interconnected as a hypercube.

VP1	VP2	VP3	VP4	VP5
b_5	b_4	b_3	b_2	b_1
	x_5			
$U_{5,5}$	$U_{4,5}$	$U_{3,5}$	$U_{2,5}$	$U_{1,5}$
		x_4		
	$U_{4,4}$	$U_{3,4}$	$U_{2,4}$	$U_{1,4}$
			x_3	
		$U_{3,3}$	$U_{2,3}$	$U_{1,3}$
				x_2
			$U_{2,2}$	$U_{1,2}$
				$U_{1,1}$

Table 3.2   Solution to $Ux = b$ using 5 virtual processors

Table 3.2 shown for $n = 5$ illustrates the partitioning and distribution of data across $n = 5$ virtual processors, $VP1$ through $VP5$. The data listed below each VP column refers to the pieces of data needed to do each calculation. Time increases as we move down the table, corresponding to increasing t in the algorithm. Thus, step one is to distribute the bs to all processors. Step two is to compute x_5 in $VP2$. Step three is to compute the Us as shown, and so on. Table 3.2 does not attempt to show how to map the steps onto a hypercube, but only serves to show how the calculations might be done in parallel.

The patterns in this table make two things clear: (1) partial columns of U are distributed across all virtual processors, and (2) the solutions must be broadcast to higher numbered VPs as soon as each x becomes available so that the next step of partial summation can be completed.

The partitioning is as follows: Partition $Ux = b$ into rows, and distribute each row to a VP. That is, row 5 consisting of $[U_{5,5} \ x_5 \ b_5]$ is placed on processor 1, row 4 consisting of $[U_{4,4} \ U_{4,5} \ x_4 \ b_4]$ is placed on $VP2$, and so forth until all rows of the partitioned problem have been assigned a VP.

The distribution is done as follows. As soon as each element of x is calculated, broadcast it to the higher-numbered VPs. Thus, x_5 is calculated first, in $VP1$, and broadcast to $VP2$, $VP3$, $VP4$, and $VP5$. When x_4 is calculated in $VP2$, it is broadcast to $VP3$, $VP4$, and $VP5$. Finally, x_2 is calculated in $VP5$ and the process stops. If each x is forwarded along a ring of VPs as they are calculated, all values end up back at $VP1$, where they can be displayed.

Suppose we map these two phases onto a two-dimensional iPSC/2 or nCUBE target machine. Let $P00$, $P01$, $P10$, and $P11$ be the four processors in a two-dimensional hypercube. For $n = 5$, we are faced with a *ragged edge problem,* i.e., the number of VPs is not a multiple of the number of physical processors. In this simple example the solution is also simple; we map $VP1$ and $VP5$ both onto $P00$. The remaining virtual processors map one-on-one as $VP2 \rightarrow P01$, $VP3 \rightarrow P10$, and $VP4 \rightarrow P11$.

The partitioning and distribution are achieved by treating the hypercube as a ring. We described a straightforward method of forming a ring from any hypercube in the previous section. We can use the ring algorithm to do the broadcasting and the fact that processors along the ring are ordered from 00 to 10 according to the gray code, e.g., 00, 01, 11, 10.

The mechanism for exchanging data as described here is called *message-passing.* In general, the message-passing operations are SEND and RECEIVE plus additional operations for inquiring about the status of messages. Chapter 5 elaborates on how to program a distributed memory machine such as the iPSC/2 and nCUBE.

SIMD Hypercubes: The Connection Machine

When the number of processors increases, e.g., the dimension of the hypercube increases, perhaps the best use of them is in massively parallel SIMD calculations like the $Ux = b$ calculation illustrated in the previous section. In such machines, memory is distributed, which means the data must be spread across the network to reduce the load on any single memory. This is the fundamental idea behind the highly successful Connection Machine (CM) family of SIMD machines from Thinking Machines, Inc. and MP-1 from MasPar Corporation. Figure 3.12 shows the general structure of the Connection Machine as described by Tucker and Robertson.

In Figure 3.12, the I/O system connects the 4 quadrants of 16,384 processors each to very large disk storage devices called data vaults and to graphics terminals. The Nexus controller also connects the quadrants to a front-end processor, typically a Digital Equipment Corporation VAX, where program development is performed.

In the iPSC and nCUBE example, we emulated data-parallel programming by duplicating the program code in each of the processor/memory nodes of the hypercube. This required that program code as well as data be distributed to the MIMD processors. Even though the computing paradigm was SIMD, the actual calculations were done in SPMD style on MIMD hardware.

The CM-1 is a true SIMD machine, so it is not necessary to duplicate program code and distribute it to all processors. Instead, one copy of the program controls numerous processors. These numerous processors execute in lockstep fashion from a single stream

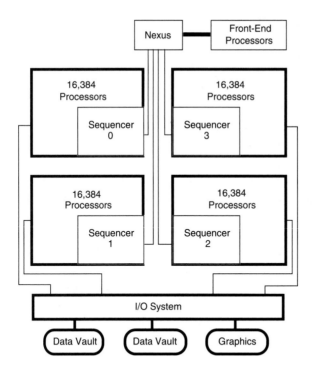

Figure 3.12   General structure of the Thinking Machines, Inc. SIMD Connection Machine for data-parallel applications

of instructions. We load program code once and then distribute data to each processor that needs it. In fact, the CM-1 has but one control unit for sequencing all processors of a quadrant.

The processors of a typical Connection Machine are imbedded in a hypercube connected IN. They are physically organized as a 12-dimensional (4096) hypercube with 16 processors at each vertex of the hypercube. Each 16-processor vertex contains a router which sends and receives messages from remote vertex processors or local vertex processors. These routers can also buffer messages in case of blocking. (The programmer, however, sees the processors as a two-dimensional mesh with Cartesian addresses.)

The Hamming difference method of routing is used. Each message has the difference appended to it, and each time the message is forwarded, the corresponding bit is set to zero so that the Hamming distance is reduced to zero when the message arrives at its destination.

Processors are bit serial CPUs that work on two-bit operands. Each operation can combine two bits from memory with one bit from a (flag) register, for example, and produce two result bits, one for memory and one for the register. To get 32-bit precision answers, the 16 processors at a vertex are combined into a 32-bit cluster. One floating point accelerator coprocessor is shared among 32 processors in the CM-2.

(The connection is as a pipeline to the cluster module.) This achieves 64-bit floating point operations at 1/64-th the speed of bit-serial scalar operations.

The CM-2 can hold from 4096 to 65,536 processors, each with from 65,536 to 262,144 bits of local memory. The front-end machine controls these processors, collectively. For example, after data are partitioned and distributed to each memory, an instruction is sent from the front-end to all CM-2 processors. Each processor executes its instruction in lockstep fashion on its own data. A processor can be inhibited by setting its context flag. All selected processors perform their instructions; all unselected processors are idle.

Extensions of Fortran and C have been used to program the Connection Machine. C*, for example, is a data-parallel version of C. These extended languages sometimes introduce a new data type called *poly data* which defines the distributed structures needed for data-parallel algorithms. At the time of this writing, C* is undergoing a revision, and the new version of C* no longer requires poly data. However, the idea has found its way into other data-parallel languages such as DataParallel C and MultiC.

Program designs like the $Ux = b$ problem employ virtual processors that are automatically mapped onto the Connection Machine's physical processors by the compilers and operating system. Each physical processor sequentially executes its *VP*s, resulting in a degradation of performance proportional to the number of *VP*s per processor.

The idea of a connectionist machine is documented in a 1985 Ph.D. thesis by Hillis, even though it originated in the 1960s. The Illiac IV, Goodyear MPP, and other machines were early examples of SIMD computers. A survey of the CM-1 and its development history is provided by Tucker and Robertson. The reader is advised to read this supplemental information for more details.

Data-Parallel Solution to Ux = b

To gain a better understanding of SIMD machines like the CM-1 and MP-1, it is worthwhile to revisit the data-parallel example used to describe how MIMD hypercubes might be programmed in SIMD style. Recall the problem is to solve the system of linear equations $Ux = b$ by back substitution when U is an upper diagonal matrix of order N.

The serial Fortran solution given earlier is repeated here for convenience.

```
      c  Initialize all X
         DO 10 I = 1, N-1
10       X(I) = B(I)
      c  Compute first solution
         X(N) = B(N) / U(N,N)
      c  Iterate backward -- X(N-1), X(N-2), ...X(1)
         DO 30 T = 1,N-1
         DO 20 I = 1,N-T
20       X(I) = X(I) - X(N-T+1) * U(I,N-T+1)
      c  Divide by diagonal element
30       X(N-T) = X(N-T) / U(N-T,N-T)
```

In this section we develop a CM Fortran data-parallel version that is very close to the final FORTRAN code that might be compiled and run on the Connection Machine. This example code sacrifices rigor for clarity, however. We provide greater programming rigor in Chapter 7, where a full discussion of data-parallel programming is presented.

The solution on a Connection Machine can immediately take advantage of the matrix operations in Fortran 8X which have been implemented for data-parallel programming in the CM Fortran compiler. Merely writing X in place of $X(I)$ tells the compiler to distribute all elements of X to N virtual processors. This is a natural data-parallel programming trait, causing N processors to implement the same operation on all elements of X.

Using the data-parallel features of Fortran 8X and the implementation on the Connection Machine, we can simplify and speed up the serial solution by replacing the initialization section with the following.

```
c  Initialize all X
   X = B
```

Next we use a new idea in programming called a stencil. A *stencil* is a subroutine that incorporates a data-parallel programming pattern. The pattern usually involves data partitioning through rearrangement of the data structures (transposing arrays, for example), and distribution of data across processors (broadcasting, for example).

The inner loop of the sequential solution is a candidate for replacement with a call to a stencil routine:

```
   DO 20 I = 1,N-T
20 X(I) = X(I) - X(N-T+1) * U(I,N-T+1)
```

The subscripts $(N-T+1)$ remain constant throughout the iteration across I, and only one column at a time of U is affected. Suppose we use a stencil routine to extract the columns from U, one at a time, and then perform a scalar multiply of the column in data-parallel fashion.

```
SUBROUTINE COLUMN (X, U, K, V, N)
DIMENSION X(N), U(N,N), V(N)
BS = X(K)
V = 0.0
V = V + U(1:K-1,K)
V = BS * V
RETURN
END
```

Here we have taken liberty with Fortran by denoting vector-column arithmetic as $V = V + U(1:K-1,K)$. This means to add the first $K-1$ elements of column K of matrix U to each element of V, in parallel. The initial values of V are all 0.0, so the partial increment of V in this statement leaves $N-K$ elements of V set to zero with each data-parallel sweep.

Similarly, the statement $V = BS * V$ means to multiply each element of V by the constant scalar BS and store the product in V. This is done on N processors in parallel, because the elements of V are distributed across N processors.

One of the differences between a stencil and an ordinary subroutine is the parallelization that is performed on the stencil routines. Normally, the operations of standard Fortran are carried out sequentially, one after the other. But, if vector operations are placed in a stencil routine, they can be carried out at once, in parallel.

Thinking Machines, Inc. provides a vast library of stencils which include most of the standard mathematical operations such as Fast Fourier Transform, Linear Algebra, and various data partitioning operations such as sum-scan and spread. A *scan*, for example, combines values from all processors along a certain coordinate. Sum-scan is used to compute the sum of a list of numbers distributed across numerous processors, in parallel. A *spread* is a generalized broadcast stencil which sends a value on one processor to all other processors. The Laplacian operator is available as a spread, as are most first and second order differential equation patterns.

Returning to the problem at hand, we can simplify the data-parallel solution to the example problem as follows.

```
      c  Initialize
         X = B
      c  Compute first solution
         X(N) = B(N)/U(N,N)
      c  Iterate backward -- X(N-1), X(N-2), ...X(1)
         DO 30 T = 1,N-1
         CALL COLUMN (X, U, N-T+1, V, N)
         X = X - V
      c  Divide by diagonal element
   30    X(N-T) = X(N-T) / U(N-T,N-T)
```

The following tableau contains only the first three steps of the data-parallel solution described above for $N = 5$.

```
Initially
X(I) = B(I)      ; I = 1,..5
X(5) = B(5)/U(5,5)
T=1:
BS = X(5)
V(1...5) = BS * [U(1,5)  U(2,5)  U(3,5)  U(4,5)  0]
X(1) = B(1) - X(5)*U(1,5)
X(2) = B(2) - X(5)*U(2,5)
X(3) = B(3) - X(5)*U(3,5)
X(4) = [B(4) - X(5)*U(4,5)] / U(4,4)
X(5) = B(5) / U(5,5) - 0
T = 2:
BS = X(4)
```

```
V(1...5) = BS * [U(1,4)  U(2,4)  U(3,4)  0  0]
X(1) = B(1) - X(5)*U(1,5) - X(4)*U(1,4)
X(2) = B(2) - X(5)*U(2,5) - X((4)*U(2,4)
X(3) = [B(3) - X(5)*U(3,5) - X(4)*U(3,4)] / U(3,3)
X(4) = [B(4) - X(5)*U(4,5)] / U(4,4) - 0
X(5) = B(5)/U(5,5) - 0
```

Clearly, the time taken to solve $Ux = b$ for very large values of N are independent of N, up to the point where we run out of processors. Assuming we have N processors, speedup is governed by the Gustafson-Barsis Law, which states that a linear speedup is possible regardless of N:

$$S = N - (N-1)\beta$$

In this example, β is very small as it is essentially the time it takes to step through the data-parallel processing operations. Assuming $\beta \ll 1$, we can ignore the $(N-1)\beta$ term. $S \approx N$.

The approximation for speedup may be inaccurate if the cost of communication is high because the Gustafson-Barsis Law ignores communication costs and other forms of overhead. The approximation becomes very accurate, however, if the grain size of the calculation is comparable with the communication overhead. For the example given here, the problem is too small to be effectively spread across $n = 4$ processors. If $n = 1,000$, however, speedups comparable to the prediction are realistic.

The SIMD and data-parallel paradigm go hand-in-hand. Distribution of data followed by lockstep parallel computation fits most scientific calculations very well. But, it has been necessary to efficiently code common communication patterns into stencil routines to achieve the highest performance.

3.3   DYNAMIC INTERCONNECTION NETWORKS

Figure 3.1 lists three forms of dynamic IN: (1) single-stage, (2) multi-stage, and (3) cross-bar. Examples of each of these are shown in Figure 3.13. The single-stage IN of Figure 3.13(a) is a simple dynamic network which connects each of the inputs on the left side to some, but not all, outputs on the right side through a single layer of binary switches represented by the rectangles. The binary switches can direct the message on the left-side input to one of two possible outputs on the right side.

Clearly, the single-stage network is limited, but if we cascade enough single-stage networks together, they form a completely connected *MIN* (Multistage Interconnection Network), as shown in Figure 3.13(b). The *omega MIN* connects 8 inputs to 8 outputs. The connection from input 010 to itself is shown as a bold path in Figure 3.13(b).

These are dynamic INs because the connection is made on-the-fly, as needed. For example, to connect input 101 to output 001 in the omega network, we simply use the bits of the destination address, 001, as instructions for dynamically selecting a path

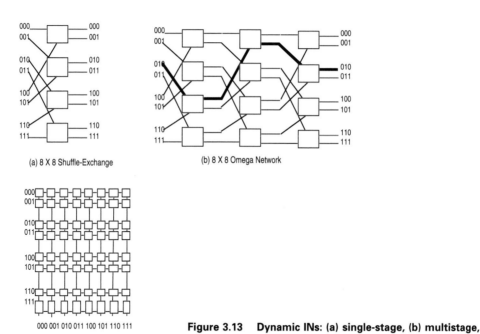

(a) 8 X 8 Shuffle-Exchange

(b) 8 X 8 Omega Network

000 001 010 011 100 101 110 111

(c) 8 X 8 Cross-bar Switch

Figure 3.13 **Dynamic INs: (a) single-stage, (b) multistage, (c) cross-bar switch**

through the switches. The destination address says to set the first two switches to 0 followed by setting the third switch to 1. This path leads to the desired destination. A path from any input side to all destination addresses from 000 to 111 can be obtained in this fashion.

Similarly, the cross-bar switch of Figure 3.13(c) provides a path from any input or source to any other output or destination by simply selecting a direction on-the-fly. To connect input 011 to itself requires only one binary switch at the intersection of the 011 input line and 011 output line to be set. (The drawing of Figure 3.13(c) is somewhat misleading, because it is not necessary for an input to pass through all intermediate binary switches to reach a certain switch, nor to flow to an output. The diagram does, however, reflect the number of components needed to make a fully connected IN.)

The cross-bar switch clearly uses more binary switching components. e.g., N^2 components are needed to connect $N \times N$ source/destination pairs. The omega MIN, on the other hand, connects $N \times N$ pairs with $N \log N$ components. The major advantage of the cross-bar switch is its potential for speed. In one clock, a connection can be made between source and destination. The diameter of the cross-bar is one. The omega MIN, on the other hand requires $\log_2 N$ clocks to make a connection. The diameter of the omega MIN is therefore $\log_2 N$.

Both networks limit the number of alternate paths between any input/output pair. This leads to limited fault-tolerance and network traffic congestion. If the single path between pairs becomes faulty, that pair cannot communicate. If two pairs attempt to

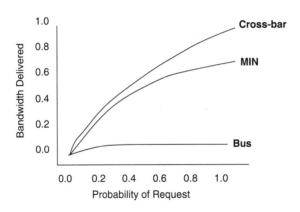

Figure 3.14   Performance of dynamic INs versus bus-structured IN

communicate at the same time along a shared path, one pair must wait for the other. This is called *blocking*, and such MINs are called *blocking networks*.

A network that can handle all possible connections without blocking is called a *non-blocking network*. One way to construct such networks is to add stages to the MIN so that alternate paths are possible. Benes networks are examples of this approach. A survey of other MINs is given by Feng.

3.3.1 Dynamic Parallel Processors

The networks described above have been used in commercial processors, but in an unusual way. Memory is distributed in these systems, but the appearance of a shared memory is given through the IN. The inputs to the IN are processors and the outputs are memories. This is in opposition to the pure distributed-memory model presented earlier.

Dynamic parallel processors are further categorized by the coupling of processors to memories. A *tightly coupled* system is one in which memory is equally accessible from all processors at high speed. (This notion is also called UMA for Uniform Memory Access, or symmetric multiprocessing because of the uniformity of access time.) Thus, a cross-bar system is tightly coupled because all processors can access all memories in the same (constant) time. Examples of tightly coupled machines are the C.mmp experimental system at Carnegie-Mellon University, and shared-memory bus-structured systems such as the Sequent Symmetry and Alliant FX/8.

A parallel computer is said to be *loosely coupled* if access times vary depending on the reference pattern. (This notion is also called *NUMA* for Non-Uniform Memory Access time.) This is the case with the BBN Butterfly system where each processor has its own local memory, but each processor can access all memories through an omega MIN. Access to a processor's local memory is fast, but access to a remote memory takes $O(1 + \log_2 N)$ cycles. Other examples are the Cm* at Carnegie-Mellon University, and the IBM RP3 research machine at IBM *T.* J. Watson Research Center.

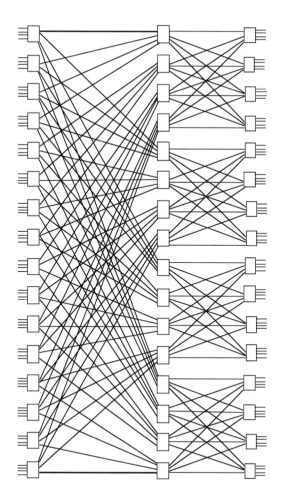

Figure 3.15   MIN for the 64-Processor BBN butterfly

The performance curves of Figure 3.14 illustrate the value of cross-bar, MIN, and bus-structured INs. The vertical axis is "bandwidth as delivered," which shows the ability of each IN to deliver responses when loaded with requests. The horizontal axis is the probability of a request for a connection. This is a measure of the load placed on the IN. The results of Figure 3.14 assume no cache memories or buffering.)

3.3.2   BBN Butterfly: A Commercial MIN Processor

A commercial example of a MIN-structured parallel computer is the BBN Butterfly manufactured by Bolt, Beranek and Newman Advanced Computers, Inc. A typical Butterfly contains 64 Motorola MC68020 processors with MC68881 floating point coprocessors connected via a MIN as shown in Figure 3.15. Each processor has its own memory, but as far as the programmer is concerned, the processors all access one large shared memory through a global address space.

All memory is local to a processor, but memory addresses are global. This means that each fetch is checked to see if the address is local to the processor. If it is, the fetch takes place in one memory cycle. If it is not, the request is put out on the MIN, which maps it onto the appropriate remote memory (attached to some other processor). Remote references take longer, about three times as long in the BBN Butterfly.

The MIN of Figure 3.15 is similar to the routing used in the butterfly FFT (Fast Fourier Transform) algorithm, hence the name of the BBN parallel computer. As you can see, each switch is four-way, leading to a diameter of $\log_4 N$, or 3 when $N = 64$. There is at least one path between processor/memory pairs.

This is also an example of a *packet-switched IN*, because the messages are sent in packets of fixed length. The destination address is appended to the block of data to be sent. As the packet flows through the MIN, each switch strips two bits from the message and uses them to compute the next link.

If a switch receives two messages at the same time, one is delayed while the other is forwarded. The delayed message is forwarded after a short delay, rather than retransmitted from its source. Thus, the MIN has limited ability to handle blocking. In larger systems, switches are added to reduce blocking and increase fault-tolerance. The complexity of this MIN increases by $N \log_4 N$ as the number of processors linearly increase.

The BBN Butterfly is programmed in traditional languages (Fortran 77 and C) much like other shared-memory machines. Locks and barriers are used to synchronize access to shared data. Tasks are spawned in much the same way as concurrent tasks in UNIX, but the Chrysalis operating system is not UNIX.

Unlike bus-structured machines, the Butterfly does not use cache memories to reduce global access frequency. This reduces the need for complex cache coherency schemes, but it can lead to hot spot contention in the global address space. A *hot spot* is a block of memory that is frequently referenced by one or more parallel processors. Hot spots reduce parallelism by forcing processors to wait for one another, e.g., serial access forces sequential task executions.

PROBLEMS FOR DISCUSSION AND SOLUTION

1   What are the cache hit rates of the Sequent S27 and S81?

2   Repeat the example in Figure 3.7 for the Producer-consumer tasks, but instead of showing the inconsistencies, show the results if the write-update policy is applied. Repeat the example for the write-invalidate policy.

3   Compute the average number of hops and number of links in the networks of Figure 3.9 for N processors.

4   Give at least two mappings from the four-dimensional hypercube of Figure 3.10(b) to a binary tree.

5   What is the diameter of the INs of Figure 3.9? What is the diameter of a 128 processor BBN Butterfly MIN?

6   How might the back substitution problem described for the iPSC and nCUBE hypercubes differ if implemented on the BBN Butterfly?

7   Redesign the MIN of Figure 3.15 using 8-way switches in place of the 4-way switches used by BBN. How many stages are required for 64 processors? Why was 4 used instead of 2, 8, or 16?

8   Give a configuration (show the switch settings) for "simulating" a three-dimensional hypercube with a cross-bar switch like the one in Figure 3.13(c). How many *I*/O ports are needed at each processor to do this?

9   How many links are needed to connect 32 processors in a binary hypercube? What is the general formula to connect $N = 2^n$ processors in an *n*-dimensional hypercube?

References

Bhuyan, L. N. (ed.), "Interconnection Networks for Parallel and Distributed Processing," (ed), special issue of *Computer*, 20, 6, pp. 9 – 75, June 1987.

Bhuyan, L. N., Yang, Q., and Agrawal, D. P., "Performance of Multiprocessor Interconnection Networks," *Computer*, 22, 2, pp. 25 – 37, February 1989.

Dubois, M., and Thakkar, S., "Cache Architectures in Tightly Coupled Multiprocessors," *Computer*, 23, 6, pp. 9 – 85, June 1990.

Duncan, R., "A Survey of Parallel Computer Architectures," *Computer*, 23, 2, pp. 5 – 16, February 1990.

Feng, T-Y., "A Survey of Interconnection Networks," *Computer*, 14, 12, pp. 12 – 27, December 1981.

Goodman, J. R., "Using Cache Memory to Reduce Processor-Memory Traffic," *Proceedings 10th Annual Symposium on Computer Architecture*, pp. 124 – 131, June 1983.

Hillis, W. D., *The Connection Machine*, MIT Press, Cambridge, Mass., 1985.

Strecker. W. D., "Analysis of the Instruction Execution Rate in Certain Computer Structures," Ph.D. Thesis, Carnegie-Mellon University, Pittsburgh, Penn., 1970.

Tucker, L. W., and Robertson, G. G., "Architecture and Applications of the Connection Machine," *Computer*, 21, 8, pp. 26 – 38, August 1988.

Chapter 4

Shared-Memory
Parallel Programming

Shared-memory parallel programming is perhaps the easiest model to understand because of its similarity with operating systems programming and general multiprogramming. Indeed, shared-memory programming is done through minor extensions to existing programming languages, operating systems, and code libraries.

In this chapter we examine the general model of applications that best take advantage of the power of shared-memory multiprocessors systems such as the Sequent Symmetry and Encore Multimax. We show that these systems are best suited for the MIMD paradigm where a supervisor task controls a number of subordinate tasks. This is the supervisor/worker model described earlier, and gives rise to a client-server structure within the application's code.

Next, we study the DYNIX parallel process model used in the Sequent Computer Systems' machines. DYNIX, an extension of UNIX, provides a number of toolbox routines to handle task creation and synchronization. Examples are given in C, but these routines are available for other programming languages.

How are processes synchronized and storage locked in these systems? We generalize the Sequent model and introduce analysis techniques based on the interleave technique and timing diagrams. These two techniques can be used to analyze any highly concurrent application to assure that it is safe, fair, and live.

Finally, we examine an application of shared-memory programming. A serial version of the simplex algorithm used to find optimal solutions to linear programming problems is parallelized by casting it in the form of the supervisor/worker paradigm. The parallel version is shown to give very good speedup performance on a shared-memory computer.

4.1 A SHARED-MEMORY PROCESS MODEL

In Chapter 1 we learned that shared-memory multiprocessors are capable of supporting the most general form of MIMD computing. That is, they can process applications whose task graph is the most general form, and whose data structures conform to traditional programming. Task partitioning and dataflow synchronization are the main concerns in this model.

A theoretical model of shared-memory multicomputers called PRAM (Parallel Random Access Memory) overlooks details such as cache coherence and synchronization. In the PRAM model, algorithms are assumed to run without interference as long as only one memory access is permitted at a time. We say that PRAM guarantees *atomic access* to data located in shared memory. Access is considered to be atomic if only one processor is allowed to read/write from/to shared memory at a time. Atomic access will be assumed in this chapter, regardless of how it is achieved.

However, task creation and access synchronization can be costly. In addition, shared-memory computers typically support a limited number of processors. In general, shared-memory computers manage only a few hundred tasks simultaneously, and consist of fewer than 100 processors.

4.1.1 Multitasks versus Microtasks

At the large-grained level, PRAM computers can provide traditional time-sharing as in UNIX. Each time a UNIX process is initiated, idle processors are supplied to run the new process. If the system is heavily loaded, the processor with the least amount of work is assigned the new process. This form of *dynamic scheduling* is typically nonoptimal, but it is fast and simple. When spread over a number of user tasks, *load balancing* is possible in-the-large, and the operating system does not need to expend much effort to match processes to processors. (The jobs are simply entered in a queue, and the next available processor takes its next job from the head of the queue.)

A major advantage of PRAM is its suitability for virtual memory and traditional input and output. Most of what we know about operating systems applies to this model. Hence, page tables and virtual memory paging hardware, disk I/O, and networking can be implemented as in any other bus-structured system.

The large-grained PRAM model is suitable for multitasking applications where the cost of task creation is rather large. Such tasks are often called *heavy-weight tasks* because of their high overhead. A heavy-weight task in a multitasking system such as UNIX consists of page tables, memory, and file descriptors in addition to program code and data.

The heavy-weight PRAM model will be called *multitasking* here. It is implemented in UNIX by invocation of fork, exec, and other related UNIX commands. Multitasking is best suited for *heterogeneous tasks*, e.g., multiprogramming as in classical time-sharing.

At the fine-grained level, the PRAM model weakens because the high cost of process creation and access synchronization must be considered. For performance reasons, *light-weight processes* are needed. MACH, a UNIX look-alike, implements light-weight processes, but most UNIX variants also support less costly *microtasking*.

Microtasking permits a finer-grained parallelism. In fact, microtasking makes parallelism within a single application practical, but on PRAM machines, microtasking is best suited to homogeneous tasks (see Figure 4.1). In this model, an applica-

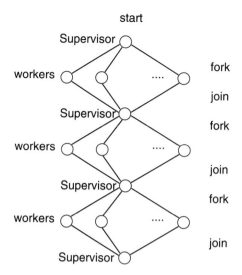

Figure 4.1   Series of fork-join tasks model supervisor/worker paradigm used in most parallel applications on shared-memory multiprocessors

tion is a series of fork-join *fans*. A fan is a collection of N worker tasks where one task is the supervisor and $N-1$ tasks are workers. In UNIX, a fan is created by forking processes as shown in Figure 4.1.

4.1.2   A UNIX Shared-Memory Model

In the standard UNIX model, the address space of an executing process has three segments called the text, data, and stack. The text is where the binary code to be executed is stored; the data segment is where the program's data are stored; and the stack is where activation records and dynamic data are stored. A simplified model of this is shown in Figure 4.2(a).

The data and stack segments expand and contract as the program executes. Therefore, a gap is purposely left in between the data and stack segments as shown in Figure 4.2(a).

Processes (multitasks) are assumed to be mutually independent and do not share addresses. The code of each serial process is allowed to access data in its own data and stack segments, only. Any attempt by another process to access other segments is trapped as a fatal error by UNIX. This is good for multiprogramming, but poses an obstacle to parallel programs.

In most UNIX systems, a new process is created by forking an existing process. Typically, this means the running program is interrupted, swapped to disk, and two copies swapped back into memory. The two copies are identical in every way, including their entire code. It is up to the programmer to interrogate the process ID returned by the fork routine to determine which process the code is executing.

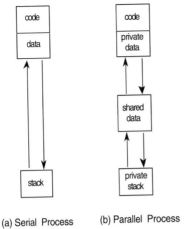

(a) Serial Process   (b) Parallel Process

Figure 4.2 (a) UNIX serial process model; (b) modified process model used by Sequent DYNIX

This swapping is costly, as mentioned before. The first time a program image is copied into memory to be executed, UNIX must set up virtual memory page tables and file buffers, for example. The initialization takes memory as well as time.

To alleviate the data access restrictions and overhead associated with multitasks in UNIX, Sequent Computer Corporation modified UNIX into DYNIX. The process model of DYNIX is shown in Figure 4.2(b).

A parallel process in DYNIX is identical to the serial model of UNIX plus an additional shared-memory data segment. This segment is allowed to grow as shown in Figure 4.2(b), and so it is placed in the hole between the private data and stack segments.

When a parallel process is created in DYNIX, the shared-memory address space as shown in Figure 4.2(b) is created. Subsequent microtasks spawned from the parent

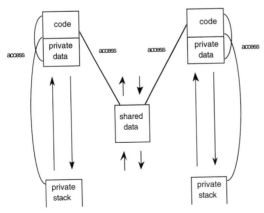

Figure 4.3 Two microtasks created by m_Fork in DYNIX share some data, do not share other data

task by the DYNIX m_fork routine copy all but the shared data segment into their address spaces. Thus, there is only one copy of the shared data segment among the worker tasks. An example for two tasks is shown in Figure 4.3.

This modification requires extensions to UNIX, languages such as C, and a library of routines to support the model. For example, in C, two keywords must be added to the language to indicate whether a data object is private or shared, e.g., *shared int x* means that *x* is shared, whereas *private int* x means *x* is a private variable.

Two new types are needed for locking and setting up barriers. Variables of type slock_t are used to set and clear access locks, and variables of type sbarrier_t are used to set and clear barriers. The appropriate operations for objects of these types are listed below.

Multitasking

Operations on variables of type slock_t:

```
s_init_lock():  initialize a lock variable
s_lock():  set the lock
s_unlock():  clear the lock
```

Operations on variables of type sbarrier_t:

```
s_init_barrier():  initialize the barrier variable
s_wait_barrier():  wait for all multitasks to reach barrier
```

The usual fork() and cpus_online() routines are used to create a multitask and query the system for the number of processors, respectively.

Microtasking

Operations on variables of type slock_t:

```
m_lock():  set the lock
m_unlock():  clear the lock
```

Operations on variables of type sbarrier_t:

```
m_sync():  wait for all microtasks to arrive
m_single():  wait for supervisor thread to call m_multi()
m_multi():  resume all workers in parallel
```

In addition, microtasks in *C* are created by calling two routines in sequence: m_set_procs(nprocs); m_fork(function); and destroyed by calling m_kill_procs().

These routines are illustrated in the following example provided by Kallstrom and Thakkar. The program creates one supervisor, and nprocs-1 workers. The code for each worker is given as function work(). The example illustrates both methods of synchronizing access to a shared variable.

```
/* Global declarations */
shared int x;
shared struct y_struct {
    int state;
    slock_t lp;     /* primitive lock */
```

```
    } y
/* Supervisor worker */
main() {
    s_init_lock (&y.1p);              /* initialize primitive lock */
    m_set_procs(nprocs);              /* initialize nprocs-1 workers */
    m_fork (work);                    /* create and run nprocs-1 microtasks */
    m_kill_procs();                   /* done, so kill worker microtasks */
    }
/* Worker microtasks */
work() {
    /* illustrate microtask locking */
    m_lock();                         /* begin mutual exclusive access to x */
    x++;                              /* increment shared variable x */
    printf ("Worker");                /* just a test message */
    m_unlock();                       /* end critical section */
    /* illustrate a barrier */
    m_single();                       /* all workers wait here until m_multi */
    printf ("Supervisor");            /* only supervisor executes this */
    m_multi();                        /* resume all workers..... */
    /* illustrate multitask locking */
    s_lock(&y.1p);                    /* lock structure y */
    y.state = 0;                      /* change the structure */
    printf ("Structure");             /* another test message */
    s_unlock(&y.1p);                  /* unlock the structure */
}
```

A *critical section* is a piece of code that accesses a shared variable. In this example, the shared variables are x and y. Note the locks in each case. These locks provide *mutual exclusion*. That is, only one task is permitted to access each shared variable at a time. Later, we look at more elaborate locks which allow multiple tasks to simultaneously access a shared variable. Most programming problems arising in shared-memory parallel programming can be solved with this handful of routines.

This is a classic example of the supervisor/worker paradigm. Microtasks are set up to execute homogeneous tasks. The function work() is identical in all microtasks, and only the data varies. This example implements one fan per Figure 4.1. More extensive applications would implement perhaps many fans in this fashion.

4.1.3 The Traveling Salesman Problem

We illustrate the use of microtasking with the famous traveling salesman problem. A traveling salesman is to visit each of N cities exactly once along a shortest path. The N cities are located at coordinates (x_i, y_i) placed on a two-dimensional map.

This is an *NP-complete* problem, but a parallel solution can be implemented which reduces the time to find an optimal path. In addition, we can employ a form of parallel *simulated annealing* to remove false minimums from the search. In simulated annealing, each iteration is an improvement over the previous iterations with a probability that is determined by a temperature parameter which simulates the cooling of atoms in a physical medium.

The pseudocode simulated annealing algorithm is given below, where a number of workers are run in parallel. This is another example of a *trivially parallel* problem.

/* Simulated Annealing Algorithm */

/* S = State of solution, calculated */

/* SN = New state of solution, calculated */

/* E = Cost function (to be minimized), calculated */

/* T = Temperature parameter, calculated */

/* TF = Final temperature parameter , input*/

/* C = Rate of change in temperature , input < 1
*/

main():

1   Start with some initial state, S
Start with some initial temperature, TF

2   Repeat until $(T \leq TF)$
  2.1   T = TF
  While (not in equilibrium) do
  Find shortest path   /* do in parallel */
  2.2   Join and elect the best path
  2.3   TF = C*T /* cool down */

Each task is given a copy of the current path, and then each task independently reduces the path to a better path after a few iterations. Then, the tasks join at a barrier to elect the best solution. The best is then redistributed to all tasks to make an even better estimate. This repeats until the change in temperature is less than or equal to *TF*.

Find Shortest Path:

1   Perturb S to get SN /* For example, select different route */

2   Calculate change in cost: Ediff = E(SN) – E(S)

3   if Ediff < 0
  then replace S with SN
  else with probability $e^{-Ediff/T}$ replace S with SN

We only provide a portion of code that implements the fan of parallel tasks. The fan implements the shortest path calculation by iterating on local copies of the current path. Following the fan, the supervisor task elects the best path. This new path is copied by the workers, who repeat the process. The path is stored as mypath[MAXPROCS]; an array of (x, y) pairs representing the location of each city.

The following C code lacks data declarations. A complete solution for the Sequent Balance multiprocessor is given by Yadav and Lewis.

```c
void iterate()
/* data declarations, here */
m_single();                                  /* single thread ..... */
n_iter = n_iter / nprocs ;                   /* divide up the work */
for (current_temp = init_temp, j = 0;
     current_temp > (TF - EPSILON) && current_temp > 0.0;
     current_temp -= drop, j++)              /* While (not in equilibrium) do
{
    m_multi();                               /* multiple workers .... */
    get_current_path(mypath[my_id));         /* get a copy of the path */
    low = 0;                                 /* Perturb S to get SN ....*/
    high = low+npts-1;
    mylow = mypath[my_id];                   /* save lowest point in path */
    beta = 1.0 / current_temp;               /* swapping temp */
    /* move cities around */
    for (i = 0L; i < n_iter; i++)
      {if (keep > 2)
        {/* swap cities within my path? Except for first city */
            for (k = low+1, tprime = mylow->next; k < high-1; k++)
              {cswap(tprime, &swapped, Eint, Erem);
                 tprime = tprime->next;
              }
         }
      /* mylow may be swapped in these two calls. Want to keep */
      /* mylow pointing to lowest one in my path */
      if (keep>1) {cswap(mylow, &swapped, Eint, Erem)}
      /* swap my first two points back to my lowest ?  */
       if (swapped){ mylow=mylow->prev;} /* yes */
      } /* end of for */
  /* Calculate length of my path and its connection to my next neighbor */
mypathlength[my_id] = 0.0;
for (i = low, t = mylow; i< = high; i++,t- > next)
  {mypathlength[my_id] += distance(t,t->next);}
/* all tasks come together — Join and elect the best path */
m_sync();                                    /* wait for all at barrier */
m_single();                                  /* sole task does election */
best = get_smallest_path_index();
pathlen = mypathlen[1];                       /* best is in mypath[1] */
put_current_path(mypath[1]);                  /* no race condition; only 1 task */
}
```

The worker tasks are started by the usual pair of microtasking toolbox calls:

```c
m_set_procs(NPROCS);
m_fork(iterate);
```

Shared-Memory Parallel Programming   Chapter 4

The multiple worker solution need not bother with checking for shared access to the data structure representing the current search path, because with one exception, the only shared access is to read the path, not change it. The annealing parameters determine how quickly and accurately the path of the salesman will converge to a solution.

4.2 ANALYSIS TECHNIQUES

The toolbox routines for parallel DYNIX make parallel programming a shared-memory computer rather similar to programming a real-time process control program in a traditional serial computer. A combination of low-level locks along with cache memories greatly simplifies application development, but all is not so simple.

First, these toolbox routines can be abused. For example, one processor can set a lock, and cause another processor to saturate the bus by *spin-waiting* for the lock to clear. This will cause the entire system to slow down to the extent that all tasks run slower than they might on one processor!

Second, simple mutual exclusion is not always the best policy. If N tasks want to read a shared variable, there is no harm in allowing free access. Yet, if one task wants to update the shared variable through write access, and (N–1) tasks want read-only access, mutual exclusion is extremely conservative and time consuming. The multiple readers problem is solved by designing a more complex but more efficient lock from the mutual exclusion building blocks.

Finally, locks raise a number of other interesting questions about the correctness of parallel programs just as they do in traditional operating systems theory. What we need are analysis tools to analyze the application code produced using the toolbox routines.

4.2.1 Safe, Live, and Fair

A *lock* is a mechanism for enforcing a policy for sharing access to data. A *policy* is a set of rules that define allowable values for shared variables. In most cases, we are concerned with two possible classes of states for shared variables: (1) the class of deterministic values, and (2) the class of nondeterministic values. The values in these states do not need to be unique.

For example, suppose we look at the four-way stop pattern found on most any country highway (see Figure 4.4). Two roads cross at an intersection consisting of four stop signs. Vehicles must stop and either travel straight ahead, or turn right or left. As long as only one vehicle arrives from any direction, the outcome is predictable (deterministic). But, if two or more automobiles arrive at the same time, the outcome is unpredictable (nondeterministic). The nondeterministic case is the most interesting for our purposes.

Suppose we select a policy that guarantees a deterministic outcome in all cases. This policy is enforced by a rule that says first priority is always given to the automobile

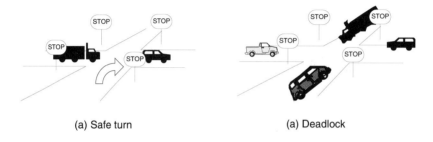

(a) Safe turn   (a) Deadlock

Figure 4.4 The four-way stop analogy illustrates access policies. The intersection (shared data) is shared by vehicles (tasks).

on the right during a trajectory. Thus, if vehicles A and B arrive and stop at the intersection at exactly the same time as shown in Figure 4.4(a), automobile B goes first because B is on the right side of truck A.

Without the "right side" policy, the outcome of any access to the intersection is nondeterministic. Each time two vehicles arrive at the intersection at exactly the same instant, a nondeterministic event occurs. This is exactly what happens in a shared-memory computer system when two or more tasks attempt to simultaneously change a shared variable. Only one task is allowed to access the variable first, but which one is left up to chance. We say the nondeterministic access is *indeterminate* because the resultant value of a shared variable after two write accesses will depend on the order of the writes, and the order is nondeterministic. An indeterminate state of a variable is a consequence of nondeterministic access.

We can summarize:

1 determinism: access order is always the same no matter how many times the program is run.

2 nondeterminism: access order is left up to chance, and so may be different each time the program is run.

3 indeterminacy: the result of nondeterminism, where the value of a shared variable is left to chance. Each time the program is run, it is possible that a different value is computed for the shared variable.

Indeterminacy was a major concern in the banking analogy of Chapter 1. As you recall, two customers wanted to access a shared account. Customers A and B could leave the shared account in one of two states, depending on the order they performed their transactions. But, without synchronized access, the ending balance of the account is left to chance. We can say the balance of the account is indeterminate, without synchronized access.

Locks can be thought of as mechanisms for carrying out policies that often require serialization of access. Thus, locks typically force parallel tasks to run in serial order during access to the shared variable. The section of program that accesses a shared variable is called a *critical section*, for obvious reasons.

A *safe policy* is one that enforces deterministic results. A lock is said to be *safe* if it enforces determinism. Thus, mutual exclusion, while often overly conservative, is a lock that enforces a safe policy because only one task is permitted access at a time. Clearly, safe access is not sufficient in many real applications, however, as we now show.

Suppose we take the four-way stop analogy even further (see Figure 4.4(a)). After automobile B passes through the intersection, suppose a long line of fast sports cars follows it, and because they are on the right side of truck A, they too are allowed to pass through the intersection. According to our policy of "right vehicle first," there is nothing that prevents a slow truck from being stopped forever by much faster sports cars.

A policy is *unfair* if it permits one task to wait indefinitely while other tasks repeatedly access shared data. A fair lock guarantees access to all tasks that have requested access, before second or third accesses are granted to any pending tasks. That is, everyone gets access before anyone gets multiple accesses.

We can add a rule to the traffic policy to guarantee fairness: Vehicles are given access to the intersection in the order they arrive, with the exception that vehicles arriving simultaneously follow the "right side goes first" rule.

This seems to solve the problem, but alas, there is one more case to resolve. Figure 4.4(b) shows a rare case where four vehicles arrive at the intersection at exactly the same time. The fair policy states that the vehicles on the right are allowed to go first, but this leads to a circular gridlock. All vehicles wait for the vehicle on their right, and since all vehicles have someone on their right side, they all must wait!

If the vehicles are tasks, then the tasks are *deadlocked*—a state where none of the tasks can continue on because they are blocked by their neighboring tasks.

We say a policy is *live* if it prevents deadlock. It must be impossible for a deadlock to ever happen for a lock to enforce liveness. Thus, even though the four-way stop gridlock is unlikely to occur, the fact that it can occur means the traffic policy is *deadlock prone*.

We can fix this problem by a number of techniques, but the simplest technique is to number the stop signs 1, 2, 3, 4, and then use these numbers as priorities whenever a deadlock happens. Thus, the vehicle at stop #1 goes first, followed by #2, and so forth. This is an example of a deadlock prevention algorithm.

Again, we can summarize what we have learned from this analogy:

1 Safe: A lock is *safe* if it is impossible for a shared value to take on indeterminate values when two or more tasks compete for access.

2 Fair: A lock is *fair* if it is impossible for one task to starve waiting tasks by repeated accesses.

3 Live: A lock is *live* if it is impossible for the lock to indefinitely postpone access by waiting tasks.

4 Critical section: A section of code that accesses a shared variable.

Typically, parallel programs employ simple mutual exclusion to guarantee safe access. This is done by forcing serial execution of a critical section. But, is it enough? The answer is generally "no," because of a number of factors that enter into a good parallel program.

First, a mutual exclusion lock cannot guarantee fairness to waiting tasks, because faster tasks are allowed to get ahead of slower tasks just as we illustrated in the four-way stop analogy.

Second, a mutual exclusion lock may on its own be live, but when used in combination with other mutual exclusion locks, it may cause a *system deadlock*. System deadlocks can occur anytime a system of tasks contain two or more locks. Such occurrences are precisely analogous to the four-way stop gridlock.

Finally, simple mutual exclusion may lead to performance problems as mentioned above.

We need to understand the way locks behave in a shared-memory computer before we can properly understand the behavior of parallel programs. This means we must look at some specific examples of algorithms for enforcing various synchronization policies.

4.2.2   The Interleave Principle

An *atomic action* is any action within a computer system that is guaranteed to be performed without interruption and without parallelism. Such actions are called atomic because they are indivisible, e.g., they cannot be decomposed into smaller actions which can be done at the same time. In serial computers, atomic actions might be single instructions, or memory read/write operations. In a shared-memory multiprocessor, instructions can be executed in parallel. Furthermore, with cache memory being updated behind the programmer's back, it is not always certain that memory read/write operations are done atomically. One of the most difficult aspects of concurrent processing is finding an atomic action to build on.

Cache coherency algorithms guarantee consistency among all copies of a shared-memory variable, so we can model memory access as an atomic action. Similarly, whenever instructions from two or more processors attempt to update a shared variable, we can assume that the cache coherency algorithm will select one processor to go first, while the others wait. That is, the shared variable is treated much like the intersection in the four-way stop analogy by the cache coherency algorithm. So, instructions that perform updates can be thought of as atomic instructions, because parallelism is restricted.

We will model the atomic actions of a task using an *interleave matrix* as shown in Figure 4.5. Each line in the matrix represents an atomic action. The horizontal lines represent atomic actions performed in order by task one, say, and the vertical lines represent task two. The line marked CR is representative of a critical section within a parallel program. This is where the access takes place. More tasks can be represented by an interleave cube, hypercube, and so forth, but this is not necessary for our purposes.

Task execution is simulated in the interleave matrix by stepping through one atomic action at a time. Steps are equivalent to crossing a line. Arrows are drawn to show all the sequences of steps possible. The cells of the matrix represent the combined state of the shared memory, and thus the state of the pair of tasks. The shaded cells are forbidden, because to enter them means the two tasks have violated determinism by running in CR at the same time.

Example

Figure 4.5 gives an analysis of a simple spin lock. A *spin lock* simply tests the lock variable over and over until some other task releases the lock. That is, the waiting task spins on the lock until the lock is cleared. Then, the waiting task sets the lock while inside of the CR. Finally, the lock is cleared, so another task can enter its critical section.

Figure 4.5(a) shows an unsafe lock, while Figure 4.5(b) illustrates a safe lock that is not live. In Figure 4.5(a), the algorithm spins on lock variable C:

```
while C do;          (* Spin until C is False *)
C := TRUE;           (* Lock(C)  so only one access *)
CR;                  (* Critical section:  access the shared variable*)
C := FALSE;            (* unLock(C) so other tasks can go *)
```

The state of a few cells in Figure 4.5(a) have been marked with the value of C (T = TRUE, F = FALSE). We can follow one of the many possible paths starting from outside of the critical region into the CR. Assume $C = F$, initially, and task P2 executes first:

```
P2: while C do;
```

Then, suppose task P1 executes a request for access:

```
P1:while C do
```

This places the interleave matrix in the (2,2) cell as shown, and the value of C is still $C = F$. Now, suppose we switch back to task P2:

```
P2: C:=TRUE
```

and likewise, task P1 executes the lock setting action:

```
P1: C:=TRUE
```

The cache coherency algorithm will prevent both of these sets from happening at exactly the same time, but one of the tasks will set C:=TRUE followed by the other task setting it to TRUE also. This is shown in the interleave matrix as two paths leading into the same cell. Regardless, the two tasks can now enter their critical sections at the same time, as shown by one possible path in Figure 4.5(a). Clearly, the lock is not safe.

The problem with this simple-minded lock is that it lets more than one task into

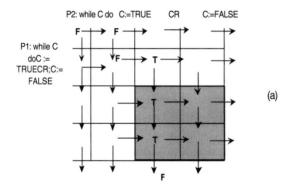

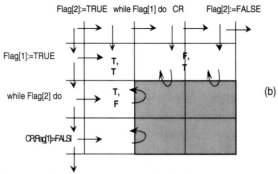

Figure 4.5   Interleave matrix analysis of two spin locks: (a) unsafe lock; (b) unlive lock

CR at the same time. This is because the lock is tested in one atomic action and set in another atomic action. If the two atomic actions were combined into a single test-and-set operation, we could guarantee safe access. Even so, an atomic test-and-set lock does not guarantee fairness.

This example illustrates a *race condition* within the lock itself. A race condition is a condition that can lead to indeterminacy. In this case, the indeterminacy occurs because we do not know which task sets C to TRUE. We say there is a *race* between the two tasks.

Example

The previous lock is unsafe, because it takes two atomic actions to set and test the lock. What happens if we provide an array of locks, and dedicate each array element to one task? The idea is to avoid a race to set and test a single lock. Unfortunately, the analysis of Figure 4.5(b) shows that the following lock is also faulty, but for a different reason.

```
Flag[me] := TRUE;      (* Set my flag.... *)
while Flag[other] do;    (* Spin on the other task's flag *)
CR;                        (* Enter one at a time *)
Flag[me] := FALSE;    (* Clear the lock *)
```

This lock is "more fair" because it forces ping-ponging between the two tasks; first me=1 accesses the data, then other=2 accesses the data, and the pattern repeats assuming the tasks make repeated requests by setting their Flags.

The problem with this improvement is that it introduces a possibility of deadlock! The deadlock state can be reached when both tasks set their flags and then simultaneously spin. When this happens, the two tasks must be terminated because they will never leave the deadlock state.

One possible path is to first set Flag[1]:=TRUE followed by setting Flag[2]:= TRUE. This can happen if we alternate between the two tasks as shown in Figure 4.5(b). Two possible paths are shown in the matrix and labeled with the values of Flag{1...2}.

4.2.3 Locks That Work

An obvious solution to the problems encountered above is to use a simple test-and-set atomic operation to implement the lock. Indeed, such instructions exist within most processors, so, why is this a poor solution? Consider a C implementation of such a lock. Let the lock be a byte in memory and initially, let the byte be UNLOCKED:

```
char *lock;
*lock = UNLOCKED
```

To prevent an interleaved read or write from another task while doing a test-and-set, we use an atomic test-and-set function which returns TRUE if the lock is already LOCKED. The function returns FALSE if the lock was changed from UNLOCKED to LOCK.

```
atomic_test_and_set(lock, LOCKED)
```

This is used to spin until the lock is UNLOCKED. The lock is then achieved by the following spin-wait.

```
while (atomic_test_and_set (lock, LOCKED));
```

The lock is cleared by the same piece of code used to initialize it. Alternately, the atomic function can be used to clear the lock as follows.

```
(void) atomic_test_and_set(lock, UNLOCKED);
```

This seems simple enough, but observe what happens. The spin-wait constantly updates the lock by changing it and then detecting if the new value actually differs from the previous value. This can cause saturation of the bus and lead to dramatic performance losses.

Graunke and Thakkar analyzed a number of locks to study their effect on caches and performance of the Sequent Symmetry multiprocessor. They found two locks that gave acceptable performance.

The backoff-reference spin lock is recommended by Graunke and Thakkar for general use when contention for multiple locks is common. However, an interleave matrix analysis shows this lock to be unfair.

The queue lock is recommended for a single lock, but it is also fair, and because it is nearly as efficient, we present it here.

Queue Lock

The general premise of a queue lock is to place requests for the CR into a first-come-first-served queue. This ordering prevents starvation of one process by another. In addition, the queue lock reduces bus activity by limiting the updates to the lock variable. Reads do not cause bus accesses, so they can be plentiful, but writes may cause a flurry of activity that saturates the bus. For a complete analysis of various forms of locks, see Graunke and Thakkar.

To implement this idea we need a hardware_lock() routine that turns off interrupts, thus making a group of statements behave like an atomic action. We designate these sections of code as atomic functions as before.

The lock variable is actually a structure consisting of a head index into a list of waiting tasks. The head index points to the next task in FIFO order. For example, we might use the following structure:

```
struct q_lock {
int head;       /* index into array of next task in FIFO order */
int tasks [NPROCS]     /* up to NPROCS-1 tasks waiting, one active */
} lock;
```

There are three atomic functions for setting, testing, and clearing the lock. Assuming each is atomic, we can create a simple spin lock that only updates the shared lock once at the beginning and once at the end of access. The spin lock only reads the lock, and does not update it.

```
void add_to_q (lock, myid);/* add task myid to end of queue lock */
while (head_of_q (lock) != myid);   /* read and wait til my turn */
CR; */ enter CR and access shared data */
void remove_from_q (lock, taskid)/* delete myid. error if myid != taskid */
```

We show that this is a fair lock by interleave analysis as shown in Figure 4.6. Not all possible paths are exhausted in the analysis. Instead, we attempt to starve task #2 by quickly repeating a second request by task #1. This is shown by assuming task #1 adds its myid to the queue before task #2 adds its myid to the queue.

We show that a lock is unfair if one task is able to pass through its critical section more times than another task, when both tasks are waiting for access. We use two interleave matrices to study fairness; each matrix represents one pass through the lock, CR, and unlock stages for a process. Clearly, Figure 4.6 shows why the queue lock is fair. The reader should apply this analysis to the simple mutual exclusion lock above to show why it is not fair.

In Figure 4.6 the cells of the matrix that are traversed are labeled with the values of the lock; head_task_id: $task_1$, $task_2$, ..., $task_{NPROCS}$ which allows you to observe the changing state of the lock as the two tasks compete for access to the shared memory.

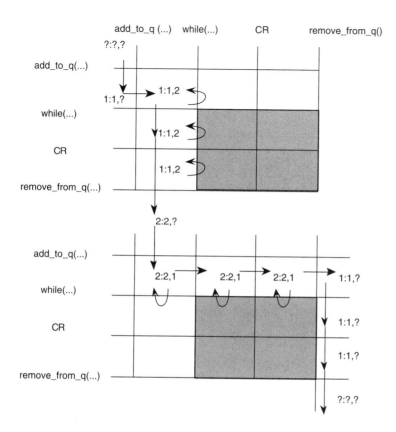

Figure 4.6 Interleave analysis of queue lock showing it is fair

The lock is fair, because access is granted to tasks in the order they request access by executing the add_to_q() routine.

If two tasks are running on different processors, and the code is duplicated for each processor, then it is possible for the add_to_q() routine to be entered and executed at exactly the same instant by the two tasks. Conceptually, it is possible for the queue lock to be updated simultaneously by the two competitors, but in practice, the cache coherency algorithm must resolve which update to the lock is allowed to happen first. If we assume the cache acts deterministically, the lock is safe.

Multiple Readers Lock

The simple mutual exclusion locks presented thus far are best suited for the case when most of the accesses are WRITE or UPDATE accesses. These do not perform as well as more elaborate locks when there is a high number of benign accesses to READ the shared memory, because only one task is allowed in the critical section at a time.

In many applications, most accesses are READ and only a few are WRITE. In fact, Baylor and Rathi studied a large number of scientific and engineering applications

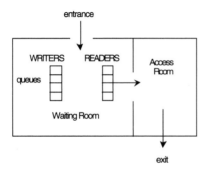

Figure 4.7　Waiting room analogy for READERS/WRITERS lock

running on a 64-processor MIN-based shared-memory computer and found that a "significant amount of explicitly shared data are accessed as either read-only by several processors, or read-write by a single processor." This suggests a lock that discriminates between READERS and WRITERS is in order.

We want a lock that gives any number of READERS simultaneous access to the shared data, but as soon as a WRITER appears on the scene, we want to stop giving out accesses to READERS, and after all READERS are flushed out, give mutually exclusive access to the sole WRITER. This seems like an easy enough algorithm, but a fair READERS/WRITER lock is extremely convoluted to design and implement.

Figure 4.7 shows an analogy with most waiting rooms (physicians, dentists, lawyers, and accountants all have waiting rooms). The access policy of this room should be fair to all, while allowing multiple READERS inside the access room. We note the following:

1 Safe: Only one WRITER is allowed in the access room at any instance in time.

2 Fair: When a WRITER is waiting in line in the waiting room, all additional READERS must allow the waiting WRITER to go in next, except when a WRITER is currently in the access room.

When a READER is waiting in the waiting room, all additional WRITERS must allow the waiting READER to go in next, except when a WRITER is currently in the access room.

3 Live: No deadlock states. That is, the lock itself must not prevent the READERS and WRITERS from entering the access room once they have entered the queues in the waiting room.

How can we enforce this policy? The following is DYNIX Pascal code for READERS/WRITERS locking on the Sequent multiprocessor system provided by Youfeng Wu of Sequent Computers. It uses a counter to enumerate the number of readers, and to monitor when all readers have been flushed out of the critical section.

In addition, you will observe its use of low-level locks to achieve locking of the counters themselves. These low-level locks use ALM (atomic lock memory) on the Sequent to achieve cache efficiency. We can ignore this detail, however, by assuming the low-level routines are safe.

```
TYPE          {Types used by the low-level lock routines}
   lockType = RECORD

                lkAlm: ^char; {lock on atomic lock memory}
                lkShadow: -128..127; {shadow lock}
           END;
   lockPtr = ^lockType;  {linked list forms a queue}


   RWLockType = RECORD
                mutexcLock, countLock:  lockPtr;
                readCount, writeCount:  integer;
                END;


VAR
   uLock:  RWLockType; {the READERS/WRTERS lock}
   {Low-level locks are written in C}
   function create_lock:  lockPtr; cexternal;
   procedure lock(p: lockPtr); cexternal;
   procedure unlock(p: lockPtr); cexternal;


PROCEDURE createRWlock(VAR x: RWlockType);
   BEGIN
     x.mutexcLock := create_lock;
     x.countLock := create_lock;
     x.readCount := 0; {no readers active}
     x.writeCount := 0; {no writers active}
   END;


FUNCTION isReadLocked(x:  RWLockType):  BOOLEAN;
   BEGIN
     lock(x.countLock); {mutual exclusive update to flag}
     isReadLocked := x.readCount > 0; {are some readers active?}
     unlock(x.countLock); {release mutual exclusion}
   END;


FUNCTION isWriteLocked(x:  RWLockType):  BOOLEAN;
   BEGIN
     lock(x.countLock); {exclusive update of flag}
     isWriteLocked := x.writeCount > 0; {is one writer active?}
     unlock(x.countLock);
   END;
PROCEDURE Readlock(VAR x: RWlockType);
   BEGIN
```

```
        lock(x.mutexcLock);
        WHILE isWriteLocked(x) DO ;
        lock(x.countLock);
        x.readCount := x.readCount + 1;
        unlock(x.countLock);
        unlock(x.mutexcLock);
    END;
  PROCEDURE ReadUnlock(VAR x: RWlockType);
    BEGIN
        lock(x.countLock);
        x.readCount := x.readCount - 1;
        unlock(x.countLock);
    END;
  PROCEDURE Writelock(VAR x: RWlockType);
    BEGIN
        lock(x.mutexcLock);
        WHILE isReadLocked(x) or isWriteLocked(x) DO ;
        x.writeCount := x.writeCount + 1;
        unlock(x.mutexcLock);
    END;
  PROCEDURE WriteUnlock(VAR x: RWlockType);
    BEGIN
        lock(x.countLock);
        x.writeCount := x.writeCount - 1; {sole writer clears out}
        unlock(x.countLock);
    END;
```

The application program interface to these routines is quite simple. Initially, the lock is created:

```
createRWlock(uLock);
```

All READER tasks execute the following sequence:

```
ReadLock (uLock);
CR;
ReadUnLock (uLock);
```

All WRITER tasks execute the sequence:

```
WriteLock (uLock);
CR;
WriteUnLock(uLock);
```

Figure 4.8 uses a timing diagram to analyze the behavior of this sophisticated lock. Clearly, the lock is safe because of the mutual exclusion locks used. It is not so obvious that the lock is fair or live. The timing diagram of Figure 4.8 analyzes only one possible configuration that could lead to unfair treatment of WRITERS.

In Figure 4.8, the timing diagram follows time from left to right and activation of routines from top to bottom. The first READER, task Reader1, enters routine ReadLock() as indicated by a jump in the timing line. A slight dip in the line indi-

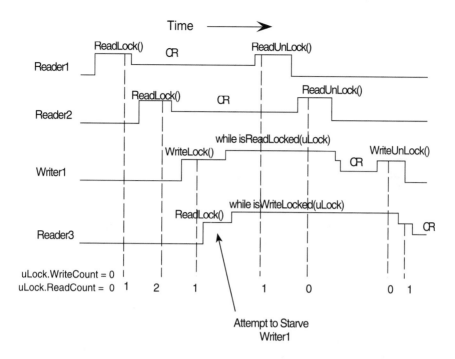

Figure 4.8 Timing diagram for READERS/WRITERS sequence Reader1, Reader2, Writer1, and Reader3. Illustrates fairness between readers and sole writer tasks.

cates that Reader1 is in its critical region, CR. Similarly, the ReadUnLock() routine is entered corresponding with a second elevated line.

The values of WriteCount and ReadCount for uLock are displayed at the bottom of the diagram. Each time a value changes, a vertical dashed line is drawn to highlight the change. These counters enumerate the number of tasks of each kind that are currently in the CR or waiting to be admitted.

Of special interest is the case where Reader3 attempts to enter the CR while the other two readers are in the CR, and Writer3 has requested access. If Reader3 is allowed to enter the CR along with its like kind, Writer3 would be starved. This unfair act is avoided because Writer3 asserts itself by setting the mutex lock WriteCount. When Reader3 attempts to set its lock, it must wait for this counter to revert to zero, thus ensuring fairness.

4.2.4 An Application to Linear Programming

Linear system optimization programs solve the following problem:

Minimize/maximize: $z = c^{\mathrm{T}} x$

Subject to the constraints: $Ax = b; \; x \geq 0$

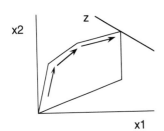

Figure 4.9 Two-dimensional region illustrating Simplex method of optimization. Path shows steepest descent search for maximum vertex

where A is a $n \times m$ matrix, c is an n-element cost vector, b is a vector of length m, and x is an n-length vector to be determined. That is, we want to find x such that z is minimized.

Typically, $n > m$. The system of equations $Ax = b$ can be analyzed by taking m of n nonsingular columns at a time and solving to find the vertex points of an enclosed polygon in hyperspace. Figure 4.9 illustrates a trivial case for $n = 2$. Each vertex corresponds to a solution of a pair of equations taken from $Ax = b$.

The vertices of the polygon in Figure 4.9 consist of feasible solutions. However, the desired optimum point (maximum as shown in the figure), coincides with the vertex intersected by the line $z = c^T x$. The problem becomes one of finding an algorithm for searching these vertices, until finding the vertex with the largest (smallest) value of z.

The famous *Simplex Algorithm* proposed by Dantzig employs a *steepest descent* method of solution. That is, beginning at the origin, we select the direction of maximal change, move to the maximal-change vertex, and compare with the previous vertex. If additional moves fail to improve the solution, the search halts. If additional moves can improve the solution, we once again select a direction that maximizes the change. The steepest descent solution in Figure 4.9 is marked with arrows.

How do we parallelize such a problem? The first inclination is to simultaneously compute all vertex points at once, and then find the maximum point among the list of values returned by the parallel tasks. Unfortunately, this approach consumes far to many tasks, because the total number of vertices grows combinatorially with n, m. (There are n columns solved, m at a time, yielding

$$C(n, m) = \frac{n!}{(n-m)!} \text{ solutions.})$$

Wu has shown that the decomposed simplex algorithm by Dantzig and Wolfe reveals a surprisingly parallel implementation on shared-memory computers due to the large number of parallel loops found within the sequential algorithm. In fact, the tasks of a straightforward implementation look precisely like the supervisor-workers paradigm given in Figure 4.1.

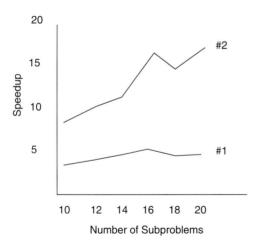

Figure 4.10 Speedup of parallel simplex algorithms vs. the number of subproblems running in parallel

Wu proposed an even better algorithm, however, which exhibits a superlinear speedup! He proposed a new implementation that runs faster than the steepest descent implementations even on a single processor! The new algorithm was obtained by noting the fact that a steepest descent direction is not always the best direction to embark from each vertex.

Figure 4.9 illustrates the point once again. If, instead of moving along the direction of steepest ascent from the origin, we had taken the less profitable direction, the optimum point would have been reached in two steps instead of three. Wu experimentally observed that most of the time, the direction selected has little impact on the speed of the search.

Using this idea, Wu implemented a modified decomposed simplex algorithm with speedup as shown in Figure 4.10. The search is partitioned into tasks that look for solutions at the same time. Each parallel solution is called a subproblem. These tasks periodically communicate their best solution to a supervisor task after a fixed period of time. The supervisor task selects the best solution from the litter, and broadcasts it to all workers, thus setting them back on the "best" path. This process repeats until there are no further improvements, yielding the solution.

Curve #1 in Figure 4.10 is obtained by the time to run Wu's new algorithm on 8 processors divided by one processor's time. Curve #2 is obtained by the time to run Wu's new algorithm on 8 processors divided by the sequential simplex running time on one processor. The curves increase to the point where the number of subproblems is a multiple of 8, and then decline slightly when the number of subproblems is not a multiple of 8. A speedup of 8 is equivalent to linear speedup, whereas a speedup of 16 is twice linear speedup.

Each task is divided into subtasks which perform the decomposed simplex algorithm in parallel according to the task graph shown in Figure 4.11. Notice the con-

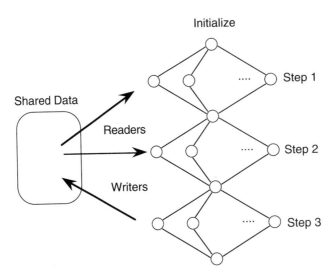

Figure 4.11   Task graph of parallel Simplex subproblem showing data accesses to shared data

current access from both READERS and WRITERS. These accesses must be locked to assure safe access. For more details, see the reference to Wu and Lewis.

4.2.5   Systemwide Synchronization

The telephone company has the longest history of dealing with complex parallel systems. People are allowed to pick up their telephone and attempt to call anyone else at any time. If the destination telephone is already in use, the caller hears a busy tone and must hang up and dial again. Callers are not allowed to call themselves, for example. Even with call-waiting service, only one connection between caller and callee is permitted at a time. This greatly simplifies systemwide synchronization problems. For example, gridlock is avoided.

Unfortunately, parallel systems that share resources such as disk files, printers, and modems are subject to the gridlock problems that we described earlier. It is possible for any parallel program that employs locks on two or more resources to fail due to gridlock. This problem is the classical deadlock problem in operating systems, and in this section we show how it can happen in a parallel program, and we briefly describe a solution.

Suppose we use the Readers/Writers lock of the previous section to control access to a data structure in RAM and a file on disk. Task T1 wants to copy the data structure from RAM to the disk file; task T2 wants to copy the file into the RAM data structure. In both cases, the accesses are to be synchronized by locks, e.g., d_lock for the data structure and f_lock for the file on disk.

Tasks T1 and T2 might be written as follows:

```
T1:      ReadLock (d_lock);              {lock RAM data for READER access}
         WriteLock (f_lock);             {lock disk file for WRITER access}
         CR;                             {copy from RAM to disk file ....}
         ReadUnLock (d_lock);            {release the RAM data}
         WriteUnLock (f_lock);           {release the File}
T2:      ReadLock (f_lock);              {lock disk file for READER access}
         WriteLock (d_lock);             {lock RAM data for WRITER access}
         CR;                             {copy from disk file to RAM....}
         ReadUnLock (f_lock);            {release the file}
         WriteUnLock (d_lock);           {release the RAM data}
```

This solution looks perfectly innocent on the surface, but if we analyze the interactions between T1 and T2 using the interleave matrix, we learn that a deadlock is possible. However, the interleave analysis requires that we know the internals of ReadLock() and WriteLock(). In general, application programmers may not know how such locks are written.

This problem does not stem from implementation of the locks, because we have just shown that these locks are safe, fair, and live. The problem is a systemwide problem. Regardless of how we implement the lock routines, the possibility of system deadlock persists.

Figure 4.12 shows a tabular analysis of this phenomenon, for one possible sequence of events. The tabular display can be used along with a *horizontal-vertical deadlock detection algorithm* to find the problem.

In Figures 4.12(a)–(c) we observe the interleaved execution of T1 and T2. The sequence is:

```
T1: ReadLock (d_lock);
T2: ReadLoc K(f_lock);
T1: WriteLock (f_lock);
T2: WriteLock (d_lock);
```

As the sequence is followed, we place a request number in the cell of the table corresponding to the task and the resource being requested. Thus, when T1 requests d_lock, we place a number in the cell corresponding to T1:Data. We start numbering each row at zero, and increment each time we place a number in a row.

The numbers increase along each row, representing the order of each request for that resource. This is the bakery system where each arriving customer takes a number and waits for his or her turn for service. As each task is served, it is removed from the table, and all numbers along the row are decremented to reflect the new priority. When a task's number reaches zero, it is permitted to lock the resource and make its access.

In this simple example, we want to find out if it is ever possible for the pattern of requests to deadlock the system. We do this with the horizontal-vertical algorithm, which is run each time a task places a number in a row. Figure 4.12(d) illustrates how this algorithm detects a deadlock caused by T1 interacting with T2.

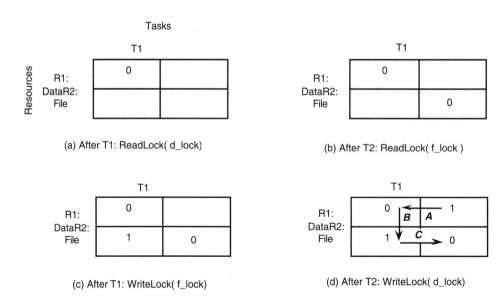

Figure 4.12   Tabular analysis of deadlocked tasks T1 and T2

After T2 places a 1 in row R1:Data, a horizontal search for the 0 is made as shown by letter A in the table. After 0 is found, a vertical search is made to locate the row containing a nonzero entry. This is shown as path B. The process is repeated, searching horizontal for a zero, and vertical for a nonzero, until the search either returns to the original column, or no further row/column can be found.

Because the horizontal-vertical algorithm is performed each time a number is placed in a row, we can always locate a circuit in the table that returns us to the original column, if one exists. This algorithm works regardless of the number of processors and the number of resources. A larger example is shown in Figure 4.13 to illustrate the generality of this method.

The horizontal-vertical algorithm works as follows:

1 Each time a request is made, the algorithm checks for a circular path in the table which leads back to the requesting task.

2 A task is given a zero number when it is allowed access, and a positive integer one greater than the current row maximum representing its order in the waiting line when it is denied immediate access.

3 Every row has at most one zero element (this can be relaxed for READERS with more effort).

4 Every column has at most one positive integer, because a task can only wait on one resource at a time.

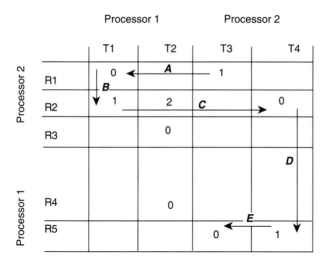

Figure 4.13 Horizontal-vertical algorithm detects deadlock in a system of 4 tasks sharing access to 5 resources

From these facts we can deduce that the algorithm will find at most one circuit in the table each time it is executed. When such a circuit is found, the requesting task must be terminated to remove the deadlock. We have shown only the detection algorithm here.

4.3 SHARED-MEMORY MULTIPROCESSOR SYSTEMS

Shared-memory computers seem to go hand in hand with bus-connected parallelism and UNIX operating systems. The bus-connection interconnection is easy to implement in hardware, and the UNIX operating system is easy to implement in software. Combined with the simplicity of matching multitasking with the hardware devices, shared-memory leads to a familiar programming model. Thus, it is no surprise that this style of parallel computing is widespread.

On the other hand, shared-memory computers cannot be easily scaled up to massively parallel levels. Furthermore, aside from vector parallel processors, shared-memory machines have not achieved the raw computing speeds of supercomputers. This places them in a nonscientific niche as compared to other very high performance systems.

Shared-memory systems are well suited to file server and backend database server systems where transaction processing speeds are more important than sustained raw performance. Therefore, it is most important that shared-memory machines also provide many parallel I/O devices for handling I/O activities, and relatively fast task switching—two topics we have not discussed. Furthermore, it is necessary for these systems to support very large virtual address spaces. We will also leave the discussion of virtual memory for another book.

Placing all data in one large global address space makes it easy to support traditional programming languages and programming paradigms of the past. However, one could argue that the corresponding need to lock and unlock access to shared data points to the need for a new paradigm. Indeed, distributed-memory message-passing paradigms have been advocated as a solution to the problems of synchronization, even on single-processor systems.

PROBLEMS FOR DISCUSSION AND SOLUTION

1 Draw the interleave matrix for the queue lock and two tasks. Show the paths for the case where no lock is set and task #1 requests and gets access, and show the paths for the case where task #2 tries to get access while task #1 already has access. Is this a safe lock? Is it live?

2 Use the interleave principle to show that the atom_test_and_set() lock is not fair.

3 The READERS/WRITERS lock is very subtle. Perform the timing analysis again as in Figure 4.8, only this time use the following code in place of the correct WriteLock() routine:

```
PROCEDURE Writelock(VAR x: RWlockType);
  BEGIN
    lock(x.mutexcLock);
    WHILE isReadLocked(x) DO ; {wait for all readers to clear out}
    unlock(x.mutexcLock);
    lock(x.countLock);
    x.writeCount := x.writeCount + 1; {one writer is in}
    unlock(x.countLock);
  END;
```

4 Can the READERS and WRITERS of Figure 4.11 deadlock? Explain your answer.

5 One proposal is to solve the linear optimization problem by simultaneous search of all vertices in the polygon. How many simplex subproblems are there in an $M \times N = 100 \times 50$ linear programming problem? Assuming each subproblem can be solved by a single processor, how many processors are needed to solve this problem in parallel?

6 Implement matrix multiply using READERS and WRITERS. Where must we place the ReadLocks and WriteLocks to assure safe access?

7 How is deadlock avoided in the public telephone system? What conditions are sufficient to cause systemwide deadlock?

8 Implement a shared-memory parallel program to compute the area under the curve $\int_{1}^{e} \frac{dx}{x}$ (hint: the area is 1.0).

References

Baylor, S. J., and Rathi, B. D., "An Evaluation of the Memory Reference Behavior of Engineering/Scientific Applications in Parallel Systems," *International Journal of High Speed Computing*, 1, 4, pp. 603 – 641, 1989.

Beck, B., and Olien, D., "A Parallel-Programming Process Model," *IEEE Software*, 6, 3, pp. 63 – 72, May 1989.

Graunke, G., and Thakkar, S. S., "Synchronization Algorithms for Shared-Memory Multiprocessors," *Computer*, 23, 6, pp. 60 – 69, June 1990.

Kallstrom, M., and Thakkar, S. S., "Programming Three Parallel Computers," *IEEE Software*, 5, 1, pp. 11 – 22, January 1988.

Wu, Y., and Lewis, T. G., "Parallel Algorithms for Decomposible Linear Programs," *Proc. Int'l Conference on Parallel Processing*, Vol. III, pp. 27 – 34, Pennsylvania State University Press, August 1990.

Wu, Youfeng, "Parallel Simplex Algorithms and Loop Spreading," Ph.D. Thesis, Computer Science Dept., Corvallis, OR 97331-3902, 1988.

Yadav, A., and Lewis, T. G., "Performance Monitoring of Parallel Applications at Large Grain Level," TR 89-60-22, Computer Science Dept., Oregon State University, Corvallis, OR 97331-3902, 1989.

Chapter 5

Distributed-Memory Parallel Programming

Shared-memory computers are relatively easy to program, but difficult to scale up to large numbers of processors. On the other hand, distributed-memory computers hold an advantage over shared-memory machines when it comes to massive parallelism. And experience has confirmed that the distributed-memory paradigm is appropriate for a wide class of applications.

There are however, at least two problems associated with using distributed-memory machines: (1) low machine efficiency due to interprocessor communication, and (2) difficulty of programming. We devote a major part of this chapter to these problems, that is, how to reduce *communication overhead*, and how to simplify distributed-memory programming.

Distributed-memory programs use message-passing among cooperating serial tasks in place of access to shared data. This paradigm is strange to a traditional serial programmer and usually requires a paradigm shift. In fact, it is strange enough to have created entirely new programming languages such as OCCAM, and entirely new hardware such as the INMOS *Transputer*. Both of these innovations are discussed as a basis for the distributed-memory programming paradigm of this chapter.

A distributed-memory system can be programmed in SIMD, SPMD, or MIMD paradigms. But which is best? Three major issues determine the best paradigm to be used: (1) the cost of communication, (2) load balancing, and (3) *processor scheduling*. If the cost of communication is too high, the distributed-memory system will spend too much time moving data around the interconnection network. If the computational load becomes unbalanced and shifts to a few of the processors, the remaining processors are idled, leading to slowdown, again. Finally, if tasks are allocated to the wrong processors, communication costs and load balancing return to penalize performance.

We address these issues and describe *OCCAM* and extensions to C and Fortran, which are languages used to program distributed-memory machines like the Transputer, nCUBE, and iPSC/2. These languages demonstrate the message-passing paradigm through examples: *FFT* on transputers, Calculation of π on hypercubes, and a computer vision application. In the final analysis, the reader will have to decide which paradigm is best for a specific application and specific machine.

Finally, an interesting problem in hypercube recognition is surveyed. Recognition is used to select a subset of processors from a larger cube in such a way that the subset of processors also forms a lower-dimensioned hypercube. This technique is used to time-share a hypercube computer by partitioning its processors into subcubes and permitting different users to use each subcube simultaneously.

5.1 MODELS FOR DISTRIBUTED-MEMORY PROGRAMMING

We begin with a general discussion of how to program distributed-memory machines. A distributed-memory machine is one in which each processor can directly address only a portion of the total memory of the system. Distributed-memory machines are also called *message-passing systems*. The concept of sharing variables does not exist in this type of architecture. Therefore, when a data structure must be shared in a distributed-memory environment, a completely different scheme is normally employed. Processes access a shared structure by sending messages to the process that owns that structure.

Figure 5.1 shows a message-passing system consisting of 4 processors, where P1 sends to and receives from both P3 and P4, P2 sends to and receives from P4, and P3 sends to P4. The idea of formulating parallel programs in terms of processes that pass messages back and forth, but share no memory, is very appealing because it removes the need for explicit synchronization as in the shared-memory paradigm. In addition, a parallel message-passing program can be implemented on a large class of machines with minimal differences in the code. For example, the same program might run on an Intel iPSC/2 hypercube or a network of workstations connected via an ethernet.

To understand the concept of message-passing, let us consider once again the shared variable example described in Chapter 4, Section 4.1.2. This code uses locks to synchronize access to shared variable x, and is reproduced here for convenience:

```
/* illustrate microtask locking  */
m_lock();                   /* begin mutual exclusive access to x  */
x++;                        /* increment shared variable x  */
printf( "Slave" );          /* just a test message    */
m_unlock();                 /* end critical section    */
```

Alternatively, the message-passing approach creates a new process that owns the shared variable x. When any other process wishes to access x, it does so by sending a message to the new process that owns x (x-owner) as shown in Figure 5.2. Process x-owner receives messages requesting access to x, and responds by sending a message back to the requestor process. For any two processes to communicate, the communicating processes must know each other's identity and the size and contents of the messages.

The basic operations needed for message-passing are *send* and *receive*. Sending and receiving messages replaces the synchronization via locking required of the shared-memory paradigm. This is the major operational difference between the message-pass-

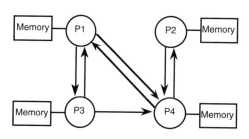

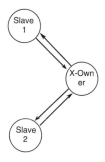

Figure 5.1 Model with 4 processors communicating via message-passing

Figure 5.2 Updating variable x in a message-passing system

ing and shared-memory paradigms. However, there are several other details that the programmer must consider when using send/receive to construct a message-passing program.

The message-passing approach is used in many languages such as Ada, CSP, and OCCAM. Because there is no shared global memory in message-passing systems, the languages that are based on this paradigm have no global shared variables. Furthermore, the style of programming is radically altered, as we will see in the following.

5.1.1 Communicating Sequential Processes (CSP)

A network of *communicating sequential processes* is a model for programming in which each process has its own locus of control, and sequential processes communicate by exchanging messages. It is straightforward to implement such a programming model on a distributed-memory architecture, as we demonstrate in this section.

The language CSP was introduced in 1978 and modified by Hoare in 1985 as a language without shared variables or common addresses. It assumes that a program is composed of $n > 1$ communicating sequential processes. Parallelism is obtained by composing a set of sequential processes that asynchronously execute as soon as they receive all of their input data from messages. Output is propagated to the next sequential process, etc., until there are no more messages to be passed, and the program terminates.

The main constructs in CSP are as follows.

Send–Receive

Communication is controlled by the following communication commands, where ? and ! designate receive and send operations, respectively.

$Pi\,?\,x$: an input request for the value of x from the process Pi

$Pj\,!\,y$: an output of the value of y to the process Pj

The requests $Pi\,?\,x$, inside Pj, and $Pj\,!\,y$, inside Pi, are activated only if Pi is ready for $Pj\,!\,y$ and Pj is ready for $Pi\,?\,x$, simultaneously. Otherwise the communication operation must wait until both are ready. This type of communication is also called *double handshaking*.

Guarded Commands

A *guarded command* is a list of statements that is prefixed by a boolean expression known as a *guard*. The statements are executed only when the guard is *true*.

$$\langle \text{ guard } \rangle \rightarrow \langle \text{ command list } \rangle$$

A set of guarded commands are grouped together and separated by the symbol []. If several guards are true, an arbitrary choice is made from among the true guards, and the corresponding list of statements are executed.

A guard may consist of a list of declarations, boolean expressions, and a message-passing statement. The guard fails if any one of its boolean expressions is false or if the process named in its message-passing command has terminated. The guard neither fails nor succeeds if the boolean expression is true but the message-passing statement cannot be executed. Consider the following process Pi.

```
Pi :: [ if  Gi1 ;  Ci1 →   Si1
        [] Gi2 ;  Ci2 →   Si2

        .

        [] Gin ;  Cin →   Sin
        fi]
```

The symbols $Gi1, \ldots, Gin$ are boolean expressions over the local variables of Pi, while $Ci1, \ldots, Cin$ are communication commands naming some process other than Pi. The symbols $Si1, \ldots, Sin$ are communication-free statements. If all guards neither succeed nor fail, the execution is delayed until some guard succeeds. If all guards fail the command aborts.

In some cases it may be required to execute a guard command repeatedly. The repetitive process has the form

```
Pi :: * [ if  Gi1 ;  Ci1 →   Si1
          [] Gi2 ;  Ci2 →   Si2

          .

          .

          [] Gin ;  Cin →   Sin
          fi]
```

This loop is executed repeatedly until all guards fail and then control is transferred to the next statement.

The Producer-Consumer Problem

To illustrate the CSP model, we show a simple solution to the classical *producer-consumer* problem in CSP. The producer-consumer problem arises because the producer

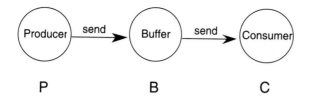

Figure 5.3   Producer-consumer model as communicating sequential processes

of data must have somewhere to store it until the consumer is ready, and the consumer must not try to consume data that is not there.

The program consists of three processes, P (producer), B (buffer), and C (consumer). We assume that buffer has finite capacity. Process P generates an item in the variable x, process B receives items from P in variable b, and process C receives items from B in variable y. Figure 5.3 illustrates the processes described in pseudocode form as follows.

```
Process P
    begin
        repeat
            generate item in x
            B!x
        forever
    end.

Process B
    B::USED:= 0, SIZE := N
    * [if  USED < SIZE; P?b  →   USED := USED +1;
    [] USED > 0; C!b →   USED := USED -1;
    fi]

Process C
    begin
        repeat
            B?y
            consume item y
        forever
    end.
```

Processes P, B, and C are independent, sequential processes that run without coordination with one another until a send (!) or receive (?) operation is attempted. Therefore, P sends a stream of values in variable x to B, as fast as P is able to run. However, $B\ !\ x$ is delayed whenever necessary in order to synchronize with process B. Waiting is necessary when B cannot keep pace.

Similarly, Process C runs on its own until it must wait for $B\ ?\ y$ to complete. Waiting is required if the value of y cannot be supplied by communication with B.

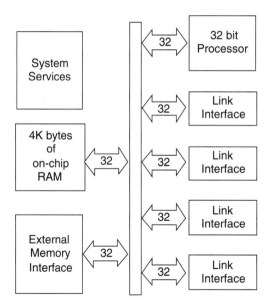

Figure 5.4 IMS T424 Transputer: Overview of a single processor

Process B is most interesting because it uses a guard to synchronize the communication of P and C. First, we note that process C runs an eternal loop containing a receive part and a send part. When USED < SIZE, the buffer b has an available space for another value, so the next value is received, and the buffer counter USED is incremented. When USED > 0, this means there is at least one value in the buffer b, so it can be sent to process C. The buffer counter USED is decremented.

Process B only pauses whenever the send must coordinate with C, or the receive must coordinate with P. What happens when the buffer is either full (USED = SIZE) or empty (USED = 0)?

5.1.2 The Transputer and OCCAM

OCCAM is a programming language based on CSP's model of concurrency and communication. This programming language has a special relationship with INMOS transputers. Therefore, a brief description of the transputer is in order.

The transputer is a high performance single-chip computer whose architecture facilitates the construction of parallel processing systems. Figure 5.4 shows an overview block diagram of a single IMS T424 transputer consisting of a 32-bit CMOS processor with 4K bytes on-chip RAM for high-speed processing, a configurable memory interface, and four standard INMOS communication links.

Up to 4 communication links per transputer allow networks of transputers to be constructed by direct point-to-point connections with no external logic. The links support the standard operating speed of 10MB per second, but also operate at 5 and 20

MB per second. More details about INMOS transputers can be found in Dettmer, INMOS IMS T414 Transputer Data Sheet, and Wilson.

OCCAM

Transputers are designed to implement the OCCAM language but also support other languages such as C, Pascal, and FORTRAN.

OCCAM is a simple language, based on the CSP model of concurrency and communication. OCCAM's processes may communicate by sending messages through interprocess data paths called channels; a process may have any number of such channels, which provide a zero-buffered, unidirectional, data path between two processes running in parallel. The channel models a simple handshaking data transfer between two hardware modules, and is efficiently implementable in special-purpose hardware.

OCCAM views processes as building blocks; a collection of processes may behave like a single process. This means an OCCAM program is a hierarchy of processes. Each collection of processes specifies the manner in which its constituent processes are to be executed.

OCCAM uses channels for communicating values among processes. A value output by one process is input to another process as in the CSP model. A single channel can only join two processes; it's like a person-to-person call rather than a conference. Channels are one-way only, so two channels are needed for two-way communication.

A transfer over a channel is actually an act of copying; if the value is output from a variable, then that variable retains its value and a copy is sent over the channel.

As in CSP, OCCAM uses the symbol ! to mean output and ? to mean input. For example, to transfer the value $V1$ in process 1 to the variable $V2$ in process 2 via channel C, we write in OCCAM:

```
Process 1              Process 2


C ! V1                 C ? V2
```

The act of transferring a value from process 1 to process 2 can only happen when both processes are ready. For example, if the output statement in process 1 is executed before the input in process 2 executes, process 1 will automatically wait for process 2 before sending its value.

A channel in OCCAM can transfer values either between two processes running on the same processor, or between two processes running on different processors. In the first case, the channel is just a location in memory, while in the second case the channel represents a real hardware link, such as a transputer link or other serial communication line.

Processes can be executed sequentially, concurrently, or selectively. Sequential processes are executed serially in the order in which they are written, while concurrent processes execute in parallel in any order. The construct SEQ is used to force sequential execution.

Example

```
SEQ
    chan1 ? his_value
    my_value := his_value + 1
    chan2 ! my_value
```

The SEQ construct forces all statements indented below it to serially execute in order. In this example, the process first inputs his_value from chan1, then assigns his_value + 1 to my_value, and finally outputs my_value to chan2.

The *PAR* construct designates parallel execution of all its components. OCCAM is sensitive to indentation of statements, because an indentation means that the statement is part of a collection of processes.

Example

```
PAR
    SEQ
        chan3 ? his_value
        his_value := his_value + 1
    SEQ
        chan4 ? her_value
        her_value := her_value + 1
```

The PAR means that the two indented SEQ constructs are executed in parallel. In other words, the parent process activates the two subprocesses simultaneously. They are allowed to run in parallel or at least at the same time as long as there is no waiting for channel communication to take place:

```
SEQ                               SEQ
    chan3 ? his_value                 chan4 ? her_value
    his_value := his_value + 1        her_value := her_value + 1
```

In this case, both subprocesses can simultaneously receive a value, increment their variables, and terminate.

In some cases, only one process is selected for execution according to some selection mechanism. That mechanism might evaluate a condition so that the first process whose associated condition evaluates to TRUE is selected. Alternately, the mechanism might evaluate a set of guards (with each guard associated with a single constituent process) and select the process whose guard is first satisfied. Selection is done with the ALT construct in OCCAM.

Example

```
ALT
    chan1 ? his_value
    ... first process
    chan2 ? his_value
    ... second process
    chan3 ? his_value
    ... third process
```

If chan2 were the first one to receive an input, then only the second process would be executed. In general, the ALT forces the parent process to wait until at least one of the channels receives a value. If more than one channel activates at the same time, an arbitrary selection is made. That is, the ALT executes non-deterministically.

The ALT may also include a test in addition to an input. The associated process can only be chosen if its input is the first to be ready and the test is TRUE.

Example

The following segment of OCCAM code illustrates the ALT with a test and an input.

```
ALT
  (my_value < 0) & chan1 ? his_value
  ... first process
  (my_value = 0) & chan2 ? his_value
  ... second process
  (my_value > 0) & chan3 ? his_value
  ... third process
```

In addition, there is a looping construct, and mechanisms called *replicators*, for creating multiple copies of a process and describing the execution behavior of the collection in the same way as for explicitly enumerated collections.

The constructs SEQ and PAR can be used to create replicated processes as many times as desired. Any process can be referred to by means of the replicator index. A replicated SEQ is very straightforward; it creates a number of replicates and executes them in sequence. A replicated PAR builds an array of structurally similar parallel processes. A replicated PAR is usually used in conjunction with an array of channels.

Example

Consider the following segment of code where an array of 21 channels called *slot* is used in conjunction with a replicated PAR.

```
[21] CHAN slot :
PAR i = 0 FOR 20
  WHILE TRUE
    INT x :
    SEQ
      slot[i] ? x
      slot[i+1] ! x
```

The replicated PAR sets up 20 parallel processes, each of which continually transfers values between two slots in an array of 21 channels. It can be noticed that the array of channels represents a queue since each value has to pass through the whole queue before leaving from slot[20].

Readers who are interested in learning more about the details of OCCAM are advised to read the suggested references [Pountain, Wilson].

The *Fourier transform* has great significance in many fields of science and engineering. It has been used in many applications such as image processing and coding theory. Thus, using parallel computers for computing the Fourier transform is of great importance. This section presents an OCCAM implementation of the Fast Fourier Transform (FFT) on a system of transputers. In the following we assume that the reader has some background on the FFT, however you can always refer to Rabiner for more details.

The FFT is a simple transformation that produces a set of points representing the frequency spectrum of a periodic signal. Inputs are n regularly spaced points sampled from one cycle of the periodic signal. Generally, the algorithm is simplified by selecting $n = 2^p$.

The FFT is made fast by organizing the calculations as repeated executions of a simple computational step that takes two inputs, A and B, and produces two outputs, X and Y. The values of X and Y are computed as follows:

$$X = A + B$$

$$Y = W * (A - B)$$

These calculations are represented in a dataflow diagram often called the *FFT butterfly* because of its resemblance to the wings of a butterfly [Rabiner, Wilson]. Figure 5.5 shows the FFT butterfly, where X, Y, A, B, and W are all complex numbers consisting of real and imaginary parts. W is known as the *twiddle factor*, its value is a function of the placement of the particular butterfly in the overall computation.

5.2.1.   The Pipelined FFT

The flow diagram of a complete FFT is constructed by connecting many butterflies in a pipelined fashion. Then a network of transputers is configured to the pipeline shape so that the hardware perfectly matches the OCCAM program. Several arrangements are possible, but we study the pipeline introduced in Wilson.

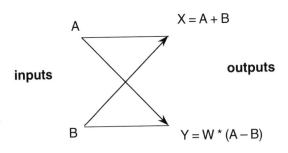

Figure 5.5   An FFT butterfly

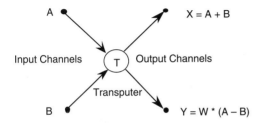

Figure 5.6   Allocating one butterfly per transputer

A pipeline can be organized as a one-, two-, or three-dimensional array using the four links per transputer. For our purposes, a two-dimensional array suffices.

For example, suppose each butterfly computation is assigned to one transputer. That of course will require two channels for input and another two for output (see Figure 5.6). That is, a transputer gets two inputs from a previous stage of the pipeline, performs the butterfly computation, and passes its two outputs to the following stage in the pipeline.

Figure 5.7 shows the pipeline arrangement for the complete FFT as a collection of butterfly computations, when the size of the problem is $n = 8$. The pipeline consists of three stages, each consists of 4 transputers. If we assume that the butterfly computation on each transputer takes t units of time, the FFT pipeline will produce a set of results every t units of time.

5.2.2   The OCCAM Program

The complex arithmetic must be expanded explicitly to obtain the real and imaginary parts of X and Y. We use the temporary locations Treal and Timag to save recomputation of (Areal − Breal) and (Aimag − Bimag), respectively. The sequential complex arithmetic to obtain X and Y can be given in OCCAM as follows. First, let us cast the butterfly computation into OCCAM.

```
WHILE TRUE
   SEQ
      Xreal := Areal + Breal
      Ximag := Aimag + Bimag
      Treal := Areal − Breal
      Timag := Aimag − Bimag
      Yreal := Treal * Wreal − Timag * Wimag
      Yimg := Treal* Wimag + Timag * Wreal
```

The butterflies input their data from their left neighbors and output to their right neighbors, so the code can be rewritten as follows.

```
WHILE TRUE
   SEQ
      PAR
        Ar ? Areal
```

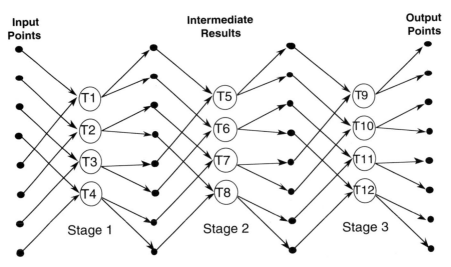

Figure 5.7   A pipelined FFT (number of input points = 8, number of transputers = 12)

```
    Ai ? Aimag
    Br ? Breal
    Bi ? Bimag
Treal := Areal - Breal
Timag := Aimag - Bimag
PAR
    Xr ! Areal + Breal
    Xi ! Aimag + Bimag
    Yr ! Treal * Wreal - Timag * Wimag
    Yi ! Treal* Wimag + Timag * Wreal
```

Looking at the code given above, we can see that the data are obtained from input channels, captured in Areal, Aimag, Breal, and Bimag, and the results of the computation are directed to the output channels. This piece of code can be improved if we reduce the number of channels needed for data transfer by using a single channel to carry the real and imaginary parts of a given complex value. This way, we need only four channels, and so will fit onto a single transputer. The following segment of code shows the change.

```
WHILE TRUE
SEQ
    PAR
        A ? Areal; Aimag
        B ? Breal; Bimag
    PAR
        X ! Areal + Breal; Aimag + Bimag
        Y !  Treal * Wreal - Timag * Wimag; Treal * Wimag + Timag * Wreal
```

5.2.3 FFT System Performance

The performance is usually measured in units of the number of FFTs that are executed per second for a given problem size, n. Using the pipeline arrangement given above, the FFT was implemented in OCCAM on a system of T424 transputers and its performance was measured by Wilson et al. [Wilson]. It was found that the butterfly computation takes about 16 microseconds to execute. Thus, the FFT pipeline produces results at approximately 16-microsecond intervals.

Table 5.1 shows the varying numbers of transputers needed for various sizes of transform, together with the sampling frequency.

FFT Size	Pipeline Size		Transputers	Sampling Frequency
	row	column		
8	4	3	12	400 KHz
16	8	4	32	800 KHz
32	16	5	80	1.6 MHz
64	32	6	192	3.2 MHz
128	64	7	448	6.4 MHz
256	128	8	1024	12.8 MHz

Table 5.1   Performance with various transputer array sizes

5.3   PROGRAMMING HYPERCUBES

In this section, we discuss some important issues associated with the hypercube architecture, and we describe some general guidelines for programming this important special case. We start by reviewing the programming characteristics common to commercial hypercubes described in Chapter 3:

• A hypercube application consists of a host program that runs on a single-processor host and one or more node programs that run on individual cube nodes. The host program executes as a conventional application. It usually initializes the application, interacts with the user, and loads the node programs onto the processors. Each node program performs calculations, communicates with other nodes, and sends data back to the host.

• Processors do not share memory. Instead, each processor has its own local memory. They can each access the file system, but otherwise operate independently of each other.

• Processors communicate with each other and the host by passing messages. There is no global data space where all processors share access to the same data.

• Each processor (node) executes its own program. In many applications, it turns out that each node executes the same program on a different set of input data, e.g., the SPMD paradigm. There may be some conditional code that identifies one or more nodes that perform some special action.

These factors all add up to special problems for distributed-memory programmers. These are the *maxmin problem*, *load balancing problem*, and *task scheduling problem*. We must determine how to solve these problems.

5.3.1 Communication versus Computation

A trivially parallel application is one that requires no interprocessor communication. Such an application achieves linear speedup. Since not all applications are trivially parallel, communication becomes inevitable and we have to deal with it. When we write programs on a MIMD hypercube multicomputer, we must be aware of the significant difference between computation and communication costs.

Tables 5.2 and 5.3 show the results of an experimental study of interprocessor communication time and the time to perform arithmetic operations on an nCUBE hypercube. Table 5.2 shows that sending an 8-byte message between two adjacent processors takes 42 times as long as an 8-byte real addition and 32 times as long as an 8-byte real multiplication. Table 5.3 shows that longer messages are transferred at a rate higher than shorter ones going the same distance. It also shows that it takes longer to send the same message to a processor four hops away than to one two hops away [Dunigan; Ranka].

Operation	Time	Comm./Comp.
8-byte transfer	47 μs	
8-byte real add	11.2 μs	42
8-byte real mult	14.7 μs	32

Table 5.2 Performance table for nCUBE [Ranka]

After taking one look at Tables 5.2 and 5.3, it becomes very clear that one of the goals of a parallel design is to develop a communication strategy that maximizes the time a processor spends computing and minimizes the time it spends communicating. It also becomes obvious that if the application requires interprocessor communication, the program designer should minimize communication between processors that are far apart. This is the classic maxmin problem described elsewhere in this book.

Length	Hops					
	1	2	3	4	5	6
8	17.2	11.7	8.9	7.1	5.9	5.1
16	33.1	22.4	16.9	13.7	11.4	9.8
32	61.6	41.7	31.4	25.2	21.1	18.1
64	106.6	72.1	54.4	43.7	36.5	31.1
128	169.5	114.4	86.1	69.1	57.6	49.4
256	241.2	162.2	121.4	97.1	81.0	69.5
512	304.8	203.4	152.4	121.9	101.6	87.1
1024	351.1	233.4	174.9	139.8	116.4	99.8
2048	380.8	252.2	188.8	150.8	125.6	107.6

Table 5.3   Communications speed on an nCUBE (Kbytes/sec)

5.3.2   Load Balancing

The goal of *load balancing* is to keep processor nodes busy and have them finish roughly at the same time. We say a program is *balanced* if its computation is equally distributed across all processors. Valuable processor cycles are wasted if some nodes have to wait on others to finish. More important, the greatest speedup is possible only when all processors are busy, all of the time.

An application should be analyzed to make sure it is balanced. If the *work load* is known beforehand, it is possible to statically determine a balanced distribution of work at compile time. On the other hand, if the work load is not known beforehand, the parallel processors must dynamically adjust the load. Static techniques can be applied by the programmer, but dynamic techniques must be applied by either the operating system or the application software during program execution.

Chapter 9 discusses a number of techniques for static and dynamic load balancing. We merely describe a few simple techniques for dynamic balancing here.

There are several heuristics for *dynamic load balancing*. In what follows, we show two variations of the same load balancing heuristic given in Ranka. In both versions, the load is balanced by averaging the load over processors that are directly connected. In heuristic H1, a processor transmits its entire work load, including the necessary data, to its neighbor processor. In heuristic H2, however, a processor transmits only the amount of work that is in excess of the average work load.

It is left as an exercise for the reader to find the differences between H1 and H2 and to determine the cases in which each heuristic is better than the other (see problem 6).

```
H1
Load_Balance_H1();

   {
   for(i=0;i<CubeSize;i++) {
      SendMyLoad to neighbor processor along dimension i;
      Receive HisLoad from neighbor processor along dimension i,
         and append to MyLoad;
      Avg = (MyLoadSize + HisLoadSize) / 2;
      if (MyLoadSize > Avg) MyLoadSize = Avg;
         else if (HisLoadSize > Avg) MyLoadSize += HisLoadSize - Avg;
         {
      }
   }

H2
Load_Balance_H2();

   {
   for(i=0;i<CubeSize;i++) {
      SendMyLoad to neighbor processor along dimension i;
      Receive HisLoad from neighbor processor along dimension i,
      Avg = (MyLoadSize + HisLoadSize) / 2;
      if (MyLoadSize > Avg) {
      Send extra load (MyLoadSize - Avg)to neighbor processor
            along dimension i;
         MyLoadSize = Avg;
      }
         else if (HisLoadSize > Avg) {
      Receive extra load (Avg - HisLoadSize) from neighbor processor
            along dimension i;
         MyLoadSize += HisLoadSize - Avg;
         }
      }
   }
```

Overhead is always associated with dynamic load balancing; therefore, we should be careful when using this technique to balance the load. Before incorporating a load balancing scheme into an algorithm, one must weigh the potential reduction in time required to complete the work against the time required to balance the load. If it takes longer to balance the load than to complete the work, it is not practical to balance the load using this method. It might be even better to perform the algorithm without dynamic load balancing.

Load balancing also depends on the way the problem is distributed in the system. Distributing a problem among the nodes in a parallel computer can be done through either *domain decomposition* or *control decomposition*. In domain decomposition, the domain of the input data are partitioned and the partitions are assigned to different processors. In control decomposition, program tasks are divided and distributed among processors.

For example, consider the problem of tree search in a game playing program. This problem can be approached as domain decomposition by distributing the branches among the processors. Each processor follows its branch down to the leaves and then returns some leaves as possible moves. Depending on the current state of the game, some of the branches may be quite involved and require more processing time than others. In this case, some nodes finish before others and this results in poor performance.

One way of control decomposing this problem is to consider the tree branches as tasks to be performed. One processor is assigned as a manager node that does some initial setup and then supervises worker tasks running on other nodes. When a node finishes its task, it reports its answer to the manager and requests another task. In this case, the decomposition is identical to the supervisor/worker paradigm.

Control decomposition achieves better load balancing than domain decomposition for this example. Control decomposition produces its best results when the tasks assigned near the end of the problem are about the same size. In general, it is not always obvious which decomposition technique is best.

5.3.3 Processor Allocation for Hypercubes

Massively parallel hypercube systems can contain thousands of processors, many of which might remain idle when a single application requires merely hundreds of processors. Can the idle processors be assigned to another user? The answer is yes, if we partition the hypercube into smaller hypercubes, thus maintaining the hypercube interconnection network for all users. This is called the *hypercube recognition* problem, and is similar to the problem of managing memory in serial computer systems. (Due to the mathematical nature of this topic, the casual reader may want to skip to Section 5.4.)

Suppose a number of users (m) share the processors of an n-dimensional hypercube. (Recall from the discussion given in Chapter 3 that the number of nodes in a hypercube is always a power of 2. That power is called the cube's dimension.) These m users make requests for subcubes of dimension k_1, k_2, ..., k_m. We seek an algorithm that recognizes these subcubes and returns their address within the larger hypercube after marking them as allocated.

A hypercube is said to be *fragmented* when there are enough processors to accommodate a subcube request but they don't form a subcube. When many candidate subcubes are recognized, the one with the minimum effect on fragmentation should be allocated. A *first-fit* subcube recognition algorithm selects the first subcube found; a *best-fit* algorithm attempts to reduce fragmentation. In general, we seek a fast and efficient algorithm for allocating subcubes that maintain the hypercube structure.

Several subcube allocation policies have been reported in the literature using different schemes [Al-Bassam; Chen 1986, 1987; Livingston 1988, 1989]. Some of these schemes are implemented on commercial machines. For example, nCUBE/6 uses an allocation method based on a scheme called the *buddy strategy*. Al-Bassam et al. [1990] have developed the best-known recognition algorithms which recognize all sub-

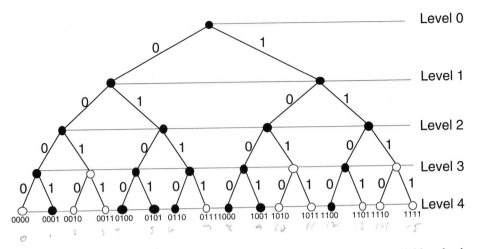

Figure 5.8   A Q_4 Buddy Tree showing allocated subcubes as dark nodes and available subcubes as light nodes

cubes, are fast, and can be parallelized. They extended the buddy system methodology [Al-Bassam] to maximize the number of recognized subcubes with low fragmentation.

The Buddy System

We first introduce some notation that is needed in this section. Let Q_n denote a hypercube of dimension n and Σ be the ternary symbol set $\{0,1,*\}$, where $*$ is a don't care symbol. Every Q_k subcube in Q_n can be represented by a string of symbols in Σ having k $*$s. For example, the address of the subcube Q_2 formed by nodes 0010, 0011, 0110, 0111 in Q_4 is $0*1*$. Let $\alpha*\alpha*$ represent the subcubes $0*0*$, $0*1*$, $1*0*$, and $1*1*$. In general, a string of length n of symbols in $\{\alpha,*\}$, where α is 0 or 1, with k $*$s and $n - k$ αs, represents 2^{n-k} subcubes of dimension k since α can be 0 or 1.

A binary tree of n levels, as shown in Figure 5.8 for $n = 4$, is used to represent the availability of some subcubes of Q_n. Note that the hypercube nodes enumerated at the leaves of this tree form subcubes according to the subtree to which they belong. Thus, one method of finding subcubes is to simply traverse this tree looking for a large enough subtree to accommodate the request. This is called the *buddy system*.

Extended Buddy System

In the buddy system, Q_k subcubes are recognized at level $n - k$. There will be 2^{n-k} recognizable subcubes at level $n - k$, namely $\alpha\alpha \ldots \alpha**\ldots*$ with $n - k$ α's and k $*$s, i.e., the subcubes $\alpha^{n-k}*^k$. For example, the Q_3s at level 1 are $0***$ and $1***$. By extending the search to more levels (levels $n - k$, $n - k + 1$, ... , etc.), more subcubes can be recognized. When the next level is searched, i.e., level $n - k + 1$, then $\binom{n-k+1}{n-k}2^{n-k}$ subcubes can be recognized. This is true since any $n - k$ bits can be chosen among the $n - k + 1$ bits in the tree, recognizing the following:

$$\leftarrow n - k + 1 \rightarrow$$
$$\alpha\,\alpha\,.\,.\,.\ \alpha\,*\,*\,.\,.\ *$$
$$\alpha\,\alpha\,.\,.\,.\ *\,\alpha\,*\,.\,.\ *$$
$$\alpha\,.\,.\,.\ *\,\alpha\,\alpha\,*\,.\,.\ *$$
$$\,.\qquad.\ .\ .\qquad.$$
$$*\,\alpha\,\alpha\,.\,.\,.\ \alpha\,*\,.\,.\ *$$

i.e., the subcubes $\{\alpha^{n-k-i} * \alpha^i *^{k-1} \mid 0 \le i < n - k\}$.

Using a similar argument, Al-Bassam et al. showed that searching to depth d yields $\binom{n-k+d}{n-k}2^{n-k}$ recognized Q_k subcubes. That is, $N(k, d)$ is the number of recognizable Q_k subcubes between levels $n - k$ and $n - k + d$, i.e., at depths 0 to d, where $0 \le d \le k$. Then in a hypercube of dimension n:

$$N(k, d) = \binom{n-k+d}{n-k}2^{n-k} \quad \text{for } 0 \le d \le k$$

It is clear that increasing the search depth (d) will increase the number of recognizable subcubes, but this takes more time due to extra searching. Al-Bassam et al. also give the maximum number of node comparisons, the *search length* of the algorithm. The maximum search length occurs when all the recognizable subcubes are not available and the search is forced to depth d. Given a hypercube of dimension n, the search length to recognize a Q_k subcube using depth parameter d is

$$\text{Length } (k, d) \le \binom{n-k+d}{n-k}2^{n-k+d}.$$

Example

Let $n = 4$ and $d = 2$. Using the tree shown in Figure 5.8, we can recognize subcubes $N(k, 2) = \binom{4-k+2}{4-k}2^{4-k}$ of size k, e.g., Q_ks, for $0 \le k \le 4$. That is, we can recognize 240 Q_0s, 80 Q_1s, 24 Q_2s, 6 Q_3s, and 1 Q_4. The maximum search length for recognizing a Q_2, for instance, is

$$\text{Length } (2, 2) = \binom{4-2+2}{4-2}2^{4-2+2} = 98 \text{ node comparisons.}$$

Efficient Subcube Recognition

To recognize the Q_k subcubes efficiently at depth d, i.e., at level $n - k + d$, we take into account two factors.

1 It is not necessary to check the subcubes that have been checked at the previous levels.

2 It is best to narrow down the recognition to candidate subcubes instead of exhaustively checking all possible $\binom{n-k+d-1}{n-k-1} 2^{n-k}$ subcubes at depth d.

A Q_k can be formed by 2^d Q_{k-d} subcubes at level $n - k + d$. Any Q_k having an "*" in bit number $n - k + d$ is generated at some level before $n - k + d$. At level $n - k + d$, we only generate subcubes that have no "*" in bit $n - k + d$. Only $n - k - 1$ α's can be chosen among the $n - k + d - 1$ positions to recognize $\binom{n-k+d-1}{n-k-1} 2^{n-k}$ subcubes at depth d.

The candidate Q_k subcubes at level $n - k + d$ are generated as follows. Let q be a Q_{k-d} subcube at level $n - k + d$. If q is available, then all the Q_k subcubes containing q are considered as candidates. When q is not available, all the Q_k subcubes containing q are not available and hence not candidates. The other $2^d - 1$ Q_{k-d} s, that form with q a candidate subcube, can then be tested for availability. This process speeds up the search considerably.

More formally, let $S_n = \{*^n\}$, $S_{n-1} = \{0 *^{n-1}, 1 *^{n-1}\}$, $S_{n-2} = \{0\,0\,*^{n-2},$ $0\,1\,*^{n-2}, 1\,0\,*^{n-2}, 1\,1\,*^{n-2}\}, \dots$, etc. In general let $S_i = \alpha^{n-i} *^i = \{0^{n-i} *^i, \dots, 1^n$ $^{-i} *^i\}$ for $0 \leq i \leq n$, i.e., S_k is the recognized Q_k subcubes at level $n - k$. Let T be the buddy system tree of Q_n. Given n, k, and d, the following algorithm recognizes $\binom{n-k+d}{n-k} 2^{n-k}$ subcubes of dimension k.

Subcube Recognition:

For $i = 0$ to d, do the following:
    For each $q = v_1 v_2 v_3 \dots v_n \in S_{k-i}$ such that $T[q] = $ "available," do
    a Let Q be the set of all Q_k subcubes that contain q.
        For each subcube $p \in Q$ do
        b If the other $2^i - 1$ Q_{k-i} s forming p are available then p is available, stop.

The set Q in step a can be formed by changing any i 0s to *s in the first $n - k + i - 1$ positions of q. Notice that if position $n - k + i$ was included, all previously recognized subcubes were formed, hence this position is avoided. Since $q = v_1 v_2 v_3 \dots v_n$ where $v_j = $ "*" for $n - k + i + 1 \leq j \leq n$, so $Q = \{p = u_1 u_2 \dots u_{n-k+i-1} v_{n-k+i} *^{k-i}\}$

where the number of $*$s in p is k, i.e., there are i $*$s in $(u_1 \, u_2 \ldots u_{n-k+i-1})$ and if $u_j = $ "$*$", then $v_j = 0$. In general, the i $*$s can be chosen in any of the positions from 1 to $n - k + i - 1$; however when only the positions containing 0s (or 1s) are considered, every Q_k at this level will be generated by exactly one Q_{k-i}.

In step b, given any subcube $p \in Q$, where $p = u_1 u_2 \ldots u_{n-k+i-1} *^{k-i}$. The other $2^i - 1 \, Q_{k-i}$ subcubes that form p are obtained by enumerating the i $*$s in the first $n - k + i - 1$ positions of p. These Q_{k-i} subcubes (having the last $k - i$ positions as $*$s) can be directly checked at level $n - k + i$ of the tree.

Example

Consider the hypercube of dimension $n = 4$ represented by the tree T in Figure 5.8 where the dark subcubes are allocated and the light ones are available. The following sequence illustrates how the subcube recognition algorithm proceeds to recognize Q_2 when $d = 2$.

When $i = 0$, the subcubes $00**$, $01**$, $10**$, $11**$ are considered but they are not all available. When $i = 1$, subcubes $0*0*$ and $*00*$ are skipped, because $q = 000*$ is allocated. But $q = 001*$ is available so we consider the candidate set $Q = \{0*1*, *01*\}$. $0*1* = 001*$ and $011*$ but $011*$ is not available, so $0*1*$ is not available either. $*01* = 001*$ and $101*$ and both are available so, $*01*$ is available. Thus, one subcube of size $k = 2$ is recognized. This is the subcube formed by leaf nodes 0010, 0011, 1010, and 1011 in Figure 5.8.

Why were the two available nodes numbered 1110 and 1111 not recognized as part of Q_2? They do not form a hypercube with the other available nodes. That is, we cannot reach nodes 1110 and 1111 from any of the other available nodes using the Hamming distance rule. Checking the recognized node numbers we note that 0010 can be reached from 0011 and 1011 by changing only one bit at a time, and 0011 can be reached from 1011 and 0010, etc.

5.4 COMPUTER VISION APPLICATION ON HYPERCUBE

The problem of matching an image to a template is one of the common problems in computer vision applications. This problem is described as follows. Given an $N \times N$ image, I, and an $M \times M$ template, T, the template is matched with the image at point (i, j) by a two-dimensional convolution ($C2D$), where:

$$C2D(i, j) = \sum_{s=0}^{M-1} \sum_{t=0}^{M-1} I(\, (i + s) \, mod \, (N, \, (j + t) \, modN) \,)^* \, T(s, t)$$

This equation requires $O(N^2 M^2)$ operations to compute the convolution at every point (i, j).

A hypercube program to compute the two-dimensional convolution assumes that the hypercube is of dimension d and the image matrix I is distributed over the 2^d processors [Ranka].

In this program, no processor has all the image values in its partition that it needs to compute the convolution. The additional values it needs are contained in its neighbor processors to the east, south, and southeast. The program can obtain these values as follows. Each processor does all the computing for the image values it has initially (this includes some of the computing for *C2D* values in the west, north, and northwest neighbor processors) and then transmits the partially computed convolution values to these neighbors.

Now we need to write two programs; the host program to be executed on the host computer and the node program to be run on each node in the hypercube processors. The high-level description of the host program is given as follows:

```
HostTemplate();
{
    Open a hypercube of the required dimension;
    Load the "node" program on all the nodes;
    Send the template to node 0;
    Receive Completion Signal from node 0;
    Deallocate the hypercube;
}
```

In what follows, we show the high-level description of the node program for each hypercube node. This program was implemented in C on nCUBE/ten hypercube [Ranka]. Table 5.4 gives the runtime of the C program to compute the convolution of images with different size using cubes with different size.

```
int TemplateAtNode;
{
    if(nodeid == 0) Receive Template from host
    Broadcast Template from node 0
    Calculate Convolution for NorthWest node
    Send Convolution for NorthWest node
    Calculate Convolution for West node
    Send Convolution for West node
    Calculate Convolution for North node
    Send Convolution for North node
    Calculate Convolution for self
    for (i=0; i < 3; i++)
    {
        Receive Convolution from a node
        Update Convolution
    }
    End Signal to node 0
    if(nodeid == 0) Send End Signal to the host
}
```

Processors	Image Size	4	8	16	32
1	32	0.505	1.857	7.000	20.450
4	32	0.139	0.482	1.417	
4	64	0.514	1.872	7.026	20.497
16	32	0.045	0.115		
16	64	0.142	0.484	1.422	
16	128	0.516	1.874	7.031	20.510
64	32	0.021			
64	64	0.047	0.188		
64	128	0.144	0.487	1.426	
64	256	0.519	1.878	7.036	20.520

Table 5.4   Runtime (in seconds) of the program given in Section 5.4 on nCUBE/ten [Ranka]

5.5   PROGRAMMING EXAMPLES

In this section we use a small example to illustrate how to program two hypercubes. We start by giving a brief introduction to the iPSC/2 programming environment, followed by a simple communication program that implements the outline of a supervisor/worker program. Then we compute π numerically using the supervisor/worker outline. A Fortran implementation of the π calculation is given for the nCUBE machine for comparison purposes.

An iPSC/2 system consists of compute nodes, I/O nodes, and a front-end processor (see Chapter 3). Each node runs the NX/2 operating system, uses message passing to communicate with the other nodes, and can access the host file system and the iPSC/2 Concurrent File System. The front-end processor is called the System Resource Manager (SRM), also referred to as the *local host*. The SRM runs the UNIX System V operating system, augmented with iPSC/2 extensions and TCP/IP networking software.

The following program is an example of a host C program that allocates a cube called *mycube*, then loads a node program called *nodeprogram* on each allocated node. The node program receives initial conditions from the host, performs its work, and then sends its answer back to the host with a message-passing call. For detailed information about using iPSC/2 hypercube, refer to the references given at the end of the chapter.

```
#include <cube.h>
```

```
#define KEEP 1
#define ALL_NODES-1
#define MSGTYPE 1
main()
{
        ..
    getcube("mycube", "64m8", " ", KEEP);
    setpid(100);
    load("nodeprogram", ALL_NODES, 0);
        ..
    csend(MSGTYPE, initial, sizeof(initial), ALL_NODES, 0);
        ..
    crecv(MSGTYPE, answer, sizeof(answer));
        ..
    reloc("mycube");
        ..
}
```

5.5.1 Computing π on the iPSC/2

The following program computes an approximation to π by finding the area under the curve $4/(1 + x^2)$ between 0 and 1. This application consists of a host program that interfaces with the user and supervises execution of the same node program on each of the worker nodes. Each node performs a portion of the integration, returning its portion of the area under the curve to the supervisor, who totals them and prints a single result.

```
/*
 * host.c 6.2 89/06/02 15:24:12
 *
 * This program calculates the value of pi, using numerical integration
 * with parallel processing, and clocks the solution time.
 *
 * The user selects the number of nodes that will do work and the
 * number of points of integration. By selecting and timing different
 * cube sizes we obtain a measure of the speedup with trivially
 * parallel problems.
 *
 */
#include "cube.h"
#define HOST_PID 100    /* process id of the host process */
#define NODE_PID   0    /* process id for node processes */
#define INIT_TYPE  0    /* type of initialization message */
#define SIZE_TYPE  2    /* type of size message */
#define PART_TYPE 10    /* type of partial integration message */
#define ALL_NODES -1    /* symbol for all nodes */
#define ALL_PIDS  -1    /* symbol for all processes */
```

```
struct msg_type {        /* structure for parameters of integration */
        double  a,       /* lower limit of integration */
                b;       /* upper limit of integration */
        long  points;    /* number of points in quadrature rule */
};
struct msg_type msg;     /* integration parameters */
int    size;             /* number of working nodes */
double integral;         /* result of integration */
long   tms, ms, tsec,    /* time calculation variables */
       sec, min;
main()
{       /* Host main */
        setpid(HOST_PID);
        /* Load all nodes with pid NODE_PID. */
        load ("node", ALL_NODES, NODE_PID);
        for (;;) {       /* Infinite loop */
                /* Get user input. */
                if (!user_input(&msg, &size)) break;
                /*
                 * Send message containing number of working
                 * nodes to all nodes.
                 */
        csend(SIZE_TYPE, &size, sizeof(size), ALL_NODES, NODE_PID);
                /*
                 * Send message containing the integration
                 * parameters to all nodes.
                 */
        csend(INIT_TYPE, &msg, sizeof(msg), ALL_NODES, NODE_PID);
                /*
                 * Wait to receive message containing the
                 * integration result and process execution time.
                 */
                crecv(PART_TYPE, &msg, sizeof(msg));
                integral =  msg.a;
                /* Calculate the time interval. */
                tms  = msg.points;
                ms   = tms % 1000;
                tsec = (tms − ms) / 1000;
                sec  = tsec % 60;
                min  = (tsec − sec) / 60;
                printf("\t\tpi is approximately : %.16f\n\n", integral);
                printf("\t\telapsed time =  %d min. %d.%d secs.\n\n",
                        min,sec,ms);
        }       /* End infinite loop */
        killcube(ALL_NODES, ALL_PIDS);
}       /* End host main */
/*
```

```
* node.c 6.2 89/06/02 15:24:14
*
* This program calculates the value of pi, using numerical integration
* with parallel processing, and clocks the solution time.
*
* The user selects the number of processors and the number of points
* of integration.  By selecting and timing different cube sizes we
* obtain a measure of the speedup with trivially parallel problems.
*
* All nodes:
* (1) Receive the message specifying the number of working nodes.
* (2) Receive the message containing the integration parameters.
* (3) Participate in the global sum operation (gdsum) which sums
*     the partial integrals.  Nonworking nodes contribute a 0 value.
*
* Each working node calculates a partial integral.
*
* Root node:
* (1) Calculates elapsed execution time.
* (2) Sends the integral result and execution time back to the host.
*/
#include "cube.h"
#define HOST_PID 100    /* process id of the host process */
#define INIT_TYPE  0    /* type of initialization message */
#define SIZE_TYPE  2    /* type of size message */
#define PART_TYPE 10    /* type of partial integration message */
#define ROOT       0    /* root node id */
int work_nodes,         /* number of nodes which will work on problem */
    my_pid,             /* process id of the nodes */
    my_node;            /* node id of each node */
long basic_slices,      /* mininum number of slices to be given each node */
     extra_slices,
     my_slices,         /* number of slices to integrate */
     starttime;         /* start time of calculation */
double x,               /* value of function to integrate */
       f(),             /* function to integrate */
       slice_size,      /* size of each integration slice */
       partial_int,     /* partial integral */
       sum,
       work,
       my_a,            /* local lower limit of integration */
       my_b;            /* local upper limit of integration */
struct msg_type {       /* structure for parameters of integration */
       double  a,       /* lower limit of integration */
               b;       /* upper limit of integration */
       long  points;    /* number of points in quadrature rule */
};
```

```
struct msg_type integral;
main()
{        /* Node main */
        int j;
        my_pid = mypid();    /* Get process id. */
        my_node = mynode();  /* Get node number. */
        for (;;) {        /* Infinite loop */
           partial_int = 0.0;
           /*
            * Receive message containing number of working
            * nodes.
            */
           crecv(SIZE_TYPE, &work_nodes, sizeof(work_nodes));
           /*
            * Receive message containing the integration
            * parameters.
            */
           crecv(INIT_TYPE, &integral, sizeof(integral));
           if (my_node < work_nodes) {   /* If I am a working node ... */
                   starttime = mclock();   /* Get initial clock value. */
                   /* Calculate size of integration slice. */
                   slice_size = (integral.b - integral.a)/integral.points;
                   basic_slices = integral.points / work_nodes;
                   extra_slices = integral.points % work_nodes;
                   /*
                    * Calculate number of slices per node and the
                    * local subinterval for each node.
                    */
                   if (my_node < extra_slices) {
                           my_slices = basic_slices + 1;
                           my_a = integral.a + slice_size * my_node *
                                   my_slices;
                   } else {
                           my_slices = basic_slices;
                           my_a = integral.a + slice_size *
                                   (my_node * my_slices + extra_slices);
                   }
                   my_b = my_a + slice_size * my_slices;
                   /* Calculate partial integral on the subinterval */
                   for (x=my_a; x < my_b - (slice_size*0.5); x+=slice_size)
                           partial_int += f(x + slice_size/2) * slice_size;
           }        /* End if I am working node */
           gdsum(&partial_int, 1, &work);  /* Sum the partial integrals */
           /*
            * If I am the root node, calculate the elapsed time and
            * send the summed partial integrals and the time to the host.
            */
```

```
              if (mynode() == ROOT) {
                      integral.a = partial_int;
                      integral.points = mclock() - starttime;
                      csend(PART_TYPE, &integral, sizeof(integral), myhost(),
                          HOST_PID);
              }
      }         /* End infinite loop */
}         /* End node main */
/*
 *   Function f for integration (pi)
 */
double f(x)
double x;
{
      return (4.0/(1.0+x*x));
}
```

5.5.2   Computing π on the nCUBE 2

For comparison purposes, we also provide the π program written in Fortran for the
nCUBE 2 computer. Notice the differences. This program was provided by John
Gustafson.

```
    PROGRAM Pi
*
*    Dsumn    System function; creates 64-bit global sum from local values
*    h        Spacing between sample points
*    sum      Sum approximating the integral
*    i        Loop counter and integer scratch variable
*    iproc    Identifying number of processor
*    lnproc   Log base 2 of the number of processors (hypercube dimension)
*    n        Global number of integration points
*    Nglobal System function; makes node 0 the conduit for all I/O
*    nloc     Local number of integration points.
*
      REAL*8 Dsumn, h, sum
      INTEGER*4 i, iproc, j, lnproc, n, Nglobal, nloc
*
*  Get node i.d. and ensemble size; compute sum in local interval;
*
      i = Nglobal ()
      CALL WhoAmI (iproc, i, i, lnproc)
      WRITE (*, *) ' Number of points per processor:'
      READ (*, *) nloc
      n = nloc * (2 ** lnproc)
      sum = 0.D0
      h = 1.D0 / DBLE (n)
      DO 1 i = iproc * nloc + 1, iproc * nloc + nloc
```

```
            sum = sum + 4.D0 / (1.D0 + ((DBLE (i) - .5) * h) ** 2)
    1    CONTINUE
    *
    *   Turn local sum into global sum, and print result:
    *
         sum = h * Dsumn (sum)
         WRITE (*, *) 'sum:', sum
         END
```

5.6 SUMMARY

The programming paradigm of distributed-memory computers is much different from that of shared-memory computers because distributed-memory computers have no global address space containing shared data. Instead, each processor has its own private address space, and processors interact by passing messages among themselves. Unlike synchronization in shared-memory systems, synchronization in distributed systems is a byproduct of message passing.

The message-passing approach has been used in many high-level programming languages such as Ada, CSP, and OCCAM. They all use the two basic operations, *send* and *receive*, to exchange messages among parallel processes.

Parallel programmers of distributed-memory computers must be aware of the trade-off between communication and computation. If the designer is not careful, communication cost can easily dominate the computation cost. One of the design goals is to maximize the time a processor spends computing and minimize the time it spends communicating. Load balancing is another issue that must be considered. Applications must be analyzed to make sure that the work load is divided evenly among parallel processors.

A hypercube of dimension d has 2^d processors, labeled 0 through $2^d - 1$. Two processors are directly connected if their binary representations differ by exactly one bit. In a hypercube of dimension d, each processor is connected to d others. This type of architecture is very popular because: (1) the average distance between two processors is shorter than in other topologies such as tree, mesh, and ring; (2) a hypercube is completely symmetric; and (3) most other popular networks are easily mapped to a hypercube.

In a multiuser environment, where users request to allocate subcubes with different sizes for their applications, a subcube allocation scheme is needed. The buddy strategy and the gray code method are two fundamental allocation schemes in hypercubes. The buddy strategy is used commercially in nCUBE/6.

PROBLEMS FOR DISCUSSION AND SOLUTION

1 Suppose that we have n different programs running on n processors in a parallel computer. The n programs communicate with each other using two basic operations: (1) *send* and (2) *receive*. Assume that communication over a link can only occur when both the sender and the receiver are ready, which means that a program on one processor might wait on another until it is ready. Design an algorithm to detect deadlock in the system. What is the complexity of your algorithm?

2 Study nondeterminism in both CSP and OCCAM. Give some example where nondeterminism arises.

3 Write an OCCAM program to sort a stream of unsorted numbers. (Hint: Use the concept of pipelining. Use as many replicated parallel processes as there are numbers.)

4 Consider the shared-memory solution of the traveling salesman problem given in Section 4.1.3. Redesign the solution to make it suitable for distributed-memory systems.

5 Synchronization in distributed-memory systems is accomplished using the two basic operations *send* and *receive*. Constructs such as locks, barriers, etc. are used for synchronization in shared-memory systems. Conduct a thorough comparison of synchronization techniques in both kinds of computers in terms of the following:
a. ease of use
b. associated overhead
c. the possibility of falling into deadlock situation
d. compatibility with the way programmers think

6 Consider the load balancing heuristics (H1 and H2) given in Section 5.3.2. Determine the cases in which:
a. H1 performs better than H2
b. H2 performs better than H1
c. H1 and H2 provide almost the same performance
(Hint: Consider the following issues: transmitted message length, number of messages to be transmitted, and data transmission setup time.)

7a How many subcubes of dimension k exist in a hypercube of dimension d, where $(k \leq d)$?
7b Count all subcubes in a hypercube of dimension d

8 Compare the buddy and the gray code subcube allocation schemes with respect to the following:
a. The number of recognized subcubes
b. The possibility of ending up with a fragmented hypercube

9 Consider the problem of matching an image to a template, discussed in Section 5.4. The image and the template matrices are distributed among the processors to do both computation and communication as shown in the given algorithm. Now suppose that we distribute the image matrix so each processor has all the image values it needs to compute the convolution at all the points assigned to it. Thus, in addition to the data a processor is assigned in the algorithm given in Section 5.4, it also receives the data that had been in its neighbors to the east, southeast, and south. Discuss the advantages and disadvantages of this way of distributing the data. Show some cases in which one data distribution method is better than the other.

10 Given a weighted graph or digraph $G = (V, E, W)$ and two specified vertices v and w, design an MIMD parallel algorithm to find a shortest path from v to w on a parallel computer.

References

Al-Bassam, S., El-Rewini, H., Bose, B., and Lewis, T., "Efficient Serial and Parallel Subcube Recognition in Hypercubes," *Proceedings of the 5th Distributed Memory Computing Conference,* pp. 64 – 71, April 1990.

Chen, M., and Shin, K. G., "Embedment of Interesting Task Modules into a Hypercube Multiprocessor," Proc. Second Hypercube Conference, pp. 121 – 129, 1986.

Chen, M., and Shin, K. G., "Processor Allocation in an N-cube Multiprocessor Using Gray Codes," *IEEE Transactions on Computers,* Vol. C-36, No.12, pp. 1396 – 1407, 1987.

Dettmer, R., "The Artful Transputer," *Electronics & Power,* The Institution of Electrical Engineers, August 1986.

Dunigan, T., "Hypercube Performance," *Proceedings Conf. Hypercube Multiprocessors,* SIAM, Philadelphia, pp. 178 – 192, 1986.

INMOS IMS T414 transputer data sheet.

Intel iPSC/2 *User's Guide.*

Livingston, M., and Stout, Q., "Fault Tolerance of Allocation Schemes in Massively Parallel Computers," *Proceedings 2nd Symp. Frontiers of Massively Parallel Computation,* pp. 491 – 494, 1988.

Livingston, M., and Stout, Q., "Parallel Allocation Algorithms for Hypercubes and Meshes," in *Proceedings of the 4th Hypercube Concurrent Computers and Applications,* Monterey, CA, 1989.

Pountain, D., *A Tutorial Introduction to OCCAM Programming,* INMOS Corporation, 1986.

Rabiner and Gold, *Theory and Applications of Digital Signal Processing,* Prentice-Hall, Englewood Cliffs, N.J., 1975.

Ranka, S., Won, Y., and Sahni, S., "Programming a Hypercube Multicomputer," *IEEE Software,* pp. 69 – 77, September 1988.

Wilson, P., "Highly Concurrent Systems Using the Transputer," *Tech Report,* INMOS Corporation.

Chapter 6

Object-Oriented Parallel Programming

Object-oriented programming has grown from a radical concept of the 1960s to routine practice among serial programmers in the 1990s. Can it be as useful in parallel programming as in serial programming? In this chapter we survey object-oriented programming concepts, illustrate them with examples, and show how parallelism introduces necessary modifications to the serial concepts.

The term *object-oriented* seems redundant in modern computer science terminology, so we use the abbreviation "object programming" which has been suggested by a number of practitioners. *Object programming* is defined as any programming technique in which the primary components of the application program are objects. *Objects* are defined as instances of a class, and a *class* is defined as a collection of procedures called *methods*, and the data types they operate on.

Perhaps the most widely known object programming language is C++. Therefore, many of our coding examples will be given in C++, even though there are many object programming languages that can be adapted to parallel programming.

We introduce the concept of a *server*, which is an object plus a task. Servers are objects in execution, and the server model is really a runtime execution model which permits execution of object programs on both distributed and shared-memory parallel computers as well as on traditional serial computers.

We begin with a survey of the concepts leading into object programming and object programming languages. This survey can be skipped by the reader who is already familiar with objects. Then we describe a low-level class hierarchy for C++ objects in a shared-memory computer. The bulk of the chapter discusses how one might adapt C++ to parallel programming, and then how to extend the object paradigm to a new model called the server model. In the server model, objects take on a life of their own, which permits them to be distributed. However, the server model does not solve all synchronization problems associated with parallelism. Because of these problems, parallel object programming remains largely a research topic.

6.1 CONCEPTS OF OBJECT PROGRAMMING

Object programming has its roots in the 1960s with the invention of Simula-67 and Smalltalk. The idea extends further into the past, and is nearly as old as computing.

Every computer is fundamentally a device with memory and circuits for modifying memory. We say a computer is in a certain *state* as defined by the contents of its memory. State is changed by instructions which are thought of as the behaviors of the computer. In object programming we talk about methods, instead of instructions, to define behavior. Thus, using the terminology of object programming, we say every computer has a state (memory) and methods (instructions) for defining its behavior. In short, a computer is an object consisting of state in the form of memory and function in the form of instructions.

When we turn to software instead of hardware, it is advantageous to classify memory according to the type of data it contains, and then restrict the "instructions" so they can modify only the types of data that make sense. For example, most programming languages manage integers and floating point numbers. Therefore, it makes sense to classify memory as containing either integer or real numbers, and to restrict each arithmetic operation to its class of data. Integer division is defined by the operations *div* and *mod*, while real division is defined by *divide*.

The concept of object programming is strongly related to the concept of data type, restricted operations on types, and information hiding in the form of encapsulation of both data and the operations that access the data. Again, using the simple example of integer numbers, we can encapsulate all integers along with *div* and *mod*, so that all accesses to integers are restricted to calls to *div* and *mod* operations. This will lead us to the concept of an object.

More formally, a type is a collection of values and the operations that are allowed on the values. A variable of type integer is a collection of all integers from the smallest to largest that a certain computer can represent. Only integers are processed by integer operations. A type character is the set of all keyboard characters, and a type boolean is the set of TRUE and FALSE values. Only character operations are permitted on characters and only boolean logic operations are permitted on booleans.

6.1.1 ADT = Data Structure + Operations

A software object has state and function much like a computer's memory and instruction set. For example, a procedure contains local variables (state variables) and performs one function (the method). In fact, in the 1970s, application programs were thought of as one monolithic object consisting of several data structures and several algorithms:

program = data structures + algorithms

This definition left too much to the imagination of the programmer, however, and was soon replaced by the concept of encapsulation found in *abstract data types*, ADTs:

ADT = encapsulated (data structure + operations)

For example, modules in Modula II, packages in Ada, and compiland files in C encapsulate data and the operations performed on the data. The notion of encapsulation is central to the concept of an ADT.

Encapsulation is done in a variety of ways in different programming languages. In all cases, the concept of information hiding is used to prevent access to an object's state by other objects, except through the methods defined on the object. We say methods and data are *visible* when they can be accessed by other objects, and invisible or *opaque* when they cannot be directly accessed by any other object.

The invisibility of an ADT's state and the separation of its interface part from its implementation part are what distinguishes an ADT from simple data types as we have defined them above. The physical structure of a type is hidden from view by users of the type.

Example

Suppose we define an object called array-like, which has as its state real elements of a mathematical vector. Suppose we want to use array-like in calculations such as random input/output, scalar multiply, and vector length. We might define the following four Fortran subroutines as methods for array-like:

```
ARRAYread(X, I)       {Return I-th element of array-like in X}
ARRAYwrite(X, I)      {Store X in element I of array-like}
ARRAYmult(A)          {Multiply all elements of array-like times A}
ARRAYlength(N)        {Return N = length of array-like}
```

These subroutines hide the details of how array-like is actually implemented. In fact, array-like could be a Fortran array, Fortran file, or a table. The implementation of the storage structure is hidden from the user of the storage structure, and thus is abstracted away from the programmer who might use it. That is, array-like is an ADT.

The encapsulation might be done in Fortran by placing the implementation data structure, say DIMENSION ARRAY-LIKE(100), in a COMMON block, and inserting the block in only these four subroutines. This would prevent the users of array-like from directly accessing ARRAY-LIKE.

6.1.2 Classes

Most applications use more than one integer, real, array-like, or other type of data. To control the growth of complexity, and simply for convenience, we can group together all objects of the same type into a class. Thus, all integers belong to the class of integers, all reals belong to the class of reals, and so forth.

The notion of a class is obviously a good idea, but it can lead to inefficiencies. For example, if an application program uses two integers, say x and y, then we need two storage cells in memory (one for x and another for y), and two identical sets of subroutines (one for x and the other for y). Thus, if there are 10 operations defined for x, there will be another 10 defined for y. Obviously, this is a waste of memory.

Perhaps it would be better to abstract the concept of a class away from the implementation of its code as well as the implementation of its data structures. That is, we can define an abstract data type class as a template for the type of its state, and the code that changes its state.

Unfortunately, we cannot do this in Fortran without bending the rules, because Fortran does not allow us to create two hidden storage structures with the same subroutines defined on them without exposing the data structures. To achieve multiple instances of a type, we must give up encapsulation.

Example

In the previous example, we defined array-like as an ADT with four methods, but only one state. Now, suppose we want to create two ADTs; they contain different state, but the same methods. We can do this by creating two arrays and then passing these arrays to the method subroutines, explicitly.

Suppose X and Y are the two ADTs of type array-like:

```
{For X.... }
ARRAYread(R, X, I)       {Return I-th element of array-like X in R}
ARRAYwrite(R, X, I)      {Store R in element I of array-like X}
ARRAYmult(A , X)         {Multiply all elements of array-like X times A}
ARRAYlength(N, X)        {Return N = length of array-like X}
{For Y .... }
ARRAYread(R, Y, I)       {Return I-th element of array-like Y in R}
ARRAYwrite(R, Y, I)      {Store R in element I of array-like Y}
ARRAYmult(A , Y)         {Multiply all elements of array-like Y times A}
ARRAYlength(N, Y)        {Return N = length of array-like Y}
```

Clearly, the subroutines of each object are identical, with the exception that X is passed in one instance and Y is passed in the other. This is a critically important feature of the object programming paradigm. An *object* is an instance of a class. When an object is created, its state variables (called *instance variables*) are created in memory, but its methods are those of the class. As such, methods never need to be created, only referenced from within the class.

A *class* is a collection of methods along with the definition of the type of data to be encapsulated by the objects which belong to that class. In a sense, a class is a template for an object. We typically denote a class as shown in Figure 6.1. Each class has a name such as BasicLock, Monitor, and Barrier. Within each class, there are named methods such as Lock(), Enter(), and Signal().

6.1.3 Object = ADT + Inheritance

The previous example suggests that we must create a set of procedures and implementation data structures for all vectors that we might want to use in an application. This could be tedious, and could also lead to errors. A better way to achieve multiple copies of an object is to use the concept of inheritance.

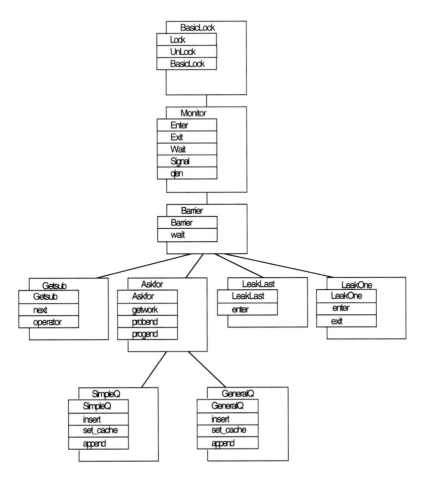

Figure 6.1   Class hierarchy of C++ Parmacs

An object *inherits* the methods of its class when it is instantiated. That is, when an object is created, unique state variables of exactly the same type as its class are created, but the class methods are merely used by the object. Two or more objects of the same type share one copy of the code for their methods.

Inheritance can be cumulative if we organize the classes along the lines of an *inheritance hierarchy*. Given a hierarchical relation, we can define a tree-structured relationship as shown in Figure 6.1. Objects are created as instances of the classes in the tree, and the objects inherit all of the methods of all classes along a path from the immediately preceding class to the root class. Thus, an object of type SimpleQ in Figure 6.1 inherits the methods defined in SimpleQ, Askfor, Barrier, Monitor, and BasicLock.

Extending the idea of an ADT to inheritance, we see an object as an instance of an ADT with the added property of method inheritance:

Object = ADT + Inheritance

The ADT hides the instance variables from direct access, and the inheritance hierarchy of the ADT classes yields methods for the object.

Example

Beck has implemented a C++ class hierarchy called Parmacs for locking mechanisms in a shared-memory computer. Figure 6.1 is part of the Parmacs hierarchy. The name of each class is given inside each box, and the names of the methods are listed within each class box. A subclass is shown as a root of a subtree below a parent class.

Class BasicLock supplies basic mutual exclusive locking. Method BasicLock() initializes the state of the object, and methods lock() and unlock() implement the mutual exclusion.

Class Monitor supplies queued waiting similar to the queue-lock of Chapter 4. Methods enter() and exit() enqueue and dequeue tasks, and methods wait() and signal() suspend and resume tasks, respectively. The length of the queue is queried by qlen().

Barrier is a class of objects that blocks all arriving tasks until all Nprocs tasks have arrived, at which point it allows all tasks to resume. Method barrier() is called to initialize the barrier with the number of tasks to wait for. Method wait() implements the barrier.

Askfor is a barrier that implements more complex locking. Method Askfor() determines the number of participating tasks; getwork() dequeues work; probend() is used to determine when a subtask finishes; and progend() determines when the entire program finishes.

The other classes are more specific and will not be fully explained here. Instead, we give the interface code for two of the classes of Figure 6.1:

```
class Getsub: Barrier{
  int    min, max;    // min and max subscripts
  int    sub;         // next subscript to return
public:
  Getsub(int Min, int Max, int Nprocs=0);
    int   next();       // return next subscript, or min-1
    int   operator()(); // nice interface to next()
};
```

Getsub is a barrier that provides atomic subscripting service. The constructor GetSub() initializes the instance variables min, max, and the parent class object Nprocs. The next() function returns the next subscript. This code is incomplete and does not handle index decrementing or error situations.

```
class  SimpleQ : public Askfor {
   SimpleList queue;
   int getprob(void *&prob) {return(prob=(void*)
queue.get())!=NULL;}
```

```
        void reset() {queue.clear();}

    public:
       int      getwork(SimpleLink*&prob) {return Askfor::getwork(prob);}
       void append(SimpleLink*prob) {enter();
    queue.append(prob);signal();}
       void insert(SimpleLink*prob)  {enter();queue.insert(prob);signal();}
       SimpleQ(int Nprocs=0) : (Nprocs)    {}
    };
```

SimpleQ is a class of simple queue objects that use the methods in its parent classes to enqueue and dequeue tasks. This class might be used to design and implement a supervisor/worker parallel program.

6.1.4 Server = Object + Task(s)

Beyond the traditional advantages of object programming for serial software, what advantages does object programming have over other kinds of parallel programming? The answer to this lies once again in the ability to encapsulate both state and function within relatively isolated objects.

Earlier we stated that an object was similar to a miniature computer complete with memory and instructions. If this is a workable analogy, and if a typical application contains many objects, then why not assign each object to a physical processor and let them run in parallel? This is the idea in the server concept of parallel programming.

A server is a task, or cluster of tasks, which implement the methods of an object as cooperating subtasks. Servers execute the methods of an object in parallel:

Server = Object + Task(s)

Servers provide a natural way to implement object programs with a minimum of synchronization and locking. That is, servers are relatively self-contained programs that implement one or more tasks of a parallel program. In the server model, a parallel program is a collection of miniature programs running independently, but occasionally interacting with one another by message passing.

We explore the server paradigm in the final section of this chapter, but first, we examine C++ as a potential object programming language. Can this popular programming language provide the functionality we seek with a minimum of bother for most programmers?

6.2 OBJECT PROGRAMMING, PARALLELISM, AND C++

Object programming features information hiding and encapsulation, meaning that (1) each object hides the implementation details from view by outside clients—only a restricted set of methods is visible, and (2) changes to the implementation of the object do not require changes to the code that uses the object, so long as the interface is stable.

Unfortunately, the C++ interface mechanism is inadequate for information hiding and encapsulation when writing parallel C++ programs, since methods are assumed to be invoked in sequence and no parallel interactions are represented by them. Also, even when method interfaces are unchanged, changes to the implementation part of methods often affect the interaction pattern of the methods, so the parallel code that uses the methods must be rewritten.

In what follows, we describe the addition of *path expressions* to the class interface, allowing for either dynamic or automatic parallelization. We survey this method, proposed by Wu and Lewis, to illustrate the power as well as shortcomings of object programming when applied to parallel problems.

For a complete explanation of object programming in C++ refer to the extensive list of references at the end of this chapter. We assume the reader is familiar with C, and point out extensions that are not obvious.

Example

Consider a program for matrix multiplication. The main body of the program inputs two matrices and computes a third matrix, which is the product of the two.

```
const N=10;
main()
{ Matrix M1(N);
  Matrix M2(N);
  Matrix *M3;
  input M1, M2;
  M3 = M1.multiply(&M2);
  print M3;
}
```

The main program uses three objects which are of class *Matrix*, and uses the *multiply* method of a *Matrix* object:

```
Class Matrix
{ vector *mat;
  int numv;

  transpose(); /* transpose m */
  public
     Matrix(int n); /* constructor */
     *Matrix multiply(&Matrix m);
     operator[];
     ...
}
*Matrix
Matrix::multiply(&Matrix m)
{ int i, j;
```

```
    Matrix *mtemp = new Matrix(m.numv);
    m.transpose(); /* transpose matrix m */
    for (i = 1; i <= numv; i++)
       for (j = 1; j <= numv; j++)
          mtemp[i][j] = mat[i].innerProd(m[j]);
    m.transpose(); /* transpose matrix m */
    return &mtemp;
}
```

Each object of class *Matrix* is implemented as an array of *Vector* objects and matrix multiplication is implemented using the *Vector* method *innerProd*:

```
Class Vector
{ real *vec;
   int numelms;
public
   Vector(int n); /* constructor */
   operator[];
   real innerProd(&Vector v);
   &Vector sum(&Vector v);
   reverse();
   ...
}
real
Vector::innerProd(&Vector v)
{ int i;
   real temp = 0.0;

   for (i = 1; i <= numelms; i++)
      temp = temp + v[i]*vec[i];
   return temp;
}
```

In this example, we see that at the top level, only the method *multiply* (of *Matrix* object) is used and no detail about its implementation is important. Similarly, when implementing the method *multiply*, the method *innerProd* of *Vector* object is used, without concern for its implementation details.

6.2.1 Parallel Programming in C++

Typically, parallelism inside a C++ program is achieved by inserting parallel primitives into the sequential code. For example, the following code implements a parallel version of matrix multiplication using Presto library objects *Thread*, *Condition*, and *Monitor* (see Bershad):

```
*Matrix
Matrix::multiply(&Matrix m)
{
   int i, j;
   Matrix *mtemp = new Matrix(m.numv);
```

```
Monitor alldonemon = new Monitor("any");
Condition alldone = new Condition(alldonemon, "waiting");
m.transpose();  /* transpose matrix m */


/* nThreads is a private variable in Matrix */
this->nThreads = numv * numv;
for (i = 1; i <= numv; i++)
   for (j = 1; j <= m.numv; j++) {
      Thread *t = new Thread("mul", i*numv+j,STKSZ);
      t->start(this,
      mat[i].innerProd,/* method */
      m[j], /* parameter */
      mtemp[i,j],/* result */
      alldone);/* a monitor */
   }
while (this->nThreads) alldone->wait();
m.transpose();  /* transpose matrix m */
return &mtemp;
}
```

In the Presto version above, all of the invocations of *innerProd* are done in parallel. This is achieved through creating and starting a thread in place of calling an *innerProd*. Busy waiting is used so that the resultant matrix is returned only when all of the threads have finished. Note that in Presto, a *condition object* contains a *monitor*. The monitor controls exclusive access to the methods in the condition object (such as *create, wait, signal*, etc.).

The parallel solution above heavily depends on an understanding of the implementation of the method *innerProd*. For the parallel program to work correctly, it is essential that different invocations of *innerProd* operate independently. Also, *innerProd* must decrement variable *nThreads* before it finishes its job, or the multiply method will wait forever. Furthermore, if the implementation of *innerProd* changes to an implementation strategy that makes different invocations of *innerProd* dependent, then all code that uses method *innerProd* must be modified. These problems effectively break the rules of information hiding and encapsulation.

Parallelizing a subject by executing the methods of the lower level objects in parallel usually requires knowledge of how the methods interact. Without a systematic mechanism to abstract parallelism and hide the low-level interaction details, the designer has no choice except to break the rules of information hiding, or to refrain from using lower level objects by putting everything in a single object. In fact, Bershad's parallel solution for matrix multiplication provided in Presto includes *innerProd* as a private method in the *Matrix* object. This is necessary to simplify the communication between the subject and objects (so that it is simple to modify and check state variable *nThreads* and to eliminate the code for matrix transpose). It is also necessary to preserve object programming principles. But *Matrix* object is the wrong place to consider vector operations. When a vector class is already

```
begin

    path a; b end;
      P1:    task a; c end;
      P2:    task c; b end;

end;
```

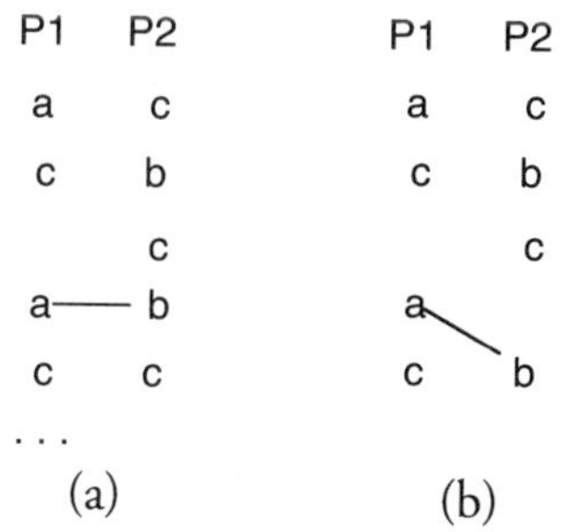

P1   P2   P1   P2

a   c   a   c

c   b   c   b

     c   c

a——— b   a⟍

c   c   c   ⟍b

. . .

   (a)   (b)

Figure 6.2   Task synchronization using path expressions: (a) not allowed; (b) allowed

available, it is wise to use it and not to use more primitive objects such as integer and real.

What we need is a way to specify the allowed parallelism between the methods inside each object and define the allowed parallelism in the interface to the outside world. This will require additional work by the programmer of the object, but the programmer is the most logical person to do this work since the programmer knows the details of the object. By forcing the programmer to specify the interaction between the methods within an object, a cleaner design will usually result. Another benefit is that the specification needs to be done only once and can be used repeatedly to save the time of all those who use this object thereafter.

6.2.2   Path Expressions

One means of controlling parallel execution of methods is to specify the allowable control paths through each object. Cambell, Lauer, Kolstad, and others proposed *path expressions,* abstractly specifying synchronization between parallel activities. The typical use of a path expression is in explicit parallel program languages in which constructs are provided for designing "tasks" that run in parallel. Path expressions constrain parallel activities.

Example

The following code specifies a parallel program in which two tasks P1 and P2 cycle through operations a; c and c; b respectively. The path expression constrains invocations of operation b so that it must be preceded by an operation a. The scenario in Figure 6.2(a) is not allowed since the second operation b cannot execute before the second operation a executes. The path expression forces a scenario such as in Figure 6.2(b).

The purpose of path expressions is to constrain parallel activities, which means they usually impose sequencing instead of indicating parallelism. For purposes of parallelism encapsulation, we are more interested in specifying parallelism, such as "*a* can run in parallel with *b*," "unlimited instances of *a* can be run in parallel," etc.

Assume *a*, *b*, *c*, . . . is a set of methods defined in an object. The parallelism between the methods can be defined using extended path expressions similar to the notion proposed by Habermann:

1 A method by itself is a path expression.

2 If e, e1, and e2 are path expressions, then the following are path expressions:

Notations	Meanings
e1 , e2	e1 and e2 can be run in parallel
{e}	0 or more e in parallel
e1 + e2	e1 and e2 must not run in parallel (e1 and e2 execute serially)

6.2.3 Expressing Parallelism with Path Expressions

Now, looking back at the matrix multiply example, *Vector* class includes methods *innerProd, sum, reverse,* and *[].* Suppose in our implementation, *innerProd, sum,* and *[]* do not alter the instance data (local data inside the object), and thus they can be done in parallel. On the other hand, *reverse* changes the private data (method *reverse* converts a vector $(x_1, x_2, \ldots, x_n)$ to a vector $(x_n, x_{n-1}, \ldots, x_1)$) so it should not be executed while the other methods are going on. Thus we can specify the following path expression between the methods.

```
{innerProd, sum, [ ]} + reverse
```

We describe a syntactical addition to the C++ class definition. That is, a path expression such as shown above must be given in the public area, and enclosed within key words PATH and END. The *Vector* class with a path expression is shown below.

```
Class Vector
{
   real *vec;
   int numelms;
public
   PATH {innerProd, sum, [ ]} + reverse END;
   Vector(int n); /* constructor */
   operator[ ];
   real innerProd(&Vector v);
   &Vector sum(&Vector v);
   reverse();
   ...
}
```

A path expression in a class describes possible interactions between the interface methods in the class. When the methods are invoked in parallel, only interaction patterns compatible with the path expression are allowed. Note that not all of the interface methods have to be included in a path expression. When a method, say *p*, is omitted, it is assumed that the method is executed mutually exclusive of all of the other methods (*p* + others). If a class does not have a path expression at all, the default assumption is that all of the interface methods are mutually exclusive.

Although a path expression is defined in a class, it specifies the parallelism between the methods that are associated with individual objects. Methods that are of the same name but associated with different objects are considered independent, except when the class has static data. For example, if we have two *Vector* objects V1 and V2. V1.reverse() only conflicts with V1.innerProd(), but not with V2.innerProd().

When a class has static data, all objects of this class share a single copy of the static data and thus the methods in different objects may have conflict access to the static data. In this case, a method can be prefixed by key word CLASSWISE indicating that the methods in different objects conflict with one another.

Note that there are two levels of parallelism being considered: that within an object, and that within a subject that uses objects. A path expression describes only the parallelism within an object. The parallelism existing in a subject is limited to the parallelism allowed by path expressions, possibly less if the subject lets one method use the result of another method.

Parallelism specified by path expressions can be used by programmers to write parallel subjects, or by automatic tools to convert sequential programs to parallel programs. Explicitly using the parallelism specified in path expressions to write parallel programs is not recommended, because the parallelism described in path expressions tends to change when implementation of the object changes. In other words, the interactions described in a path expression are not as stable as the method interfaces. Explicit use of the parallelism may require that the parallel program be frequently modified. So, path expressions provide a mechanism for parallel information hiding and not for parallelism encapsulation. Parallelism encapsulation requires that changes to the parallelism within an object do not affect the rest of the world that uses the object. There are two ways to achieve parallelism encapsulation: dynamic parallelization and automatic parallelization. The next section may be skipped by the casual reader.

6.2.4 Encapsulation Through Dynamic Parallelization

Dynamic parallelization was used in Path Pascal by Cambell to achieve parallelism encapsulation. In this approach, explicit parallel constructs are used to express parallelism so multiple methods from the same object can be run simultaneously. At compile time, each path expression is converted into a control engine (think of a control engine as a Hoare monitor).

At runtime, whenever an object is created, a control engine is implicitly created for it. Every invocation of a method is passed through the control engine, which may grant the invocation, or delay it, depending on the current state of the control engine. Also, every termination of a method must pass through the control engine to update the state of the control engine.

For example, assume an object has the following methods and path expression:

```
Class Sample
{ public
  PATH {a} + b END;
  a();
  b();
}
```

The path expression PATH {a} + b END is compiled into a control engine consisting of the following two procedures, start and depart, and the two state variables, #a for the number of active a operations and #b for the number of active b operations.

```
start(operation)
{
    case operation {
    a: if (#b == 0)
        #a++;
      else
        wait;
      break;
    b: if (#a == 0 && #b == 0)
        #b++;
      else
        wait;
      break;
  }   }
depart(operation)
{
    case operation {
        a: #a--; signal; break;
        b: #b--; signal; break;
    }
}
```

The state variables #a and #b are added to the private data of the object and the procedures *start* and *depart* are two private methods of every object of class *Sample*. Every method of a *Sample* object invokes the *start* method as its first operation and invokes the *depart* method as its last operation.

With dynamic parallelization, parallelism is completely encapsulated inside the object, and any change to the path expression of an object requires only a recompilation of the object (recoding the control engine). However, this method assumes that there are parallel constructs for specifying parallel tasks that issue parallel operations to the control engine. In C++ we don't have language constructs for specifying tasks.

Paths Through Automatic Parallelization

Another approach for parallelism encapsulation is *Automatic Parallelization.* Given a C++ program (or a subject) that uses objects whose parallelism is described by path expressions, a restructuring tool converts the sequential program to a parallel one by consulting the parallelism described in the path expressions. When the parallel pattern in an object changes, only recompilation of the parts of the program that use the object needs to be done to ensure correct parallelization of the program, without any global code modification by the programmer.

Parallelism encapsulation through automatic parallelization takes advantage of both explicit parallelization (path expression) and implicit restructuring technology. Without parallelization tools, parallel programming is tedious according to Appleby, and Lubeck. On the other hand, achievable parallelism is very limited without explicit parallel programming effort, according to Wolfe, and Lee. Path expressions seem to be a middle ground between these two extremes. Specifying a path expression is relatively easy since it is only necessary to consider object-local parallel activities. Still, we anticipate that highly parallel objects will result in highly parallel programs when objects are used properly, although statistics are needed to support this expectation.

When path expressions have been specified, automatic restructuring becomes much easier. Parallelism encapsulation through automatic parallelization offers a natural combination of explicit and implicit parallel programming efforts.

Restructuring is centered around *data dependence* analysis. Normally, to analyze whether two statements S1 and S2 are dependent, the sets of used variables, S1.U and S2.U, and the sets of modified variables, S1.M and S2.M, are first determined. S1 and S2 are independent if S1.U $\cap$ S2.M, S1.M $\cap$ S2.U, and S1.M $\cap$ S2.M are empty. To analyze data dependence between the statements that involve procedure calls, interprocedural analysis is required to find summary information, namely the sets of variables that may be used or modified by the procedure. This problem has been studied by Barth, Cooper, and Li.

Interprocedural analysis is difficult because procedural side effects force the analysis to make conservative assumptions and often the summary information is far from precise at the site where it is used.

In C++, all accesses to data take the form of procedure (method) calls. This implies that analyzing any data dependence requires interprocedural analysis which gives no precise data dependence information. However, once parallelism has been described by path expressions, the side effects of calling the methods of an object are limited to the object itself and all the methods that are affected by side effects have their interaction specified in the path expression. So, if calls to methods take no reference parameters (this is the dominant use of methods, namely sending messages to methods), path expressions encapsulate completely the information about the interactions between methods and data dependence analysis is trivial.

If calls do take reference parameters, we may need additional analysis to find the set of indirectly called methods of the parameter objects. This analysis resembles normal interprocedural analysis, but it is simpler since no global variables need to be considered (see Cooper). Note that, even if a call to a method takes reference parameters, programmers who design the method may know that the indirectly called methods are side-effect free and so they can help to avoid the difficulty of finding the set of indirectly called methods by classifying the method as, say, IGNOREINDIRECT.

Example

Data dependence analysis techniques can be used in any of the restructuring algorithms that are based on dependence analysis [Padua; Ferrante; Wolfe]. Detailed descriptions of these algorithms are outside the scope of this chapter, so we only show how the matrix multiplication method can be parallelized.

The matrix multiplication method presented earlier is duplicated below:

```
*Matrix
Matrix::multiply(&Matrix m)
{
    int i, j;
    Matrix *mtemp = new Matrix(m.numv);
    m.transpose();  /* transpose matrix m */
    for (i = 1; i <= numv; i++)
        for (j = 1; j <= numv; j++)
            mtemp[i][j] = mat[i].innerProd(m[j]);
    m.transpose();  /* transpose matrix m */
    return &mtemp;
}
```

The statement inside the nested loop calls the following methods (directly and indirectly):

```
mtemp.[]
mtemp.[i].[]
mtemp.[i].[j].=
mat.[]
mat.[i].innerProd
m.[]
```

The following table categorizes the calls according to their base classes and determines whether any of the calls are in conflict.

class	path expression	object.calls	conflict calls
matrix	{multiply, []}	mtemp.[]	none
		mat.[]	
		m.[]	

class	path expression	object.calls	conflict calls
vector	{[], innerProd,	mtemp.[i].[]	none
	sum}+reverse	mat.[i].innerProd	
real	=+access	mtemp.[i].[j]	none

Since there are no conflicting calls involved in the statement of the nested loop, we conclude that the statement has no loop carried dependence on itself and the iterations of the outer loop can be run in parallel (see Allen). Thus, we can parallelize the matrix multiplication method as follows:

```
*Matrix
Matrix::multiply(&Matrix m)
{
   int i, j;
   Matrix *mtemp = new Matrix(m.numv);
   m.transpose();   /* transpose matrix m */
   PARALLEL (i = 1; i <= numv; i++)
      for (j = 1; j <= numv; j++)
         mtemp[i][j] = mat[i].innerProd(m[j]);
   m.transpose();   /* transpose matrix m */
   return &mtemp;
}
```

6.3 The Server Paradigm

Perhaps the most natural extension of object programming is that of the server paradigm. In this view of parallel programming, every object is a miniature program that communicates with other objects by message passing. When objects are activated in this manner, we call them *servers*. In the remainder of this discussion, a server is defined as an instance of a class such that the resulting object is implemented as a collection of one or more tasks: one task for each message, and one task for each active method of the object. A server is an object in motion.

The server paradigm faces the same problems described for C++ in the previous section of this chapter. First, servers must be constrained to execute in parallel only when no data dependencies exist. Second, we need some rules for identifying servers. This brings up the issue of how to partition the application. We illustrate these issues with SS/1 (Server System/One), a tool for parallel programming using the server paradigm.

SS/1 is a tool for dealing with class hierarchies, partitioning, and server coordination. Two graphical editors are provided: (1) a class hierarchy editor for specifying the hierarchical relationship between servers, and (2) a communication structure editor for specifying constraints on servers, in effect telling when servers can be executed in parallel.

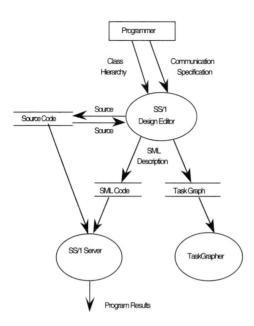

Figure 6.3   SS/1 Components and dataflow relationships

SS/1 allows a programmer to first define a class hierarchy and then describe a program as a parallel sequence of messages. By displaying the message sequence graphically in two dimensions, the SS/1 Design Editor makes the job of programming in parallel much easier. Because the resultant program is based on object programming concepts, communication between servers is minimized.

Once an application is designed, the methods of each server must be defined as a subroutine or procedure in Fortran, C, or some other language. The class hierarchy, communication structure, and methods provided for each server are automatically analyzed by SS/1 to generate all synchronization code, creation and coordination of tasks within all servers, and all message passing. This process is shown in Figure 6.3.

Finally, the program descriptions generated by the SS/1 Design Editor are executed using a "master" SS/1 server on the target parallel computer. Currently, SS/1 generates parallel code for Sequent parallel computers using UNIX "exec" and "fork" primitives.

Optionally, the output from SS/1 can be analyzed by the Task Grapher program discussed in Chapter 9. This program attempts to optimally schedule the servers onto processors in a manner that minimizes overall execution time. We defer discussion of scheduling techniques until Chapter 9.

6.3.1   Class Definition in SS/1

Programming in SS/1 proceeds in two stages. In the "Class Definition" stage, the programmer defines a class hierarchy graphically as a tree. This is a natural way to

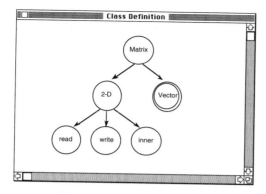

Figure 6.4 Class definition diagram for matrix objects. The arcs indicate a superclass/subclass relationship. Leafs are methods, and internal nodes are classes

```
read (theMatrix, inFile, row, col)
char *inFile
int theMatrix[][]. row, col,

{
    FILE *fp
    int i, j;

    if ( (fp = fopen(inFile, "r")) == (FILE *) NULL)
        return (1)

    for (i = 1, i <= row, i ++) {
        for (j = 1 ; j <= col ; j ++0
            fscanf (fp, theMatrix{i,j]);
        fscanf(fp, "\n");
    }
}
```

Figure 6.5 Text window for method read

view the hierarchy, and makes the inheritance patterns easy to see as illustrated by a sample hierarchy shown in Figure 6.4.

The inner nodes of the class definition tree are truly classes, while the leaf nodes are methods. In Figure 6.4 the parent class "matrix" has descendants "2-D" and "vector," The methods of "2-D" are read(), write(), and inner(). Class "vector" is decomposable into lower classes. This is shown as a double circle to indicate that "vector" is actually composed of a sub-tree that is not shown in the diagram. (The double circle is strictly a convenience for dealing with very large class hierarchies.)

Each method node is associated with a source file containing the source code to implement the method. Methods in these source files may be implemented in any compilable programming language. This makes it very easy to reuse existing code when developing SS/1 programs. The Design Editor supports basic text editing functions so that the source may be viewed and/or edited during the class definition phase.

Example

We illustrate the SS/1 technique by implementing yet another matrix multiply program. If source for a given method already exists, simply "link" that source to the appropriate method in the class definition diagram. Otherwise, a text window is provided for entering the text of each method. In either case, the method will appear as in Figure 6.5.

Text for each method of matrix multiply is supplied by either reusing a definition or entering the definitions as shown in Figure 6.5. For completeness, we provide the other methods of Figure 6.4 in C:

```
write(theMat, row, col)
float theMat[][];
int row, col;
{   int i, j;
    for (i = 0; i < row; i++) {
        for (j = 0; j < col; j++)
            printf("%d", theMat[i][j]);
        printf("\n");
    }
}

inner(MatA, MatB, MatC, rowCol, row, col)
float MatA[][], MatB[][], MatC[][];
int rowCol, row, col;
{   int i;
    MatC[row][col] = 0.0;
    for (i = 0; i < row; i++)
        MatC[row][col] += MatA[row][i] * MatB[i][col];
}
```

6.3.2 Communication Specification in SS/1

The purpose of the communication specification diagram is to constrain servers as necessary to prevent data race conditions. This diagram determines the parallelism in the application. It must be explicitly supplied by the programmer for each application.

The communication specification diagram shown in Figure 6.6 uses four types of rectangles to represent messages, and arcs to represent temporal dependency. A basic rectangle is a single unrepeated message. A double rectangle is a compound unrepeated message, an abstraction representing a number of messages. A rectangle with a vertical bar at the right side is a compound parallel replicated message. The messages it represents can be replicated concurrently. Finally, a rectangle with a horizontal bar is a compound, sequential replicated message. The messages it represents must be replicated sequentially. Compound messages may have only a single incoming arc and a single outgoing arc. This single-entry, single-exit restriction removes any chance of ambiguity over the message sequencing.

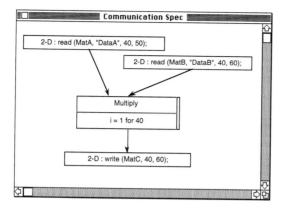

Figure 6.6 Communication specification diagram for matrix multiplication

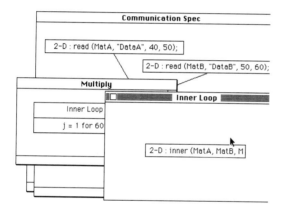

Figure 6.7   Nested levels in the communication specification of matrix multiply. The inner product method is invoked 60 times

Information for each message in the diagram must be supplied by the programmer. For basic messages, the programmer must specify the receiving class, the method name, and the parameters. The number and types of the parameters will be checked against the method's parameter list in the source file. For compound messages, the programmer must specify a display label which will be useful for identifying the contents of the message. For replicated messages, the programmer must provide a display label and the loop bounds.

Example

Figure 6.6 shows the top-level communication diagram for the well-worn matrix multiply program. But the parallelism is hidden in the repeated box labeled "Multiply." To complete the specification, we must also specify what is inside this box.

Figure 6.7 shows the lower level specification of "Multiply." In this simple example only one method is needed to specify the "Multiply." However, it should be noted that this method is called 60 times in parallel, achieving a great deal of parallelism. (In Figure 6.6 the method is invoked 40 times. This illustrates the limitation of this technique—each time we want to change the number of parallel invocations of a method, we must alter the design, or else leave the value undefined until task creation.) The performance of this version of matrix multiply is given in Table 6.1.

matrix size	SS/1	Parallel C
50	6.70	4.52
100	15.33	13.46
200	60.74	59.12
300	158.82	154.32

Table 6.1 Performance data for matrix multiply example written in C and SS/1. Times are reported in seconds, and matrix size equals number of rows and columns of each square matrix. The number of processors used is 20

6.3.3 How SS/1 Works

SS/1 introduced new parallel programming constructs called *servers*, which are self-contained parallel agents communicating with each other by sending messages. Once a server is instantiated from a class, the server becomes an active computational agent which carries out its actions in response to incoming messages.

A server consists of an event-handler task and one or more method tasks (see Figure 6.8). The event-handler task reads messages from its message queue and looks for appropriate methods in its method table. If the requested method exists, the event-handler task spawns another task for executing the method. If no method is found, a search up the class hierarchy is made to find the appropriate method to be inherited from a superclass. The class hierarchy diagram is used by SS/1 to facilitate this search.

A method task can be duplicated as many times as the application demands. In contrast to other object programming paradigms, method tasks may not have persistent state, because they may be executed only once and then may lose their state information. All transient state information is stored in a global communication server set up by SS/1 prior to launching the application.

Each server maintains a scheduler which schedules its method tasks by determining processor and communication overhead. Incoming messages are queued in the message queue and scheduled dynamically according to the current system overhead. This kind of distributed scheduling finds local and current optimal scheduling. An optimal static schedule may be estimated by the Task Grapher static scheduler, discussed in Chapter 9.

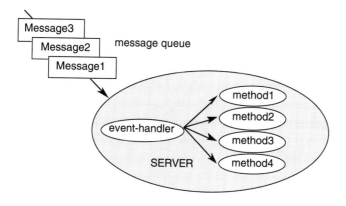

Figure 6.8 Servers and messages. Each bubble is a method task, and each box is a message task. Both message passing and method invocation result in parallel task creation and execution

Messages and Synchronization

A message handler is a self-contained task which is responsible for the delivery of messages and the synchronization of the system (see Figure 6.9). A message handler task is activated by SS/1 for each message sent by a method task. The message handler task sends its message to the target server, which copies the content information, and then tells the message handler task to terminate itself.

Messages are queued in the message queue of the target server until the event-handler of the target server reads that message and creates and activates the appropriate method tasks. The message handler tasks wait for termination signals from the methods. After the termination signal arrives from the target server, the message handler task terminates itself.

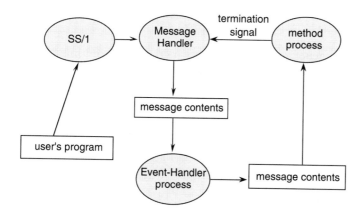

Figure 6.9 Messages are processed by a message handler task

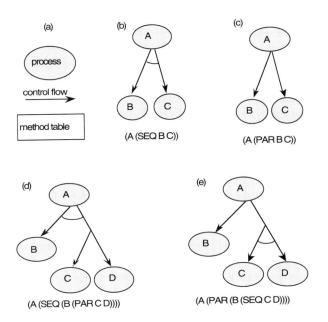

Figure 6.10 PAR-SEQ tree for representing communication specifications in SS/1. And/Or branches are indicated with arcs across the edges of the tree

SS/1 is synchronous, which means that whenever a message task is created, SS/1 waits for its termination. However, asynchronous tasks can also be created by parallelizing message handler task activation.

In a message-passing machine, the message handler task can be a communication manager which controls the routing of its messages and data depending on its interconnection topology and communication overhead. Even in a shared-memory machine, message handler tasks have information about shared memory and can guarantee mutual exclusion and prevention of deadlock.

Routine Environment

SS/1 applications are generated from the class hierarchy, communication specification diagrams, and source code for each method. The generated code is embedded in a shell program which interprets the communication diagram in order to provide runtime synchronization and scheduling. This shell is the runtime environment of all SS/1-produced applications.

To reduce the overhead in interpreting the communication specification diagram, SS/1 translates the diagram into an intermediate form called SML (Server Meta Language). SML is an OCCAM derivative with constructs for explicit parallel/sequential task control.

SML essentially defines a "PAR-SEQ tree" which is the mapping of the communication specification into a textual representation of PARallel-SEQuential code.

This looks like an "and-or tree," representing task creation order. The nodes represent tasks, and the edges indicate control flow. Several examples are given in Figure 6.10(a). A child node is always created by its parent node. Once the parent node wakes up its child task, it waits for the termination of the task.

There are two ways to create children nodes. The "SEQ" subtree as in Figure 6.10(b), which has arcs across the edges to show sequential task creation order, from left to right. In this case, the parent task creates its child tasks and waits for them to terminate one by one. This corresponds to the SML construct, "SEQ," which represents the serial execution of its substructures.

The "PAR" subtree in Fig 6.10(b) denotes the parallel creation of child task nodes. The parent task wakes up all its children tasks at the same time and waits for the terminations of all the created tasks. This corresponds to the SML construct "PAR" which represents the parallel execution of its substructures.

6.4   APPLICATION TO SIMULATION

Object programming is an especially appropriate paradigm for simulations. After all, the original object programming language was Simula-67, a simulation language. We use the simulation of a computer store as a vehicle to illustrate the use of object programming. The Computer Store Simulation is a program written in the SS/1 language. The methods were implemented in C, and the remainder of the code automatically generated by SS/1.

This simulation is a simple representation of a computer store with classes of objects such as products, people, and store facilities. The example illustrates the power of object programming for modeling, and shows how typical simulation models can be carried out on parallel computers.

6.4.1   Computer Store Class Definition

The class hierarchy for the Computer Store Simulation contains three distinct classes: Ware, People, and Environment. The class Ware includes all products carried by the store and has subclasses Software and Hardware. The classes Customer, Sales, and Service are all subclasses of class people. The classes each have methods associated with them, as shown in Figure 6.11. Note that the subtrees for classes Hardware and Software are nested within double-bubbles.

6.4.2   Communication Specification

The top level for the Computer Store simulation communication specification is shown in Figure 6.12. This diagram should be interpreted as follows:

1   Open the store.

2   Customers, sales, and service personnel do their actions in parallel.

3 Close the store.

Nested within each parallel loop is a sequential event loop. Each person in the simulation is generating and/or processing events independent on all others. The loop for an individual salesperson is shown in Figure 6.13. This is interpreted as:

1 Get an event from the system.

2 Depending on the event, give a demo or sell some ware.

Since SS/1 does not support a conditional branch, the demo and sell messages will both be sent. It is thus the responsibility of the demo and sell methods to make sure that the event was meant for them.

The SML description for this program is:

```
/* Class Definition */
(
    Ware (HardWare SoftWare)
    People (
        Sales (demo sell)
        Service (fix)
        Customer (buy demoReq fixReq)
    )
    Environment (open close getEvent moneyIn)
)
/* Communication Specification */
(SEQ
    (Environment, open)
    (SEQ
        (PAR
            (PAR k = 1 for MAX_CUST
                (SEQ k1 = 1 for forever
                    (SEQ
                        (Environment, (getEvent,TheEvent))
                        (PAR
                            (Customer, (fixReq,TheEvent))
                            (Customer, (demoReq,TheEvent))
                            (Customer, (buy,TheEvent))
            ) ) ) )
            (PAR j = 1 for MAX_SERVICE
                (SEQ j1 = 1 for forever
                    (SEQ
                        (Environment, (getEvent,TheEvent))
                        (Service, (fix,TheEvent))
            ) ) )
            (PAR i = 1 for MAX_SALES    /* Demo this part, below */
                (SEQ i1 = 1 for forever
                    (SEQ
                        (Environment, (getEvent,TheEvent))
```

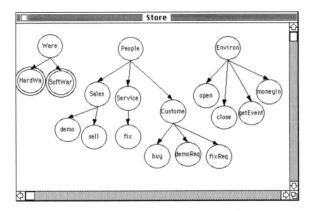

Figure 6.11 Class definition for computer store simulation

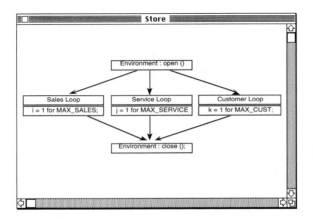

Figure 6.12 Computer store simulation communication specification, level 1

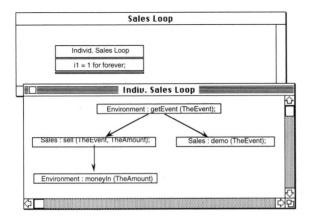

Figure 6.13 Computer store simulation communication specification, levels 2 and 3

```
                    (PAR
                        (Sales, (demo,TheEvent))
                    (SEQ
                        (Sales, (sell,TheEvent, TheAmount))
                        (Environment, (moneyIn,TheAmount))
        )  )  )  )   )  )
        (Environment, close)
)   )
```

The SML description also holds the class hierarchy definition and the message communication structure for specifying the control and dataflow of the messages to be sent.

To execute the SML code in the SS/1 environment the methods are compiled and linked with a communication handler which handles the message-passing mechanism in the methods. Once all of the methods are assembled according to the class definition part, the system can be executed.

6.4.3 Server Activation

A portion of the simulation model can be traced through some of the SS/1 execution steps to illustrate server activation. The superclass "Store" has subclass "People." The class "People" has "Sales." And the class "Sales" has two methods, "demo" and "sell." According to the SML definition, SS/1 will set up the task class hierarchy in the order indicated below and shown in Figure 6.14.

1　SS/1 activates tasks for each class as defined in the class hierarchy.

2　Each class task sets up a method table using the information from its methods. We have illustrated this table for "Sales" only.

3　SS/1 sets up the communication buffer and unique process IDs.

Next, SS/1 interprets the SML code as shown in Figure 6.15 and annotated below. (We follow only the activation of "Sales," which corresponds to only one of the PAR statements in the SML definition.)

1　PAR i=1 for MAX_SALES: SS/1 forks MAX_SALES message handlers as in level (a) of Figure 6.15.

2　SEQ i1 = 1 for forever: Each message handler executes as shown in level (b) of Figure 6.15.

3　Each message handler sends a "getEvent, theEvent" message to the server "Environment," per the class hierarchy specification.

4　Each message handler forks two other message handlers as shown in level (c).

5　One message handler at level (c) executes from the "SEQ" of the SML specification, and sends the message "sell, theEvent, theAmount" to the "Sales" server. Server "Sales" forks a task to perform the "Sell" method. After the message is processed, the

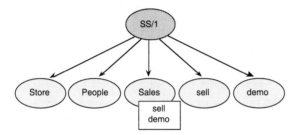

Figure 6.14 Initialization phase of computer store simulation. SS/1 initiates servers.

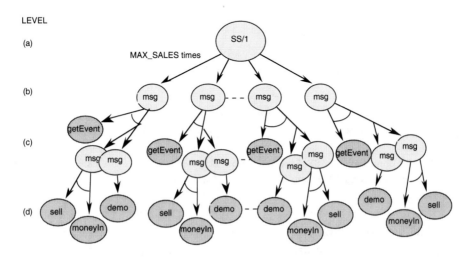

Figure 6.15 Message flow and process creation

message handler sends "moneyIn, theAmount" to server "Environment." Server "Environment" forks a task to perform "MoneyIn." The message handler is terminated in level (c), (d).

6 The other message handler sends the "demo, theEvent" to the "Sales" server at levels (c) and (d). The "Sales" server activates method "Demo" as a task to perform the demo simulation.

6.5 OTHER PARALLEL OBJECT LANGUAGES

Because the object programming approach to large-grained parallelism has many benefits, a number of object programming languages have been developed during the 1980s. See the extensive literature in the references at the end of this chapter. As in SS/1, many of these languages implement "objects" as independent processing agents which communicate by sending messages.

Act 1 is an implementation of the Actor [Agha and Hewitt] model. In this model, objects (called "actors") are separate tasks that respond to incoming messages. Each actor maintains a message queue so that messages are handled first-come, first-served. "Future actors" are used as place holders for results being computed. This tends to increase parallelism because an actor must only wait for the future value if a read operation is requested before the value is computed.

Language	Activation	Synchronization	Interconnection	Communication
CSP	parbegin/ parend	blocking send and receive	static	I/O commands through channels
DF	receiving data	data	static	data path
Actor	receiving a message	future message	dynamic	message passing and remote procedure call
SS/1	receiving a message	message	dynamic	message passing

Table 6.2 Comparison of SS/1 with other parallel programming systems. CSP = Cooperating Sequential Processes, DF = Data Flow, Actor = Actor model of parallel objects, and SS/1 = Server System/One

ABCL/1 [Yonezawa] is similar to Act 1, but contains some extra features. Messages can be sent in "normal" or "express" mode. An express message will interrupt an object handling a normal message. Message passing can be one of three types: "past" type is asynchronous, "now" type is synchronous, and "future" type is asynchronous and creates a future object for the return value. As in SS/1, the actual methods in ABCL/1 can be written in various languages including C, FORTRAN, LISP, etc.

ConcurrentSmalltalk [Yokote] is a superset of Smalltalk-80 which expands the message-passing semantics to include asynchronous (in addition to the standard synchronous) message passing. Results from asynchronous messages are returned to "future objects," similar to the future actors used in Act 1.

Linda Smalltalk [Chun] is an implementation of Smalltalk using Linda tuple-space communication. Implicit parallelism is achieved through concurrent execution of message arguments.

PROBLEMS FOR DISCUSSION AND SOLUTION

1   Define these terms: object, class, method, message, server, ADT, inheritance, type, message handler, and communication specification.

2   Describe the relationship between encapsulation and visibility. Define both

terms. Give an example of each in two programming languages.

3 Does Parmacs include a "READERS/WRITER" lock class? Where would you place a multiple readers, single writer class in the Parmacs hierarchy?

4 Extend the C++ matrix multiply example to include an operation to perform matrix transpose.

5 Extend problem five above by giving a path expression in the interface of the matrix transpose class to allow parallel computation of the transpose operation.

6 Give an SS/1 solution to matrix transpose. Can you find an SS/1 solution to matrix inversion? What are the difficulties with matrix inversion within SS/1?

7 What are the major problems with implicit parallelization of C++ programs? Is this a general problem for most serial languages, or specific to C++?

8 Give an example of a loop carried dependence. An indirect method call dependence. Why do these pose a problem for object programming?

9 Why do we sometimes claim that C++ is not a "pure" object programming language? What is wrong with it?

10 Give an SS/1 design in terms of the hierarchy of classes with methods attached at the lowest level in the hierarchy, and a communication structure for a simulation of an airport. The airport has aircraft, runways, people, and a tower. Explain what must proceed serially, and what can occur in parallel.

11 Draw a speedup line graph for the data in Table 6.1. What can you say about the overhead of SS/1 versus parallel C implementations as the size of the problem increases? Why do you observe this phenomenon?

References

Agerwala, T., Arvind, T., "Data Flow Systems," *Computer* 15:2, February 1982.

Agha, G. A., *ACTORS: A Model of Concurrent Computation in Distributed Systems*, MIT Press, Cambridge, MA, 1986.

Alan Kay, A., "Microelectronics and the Personal Computer," *Scientific American*, Vol. 237: 230, 244, September 1977.

Allen, J. R., *Dependence Analysis for Subscripted Variables and Its Applications to Program Transformations*, Ph.D. Thesis, Rice University, Houston, TX, April 1983.

Andler, S., *Predicate Path Expressions: A High-Level Synchronization Mechanism*, Ph.D. Thesis, Carnegie Mellon University, Pittsburgh, PA, August 1979.

Appelby, W. F., and McDowell, C., "Anomaly Detection in Parallel Fortran Programs," *Proceedings Workshop on Parallel Processing Using the HEP*, May 1985.

Barth, J. M., *A Practical Interprocedural Data Flow Analysis Algorithm*, CACM 21(9), September 1978.

Beck, B., "Shared-Memory Parallel Programming in C++," *IEEE Software,* 7(4), pp. 38 – 48, July 1990.

Bershad, B. N., Lazowska, E. D., and Levy, H. M., "PRESTO: A System for Object-Oriented Parallel Programming," *Software—Practice and Experience,* 18(8), pp. 713 – 732, August 1988.

Bruegger, B., and Hibbard, P., "Generalized Path Expressions: A High Level Debugging Mechanism," *Journal of System and Software* II(III), pp. 265 – 276, 1983.

Cambell, R. H., and Kostad, R. B., "A Practical Implementation of Path Pascal," *Tech Report,* Dept. of Computer Science, University of Illinois at Urbana-Champaign, UIUCDCS-R-80-1008, 1980.

Cambell, R. H., and Habermann, A. M., "The Specification of Process Synchronization by Path Expressions," in G. Goos and J. Hartmanis, eds., *Lecture Notes in Computer Science,* Vol. 16, Operating Systems, Springer-Verlag, Berlin, pp. 89 – 102, 1974.

Choi, S., Sturtevant, T., and Lewis, T. G., *The SS/1 Design Editor: A Graphical Interface For Object Oriented Parallel Programming With Server System/1,* TR 90-60-15, Department of Computer Science, Oregon State University, Corvallis, OR, 97331, 1990.

Choi, S., Sturtevant, T., and Lewis, T. G., "Parallel Programming and Designing in Object Oriented Environment SS/1," *Technical Report,* Computer Science Department, Oregon State University, April 1990.

Chung, J., "Implicit Parallelism in Object Oriented Programming," *Technical Report,* Computer Science Department, Oregon State University, May 1990.

Cooper, K. D., *Fast Interprocedural Alias Analysis,* Dept. of Computer Science, Rice University, Rice COMP TR88-80, November 1988.

Cox, B., *Object Oriented Programming—An Evolutionary Approach,* Addison-Wesley, Reading, MA, 1986.

DiNucci, D. C., Babb, R. G., II, "Design and Implementation of Parallel Programs with LGDF2," *Characteristics of Parallel Algorithms,* MIT Press, Cambridge, MA, 1985.

El-Rewini, H., *Task Partitioning and Scheduling on Arbitrary Parallel Processing,* Ph.D. Dissertation, Oregon State University, November 1989.

Ferrante, J., Ottenstein, K. J., and Warran, J. D., "The Program Dependence Graph and its Use in Optimization," *ACM Trans. Programming Language Sys.* Vol. 9, No. 3, pp. 319 – 349, July.

Goldberg, A., Robson, D., *Smalltalk-80: The Language and its Implementation,* Addison-Wesley, Reading, MA, 1983.

Habermann, A. N., "Path Expressions," *Tech Report,* Dept. of Computer Science, Carnegie-Mellon University, Pittsburgh, PA, June 1975.

Hewitt, C., Baker, H., "Laws of Communicating Parallel Processes," *1977 IFIP Congress Proceedings,* pp. 987 – 992, IFIP, August 1977.

Hewitt, C., et al., "A Universal, Modular Actor Formalism for Artificial Intelligence," *Proceedings of IJCAI,* 1973.

Hillis, W. D., and Steele, G. L., Jr., "Data Parallel Algorithms," *Communications of the ACM,* 29(12), December 1986.

Hoare, C.A.R., "Communicating Sequential Processes," *CACM* 21:8, pp. 666 – 677, August 1978.

Hoare, C.A.R., "Monitors: An Operating System Structuring Concept," *CACM,* Vol. 17, No. 10, pp. 549 – 557, October 1974.

Kolstad, R. B., and Cambell, R. H., "Path Pascal User Manual," *ACM SIGPLAN Notices,* 15(9), pp. 15 – 25, September 1980.

Kuck, D. J., Kuhn, R. H., Padua, D. A., Leasure, B., and Wolfe, M., "Dependence Graphs and Compiler Optimizations," *Proceedings 8th ACM Symp. Principles Programming Languages,* pp. 207 – 218, January 1981.

Lauer, P. E, Torrigian, P. R., and Shields, M. W., "COSY—A System Specification Language Based on Paths and Processes," *Acta Informatica* 12, pp. 109 – 158, 1979.

Lee, G., Kruskal, C. P., and Kuck, D. J., "An Empirical Study of Automatic Restructuring of Nonnumerical Programs for Parallel Processors," *IEEE Trans. on Computers,* Vol. C-34, No. 10, October 1985.

Li, Z., Yew, P. C., "Interprocedural Analysis for Parallel Computing," *Proceedings of 1988 ICPP,* Vol. II, pp. 221 – 228.

Lubeck, O. M., Frederickson, P. O., Hiromoto, R. E., and Moore, J. W., "Los Alamos Experiences with the HEP Computer," in *Parallel MIMD Computation: HEP Supercomputer and Its Applications,* MIT Press, Cambridge, MA, 1985.

Meyer, B., *Object-Oriented Software Construction,* Prentice Hall, Englewood Cliffs, NJ, 1988.

Padua, D. A., and Wolfe, M. J., "Advanced Compiler Optimizations for Supercomputers," *CACM,* 29(12), December 1986.

Pountain, D., *A Tutorial Introduction to OCCAM Programming,* INMOS Ltd., March 1987.

Sequent Computer Systems, *Guide to Parallel Programming,* Sequent Computer Systems, Inc. 1987.

Snyder, A., "Inheritance and the Development of Encapsulated Software Systems," *Research Directions in Object-Oriented Programming,* MIT Press, Cambridge, MA, 1987.

Stroustrup, B., *The C++ Programming Language,* Addison-Wesley, Reading, MA, 1986.

Stroustrup, B., "Multiple Inheritance for C++," *Proceedings of the Spring 1987 BUUG Conference,* Helsinki, May 1987.

Stroustrup, B., "What is Object Oriented Programming?" *IEEE Software,* Vol. 5 No. 3, pp. 10 – 20, May 1988.

Stroustrup, B., "A Better C?" *Byte Magazine,* pp. 215 – 216D, August 1988.

Wiener, R. S., Pinson, L. J., *An Introduction to Object-Oriented Programming and C++*, Addison-Wesley, Reading, MA, 1988.

Wolfe, M. J., and Banerjee, U., "Data Dependence for Parallelism Detection," *International Journal of Parallel Programming*, XV(II), April 1987.

Wolfe, M. J., *Optimizing Supercompilers for Supercomputers*, MIT Press, Cambridge, MA, 1989.

Wu, Y., *Parallel Simplex Algorithms and Loop Spreading*, Ph.D. Dissertation, Oregon State University, 1988.

Wu, Y., and Lewis, T. G., "Parallelism Encapsulation in C++," *Proceedings International Conference on Parallel Processing*, Vol. II, Pennsylvania State University Press, pp. 35 – 42, August 1990.

Yokote, Y., and Tokoro, M., "Concurrent Programming in Concurrent Smalltalk," in *Object-Oriented Concurrent Programming*, MIT Press, Cambridge, MA, 1987.

Yonezawa A., and Tokoro, M., *Object-Oriented Concurrent Programming*, pp. 1 – 7, MIT Press, Cambridge, MA, 1987.

Chapter 7

Data Parallel Programming

In this chapter we study a paradigm called *data parallel programming*, in which parallel computers are programmed in SIMD or SPMD style. The parallelism in this style comes from simultaneous operations across large sets of data, rather than from multiple threads of control. This style of programming is appropriate for a machine with tens of thousands or even millions of processors.

A number of commercial parallel machines typically programmed in the data parallel paradigm are available. The names of the companies and their machines follow: Thinking Machines Corporation, The Connection Machine (CM); Mas-Par Computer, MP series; Active Memory Technology, Distributed Array Processor (DAP); and Wavetracer Corporation, Data Transport Computer (DTC).

Data parallelism is usually associated with fine-grained parallelism. Because the Connection Machine introduced in Chapter 3 is an example of a fine-grained SIMD computer, we revisit it and give more programming details this time. Then we present several applications of the Connection Machine in various fields.

A major portion of this chapter discusses the data parallel language C*, which is a C extended to support data parallel programming. Other languages, such as MultiC, and DataParallel C have extended C to data parallel capability, too. We give samples of DataParallel C in Appendix B. In all cases, the goal of data parallel languages is to simplify parallel programming by making a data parallel program look very much like a serial program. This is done by retaining the control flow of a serial program, but allowing operations to be performed on many different pieces of data.

We conclude with a section on data parallel programming on meduim-grained MIMD machines, and explain the subtle differences between SIMD and SPMD paradigms. SPMD is a subtle variation on SIMD that works best on meduim-grained applications where the computation can mask communication delays.

7.1   THE DATA PARALLEL PARADIGM

The parallelism in data parallel algorithms comes from simultaneous operations across large sets of data. In most cases, the data parallelism is at the statement level of a program. That is, data parallelism is fine-grained parallelism. Therefore, this style of programming is appropriate for fine-grained parallel computers with very high-speed communication. A parallel machine of this type is typically *massively parallel*, i.e., it has tens of thousands or even millions of processors and is operated in SIMD mode.

Our model of a fine-grained, massively parallel computer consists of two parts: a front-end computer of the usual von Neumann style, and a *processor array*. A processor array is a set of identical synchronized processing elements capable of simultaneously performing the same operation on different data. Each processor in the array has a small amount of local memory where the distributed data reside while being processed in parallel.

The processor array is connected to the memory bus of the front-end so that the front-end can randomly access the local processor memories as if it were another memory. Thus, the front-end can issue special commands that cause parts of the memory to be operated on simultaneously or cause data to move around in the memory. A program can be developed and executed on the front-end using a traditional serial programming language. The application program is executed by the front-end in the usual serial way but issues commands to the processor array to carry out SIMD operations in parallel. The similarity between serial and data parallel programming is one of the strong points of data parallelism.

Some fine-grained SIMD parallel computers use INs (interconnection networks) which restrict the communication to certain patterns wired into the hardware. Typically the pattern is a two-dimensional grid or a tree. Our machine model is based on the Connection Machine, which uses a modified form of a hypercube.

In general, data parallel programming applies to distributed-memory machines with very high bandwidth interconnections such as found in SIMD machines. However, if we are careful, MIMD machines can be programmed in this paradigm. In the final section we describe how data parallelism is used to program MIMD machines, but in the subtle variation of SIMD called SPMD.

7.2 THE CONNECTION MACHINE

The Connection Machine Model CM-1 was first introduced commercially by Thinking Machines Corporation in April 1986. Experience gained during the use of the CM-1 led to an improved version of the machine called the CM-2. The CM-2 kept the basic architecture of the CM-1 with modifications to increase memory capacity, performance, and overall reliability. Although part of the original Connection Machine, the I/O system was not implemented until the introduction of CM-2. The company commercially introduced the CM-2 in April 1987, and the CM-5 in 1991.

The hardware architecture of the Connection Machine is discussed in Chapter 3. In this chapter we focus attention on the software architecture, and how the machine is programmed using the data parallel paradigm and C*. The important principles illustrated are: (1) parallelism is in the data, not the control portion of the application, (2) processors either do nothing or exactly the same operations at the same time as all other procesors, and (3) synchronization is done by neither message passing nor locks; instead, it is made irrelevant by the lockstep synchronization of the processors.

7.2.1 Software Architecture of the Connection Machine

The system software of the Connection Machine is based on the operating system of its front end computer, with minimal visible software extensions to handle the back-end Connection Machine. The front-end executes the control structure of parallel programs, issuing commands to the CM-2 processors whenever necessary. Programs have normal sequential control flow and do not need new synchronization structures. In fact, programmers use familiar languages and programming constructs.

The front end can read (write) data from (to) the local memories of the Connection Machine's processors. In addition, the front-end can issue instructions to the processors via a microcontroller, asking them to manipulate their data in some specified way.

CM Virtual Machine Model

The CM *virtual-machine* parallel instruction set, called PARIS (Parallel Instruction Set), presents the low-level programmer with an abstract machine architecture very much like the physical Connection Machine hardware architecture, but with two important extensions: (1) a much richer instruction set, and (2) a virtual-processor abstraction.

PARIS provides a rich set of parallel primitives ranging from simple arithmetic and logical operations to sorting and communications operations. The interface to PARIS between the front-end and the rest of the machine is a simple stream of operation codes and arguments. The arguments usually describe fields to operate on in the form of a start address and bit length. Arguments can also be immediate data, broadcast to all data processors.

Virtual Processors

Data parallel applications often call for many more individual processors than are physically available on a given machine. The Connection Machine software provides for this through its virtual-processor mechanism, supported at the PARIS level and transparent to the programmer. If the number of processors required by an application exceeds the number of available physical processors, the local memory of each processor splits into as many regions as necessary, with the processors automatically time-sliced among regions. If V is the number of virtual processors and P is the number of physical processors, each physical processor would support V/P virtual processors. The ratio V/P, usually denoted N, is called the *virtual-processors ratio*, or *VP ratio*.

Interprocessor communication really means inter-*virtual*-processor communication, and on-processor operations are really on-*virtual*-processor operations. Thus, the same program will run unchanged on different-sized Connection Machines. One simply specifies the desired number of (virtual) processors and the *VP* ratio is set accordingly.

Parallel variables are the variables spread across the virtual processors running the parallel program. For example, in a finite-difference calculation the *x* coordinate of each gridpoint comprises a parallel variable. Parallel variables have three attributes: their memory location, their length in bits, and the *VP* set to which they belong.

Parallel variables in different *VP* sets can coexist in the same computer program. For example, in a molecular dynamics simulation, we can set up two *VP* sets; one that associates a processor to each molecule, and another that associates a processor to every spatial gridpoint in a grid that can be used to keep track of thermodynamic quantities such as the particles' local density, temperature, pressure, etc. Parallel variables such as molecular position and velocity are in the first set while parallel variables such as density, temperature, and pressure are in the second.

The programmer must also specify the *geometry* of a *VP* set, which defines the processor interconnection topology. The concept of geometries is supported by low-level system software as well as the actual hardware of the Connection Machine. Even though the underlying hardware IN topology is a hypercube, multidimensional Cartesian grids with periodic boundary conditions can be mapped into a hypercube in a nearest-neighbor-preserving fashion.

Software Primitives

In this section, we present a set of software primitives that map efficiently onto the hardware of the Connection Machine. The primitives are given in terms of familiar mathematical operations on functions. We place processors in a multidimensional Cartesian grid addressed by Cartesian coordinates $X = (x, y, \ldots)$. Note that if the geometry is of N dimensions, X denotes N different coordinates.

A parallel variable is simply a scalar function of X, $f(X)$, which denotes the value of the parallel variables on processor X.

The following set of primitives is not meant to be exhaustive. For more details, refer to Hillis [1985]; Tucker [June 1988], and Thinking [1986, 1990].

Read (write) data from (to) a specified processor
To read data, the programmer specifies the processor's address X and the name of the parallel variable *f*. The value $f(X)$ is returned as a front-end scalar. Similarly, one can write any given scalar into the value of a parallel variable in a particular processor. Other system routines exist for reading *all* the values of a parallel variable into a front-end array, or vice versa.

Access to the ith Cartesian coordinate of a processor
The programmer specifies *i*, and the parallel variable $f(X) = x_i$ is returned.

Local processor operations

Software primitives exist for all basic mathematical operations such as addition, subtraction, multiplication, division. For example, to add two parallel variables, the programmer gives the names of the two variables to be added, say $f(X)$ and $g(X)$. The result is calculated by all the processors in parallel. Similar routines exist for adding front-end constants to parallel variables in all processors; that is, they might return the parallel variable $f(X) + c$, where c is a scalar.

Regular nearest neighbor communication

This is supported by software that returns the parallel variable $f(X \pm e_j)$, where e_j is a unit vector in dimension j; the programmer supplies the name of the parallel variable f, the dimension j, and the direction of the communication (the $\pm$ sign result).

Communication with several neighbors simultaneously

Fast *stencil* software exists for doing communication with several neighbors simultaneously, weighting the incoming results with either scalars or other parallel variables. For example, software is available to return $f(X + e_j) - f(X)$, which is obviously just a discretized version of the jth component of the gradient operator $\nabla_j f(X)$. Similarly, fast stencil software is available for the Laplacian operator $\nabla^2 f(X)$. General stencil software is available for the construction of any first- or second-order differential operator. Finite difference calculations based on these routines achieve speeds between 5 and 8 Gflops [Boghosian].

Broadcasting

This primitive helps to *broadcast* the value of a parallel variable in one processor to all the other processors. Given the name of a parallel variable f and a particular processor address X, there are *spreads* that return a new parallel variable whose value is $f(X)$ in all processors.

Global Commands

Global commands exist for many associative binary operations. An example might be global addition for which the values of a parallel variable in all processors are added and returned as a front-end scalar.

Fast Fourier Transforms

There are packaged routines for Fast Fourier Transform (FFT) in which the butterfly network of the standard Cooley-Tukey algorithm is mapped to the hypercube architecture efficiently, and transparently to the high-level language programmer.

7.3 DATA PARALLEL PROGRAMMING LANGUAGES

The high-level languages for the Connection Machine are built on top of PARIS. There are currently several high-level languages such as CM FORTRAN, C*, and *LISP.

CM FORTRAN is a Connection Machine implementation of the FORTRAN 8x array extensions. In CM FORTRAN, a standard array is used as a data type for parallel variables. Even though the actual programming is different from the well-known standard FORTRAN 77, it is much simpler and more compact. For example, in FORTRAN 77, addition of two arrays is done with a DO-loop as follows:

```
      DO 100 I = 1,N
      C(I) = A(I) + B(I)
 100  CONTINUE
```

In CM FORTRAN, assuming that A, B, and C are declared to be arrays, this is accomplished in one statement:

```
   C = A + B
```

Nearest-neighbor communication can be invoked by the CSHIFT and EOSHIFT commands of the CM FORTRAN extensions. These shift operators cause a copy of each element of an array to be "shifted" one or more positions along an axis.

Broadcasting primitives described earlier are invoked by the SPREAD command.

General communication is invoked by vector-valued subscripts. That is, if A is the array

$$A = \{1.5, 2.1, 3.6, 4.8, 2.0\}$$

and B is the array

$$B = \{2, 5, 1, 4, 4, 3\}$$

then the single command C = A(B) yields the result

$$C = \{2.1, 2.0, 1.5, 4.8, 4.8, 3.6\}$$

Once again, this single command in CM FORTRAN would have required a loop in FORTRAN 77.

The languages C* and *LISP are parallel extensions of C and LISP respectively. Unlike CM FORTRAN, both C* and *LISP introduce a new data type for parallel variables. In fact, C* and *LISP extend their base languages into the realm of data parallelism far beyond what is possible with CM FORTRAN.

7.3.1 C*: An Extended C for Data Parallel Programming

C* is an extension of the C programming language designed to support data parallel programming. The C* language is based on the standard C specified by the American National Standards Institute (ANSI).

C* is a small extension of C adding only a few new features that support broadcasting, reduction, and interprocessor communication in both regular and irregular patterns. C programmers will find most aspects of C* familiar. C language constructs such as data types, operators, structures, pointers, and functions are all maintained in C*.

C* is well suited for applications that require dynamic behavior, since it allows the size and shape of parallel data to be determined at runtime. C* also provides a straightforward method of calling PARIS functions and CM FORTRAN subroutines from a C* program, thus allowing access to these languages when appropriate.

The C* language underwent a radical revision in 1990, and seems to be evolving. Therefore we only highlight a few important features of C* valid circa 1991. A detailed description of the most recent version of the language can be found in Thinking [November 1990].

A parallel variable in C* is similar to a standard C variable, except that it has a *shape* in addition to its type. The shape defines how many *elements* of a parallel variable exist, and how they are organized. Each element occupies one position within the shape and contains a single value. Each element of a parallel variable can be thought of as a single scalar variable.

In C*, data are allocated only when it is tagged with a shape template. A shape is defined by specifying how many dimensions it has, which is referred to as its *rank*, and the number of elements or *positions* in each of its dimensions. In C*, a dimension is also referred to as an *axis*.

For example, the following statement declares a shape called employees with one dimension (a rank of 1) and 16348 positions.

```
shape [16384] employees;
```

Typically, the choice of a shape reflects the natural organization of the data. For example, a graphics program might use a shape representing the two-dimensional images that the program is to process.

Left indexing is another important new concept in C*. A shape can have multiple axes. The left-most axis is referred to as axis 0; the next axis to the right is axis 1, and so on. Dimensions, or axes, are specified in brackets to the left of the shape name. For example, consider the following declaration of a two-dimensional shape.

```
shape [256] [512] image;
```

In C* a single shape statement can be used to declare multiple shapes. For example, the previous two shape statements can be combined into one as follows.

```
shape [16384] employees, [256] [512] image;
```

Parallel Variables

Once a shape has been fully specified, one can declare parallel variables of that shape. For example, once the shape employees has been declared as in the example above, we can declare a parallel variable named employee_id as an unsigned integer as follows.

```
unsigned int: employees employee_id;
```

Left indexing is used to specify an individual element of employee_id. For example, [2]employee_id refers to the third element of employee_id. [2] is referred to as the coordinate for this element.

We can also declare many parallel variables of the same shape. If they are of the same type, we declare them in the same statement as follows.

```
unsigned int: employees employee_id, age, salary;
```

The three parallel variables employee_id, age, and salary are of shape employees and type unsigned integer.

In addition to parallel variables, C* provides a parallel version of C aggregate types such as parallel structures and parallel arrays. We can declare an entire structure as a parallel variable. For example, consider the following shape and structure declaration.

```
shape [16384] employees;
Struct date {
    int month;
    int day;
    int year;
    };
```

A parallel structure birthday of type struct date and of shape employees can be declared as follows.

```
struct date: employees birthday;
```

Each element of the parallel structure contains a scalar structure, which in turn will contain the birthday of an employee. Accessing a member of a parallel structure works the same way as accessing a member of a scalar structure. For example, birthday.month specifies all elements of structure member month in the parallel structure birthday.

Similarly, an array of parallel variables can be declared as follows.

```
shape [16384] employees;
int:employees ratings[3];
```

This piece of code declares an array of three parallel variables of shape employees.

7.3.2 Parallel Operations

C* extends the use of standard C operators, through overloading, to apply to parallel data as well as scalar data. For example if x, y, and z are all parallel variables of the same shape, the statement

```
x = y + z;
```

performs a separate addition of the values of y and z in each position of the shape, and assigns the result to the element of x in that position. All the additions take place in parallel. If y and z were not parallel variables, they would first be promoted to parallel, with their value replicated in each element.

C* also adds a few new operators to standard C. For example, the <? and >? operators are available to obtain the minimum and maximum of two variables (either scalar or parallel).

7.3.3 Choosing a Shape: The *with* Statement

The *with* statement is one of the statements that C* adds to standard C to allow operations on parallel data. Before we can carry out most operations on parallel variables, they must be of the *current shape*. The *with* statement selects a current shape. For example, code like the following is required to perform a parallel addition:

```
shape [16384] numbers;
int: numbers x, y, z;
with (numbers)
    x = y + z;
```

We can have many *with* statements in a program, making different shapes current at different times.

7.3.4 Setting the Context: The *where* Statement

C* also adds a *where* statement to restrict the set of positions on which operations are to take place. The positions to be operated on are called the *active positions*. Selecting the active positions of a shape is known as *setting the context*. For example, the *where* statement in the following code ensures that division by 0 is not attempted:

```
with (numbers)
    where (z != 0)
        x = y / z;
```

Like the *if* statement in standard C, the *where* statement can include an *else* clause. The *else* clause reverses the set of active positions; that is, those positions that were active when the *where* statement was executed are made inactive, and those that were made inactive are made active. For example:

```
with (numbers)
    where (z != 0)
        x = y / z;
    else
        x = y
```

C* also provides an *everywhere* statement. This statement makes all positions of the current shape active. Parallel code within the scope of an *everywhere* statement operates on all positions of the current shape, no matter what context has been set by previous where statements. After the *everywhere* statement, the context returns to what it was before.

7.3.5 Parallel Functions

C* adds support for parallel variables and shapes to standard C functions. Parallel variables and shapes can be passed as arguments to and returned from functions. For example, the following function takes a parallel variable of type int and shape numbers as an argument:

```
void print_sum (int:numbers x)
   {
       printf ("The sum of the elements is %d. \n", +=x);
   }
```

Note that the operator += is called a *reduction operator.* If x is a parallel variable of the current shape, +=x sums the values of all active elements of the parallel variable x.

If it is not known what the current shape is when the function is called, the new keyword *current* is put in place of a specific shape name. *Current* always means the current shape.

Another useful feature of C* is *overloading* of functions. C* allows you to declare more than one version of a function with the same name. For example, the following versions of function f are overloaded—there are three different meanings of f:

```
void f(int x);
void f(int x, int y);
void f(int:current x);
```

We use the *overload statement* to specify the names of the functions to be overloaded. For example, the following statement specifies that there may be more than one version of the function f:

```
overload f;
```

The overload statement must precede an overloaded declaration. Typically, it is put at the beginning of the file that contains the function's declaration.

7.3.6 Communicating in Parallel

C* provides two methods of parallel communication. The first method is called *grid communication,* in which parallel variables of the same shape can communicate in regular patterns by using their coordinates. The other method is known as *general communication,* in which the value of any element of a parallel variable can be sent to any element of any other parallel variable, whether or not the parallel variables are of the same shape. Grid communication is faster than general communication.

Grid Communication

C* uses the intrinsic function *pcoord* to provide a self-index for a parallel variable along a specified axis of its shape. The pcoord function is typically used to provide grid communication along the axes of a shape. For example, the following code sends values of source to the elements of dest that are one coordinate higher along axis 0:

```
[pcoord(0) + 1]dest = source;
```

In the common case where pcoord is called within a left index expression, and the argument to pcoord specifies the axis indexed by the left index, C* allows a shortcut. The call to pcoord can be replaced by a period. Thus, for a two-dimensional shape, the following provides grid communication along both axis 0 and axis 1:

```
[ . + 1][. - 2]dest = source;
```

General Communication

C* uses the concept of left indexing to provide communication between different shapes, as well as within-shape communication that does not necessarily occur in regular patterns. A left index can be applied to a parallel variable. If the index itself is a parallel variable, the result is a rearrangement of the values of the parallel variable being indexed, based on the values in the index. If the index is of one shape and the parallel variable being indexed is of another shape, the result is a remapping of the parallel variable into the shape of the index. Thus, in the following code

```
dest = [index]source;
```

the parallel variable dest gets values from source; the values in index tell dest which element of source is to go to which element of dest.

7.3.7 Computing an Approximation to π in C*

The C* program presented here computes an approximation to π by finding the area under the curve $\dfrac{4}{1 + x^2}$ between 0 and 1 by computing the sum shown below.

$$\pi \approx \frac{1}{N} \sum_{i=0}^{N-1} \frac{4}{1 + x_i^2} \text{, where } x_i = \frac{(i + \frac{1}{2})}{N} \text{ is the midpoint of the } i\text{th interval.}$$

The data parallel programming solution to this problem associates one virtual processor with every interval. Each virtual processor computes the area of its rectangle, and then all the individual areas are added to form a global sum.

```
/* Estimation of pi using rectangle rule */
#define INTERVALS 400000
shape [INTERVALS] chunk; /* Declare the shape */
double:chunk x; /* Midpoint of rectangle on x axis */
main ()
{
    double sum;        /* Sum of areas */
    double width;      /* Width of interval */
    width = 1.0 / INTERVALS;
    with (chunk) /* Select the shape */

    {
        x = (pcoord(0)+0.5)*width;
        sum = (+= (4.0/(1.0+x*x)));
```

```
    }
    sum *= width;
    printf ("Estimation of pi is %14.12f\n", sum);
}
```

In this simple program, the calculation takes place in 400,000 virtual processors which are mapped onto many fewer physical processors (depending on how large the Connection Machine is). Each *VP* performs the calculation of one chunk:

```
    {
        x = (pcoord(0)+0.5)*width;
        sum = (+= (4.0/(1.0+x*x)));
    }
```

This simple example serves as an introduction to C*. The advantages of data parallelism are better demonstrated, however, by more elaborate examples.

7.4 DATA PARALLEL ALGORITHMS

Data parallelism has an effect on the design of algorithms that cannot be ignored or passed on to the compiler to "take care of." The next few algorithms were chosen to demonstrate the data parallel programming style, and how it affects algorithm design. Remember, this style of programming is appropriate for fine-grained parallel computers with fast communication.

To make matters more concrete, suppose we design a data parallel algorithm to compute all partial sums of an array of numbers. That is, given n numbers, stored in array $x = (x_0, x_1, \ldots, x_{n-1})$, compute the partial sums $x_0, x_0 + x_1, x_0 + x_1 + x_2, \ldots, x_0 + x_1 + \ldots + x_{n-1}$.

At first glance, one might think that accumulating sums is an inherently serial process, because one must add up the first k elements before adding in element $k + 1$. However, we can avoid serialization by performing some redundant additions, and illustrate some interesting features of data parallelism along the way.

To make it easy for the reader to understand the algorithm, we start by developing a similar algorithm for the simpler problem of computing the simple sum of an array of n values. Then we extend the algorithm to compute all partial sums using what is learned from the simple summation problem. In all cases we provide a picture of the algorithm, description of the algorithm in Pascal-like pseudocode, and finally the C* code.

7.4.1 Sum of an Array of Numbers

The sum of n numbers can be computed in time O(log n) by organizing the numbers at the leaves of a binary tree and performing the sums at each level of the tree in parallel. For simplicity, we assume that n is an integral power of two. We also assume that there are as many processors as elements. The elements of the array $x = (x_0, x_1, \ldots, x_{n-1})$ are distributed one value per processor.

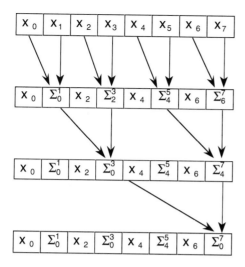

Figure 7.1 Computing the sum of an array of 8 elements

Figure 7.1 illustrates the algorithm on an array of 8 elements named x_0 through x_7. In order to sum 8 elements, 3 iterations are needed as follows. In the first iteration, processors 1, 3, 5, and 7 add to their values the numbers stored at processors 0, 2, 4, and 6, respectively. In the second iteration, processors 3 and 7 add the values stored at processors 1 and 5, respectively, to their values. Finally, in the third iteration processor 7 adds the value stored at processor 3 to its value. Thus, processor 7 contains the sum of all numbers in the array.

The algorithm can be expressed in Pascal-like pseudocode as follows.

```
Distribute array values to processor, one value per processor
    for i = 1 to log n do
        forall k where 1 ≤ k ≤ n
            if (k+1 mod 2^i) = 0 then
                x[k] ← x[k - 2^(i-1)] + x[k]
            endif
        endforall
    endfor
```

The parallelism is indicated by the use of the forall statement which activates a set of processors to concurrently execute the statements before endforall. All the processors work in synchrony and execute the statements in lockstep. At the end of the process, x_{n-1} contains the sum of the elements. The C* code that implements this pseudocode is given as follows.

```
/* Sum of an Array of N Numbers */
#define N 1024
shape [N] ArrayShape; /* Declare the shape ArrayShape*/
int: ArrayShape x; /* Declare the variable x */
```

```
int i;
main ()
{
/* initializing of x omitted */
   with (ArrayShape)                          /* Select the shape */
      for (i = 1; i <= log(N); i++)           /* Iterate log(N) times */
         where ((pcoord(0) +1) % pow(2,i) == 0)  /*Set active positions*/
            x += [pcoord(0) - pow(2,i-1)] x;/* add to x */
/* Position [N-1]x contains the sum of all numbers */


/* print the sum of numbers */
printf ("The sum of all numbers is %d. \n", [N-1]x);
}
```

In C*, several operators can be used to reduce the values of all elements of a parallel variable to a single scalar value. Thus, the previous C* program can be written in a more compact form using the C* reduction operators +=. Assuming that the variable sum was declared, the *with* statement in the program given above can be replaced by the following:

```
with (ArrayShape) /* Select the shape */
/* calculate the sum of all numbers using reduction operator += */
sum  += x;
```

7.4.2 All Partial Sums of an Array

Take a closer look at the algorithm to find the sum of n values and notice that most of the processors are idle most of the time. However, by exploiting the idle processors, we should be able to compute all partial sums of the array in the same amount of time it takes to compute the single sum.

Again, the elements of the array $x = (x_0, x_1, \ldots, x_{n-1})$ are distributed one value per processor. The partial sum algorithm replaces each x_k by the sum of all elements preceding and including x_k. The picture given in Figure 7.2 illustrates the three iterations of the algorithm on an array of 8 elements named x_0 through x_7.

The only difference between this algorithm and the earlier one is the test that determines whether a processor is to perform the operation or not. In the earlier algorithm during iteration i, only $n/2^i$ processors are active, while in this one, nearly all processors are in use. After step i, element number k has become

$$\sum_{j=a}^{k} x_j, \text{ where a} = (\max(0, k - 2^i + 1)).$$

It is left as an exercise for the reader to prove that the time complexity of this algorithm is $O(\log n)$ on n processors. The algorithm is described in pseudocode as follows:

```
Distribute array values to processor, one value per processor
for i = 1 to log n do
   forall k where 1 ≤ k ≤ n
```

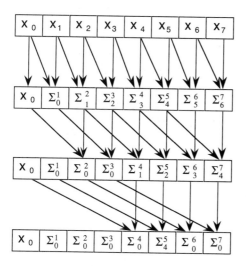

Figure 7.2   Computing partial sums of an array of 8 elements

```
        if k ≥ 2^i then
        x[k] ⟵ x[k - 2^{i-1}] + x[k]
        endif
    endforall
endfor
```

The C* program for the partial sums problem is given below.

```
/* Partial Sums of an Array of  N Numbers */
#define N 1024
shape [N] ArrayShape; /* Declare the shape ArrayShape*/
int: ArrayShape x; /* Declare the variable x */
int i;
main ()
{
/* initializing of x omitted */
    with (ArrayShape)    /* Select the shape */
        for (i = 1; i <= log(N); i++)    /* Iterate log(N) times */
            where (pcoord(0) >= pow(2,i))  /* Set active positions */
                x += [pcoord(0) - pow(2, i-1)] x;/* add to x */

/* print the partial sums */
for (i = 0; i < N; i++)
printf ("The sum of all numbers up to index %d  is  %d. \n", i, [i]x);
}
```

7.5 APPLICATIONS OF DATA PARALLELISM

One of the significant advantages of SIMD parallel computers and data parallelism is the large number of different application areas suitable for this technology. Examples of these applications are: geophysics, VLSI design, particle simulation, fluid-flow modeling, computer vision, protein-sequence matching, information retrieval, machine learning, and computer graphics. The details of these applications can be found in Batcher [1980]; Boghosian; Hillis [1986]; Pang; Stanfill; Tucker [June 1988, August 1988]; Thinking [1990]; Waltz.

In this section, we include brief descriptions of several applications from the fields of computer graphics, finite-difference and finite element codes, VLSI design and simulation, and computer vision.

7.5.1 Data Parallel Line Drawing in Computer Graphics

Many computer graphics algorithms define component lines of a picture by specifying pairs of endpoint coordinates for each line. The output device is directed to fill in the straight-line path between each pair of endpoints. Simply drawing a picture on a screen can become very compute intensive due to the high number of lines typically drawn in a picture. Therefore, we seek a parallel algorithm that can do this much faster than a serial algorithm.

We begin with a brief description of a sequential algorithm, called digital differential analyzer (DDA), for line drawing. The simple DDA, as described in Newman, initially selects the driving axis determined by the larger displacement between the endpoints. The DDA then plots a point for each pixel along the driving axis, displaced proportionally by an amount equal to the slope. The sequential algorithm is described as follows.

1 Given the endpoints (x_1, y_1) and (x_2, y_2),
length = max (abs $(x_2 - x_1)$, abs $(y_2 - y_1)$)

2 dx = $(x_2 - x_1)$/length, dy = $(y_2 - y_1)$/length

3 $x = x_1$ $y = y_1$
Perform the following *length* times:
plot(x, y)
$x = x + dx$
$y = y + dy$

One way to write a data parallel version of the DDA algorithm is to decompose the line into segments. The number of segments necessary to draw a line can be determined from the length of the driving axis. Each segment on the line gets assigned to a processor. The number of active processors will depend on the length of the line. In most cases, the number of required processors greatly exceeds the number of segments. In addition, the processors may not all be equally busy, leading to a balance problem. Therefore, this decomposition does not use multiple processors efficiently.

We give a parallel version of a line drawing algorithm implemented on the Connection Machine using the *distance method*. The distance method makes each point compute its distance to a given line. If a point lies close enough, then it is on the line. We use the shortest perpendicular distance from a point to the line to determine how close a pixel is from the line.

The algorithm, which was introduced in Pang, dedicates a virtual processor to each pixel on the display and lets each pixel decide whether it lies on the line or not. This strategy is workable only if the number of processors approaches that of the display resolution. In other words, the *VP* ratio must be sufficiently low. After the pixels are marked as either on the line or not, dumping the appropriate contents from each virtual processor onto the frame buffer renders the line.

The shape of the screen can be declared in C* as follows:

```
/* display, represented as an array of pixels */
shape[512][512] pixels;
```

Each element in the screen needs to maintain a single-bit variable to contain the information about whether it is on the line or not. The parallel variable Am_I_on_- Line of type bool and shape pixels is declared as follows:

```
/* declare the parallel variable Am_I_on_Line */
bool: pixels Am_I_on_Line;
```

The algorithm as shown below splits into serial and parallel sections. The front-end host computer executes the serial code, while the parallel processing unit executes the parallel code.

Serial code

1. Read the endpoints (x_1, y_1) and (x_2, y_2), and Line_Thickness.

2. Calculate $\Delta_x = x_2 - x_1$ and $\Delta_y = y_2 - y_1$.

3. Calculate $A = -\Delta_y$, $B = \Delta_x$, and $C = x_2{}^*\Delta_y - y_2{}^*\Delta_x$ /* the coefficient for the implicit line form */.

4. Normalize the line by dividing the coefficients by $r(A^2 + B^2)$.

Parallel code

1. Each virtual processor uses the row and column numbers for the pixel it represents to compute the distance from the line as A^*column + B^*row + C.

2. If distance is less than the line thickness, then the processor declares itself to be on the line.

The C* segment for the parallel part can be given as follows:

```
with(pixels)
```

```
where ( (pcoord(0)*A + pcoord(1)*B + C) <= Line_Thickness)
    Am_I_on_Line = TRUE;
```

7.5.2   VLSI Design and Circuit Simulation

It is quite common for a VLSI circuit to consist of a large number of parts or cells (10,000 or more). The problem of placing such a number of parts on a chip while minimizing the area taken up by interconnecting wires is considered one of the most difficult and time-consuming problems in the VLSI area. This is a perfect application for parallel computers because of the high demands on computing power needed to solve this optimization problem.

One way to solve this problem is to start with some initial solution and go greedily for the quick nearby optimum. That is, from the starting point, we go immediately downhill as far as we can go. This approach leads to a local, but not necessarily a global, minimum. This is an example of a technique called Local Neighborhood Search.

Another approach is called *simulated annealing* and works on the basis of a probabilistic search. Simulated annealing is a mathematical technique derived from the physical phenomenon of cooling in metallurgy. When properly cooled, the molecules in a metal arrange themselves into a minimum energy state, thus finding an optimum. The optimum seeking properties of molecules in metals are an analog for the mathematical technique.

Simulated annealing is a probabilistic modification of traditional neighborhood search techniques [Kirkpatrick]. Both approaches find a solution to a combinatorial optimization problem by starting with some initial solution and making a series of modifications to the solution. In neighborhood search algorithms, modifications that improve the solution by some given cost criterion are accepted and others are rejected. The acceptance criterion in simulated annealing is more complex. All modifications that lead to a better solution are accepted. All modifications that result in a poorer solution (higher cost) are accepted with probability $\exp(-\Delta E / T)$ where ΔE is the difference between the costs of the solutions before and after the update, and T is a parameter known as temperature. Over time, the parameter T is slowly reduced, causing a reduction in the probability that a modification which results in a poorer solution will be accepted.

Employing simulated annealing produces good optimization results on a broad spectrum of placement problems. For circuits having 15,000 parts, simulated annealing may require 100 to 360 hours on a conventional computer. On a 64K-processor Connection Machine, the time required is less than two hours [Tucker, August 1988].

Designers apply simulated annealing to VLSI placement as follows. Given an initial arbitrary placement of cells for a VLSI circuit, the designer first computes the size of the silicon chip required. Improvement in the layout results from swapping cells to reduce the total wire length (see Figure 7.3).

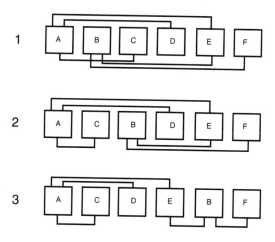

Figure 7.3 VLSI cell placement

Implementing the simulated annealing in parallel on the Connection Machine is quite straightforward. Individual cells, potential locations for cells, and nodes where wires between cells connect are represented in individual processors. The need to exchange information between cells at arbitrary locations illustrates the utility of the general router-based communications mechanism of the Connection Machine. According to the given temperature parameter, a certain percentage of cells initiate a swap, calculate the expected change in wire length, and accept or reject the move. Potential exchanges are chosen by randomly generating the addresses of the other cells.

7.5.3 Finite-Difference Codes

Finite-difference techniques are used to study viscous fluid flow, stress and strain computation, heat transport, and so on. We briefly outline one such problem on the Connection Machine to illustrate how data parallelism can be used to solve this class of problem.

Suppose the problem is to solve the heat equation in a given domain such as a simple parallelepiped. The parallelpiped is divided into cells using the familiar grid technique. If we defer the discussion of boundary conditions, an *explicit* finite-difference algorithm can be mapped to the Connection Machine as follows. Each node in the grid is mapped to one processor which updates its parallel variable, e.g., temperature in the heat equation, by averaging the values of the temperature variables received from its neighbors on the grid. In general, we can solve for any dependent variable. Temperature will be used as an example here.

Now suppose that it is desired to use an implicit method which involves the solution to a banded matrix equation $Ax = b$ at each time step. Each row of the matrix may

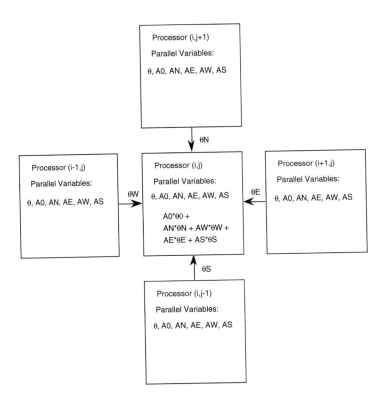

Figure 7.4 **Implicit finite-difference data structure**

be thought of as specifying a single linear equation that must be satisfied at a given node.

For a three-dimensional problem D_x, this translates to a seven-banded matrix. The Connection Machine solution configures the shape of the parallel variables as a three-dimensional grid to match the domain of the problem. The resulting linear equation at each node is represented on each processor as seven coefficients that weight the local and neighboring values of the temperature variable. Values of the load vector bare needed at each node.

Figure 7.4 shows the data structure of the explicit finite-difference problem on the Connection Machine. Notice how the information on the seven-banded matrix is mapped onto the Connection Machine as a simple data structure that looks like the domain of the actual problem.

Now let's generalize the problem somewhat and consider the boundary conditions as well as other possible dependent variables. They might be Dirichlet (prescribed temperature), Newmann (prescribed heat flux), radiative (a nonlinear boundary condition for which heat flux is proportional to the fourth power of temperature according to the Stefan-Boltzmann law), or a mixture of all of the above [Boghosian].

In Figure 7.4, we show one linear equation per node. The coefficients of this equation can themselves be parallel variables. Thus, Dirichlet boundary conditions at a given node can be implemented by setting $A_0 = 1$, setting all the other A's to zero, and setting the load vector to the specified value of θ at that node. Similarly, Newmann boundary conditions at an eastern boundary might be implemented by taking $A_0 = 1$ and $A_w = -1$, setting all other A's to zero, and setting the load vector to the desired value of the flux (times the grid spacing Δ_x). By making the A coefficients themselves parallel variables, different boundary conditions can be dealt with on the Connection Machine.

7.5.4 Computer Vision

Applications in computer vision are considered good candidates for massively parallel computers because of the inherent parallelism in image processing. Examples of vision applications are production of a depth map from stereo images and two-dimensional object recognition [Tucker, August 1988]. We give a very brief discussion of object recognition on the Connection Machine.

The problem is to recognize an object imbedded within an image. A *model* object is given as the pattern to be matched, and the parallel program must compare the model features with the features of objects in the image until a match occurs. If no match occurs, the model object must not be in the image.

On the Connection Machine, objects known to the system are represented as a collection of features—straight line segments and their intersections at corners. Each feature is assigned to its own processor. Therefore, a single object is distributed over a number of processors, enabling each feature to be actively used in the search.

Traditionally, object recognition algorithms use some form of *tree search,* but in this example searching is replaced by *hypothesis generation.* Features useful for hypothesis generation are those that constrain the position and orientation of a matching model object. The intersection of two lines that matches an expected model corner can be used to generate a hypothesis that an instance of the model object exists.

An unknown scene is first digitized and loaded into the Connection Machine memory as an array of pixels, one per processor. Edge points are marked and straight line segments are fitted to edge points using a least-squares estimate. Interesting lines are grouped into corner features and matched in parallel with corresponding corner features in the model. Whenever a match between an image and model feature occurs, a hypothetical instance of the corresponding model object is created and projected into the image plane. A hypothesis-clustering scheme is next applied to order the hypotheses.

Figure 7.5 illustrates parallel hypothesis generation and verification. The time required from initial image acquisition to display of recognized objects of sizes ranging from 10 to 100 is approximately 6 seconds on a 64K-processor Connection Machine [Tucker, August 1988].

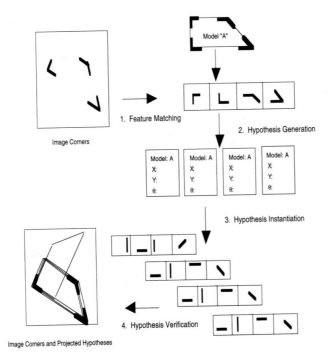

Figure 7.5 Parallel object recognition steps

7.6 DATA PARALLEL PROGRAMMING ON MIMD COMPUTERS

Data parallelism is not restricted to SIMD machines, nor is it appropriate only for fine-grained applications. In fact, SIMD machines are sometimes inefficient because each processor must do nothing whenever it is unable to perform an identical operation in lockstep with all other processors. What happens when we combine the multiple control units of an MIMD machine with the data parallel paradigm? In this section we report some results on implementing data parallel programming languages on MIMD hardware. The details of these results can be found in [Quinn].

The data parallel paradigm is a simple and natural paradigm for solving many scientific problems, but it also appears to be useful for solving large-grained problems, if we can overcome the loss in efficiency that is a byproduct of grain size and lockstep operation. MIMD machines are more general than SIMD machines because they have multiple control units. This capability can be used to advantage when combined with the data parallel programming paradigm and large-grained applications.

The researchers listed under Hatcher have implemented two compilers for an earlier version of C* called DataParallel C. One compiler generates code for the distributed-memory nCUBE 3200 and the other generates code for the shared-mem-

Data Parallel Programming   Chapter 7

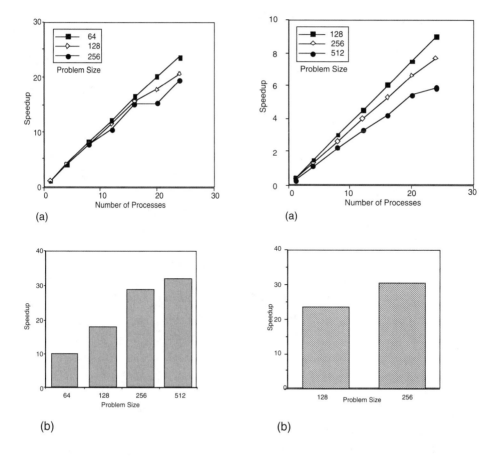

Figure 7.6 Performance of data parallel algorithm for matrix multiply computation on (a) shared-memory, and (b) distributed-memory machines.

Figure 7.7 Performance of data parallel algorithm for relatively prime number computation on (a) shared-memory; (b) distributed-memory machines

ory Sequent Balance 2100. These compilers achieve a high degree of portability across radically different parallel processor architectures. Furthermore, they implement a form of data parallelism called SPMD, because each program executes in lockstep, but within each program processors are permitted to execute different instructions than their peers.

Consider the simple pseudocode fragment running on two processors at the same time. The value of p will be determined by the particular values of data at each processor.

```
if p
  then S1
  else S2
```

Suppose the first processor finds p TRUE and executes S_1. Also suppose processor two finds p FALSE. In a SIMD machine, processor two would do nothing. In the SPMD paradigm, the second processor executes statement S_2 while processor one executes S_1. This is the consequence of running on a MIMD machine with multiple control units. This is also the idea behind data parallel languages for MIMD machines.

Figures 7.6 and 7.7 show speedups for two data parallel programs executing on the 64-processor nCUBE 3200 and Sequent Balance 2100. Portability of the data parallel programs in Figures 7.6 and 7.7 is demonstrated by running the same programs on two radically different machines. The code was reported for C*, but was actually written in DataParallel C.

The Gustafson-Barsis Law should apply to data parallel programs. Does it predict the performance of these sample applications? Figures 7.6(b) and 7.7.(b) give speedup as a function of problem size. According to the Gustafson-Barsis Law, doubling the problem size should double the speedup. As you can see, this is nearly the case, with some loss due to communication overhead in the case of the nCUBE, and loss due to synchronization overhead in the case of the Sequent.

A data parallel solution to Gaussian Elimination is given in Appendix B, for the reader who wants to study a complete programming example in DataParallel C.

7.7 SUMMARY

In data parallel computing, there are many processors, each with some associated memory, all acting under the control of a single program. All processors can then perform the same operation on all the items of data at the same time. Think of a SIMD computer as a single control unit directing the activities of a number of processing elements, each fetching and manipulating its own local data. A number of parallel computers that fit this category are commercially available, such as Thinking Machines CM series and MasPar Mp series.

The Connection Machine was studied as an example of a SIMD data parallel computing system. Programs written for the Connection Machine have normal sequential control flow and do not need synchronization structures. All operations happen in parallel on all processors.

The language C* is a major language for data parallel programming. C* adds new features to C to make possible data parallel computing. For example, C* provides a shape keyword that lets the programmer describe the shape and the size of parallel data.

The SPMD paradigm is actually a MIMD computer programmed in the data parallel paradigm. To a programmer, a SPMD program is sequenced by many controllers, but they are all coordinated to achieve a form of SIMD parallelism at the procedure level of a program. Examples of this form of computing are given whenever a MIMD machine like the nCUBE is programmed in data parallel style.

Although C* was designed for SIMD machines, it has been implemented on a number of MIMD machines. We report the results of implementing an early version of C* on two MIMD machines, an nCUBE 3200 hypercube and Sequent Balance 2100. This approach achieves portability across distributed-memory and shared-memory machines.

PROBLEMS FOR DISCUSSION AND SOLUTION

1 Consider the algorithm to obtain the sum of an array of n numbers. Modify the algorithm to make it run on the following:
(a) A hypercube with n processors, where $n = 2^k$, and k is any positive integer.
(b) A mesh-connected machine with n processors, where $n = k^2$, and k is any positive integer.

2 Find the time complexity of the algorithms you came up with in problem 1.

3 A shuffle-exchange network consists of $n = 2^k$ nodes, numbered 0, 1, ..., $n - 1$, and two kinds of connections, called shuffle and exchange. A shuffle link connects node i with node 2^i modulo $(n - 1)$, except that node $n - 1$ is connected to itself. Exchange connections link pairs of nodes whose numbers differ in their least significant bit. Write a data parallel algorithm on a shuffle-exhange network to do each of the following:
(a) Sort a list of n numbers.
(b) Find the sum of n values.

4 Implement a data parallel program to use the Sieve of Eratosthenes to determine all prime numbers $\leq n$. The Sieve of Eratosthenes is initialized by assuming all values in the range 2, ..., n are primes. The sieve repeatedly finds the next prime value and then sets to "not prime" all multiples of that value. The algorithm terminates when all primes $\leq \sqrt{n}$ have been found.

5 Write a C* program for matrix multiplication.

6 Write a short essay comparing the parallel programming paradigms discussed in Chapters 4 through 7. Consider the following questions:
(a) How do they differ?
(b) What do they have in common?
(c) Which paradigm is more convenient from the programmer's viewpoint?
Your essay should cover topics beyond those suggested here.

7 Modify the partial sum algorithm, written above in C*, to compute the following:
(a) The largest element of an array.
(b) The smallest element of an array.
(c) A certain element in a linked list of length n.

8 Modify the line drawing algorithm so that each processor processes a rectangular region of a picture of size $M \times N$.

References

Batcher, K., "Design of a Massively Parallel Processor," *IEEE Trans. Computers,* Vol. C-29, No. 9, 1980.

Batcher, K., "Sorting Networks and Their Applications," *Proceedings of the 1968 Spring Joint Computer Conference,* April, AFIPS, Reston, VA., pp. 307, 314, 1968.

Boghosian, B., "Computational Physics on the Connection Machine," *Computers in Physics,* American Institute of Physics, January/February 1990.

Hatcher, P., Lapadula, A., Jones, R., Quinn, M., Seevers, B., and Anderson, R., "Data-Parallel Programming on MIMD Computers," TR 90-80-4, Dept. of Computer Science, Oregon State University, 1990.

Hillis, W., and Steele, G., "Data-Parallel Algorithms," *Comm. ACM,* Vol. 29, No. 12, pp. 1170 – 1183, 1986.

Hillis, W., *The Connection Machine,* MIT Press, Cambridge, MA, 1985.

Kirkpatrick, C., Gelatt, C., and Vecchi, M., "Optimization by Simulated Annealing," *Science,* Vol. 220, pp. 671 – 680, May 1983.

Newman, W., and Sproull, R., *Principles of Interactive Computer Graphics,* McGraw-Hill, Hightstown, NJ, 1979.

Newton, R., and Sangiovanni-Vincentelli, A., "Relaxation-Based Electrical Simulation," *IEEE Trans. Computer-Aided Design,* Vol. CAD-3, No. 4, 1984.

Pang, A., "Line-Drawing Algorithms for Parallel Machine," *IEEE Computer Graphics & Applications,* pp. 54 – 59, September 1990.

Stanfill, C., and Kahle, B., "Parallel Free Text Search on the Connection Machine System," *Comm. ACM,* Vol. 29, No. 12, December 1986.

Tucker, L., and Robertson, G., "Architecture and Applications of the Connection Machine," *IEEE Computer,* pp. 26 – 38, August 1988.

Tucker, L., Feynman, C., and Fritzche, D., "Object Recognition Using the Connection Machine," *Proceedings IEEE Conference Computer Vision and Pattern Recognition,* pp. 871 – 877, June 1988.

Thinking Machines Corporation, *C* Programming Guide Version 6.0,* Cambridge, MA, November 1990.

Thinking Machines Corporation, *Implementing Fine-grained Scientific Algorithms on the Connection Machine Supercomputer,* TR90-1, Cambridge, MA, 1990.

Thinking Machines Corporation, *Introduction to Data Level Parallelism,* Cambridge, MA, 1986.

Quinn, M., and Hatcher, P., "Data-Parallel Programming on Multicomputers," *IEEE Software,* pp. 69 – 76, September 1990.

Waltz, D., "Applications of the Connection Machine," *IEEE Computer,* pp. 85 – 97, January 1987.

Chapter 8

Functional
Dataflow Programming

The dataflow/functional paradigm is one of the favorites of computer scientists because it appears to naturally lend itself to parallelism. However, it has not gained widespread acceptance among application developers. Why? The answer is found in this chapter.

We begin by describing the duality between control flow and dataflow. These two views of computing have been around for decades, but until parallel computers became widely available, the dataflow view has lived in the shadow of the control flow view. We show that these are different sides of the same coin, and that, in fact, any program that can be written in one paradigm can also be written in the other.

Next, the equivalence of functional programming and dataflow programming is demonstrated by "inverting" dataflow to obtain functional or procedural parallelism. This is a powerful idea which we exploit in a functional language called Strand. Strand combines the best of functional programming with dataflow programming to arrive at a solution to the "parallel programming problem." The reader will have to judge whether this solution is to his or her liking; but Strand does have an important feature: it is able to express parallelism without machine dependent constructs. This means that applications written in STRAND run equally well on parallel and serial computers. It also means that applications are portable across a wide variety of parallel computers.

Strand has been implemented in a commercially available language called STRAND88 by Strand Software Technologies, Inc., and is available on numerous parallel and serial computers. In the remainder of this chapter, we define a major portion of the STRAND88 language through several examples. In the final sections, we develop and present an application of functional/dataflow programming in STRAND88 . Convolution, given in both STRAND88 and in a graphical functional/dataflow design language, gives a speedup of 4× on an 8-processor hypercube.

8.1 A DUALITY PRINCIPLE

Computing is a young science and so it is perhaps too early to tell if there are any profound laws that govern the behavior of computer software. But, a number of pioneers have attempted to quantify what it is that a computer does, and how humans write programs. One of the immediate roadblocks encountered when attempting to describe fundamentals of computing is that of a basic underlying computational model. What exactly is a "computer"?

Theoretically, anything that can be computed can be computed by a Turing machine. (A Turing machine consists of a READ/WRITE head, control unit, and an infinitely long input/output tape. At each instruction step, the machine can read a bit from the tape, and decide to move the tape left or right, and read or write another bit.) Turing machines are extremely low level computers, unsuitable for more than theoretical discussion.

Most electronic digital computers are based on the von Neumann model described in Chapter 1. The von Neumann computer is fundamentally a *control flow* computer, because it is programmed by specifying flow of control, i.e., which instruction is done at each step of the program.

There is a dual model of computation, called *dataflow*. In this model, computations move forward by nature of the availability of data values instead of the availability of instructions. A *dataflow computer* is programmed by specifying what happens to data, and ignores instruction order. To get a feeling for the differences, consider the following example.

Example

Suppose we have a simple calculation to perform as given by the mathematical equation $X = B^2 - 4*A*C$, where * is multiply and = is assumed to be value assignment. The control flow steps for computing X given inputs $A = 1$, $B = -2$, and $C = 1$ must be decomposed into single operations of *, +, −, etc. The steps might be generated by a high-level language compiler, and look like this:

Steps	Calculations
1	$C = 1$
2	$A = 1$
3	$B = -2$
4	$T1 = A*C = 1$
5	$T2 = 4*T1 = 4$
6	$T3 = B^2 = 4$
7	$X = T3 - T2 = 0$

Here we have introduced temporary variables T1, T2, and T3 much like a compiler code generator would to hold intermediate results of the calculation. The sequence of instructions are assumed to be executed in the order they are written. That is, each instruction is performed, one at a time, in time-step order. Note that 7 time steps were required, corresponding to the task graph shown in Figure 8.1(a).

Now, suppose the same calculations were driven by the availability of data instead of the order of the instructions. The same calculations would be done in a different order:

Steps	Calculations
1	$C = 1; A = 1; B = -2$
2	$T1 = A*C = 1; T3 = B^2 = 4$
3	$T2 = 4*T1 = 4$
4	$X = T3 - T2 = 0$

The task graph of this model is shown in Figure 8.1(b). The arcs in this task graph show dataflow from one operation to the next. Arcs connect bubbles that must wait for the availability of data values before they can proceed. For example, in step 2, T1 must wait for the availability of A and C before the product $A*C$ can be computed.

The task graph is a precedence ordering of *small-grained tasks*, showing what

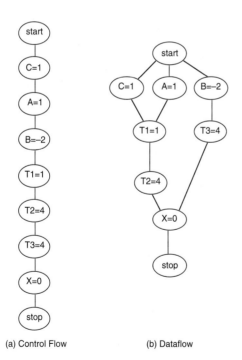

(a) Control Flow   (b) Dataflow

Figure 8.1 Task graphs of control flow vs. dataflow computation of $A = 1$, $B = -2$, $C = 1$, $X = B^2 - 4*A*C$

data are available in each step. In other words, the order of instruction execution is dictated by the precedence relations among instructions rather than an arbitrary control ordering. Sequential programming is simply the arbitrary placement of instructions into a sequence such that values are available when needed.

The important point of this example is that the two forms of calculation yield the same result. The only difference between these two forms is the underlying model used to represent computation. Control flow and dataflow are alternate computational models that yield identical numerical values.

The previous example illustrates a duality of computational models. This two-fold view of computation is not unlike the twofold model of light (waves versus particles), reality (mind versus matter), or morality (good versus bad). In a dual system, both models are simply alternate views of the same phenomenon.

We have used the *duality principle of computation* to advantage in this book. The control flow model is employed when appropriate, and the dataflow model used when it serves our needs. In most cases, the dataflow model is more appropriate for revealing parallelism. This is obvious in Figure 8.1, which shows how a dataflow program computes the same result as a control flow program, but in fewer time steps. Of course, the dataflow program used more hardware to do the calculation.

8.1.1 Conversion of Serial Programs

Most dual systems are simply representations; it is possible to convert from one dual system to the other, and back again. The duality between control flow and dataflow is no exception. It is possible to translate a control flow program into a dataflow equivalent, and conversely. Algorithms for doing this have long been known. For example, Allan and Oldehoeft gave algorithms for conversion of control flow programs to equivalent dataflow programs in 1980.

The feasibility of converting a serial control flow program into its dual dataflow program intrigues computer scientists. Might it be possible to program in the comfortable control flow languages we have grown accustomed to, and then let the compiler convert the serial program into an equivalent parallel dataflow program? The answer is yes, and we show how, in Chapters 11 and 12.

While it is possible to automatically convert control flow programs into dataflow programs, it is not always desirable. Why? It turns out that the control flow paradigm biases programmers so that many algorithms that might perform better as parallel programs are overlooked by the serial-thinking programmer. Hence, the control flow representation tends to obscure parallelism.

In addition, control flow programming minimizes the use of hardware, and this causes programmers to invent conservative algorithms. If, on the other hand, parallelism were made explicit in the programming language, better and faster algorithms might be invented. For maximum speed, it is better to program in a language that explicitly expresses parallelism than to rely on a compiler to find and express the parallelism for you.

8.1.2 Functions and Dataflow

The duality of control flow and dataflow has divided the world into two camps: the serial programmers who seek a "genius compiler" that can automatically convert their serial programs into parallel programs, and the parallel programmers who invent new programming languages that require the human programmer to express parallelism explicitly.

While searching for "good" parallel languages, designers have observed the following:

1 The dataflow computation model is very nearly equivalent to the functional programming language model of computation.

2 In the functional paradigm, computation can be expressed in a serial fashion, but interpreted in a parallel fashion.

The consequences of these two observations are profound, because they seem to remove the duality between control and data. That is, functional programming appears to unify the two theories of computation into one. Can this be true? If it is, then functional programming is analogous to the quantum theory of matter, yielding an explanation of why light is both wave and particle.

In the functional paradigm, we think in terms of functions only. A function is simply a mapping from a tuple to a value

```
value ← F(tuple)
```

where a tuple is an ordered set of values, $<x_1, x_2, \ldots, x_n>$. Actually, $<x_1, x_2, \ldots, x_n>$ is an n-ary tuple, or simply an n-tuple. An n-ary function is a mapping from an n-tuple to a value. This is the basis of functional programming, where each function returns a value which is in turn used as an input to other functions, and so on.

The function's value can be denoted by the function name itself, in which case we think of the function name as a variable containing a value

$$F(<x_1, x_2, \ldots, x_n>)$$

When this form is used, it is easy to see that any of the values in the n-tuple can be either a simple (primitive) value, or else a function itself. In this way, we compose complex calculations (programs?) without explicit control. That is, a function can call a function, which in turn can call another function, and so forth.

There are two rules for composing a calculation in functional form: (1) concatenation, and (2) functional composition. Concatenation simply permits the construction of a collection of function evaluations, in any order, by concatenating the functions. We will employ the punctuation mark "," to designate concatenation. Thus, F1, F2, F3 means to calculate all three functions in any order.

The second rule permits composition as suggested by the function-as-value convention. Since each function is allowed to take on the value returned from the function's activation, we simply use F1(F2(F3)) to indicate composition. This form means to compute F3 and use its value as the input to F2, which returns a value to F1, which returns the final value.

Example

Suppose the previous example is recast in functional form. All steps are represented as functions instead of control flow statements. In place of control flow, we use either concatenation or else call each function from within another function, and let the compiler decide how to "execute" the functions.

We need functional equivalents to the usual arithmetic operations "+", "∧", "−", and ":=". For simplicity, we use obvious function names in place of these operators. In each case, the arguments of each function are either simple variables or the name of another function.

```
ASSIGN(C, 1), ASSIGN(A, 1), ASSIGN(B, -2),
ASSIGN(X, (MINUS(POWER(B,2), MULTIPLY(4, MULTIPLY(A, C)))))
```

The compiler will most likely unravel these nested expressions and generate code for the expected computations, which are exactly the computations illustrated in Figure 8.1(b). Here they are in functional form.

Step	Calculations
1	ASSIGN(C, 1), ASSIGN(A, 1), ASSIGN(B, –2),
2	MULTIPLY(1, 1), POWER(–2, 2)
3	MULTIPLY(4, 1)
4	MINUS(4, 4)
5	0

An important point to note here is that the choice of parallel or serial execution of these functions is determined by the compiler and not the programmer. That is, the compiler can evaluate functions in parallel even though the programmer may have written the functions in a certain order.

The reader should also note the functional program's similarity to the dataflow program for the same calculation. We have literally rewritten the dataflow version in a functional form, and retained the same model. Thus, functional programming might be interpreted as another way to write dataflow programs (this is not accurate, but the resemblance is difficult to ignore).

The functional paradigm seems to hold the key to parallel programming, but even this simple example shows some difficulty with the approach. For example, the excessive use of parentheses can obscure the program. How does a programmer deal with complex data structures? And what about decision making? Rather than ignore these perennial complaints against LISP and other traditional functional languages, we advocate a new functional language called STRAND[88], which overcomes most of these shortcomings.

8.2 THE FUNCTIONAL PROGRAMMING PARADIGM

Functional and dataflow programming appear to go hand in hand, but all is not as straightforward as we might hope. In particular, we still have to deal with control flow, data dependencies, and concurrency to a limited extent. In this section, we develop these ideas further, and introduce Strand, a functional language that executes programs on both serial and parallel computers.

In Strand, a program is a collection of functions that consumes a varying number of processors. When only one processor is available, a Strand program runs like any other serial program. When more than one processor is available, a Strand program dynamically "uses up" as many processors as it needs.

The word "STRAND" is a play on words: STReam/AND is contracted to form the name of a language that supports streams (continuous dataflows between tasks) and AND parallelism (adjacent tasks are executed in parallel as in the supervisor/worker paradigm). Strands are also the threads of a rope. To complete the play on words, *thread* is used in computing to denote light-weight processes.

8.2.1 And/Or Graphs

Clearly, the pure functional form of the previous example has severe limitations. How, for example, can we write a looping program? And, what about decision branches? We can relax the pure functional form without sacrificing the utility of functional programming, and accommodate loops and branches. This will lead us to the concept of an and/or execution tree.

Functional programs use *guards* in place of branches, and *recursion* in place of loops. A guard is a boolean expression that allows a function to be executed when it is TRUE, and prevents the function from executing when it is FALSE. A recursive function is simply any function that calls itself.

We use the Strand notation to illustrate the ideas of recursion and guards. The reader should be aware that other functional languages are similar, and differ mainly in the syntactic structures used to express these ideas.

Suppose we want to write a function to compute POWER(X, N, R), where the parameters are all assumed to be integers, for simplicity, and R is the returned value

$$R = X^N;\ \ X > 0,\ \ N \geq 0$$

In a procedural language such as Pascal, C, Fortran, or BASIC, the routine will employ a loop and might look similar to the Pascal procedure below.

```
Procedure Power(X, N : integer; var R : integer);
R := X;        {Awkward, but useful, later}
If N = 0          {Assume N ≥ 0}
    then R = 1;
If N = 1        {The reason for this will be clear later}
    then R = X;
If N > 1        {Iterative solution . . .}
```

```
        then For I:= 2 to N do
              R := R * X;
  end.
```

How does this solution appear in functional form? The following Strand code does exactly the same as the code above, but in an entirely different manner.

```
POWER(X, N, R):-
N == 0 | R := 1.     % Similar to If N = 0 then R :=1


POWER(X, N, R):-
N == 1 | R := X.      % Similar to If N = 1 then R := X


POWER(X, N, R):-
N > 1 | N1 is N - 1,  % Similar to For I:=1 to N do R := R*X
        POWER(X, N1, R1),
        R is X * R1.
```

First, some syntactic notation. All Strand functions are procedures because they do not return a value. A procedure has a header consisting of its name and parameters followed by the ":–" symbol to designate "is defined as . . . ."

The (optional) guard is a boolean expression separated from the body of the procedure by "|". Thus, $N == 0$ | designates a guard. Only one guard is allowed per clause, but as you can see, a procedure may have more than one clause. In this example, there are three clauses for POWER.

The statements in each clause are separated by "," to designate additional procedure calls or primitive statements. Thus, $R := 1$ is a primitive statement meaning to assign the value one to R, and

```
        N1 is N - 1,
        POWER(X, N1, R1),
        R is X * R1.
```

are two primitive statements and one procedure call which define the actions of one of the clauses. The "is" operator specifies a calculation, while the ":=" operator simply assigns a value to a variable.

Notice the order of these statements is irrelevant. N1, R1, and R are computed by this body, but *not* in the order in which they appear. That is, the comma separator also designates potential parallelism in the execution of the body of a procedure.

In place of serial execution of statements in the order they are written, Strand statements are executed as soon as their input parameters are available, and as soon as their guards are TRUE. The reason we have three clauses for POWER is quite clear now. We need one body for each of the conditions that might occur, i. e., $N = 0$, $N = 1$, or $N > 1$. The three clauses specify *OR-parallelism* and the comma specifies *AND-parallelism* in the program. Each body is terminated by a period, ".".

This idea is exploited in many functional languages to achieve parallel execution without programmer effort. The following example illustrates this in detail.

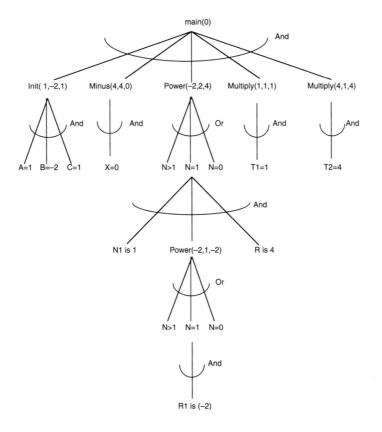

Figure 8.2 AND/OR graph of *X*:= *B*^2 – 4*A*C in functional form

Example

Consider again the discriminate $X = B^2 - 4*A*C$. Figure 8.2 shows the AND/OR tree for this problem.

A Strand program, and most functional programs, execute by traversing an AND/OR tree. The OR branches of the tree are selected by examining the guards of the procedure clauses (and the parameters of the functions, too, but we simplify for the time being). The AND branches of the tree are candidates for AND parallelism, but for our purposes, they tell the program to execute all of the branches. In short, a Strand program attempts to execute all AND branches simultaneously, and only one OR branch at a time.

Now, consider the code for the problem. We use Strand notation to express the calculation discussed in the previous example. The main program goes something like this.

```
MAIN( ):-
    INIT(A, B, C),        % A set to 1, B to -2, and C to 1
    MINUS(T3, T2, X),     % Computer X as soon as possible
```

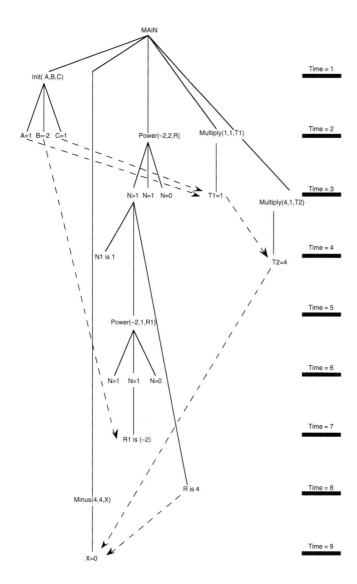

Figure 8.3 Dataflow within the Strand example of Figure 8.2

```
POWER(B, 2, T3),       % B^2, can be done anytime
MULTIPLY(A, C, T1),    % T1 = A*C
MULTIPLY(4, T1, T2).   % T2 = 4*T1
```

The MAIN procedure computes zero for X, and is represented by the root of the AND/OR tree in Figure 8.2. The AND-parallel branches of the tree are searched for one or more functions which can be executed next. This is shown at the next level in the tree. Here is the code for these functions.

```
INIT(A, B, C):-
```

```
     C:= 1,
     A:= 1,
     B:= -2.
```

These simple assignments can also be done in parallel. Even if they are performed serially, the order of execution is unimportant. The POWER procedure was given earlier and is not repeated here.

```
MULTIPLY(X, Y, PRODUCT):-
   PRODUCT is X * Y.
MINUS(X, Y, DIFF) :-
    DIFF is X - Y.
```

Clearly, this problem is solved without loops or branches. The recursive call within POWER replaces loops, and the guards remove the need for decision branching in the program. When coupled with the AND/OR tree model, functional programming is as capable as a procedural language with loops and branches.

8.2.2   Parallelism in Strand

The previous example did not make clear how Strand handles parallelism. Indeed, a Strand program appears to require explicit synchronization to avoid race conditions on shared variables. This, however, is not the case. Strand employs two rules to avoid such messy details: (1) single-assignment, and (2) dataflow constraints.

First, it is clear that restricting the programmer to single-assignment solves many problems. In *single-assignment* languages, a variable is allowed to be assigned a value only once in its life. That is, we are prevented from using the variable more than once to hold a certain value.

Again, we can use the POWER procedure to illustrate single-assignment. The value of N can be assigned only once, so we used N1 in place of N, and R1 in place of reusing R. Compare the following two implementations of one body of POWER to see how single assignment forces the programmer to introduce more variables than required in a multiple-assignment language.

Single-Assignment   Multiple-Assignment
```
N > 1 | N1 is N - 1,                N > 1 | N is N - 1,
   POWER(X, N1, R1),                   POWER(X, N, R),
   R is X * R1.                        R is X * R.
```

The second restriction placed on us by Strand is the hidden dataflow analysis. The idea is to prevent a procedure from "firing" until the data it wants are available. We illustrate this by making the dataflow constraints explicit in the sample problem of Figure 8.2, as shown in Figure 8.3.

Below is the main program as written originally, and the program as it is executed, given the dataflow constraints of Figure 8.3. The version titled "DataFlow Ordered" is how a serial programmer might see the code if each statement is run in order from top to bottom of the listing. The two statements listed side by side are assumed to be executed at the same time, if two processors are available.

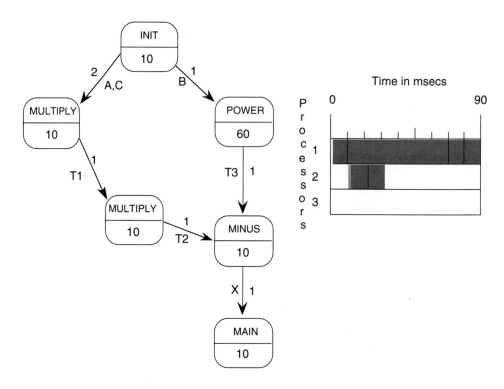

Figure 8.4 Task graph and Gantt chart schedule for sample Strand program

Original Order

```
MAIN(X):-
    INIT(A, B, C),
    MINUS(T3, T2, X),
    POWER(B, 2, T3),
    MULTIPLY(A, C, T1),
    MULTIPLY(4, T1, T2).
```

Dataflow Order

```
INIT(A, B, C),
MULTIPLY(A, C, T1), POWER(B, 2, T3),

MULTIPLY(4, T1, T2),
MINUS(T3, T2, X).
```

The job of blocking a procedure until its data are ready to be accessed is hidden within the runtime support environment of Strand. The programmer never needs to be aware of the parallel execution, but of course, it is hoped that parallelism is exploited whenever possible.

8.2.3 Scheduling Strand Programs

We can compare the functional program of the previous example with the more traditional MIMD task graph as shown in Figure 8.4. The task graph is obtained from the dataflow constraints discussed above, and illustrated in Figure 8.3. The start task is INIT, and we can see that the two MULTIPLY functions can be run in parallel with the POWER procedure.

The task graph of Figure 8.4 assumes execution times of 10ms for MULTIPLY, INIT, and MAIN, and 60ms for POWER. Communication delays are also assumed to be known as shown. These times will vary depending on the machine that executes this program.

The best schedule is shown in the Gantt chart of Figure 8.4. According to the Gantt chart, the two MULITPLY functions should be run on a second processor in parallel with the POWER procedure. This is optimal because of the 60ms execution time of POWER as compared with the 10ms times for each of the MULTIPLY functions, see Figure 8.4.

Strand will always attempt to use as many processors as it can, regardless of the wisdom of dynamic scheduling. That is, if a processor is available, Strand will employ it to run even the smallest task. In some cases, this is good, but most of the time it leads to high overhead. Accordingly, we should always study the problem and decide whether to force tasks onto fewer processors or not.

The commercial implementation of Strand, STRAND88, requires the programmer to explicitly map each Strand procedure onto a certain processor. To force a procedure onto a processor, STRAND88 provides the "@" specifier. Appending "@1" to a procedure forces it to run on processor #1, and appending "@2" forces a procedure to be executed on processor #2. Using this notation, we get a tuned example from the previous problem, and the Gantt chart of Figure 8.4.

Example

The code of the previous example can be modified to force task instantiation on two processors. The following code for main shows how this is done. Notice the use of lowercase letters for procedure names and initial-letter uppercase for variable names. This is also required by STRAND88.

```
main( ):-
  init(A, B, C)@1,
  minus(T3, T2, X)@1,
  power(B, 2, T3)@1,
  multiply(A, C, T1)@2,
  multiply(4, T1, T2)@2.
```

This version of the sample program instantiates all functions as tasks on two processors. The time to compute power() on processor #1 is overlapped with the time to compute the two multiply() procedure/tasks on processor #2.

8.2.4 Data Types

Data is not strongly typed in STRAND88 like it is in most modern languages. Instead, types are determined during execution of the program. In addition, "data structures" are composed of simple scalars, lists, and tuples. A list of data types and examples of each follow.

```
integer32
real3.14159
string"hello", 'hello'
```

```
tuple(first, second, last)
list[], [first, second, last], [Head | Tail]
```

In the case of a list, the vertical bar "|" designates concatenation of list items. For example, [Head | Tail] means a list consisting of a head item, and a sublist called tail with all other items in it. Variables are designated by an uppercase initial letter. All procedure names must begin with a lowercase letter.

Example

Suppose we want to total up a list of numbers such as [2, 3, 5, 7, 11, 13]. This numerical list can also be thought of as a concatenation of a head item, 2, followed by a tail list [3, 5, 7, 11, 13]. In turn, the tail list can be thought of as a head item 3 followed by a tail list [5, 11, 13]. This decomposition into head and tail is used to advantage in many list processing applications. Simple summation uses decomposition of the input list of numbers.

The total of the list is computed by calling Sum ([2, 3, 5, 7, 11, 13], Answer) to start the chain of actions as follows.

```
sum(List, Result) :-
  tally(List, 0, Result).        % OR-Parallelism. Start with one case
tally([Head | Tail], SumIn, R):-
  integer(Head) | Sum is SumIn + Head,    % test if it is a number
              tally(Tail, Sum, R).    % Recursion in place of loop
tally([], SumIn, R):-
    R:= SumIn.            % Finally, the list runs dry
```

Here we have used integer(Head) as a function which returns TRUE if its argument is an integer, and FALSE otherwise. We have also used a short-cut method of making decisions in place of an explicit guard. One body of tally() is executed if the List is not empty, and the other is executed if it is empty. The empty List is denoted by a [] parameter.

Additionally, we used recursion in place of iteration to scan the list. Each recursion consumes the Head of the list, and recursively processes its Tail.

Note the way R is passed through several layers of recursion. The table below gives a trace of the program as it sums [2, 3, 5, 7, 11, 13].

Procedure	SumIn	Head	Tail	R
sum	?	2	[3, 5, 7, 11, 13]	
Tally	2	3	[5, 7, 11, 13]	
Tally	5	5	[7, 11, 13]	
Tally	10	7	[11, 13]	
Tally	17	11	[13]	
Tally	28	13	[]	
Tally	41	[]	?	41

8.2.5 Streams

We have seen where the AND portion of the name "Strand" comes from, but what about the STReams portion? A stream is a continuous dataflow between tasks. In STRAND[88], this is usually achieved by shared lists containing variables. In the following example, we show how to write a producer-consumer pair of tasks in STRAND[88].

Example

A producer continuously passes items of a list to a consumer task. Thus, the idea of a continuous stream of data is born. Suppose these two tasks share access to a buffer of length 100 items. The shared buffer is write-accessed by the producer and read-accessed by the consumer. We must be careful not to overflow the buffer, nor underflow it by attempting to remove items that are not in the list.

The comma punctuation of STRAND[88] denotes instantiation of tasks, so we can instantiate a producer-consumer pair of tasks simply by calling them from the body of a main procedure.

```
main() :-
    producer(100, Buffer),   % Shared Buffer of size 100 items
    consumer (Buffer).       % Take from the Buffer until it runs dry
```

The producer task runs whenever it can, and continues to run in a somewhat sporadic manner until all 100 items have been placed in the Buffer. Pseudovariable "input" designates input from the keyboard.

```
producer(Count, Buffer):-
  Count > 0 |
          get_input(Input),          % keyboard input
          Buffer := [input | Buffer],  % Concatenate to existing list
          Count1 is Count - 1,       % Single-assignment countdown
          producer(Count1, Buffer).  % Do it again.
consumer([Head | Tail]) :-           % If Buffer is not empty...
       Output := Head,               % Display on screen
       consumer(Tail).               % Recurse on the tail
consumer([]) :-                      % If Buffer is empty...
       Output := "Finished".
```

8.2.6 Supervisor/Worker Paradigm

The supervisor/worker paradigm is one of the most frequently recurring patterns in parallel computing. It would seem that it is difficult to program in STRAND[88]. The problem is solved, however, by a powerful pattern-matching feature of STRAND[88]. In this section, we illustrate the paradigm by revisiting the Bank Tellers problem of Chapter 1.

Recall from Chapter 1, a bank consists of a supervisor and several workers. In this case, the tellers are workers, and they are governed by a stream task (the supervisor) which directs customers to the next available teller. In our analogy, a teller is a processor that is equipped with the necessary code to do either a withdrawal or deposit on the customer's account.

We will achieve an elegant solution by noting that a STRAND88 pattern may appear in the parameter list of a procedure. This pattern will be the processing procedure we want to perform, and the processor that takes on the job of the procedure becomes a worker.

Example

Suppose the Deposit and Withdraw functions are given with the following interfaces.

```
deposit(Amount, Status_of_Account)
withdraw(Amount, Status_of_Account)
```

Then we can define optional clauses for each case of the Update procedure:

```
update(Bal, [deposit(Amount, Status_of_Account) | Tail]):-
  NewBal is Bal + Amount,
  Status_of_Account := ok,
  update(NewBal, Tail).
update(Bal, [withdraw(Amount, Status_of_Account) | Tail]):-
  Amount < Bal |
          NewBal is Bal - Amount,
          Status_of_Account := ok,
          update(NewBal, Tail).
```

Clearly, additional code should be added to handle the case where Status_of_Account is NotOk. But, the idea of a supervisor/worker paradigm holds, by using the patterns and recursion to process the streams of transactions.

The reader should work out the details of this paradigm by adapting the producer-consumer paradigm to this code. The result is a server model similar to the one discussed in Chapter 6.

8.2.7 The STRAND88 Runtime Model

If elegance is the right combination of simplicity and power, then the runtime environment of STRAND88 is elegant. Coordination of tasks and synchronization of data access are achieved with one simple technique—the *process pool*.

All data and functions are named in STRAND88. In fact, one can think of functions as named data, where the value of a function name is obtained by exercising a function's clause. A data name gets a value by assignment, parameter passing, or calculation. In either case, the name along with its value is held in a pool, waiting to be used.

Data names are removed from the pool whenever they are accessed (used) by a procedure. If another procedure needs the data, it must wait until the data are placed back in the pool. Thus, mutual exclusion is achieved by mere presence or absence of the named data.

Functions are executed whenever all their inputs are also in the pool, and a guard is TRUE. A ready procedure is removed from the pool by a processor that instantiates it as a task. The activated procedure/task is quickly decomposed into its AND-parallel parts (the statements separated by commas), and each AND-parallel part is placed back into the pool.

The AND-parallel functions remain in the pool until their parameters are available and a guard is found to be TRUE. When this condition occurs, we once again remove the ready procedure, assign it to a processor, activate it as a task, and decompose it into its constituent AND-parallel functions. Eventually, all functions in the AND-parallel clause of a procedure complete their tasks, and the parent procedure is placed back in the pool to await another "call."

These duties are carried out by SAM (STRAND88 Abstract Machine) which is an interpreter. SAM obtains resources from the parallel computer's operating system, and manages these resources on behalf of applications.

8.2.8 Foreign Function Interface

Procedures in a STRAND88 program are not restricted to STRAND88 defined functions. In general, any Fortran or C function that can be compiled into binary format is eligible to be called from a STRAND88 program. Importing subroutines from Fortran or functions from C is a powerful feature for any functional language. It has several useful applications.

First, it is clear that Fortran and C programmers will prefer to continue coding in Fortran and C. The resulting routines can be linked in with a STRAND88 superstructure with the result that parallelization of most programs can be quickly achieved. A valuable side effect is that the parallel program is portable across a number of parallel computers.

Second, existing Fortran and C programs can be parallelized by reusing their existing routines, writing a small amount of STRAND88 code to handle the "calls," and recompiling it all on a parallel computer. This is a simple way to achieve 2×– 5× speedups of old applications with minimal effort.

Finally, STRAND88 makes an excellent gluecode language for constructing large applications from reusable components. The functional notation is extremely lucid, and because the language takes care of most of the details of synchronization and parallelism, parallel programming is made easy. STRAND88 can often be generated automatically from graphical specifications so that the programmer is not even aware of its existence! (see Chapter 12 for details on this approach.)

8.3 DESIGNING FUNCTIONAL PROGRAMS

Functional programs make good dataflow programs because function calls produce limited side effects on program variables. Indeed, the functional paradigm is tied to the dataflow paradigm by noting that a function takes input flows and converts them

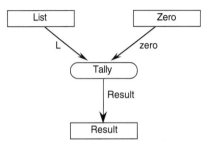

Figure 8.5 Functional/Dataflow design of sum program in STRAND[88]

into output flows as does pure dataflow. In other words, functions can be thought of as side effect-producing operators in the dataflow paradigm.

A very simple design methodology can be established by combining functional and dataflow programming as follows:

1 Functions are operators that "fire" as soon as all inputs are available and all appropriate guards are TRUE.

2 Dataflows are values that provide inputs to functions and outputs from functions.

3 A program is a dataflow graph consisting of dataflow arcs connecting functional operations which operate on the values flowing along the arcs in accordance with 1 and 2 above.

Figure 8.5 illustrates these rules for the simple summation program given earlier and repeated here. Function sum() uses recursive calls to tally() to add a list of numbers and produce the summation in variable Result:

```
sum(List, Result) :
  tally(List, 0, Result).
```

Each function is designated by an oval "bubble" consisting of the function's name and input/output ports. *Ports* are places to plug in dataflows, that is, ports are place holders for the parameters of a function. In this example, function tally() has three ports: two input and one output.

Storage boxes designate static data or named variables for holding values. Again, in Figure 8.5 there are three storage boxes named List, Zero, and Result. They too contain ports to show the flow of their values.

The data arcs in Figure 8.5 show how the data are allowed to flow from one function to another via ports. The values stored in data boxes List and Zero flow into function tally(), and the value Result is provided by an output from Tally().

8.3.1 Parallax CASE

The visual diagram of a parallel program is very helpful in program design. Indeed, in Chapter 12 we discuss more generally the idea of a computer-aided software engineering (CASE) tool for design and implementation of parallel programs. A *CASE* tool is any program for automating a portion of the programming process. The program design in Figure 8.5 can be thought of as an input to a CASE tool for drawing the design of the Sum() procedure in STRAND[88].

The power of most CASE tools derives from their ability to automatically produce documentation, design checks, and portions of the source code, and assist in testing the final application. We will exploit this power in the design of parallel STRAND[88] applications through the use of Parallax™ .

Parallax is a collection of parallel programming tools for design and implementation of parallel programs. It consists of design entry and analysis, task scheduling, and code generation tools which can speed development of applications for a variety of parallel computers. (See Chapter 12 for more detail).

CASE tools typically employ *hierarchical decomposition* to reduce the complexity of large applications. Parallax is no exception, and in fact uses the natural hierarchical structure of most STRAND[88] applications to hide details. These details can be revealed in levels, as the designer wishes.

Example

Again, the simple summation example will be used to illustrate hierarchical decomposition in the design of functional/dataflow programs. Consider Figure 8.5 to be at the top level of the design and Figure 8.6 to be a decomposition of the tally() procedure. Recall the code for tally():

```
tally([Head | Tail], SumIn, R):-
  integer(Head) | Sum is SumIn + Head,          % test if it is a number
                  Tally(Tail, Sum, R).           % Recursion in place of loop
tally([], SumIn, R):-
    R:= SumIn.                                   % Finally, the list runs dry
```

There are two versions of Tally();—one for each guard. These conditions are reflected in the design as functional operators Integer(*H*) and Empty(L). The output ports of these boolean functions are of type boolean. That is, they carry T =TRUE or F = FALSE values rather than numerical values. This means that only one of the two functions named IS and EQUAL are executed—not both.

The second interesting feature is the recursive call to tally() itself. This is how we achieve parallelism in STRAND[88]. In place of a loop, we use recursion to produce partial sums. To reveal the parallelism between two adjacent tally() functions, replace the tally() bubble with itself, and you will see that the two instances of tally() can be executed in parallel. This is left as an exercise for the reader.

8.4   AN APPLICATION IN STRAND[88]

In this section we illustrate the ideas of the previous sections with an application of functional/dataflow parallel programming. We will show how STRAND[88] is

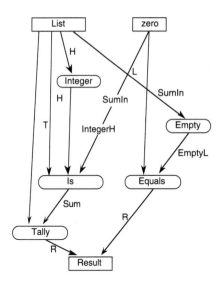

Figure 8.6 Decomposition of the STRAND[88] tally() procedure as it would appear in a parallax design

used along with a C function to write a portable parallel program for computing convolutions useful in signal processing.

Convolution is an important operation with many applications in communications, signal detection, spectral analysis, image processing, and various areas of science such as physics and chemistry.

Convolution is a key calculation in these diverse fields because from the output of a linear system that has been stimulated by an impulse signal, we can determine the output from nearly any stimulus. That is, the output of an arbitrary linear system can be determined for any stimulus by study of the output caused by a simple impulse (a spike that has some magnitude at one point in time, but is zero everywhere else).

In addition, the convolution can be used to find the Fourier transform of signals without taking the Fourier transform directly. As the reader probably knows, the Fourier transform has many applications in signal, speech, radar, and image processing.

The following application was designed and written by Tim Mattson of Strand Software Technologies, Inc. It operates on any serial or parallel machine that supports C and STRAND[88]. It is an example of a portable parallel program in addition to illustrating the ideas of functional/dataflow programming.

8.4.1 The Convolution Procedure

Let an input signal be represented in digital form by the sequence of values $X[i]$, $i = 1$ to NX. Furthermore, let the unit impulse response $H[j]$, $j = 1$ to NH be the output of a linear system when stimulated by a unit impulse, e.g., 1 at $i = 0$, and 0 everywhere else.

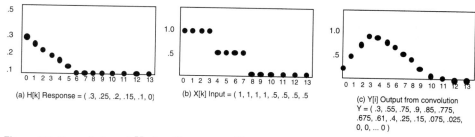

(a) H[k] Response = (.3, .25, .2, .15, .1, 0)

(b) X[k] Input = (1, 1, 1, 1, .5, .5, .5, .5)

(c) Y[i] Output from convolution
Y = (.3, .55, .75, .9, .85, .775,
.675, .61, .4, .25, .15, .075, .025,
0, 0, ... 0)

Figure 8.7 Convolution of X **with** H **to obtain** Y

The output of a linear system $Y[k]$, is completely determined by its response function H and its input function X by the convolution formula below.

$$Y[i] = \sum_{k=-\infty}^{\infty} (X[k]*H[i-k])$$

Typically, the signals are valid only within a window, so the infinity of points can be dropped and the convolution formula becomes:

$$Y[i] = \sum_{k=0}^{N-1} (X[k]*H[i-k])$$

An example of the effects of convolution of X with H is shown in Figure 8.7. In this figure, H is the output of some linear system when stimulated by an impulse function, X is a new stimulus function whose effect on the linear system we wish to determine, and Y is the resulting output.

In terms of signal processing, the convolution of a signal in frequency domain is equivalent to multiplication of the time domain signal. This feature makes convolution an extremely useful calculation for many applications.

8.4.2 Foreign Function Conv

The convolution procedure can be carried out in parallel by noting that it is essentially a collection of summations—one for each value of $Y[i]$. Therefore, we can design a parallel summation program similar to the tally() procedure described earlier.

The plan is as follows: Given fewer parallel processors than we have $Y[i]$'s to compute, we assign a number of $Y[i]$'s to each of NodesUsed processors. Each processor will carry out the convolution on its portion of the $Y[i]$'s, using a C function called from STRAND88. This is essentially the supervisor/worker paradigm in a functional/dataflow format.

The plan uses STRAND88 as a parallelizing framework, and the C function to quickly compute the partial sums. The C function called conv is given below. It is somewhat more complicated than a simple summation might be, because it is generalized to handle the segmentation of summations, and because the boundaries of X and H must be considered. The documentation was provided by Tim Mattson.

```
/*--------------------------------------------------------------------
   NAME:
        conv
   CALLING FORMAT:

        conv(IND, NUMB, N, NH, H, NX, X, NY, Y)

   PARAMETERS:

        IND     int input.  First desired element of Y
        NUMB    int input.  Number of desired Y elements
        N       int input.  Length of H and X for the convolution.
        NH      Int input. Length of full array, H
        H       double Array of length N.
        NX      Int input. Length of full array, X
        X       double Array of length N.
        NY      Int input. Length of full array, Y
        Y       double Array of max length 2N-1.  The NUMB desired
                output values fill Y[0] through Y[NUMB-1].


   DESCRIPTION:
                This subroutine will compute NUMB elements of Y starting
        with the IND'th Y element where Y is defined as the
        convolution of the input arrays, H and X
                Y = H * X
        The two arrays, H and X, are assumed to be of length N
        and the output array, Y, is of length Numb. The algorithm
        assumes that H and X outside of the range of indices 1..N
        are zero. This corresponds to what is commonly known as
        "linear convolution."
--------------------------------------------------------------------*/
void conv (ind, numb, n, nh, h, nx, x, ny, y)
int ind, numb, n, nx, nh, *ny;
double h[], x[], **y;
{
        int     i,   k,    klast,   koff;
        double sum;
        float  t_init;
        int    yind = 0;
        int    i_start_1, i_end_1; /* segment 1 index ranges */
        int    i_start_2, i_end_2; /* segment 2 index ranges */
        static double *temp = 0;
        if(temp) free(temp);
        temp = (double*)malloc(numb*sizeof(double));
```

```
/*
   Test input parameters, return immediately if an error
*/
   if ((ind > 2*n-1) || ((ind + numb) > 2*n) || (ind < 0)) return;
/*
   NOTES:  The convolution is split into two parts. The need for
   this is best understood by thinking of the convolution algorithm
   as reversing the first array (H)  and "sliding it past" the
   fixed second array (X).  Summing occurs for the parts of the
   arrays that overlap. The first part of the convolution handles
   the portion where the H runs off the low edge of X. The second
   part handles the case of H overrunning the high edge of X.
   For the case of restricted output ranges, we need to construct
   the index ranges for each part of the convolution.
*/
       if (ind < n) {
           i_start_1 = ind;
           if ( (i_start_1 + numb)>n){
               i_end_1   = n; i_start_2 = n;
               i_end_2   = n + numb - (i_end_1 - i_start_1);
           }
           else {
               i_end_1   = ind + numb;  i_start_2 = 0;
               i_end_2   = 0;
           }
       }
       else {
           i_start_1 = 0;  i_end_1 = 0;
           i_start_2 = ind;  i_end_2 = ind + numb;
       }
/*
   Do the convolution.
*/
       for (i=i_start_1; i<i_end_1; i++) {
           sum = 0.0;
           for (k = 0; k<= i; k++)
               sum + = h[i-k] * x[k];
           *(temp+yind) = sum;
           yind++;
       }
       koff  = i_start_2-n+1;
       klast = n-koff;
       for (i=i_start_2; i<i_end_2; i++) {
           sum = 0.0;
           for (k=0; k<klast; k++)
               sum += h[n-k-1] * x[k+koff];
           *(temp+yind) = sum;
```

```
        yind++;
        klast--;
        koff++;
    }
    *ny = numb;
    *y  = temp;
}
```

8.4.3 STRAND[88] Functions for Convolution

The C function computes only a portion of the outputs $Y[i]$, depending on how many workers we have. If we divide up the work equally (except for the last worker), the summations all take roughly the same amount of time, and so the calculation can be done linearly faster.

The following STRAND[88] code, also provided by Tim Mattson, uses recursive calls to spawn parallel workers as we have illustrated many times before.

```
-compile(free).
%-------------------------------------------------------------
% Module Name: convolve
%
% Description: This module will convolve two vectors of equal
%              length. A vector is represented as a list of
%              real values manipulated through the C function,
%              conv.
%
%              This version is simplified so it will fit on a
%              single page (a nice feature for inclusion in papers
%              and other presentations). Because of this, the
%              code is not as fault tolerant as "good" Strand code
%              should be.
%
% HISTORY:     Written by Tim Mattson, May 7, 1990
%
%-------------------------------------------------------------
-exports([
   convolution/5, % the parallel convolution routine
   worker/6       % convolution worker
]).

%-------------------------------------------------------------
%
% NAME:        convolution(int?, int?, list?, list?, list^)
%
% Description: Will convolve the two input vectors to produce
%              an output vector. The input vectors are input
%              as lists while the output vector is represented
%              as a list of lists—one list for each block of
```

```
%              computation.
%
%              This version of the procedure has been shortened
%              to be as simple as possible. Hence, certain
%              assumptions have been made about the data.
%                   1.  The vectors are of length NX.
%                   2.  All input data are reasonable (Nodes > 0, etc).
%
%  USAGE:  To convolve two vectors (A and B) of length NX = 10
%              using 3 nodes to produce a vector Y containing
%              2*NX-1 values:
%
%                   convolution(3, 10, A, B, Y)
%
%-------------------------------------------------------------
convolution(Nodes, NX, X, H, Y) :-
    NY    is 2 * NX - 1,          % Length of X and H is NX
    ModNY is NY // Nodes,         % // is the MOD operation
    comp_bsize(Nodes, NY, ModNY, Size, NodesToUse),
    conv1(NodesToUse, 0, NY, Size, NX, X, H, Y).
conv1(Node, Index, NY, Size, NX, X, H, Y) :-
  Node > 0 |
    NewInd  is Index + Size,
    NewNode is Node - 1,
    worker(Size, Index, NX, X, H, YHere)@Node,
    Y := [YHere | YRest],
    conv1(NewNode, NewInd, NY, Size, NX, X, H, YRest).
conv1(0, Index, NY, _Size, NX, X, H, Y) :-
    Length is NY - Index,
    worker(Length, Index, NX, X, H, Y)@0.
worker(Length, Index, NY, X, H, Y) :-
    ground(X,Xready),      % Test that all of X has arrived
    ground(H,Hready),      % Test that all of H has arrived
    do_conv(Xready, Hready, Index, Length, NY, H, X, Y).

do_conv(Xready, Hready, Index, Length, NY, H, X, Y):-
  Xready == [],  Hready == [] |
    conv(Index, Length, NY, H, X, Y).
comp_bsize(Nodes, NY, 0, Size, NodesToUse) :-
    NodesToUse := Nodes,
    Size  is NY / Nodes.
comp_bsize(Nodes, NY, ModNY, Size, NodesToUse) :-
  ModNY > 0 |
    Size  is 1 + NY / Nodes,
    NodesToUse is NY / Size.
```

The STRAND[88] code is straightforward except for a few statements which need to be clarified. First, the placement of tasks onto processors is forced on the solution using the @ operator.

```
worker(Size, Index, NX, X, H, YHere)@Node,
```

Secondly, the vectors X and H are grounded inside the worker tasks as shown in the program:

```
ground(X,Xready),    % Test that all of X has arrived
```

This forces the parallel tasks to wait for all elements needed by the C function conv. This is needed because each parallel C function is without synchronization and so will access its portion of X and H without delay. The ground function is like a barrier because it makes the C function wait until all tasks have provided the needed values.

8.4.4 Parallax Design of Convolution Application

The C code above is used as a foreign function in a STRAND[88] program. This program can be designed as a functional/dataflow application, independent of STRAND[88]. In this section, we give such a design in the notation of PPSE. Chapter 12 more fully describes the PPSE (Parallel Programming Support Environment) tools.

The design shown in Figure 8.8 is hierarchical. That is, each function is decomposed into a second layer possibly containing additional functions. The functions at each layer may optionally be decomposed into other layers, and so forth. The final layer contains only functions whose definition is given as a foreign function in C. Thus, in the convolution example, the conv() function is actually textually defined in C.

We have purposely made the design conform to the textual program given in the previous section. However, there are a number of distinct differences. The most glaring difference is the way the design represents branching. In the design, we had to introduce additional functions to compute the guards, and then create control arcs from the guard functions to the worker functions. This is in effect a kind of "if-then" branch, as shown in Figure 8.8(c).

The top level is designated as level 0, and each layer is labeled with an increasing integer. The decomposition of the main function called Convolution in Figure 8.8(a) is shown in Figure 8.8(b). Notice how all the inputs and outputs from level 0 are carried over to level 1. This is an important feature of design notations such as this—leveling of inputs and outputs guarantees the correctness of dataflow across layers.

In Figure 8.8(c), the worker() functions are identical, but one is called if ChkNodeVal() returns TRUE, and the other is called if the returned result is FALSE. In effect, the control value computed by ChkNodeVal is used to "gate" the activation of a worker with one set of inputs, or "gate" the other set.

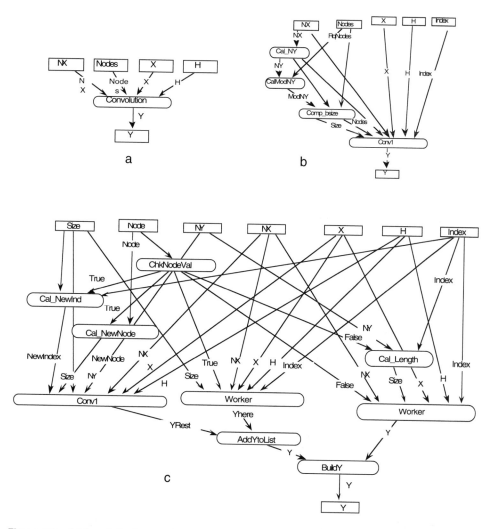

Figure 8.8 (a) Level 0 of convolution showing inputs, main program, and output result; (b) Level 1 of convolution showing the structure of the main function; (c) Level 2 of convolution showing the ChkNodeVal function used to compute a guard and cause an IF-THEN branch in the dataflow, depending on the TRUE/FALSE result

In either case, a value of *Y* is returned, but which one should be used? The BuildY function is used to select one or the other, but not both.

Also, note in Figure 8.8(c) how conv1() calls itself, recursively, to achieve a kind of iteration. Because functional programming replaces looping with recursion, and branching with guards, the design shown here is pure functional/dataflow parallel programming.

The worker() function is instantiated many times, according to the programmer's intent. This parallelism is not shown explicitly here, because we used recursion in

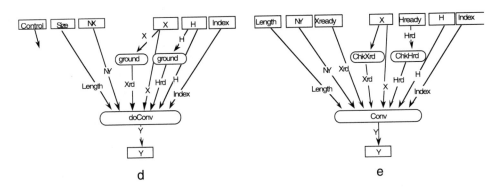

d

e

Figure 8.8(Continued) **(d) Level 3 of convolution showing the structure of a worker task. The control input is either TRUE or FALSE, but is not used. Instead, the control value is used to decide which inputs are passed to a worker; (e) Level 4 of convolution showing the structure of each worker function. The Conv function is implemented as a C function**

place of iteration. But, in fact, the multiple instances of worker() cause some problems for this design.

First, the parallelism is not explicit, and therefore might be overlooked. This shortcoming will be remedied in Chapter 12, where we show how to expose the parallelism.

Second, the dataflows do not show how to coordinate access to the shared input vectors X and H. We must be careful not to begin processing each segment of the data until they are all available. The ground() functions for X and H are shown in Figure 8.8(d). They return Xrd and Hrd (X-ready and H-ready) as control values. When these two vectors are "full," the "ready" signals Xrd, and Hrd are sent to doConv(). This allows doConv() to begin, and a possible fault due to an unexpected race condition is averted.

Clearly, this kind of detail should not be allowed to creep into a design. This example serves to show that the functional/dataflow paradigm as advanced by STRAND[88] is not perfect.

Figure 8.8(e) shows the final layer in the 5-level hierarchy. The control signals from above have been passed on to this level as Xready and Hready. These are necessary details because of STRAND[88].

The Conv() function decomposes as text, and is given in the previous section as a C function. Notice that the interface to this version of the C function will have to be modified to accommodate the control signals.

Clearly, the design of Convolution is more complex and cluttered than the source text given earlier. So why bother with the layered design? The payoff for this added effort is very small if we intend to discard the program after it is used once or twice. We can benefit from this effort if analysis and code generation tools are made available as in a programming environment. For example, if this design is automatically scheduled onto a specific parallel computer in some optimal manner, then the time

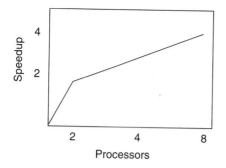

Figure 8.9 Speedup vs. number of processors for convolution running on an Intel iPSC/2 hypercube processor

and effort to construct the dataflow design is made worthwhile. Other analysis and code generation tools make this approach even more attractive.

8.4.5 Performance of Convolution

The performance of the convolution program, as implemented by Tim Mattson on an iPSC/2 hypercube, can be measured directly by running it. For the speedup curve shown in Figure 8.9, Tim used 5,000 element vectors and up to 8 nodes.

The speedup of convolution on a hypercube is sublinear. A speedup of 1.94 was obtained with 2 processors; 2.55 with 4; and 4.17 with 8 processors. The empirical data were obtained for $Y = H * X$, with vector lengths of 5,000 elements.

PROBLEMS FOR DISCUSSION AND SOLUTION

1 Write a STRAND88 program to find the maximum from a list of integers.

2 Modify the sample STRAND88 program for computing $X = B^2 - 4*A*C$ to compute the roots of a quadratic equation. Analyze your solution using the techniques shown in Figures 8.3 and 8.4.

3 Complete the supervisor/worker example of a Bank with Tellers by adding code to supply a stream of transactions and other code to provide a collection of workers (consumers) to complete the transactions.

4 Write a STRAND88 program to solve the steady state wave equation by SOR (Successive Overrelaxation). Recall this is done by averaging the N, E, W, S neighbors within a finite element grid.

5 Expand Figure 8.6 into two parallel tally() operations by replacing the tally() bubble in Figure 8.6 with another Figure 8.6 definition of Tally(). Can you identify the parallelism in this expanded diagram?

6 Compute the convolution function of Figure 8.7 and compare your results with the results given. Write a parallel program to compute convolutions.

7 Modify the STRAND$\underline{88}$ solution to the convolution problem so that there are $2*NX - 1$ parallel worker tasks, one for each $Y[i]$.

8 Redesign the convolution application given in the graphical notation of Figure 8.8 to make it even simpler.

9 Implement the design of Figure 8.8 by manually converting each function into a STRAND$\underline{88}$ function, and each data arc into a variable.

10 Can the convolution application be "parallelized" more than we have shown in its design? Discuss the opportunities to parallelize this application.

References

Allan, S. J., Oldehoeft, A. E., "A Flow Analysis Procedure for the Translation of High-Level Languages to a Dataflow Language," *IEEE Trans. Computers,* C–29, 9, pp. 826 – 831, September 1980.

Dennis, J. B., "Dataflow Supercomputers," *Computer,* 13, 11, pp. 48 – 56, November 1980.

Dennis, J. B., Leung, D. K., Misunas, D. P., "A Highly Parallel Processor Using a Dataflow Machine Language," *MIT Laboratory for Computer Science, Computation Structures Group Memo 134,* June 1977 (revised June 1979).

Foster, I., Taylor, S., *Strand: New Concepts in Parallel Programming,* Prentice Hall, Englewood Cliffs, NJ, 1990.

STRAND$\underline{88}$ User Manual, Buckingham Release 1990, Artificial Intelligence Limited, Greycaine Rd., Watford, Hertfordshire, WD2 4JP, England.

Chapter 9
Scheduling Parallel Programs

A MIMD parallel program is a collection of tasks that may run serially or in parallel. These tasks must be optimally placed on the processors of a particular parallel machine if the shortest execution time is to be realized. This problem is known as the *scheduling problem* of parallel computing and has received considerable attention in recent years. It is one of the most challenging problems in parallel computing and known to be *NP-complete* in its general form [Ullman]. Regardless, many researchers have studied restricted forms of the problem by constraining either the task graph representing the parallel program or the parallel system model. For example, when communication between tasks is not considered, a polynomial time algorithm can be found for scheduling tree-structured task graphs wherein all tasks execute in one time unit [Hu].

An *optimal schedule* determines both the *allocation* and the execution order of each task such that the tasks complete in the shortest time. An allocation is an assignment of the program tasks to the processors. Allocation alone may result in a nonoptimal schedule, because the order of execution of each task plays an important role in determining the completion time of the parallel program.

In this chapter we bring together the different views and ideas in the area of scheduling. In Section 9.1, we define the scheduling problem as a general problem. We then categorize the different scheduling techniques in Sections 9.2 and 9.3. Section 9.4 focuses on static scheduling as an important category in the scheduling problem. Several optimal scheduling algorithms are presented in Section 9.5. Section 9.6 is dedicated to scheduling heuristics that provide fast but suboptimal algorithms when an optimal solution cannot be found in real time. In Section 9.7, we show a scheduling example. In Section 9.8 we describe a practical tool called Task Grapher for studying various approaches to scheduling and its effect on system performance. At the end of the chapter we provide some references that cover most of the issues in the scheduling problem.

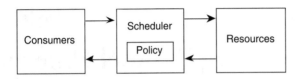

Figure 9.1 Scheduling system

9.1 THE SCHEDULING PROBLEM

The *scheduling problem* has been described in a number of different ways in different fields. The classical problem of job sequencing in production management has influenced most of what has been written about this problem.

The scheduling problem assumes a set of resources and another set of consumers that is to be serviced by these resources according to a certain policy. Based on the nature of and constraints on the consumers and the resources, the problem is to find an efficient policy for managing the access to and the use of the resources by various consumers to optimize some desired performance measure. *Schedule length* and the *mean time* spent in the system by the consumers are two examples of performance measures.

A scheduling system can be considered as consisting of consumer(s), resource(s), and policy as shown in Figure 9.1. Using the same analogy given in the bank example introduced in Chapter 1, the bank customers can be looked at as the consumers and the tellers as the resources. The policy in the scheduling model is analogous to any systematic way used to assign customers to tellers.

Performance and efficiency are two characteristics that must be used to evaluate a scheduling system. In other words, we are concerned with how good the produced schedule is and how efficient the policy itself is.

In this chapter we focus on scheduling parallel program tasks onto parallel computers. The terms jobs, tasks, and modules will be regarded as equivalent to the term consumers. Also, resources may be referred to as processors.

9.2 SCHEDULING TAXONOMY

Scheduling techniques can be classified as local and global. *Local scheduling* is used in scheduling concurrent processes to the time slices of a single processor. The operating system normally handles local scheduling. We are concerned with *global scheduling*, which deals with the assignment of tasks to processors in parallel systems.

As shown in Figure 9.2, at the highest level, we distinguish between static and dynamic scheduling. The distinction indicates the time at which the scheduling decisions are made. With *static scheduling*, information regarding the precedence-constrained task graph must be known beforehand. Hence, each task in the task graph has a static assignment to a particular processor, and each time that task is submitted for execution, it is assigned to that processor.

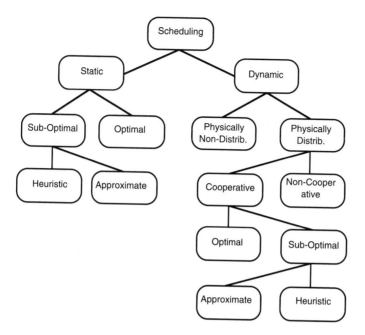

Figure 9.2 Taxonomy of scheduling approaches

Clearly, the major disadvantage of static scheduling is its inadequacy in handling nondeterminism in program execution. Conditional branches and loops are two program constructs that may cause nondeterminism. For example, the direction of a branch may be unknown until the program is midway in execution. Also, loop upper bounds could be unknown before a program starts execution. Thus, the term *deterministic scheduling* is sometimes used, meaning static scheduling.

When the task graph topology and labels are not known before the program executes due to branches and loops, the parallel processor system must attempt to schedule tasks on the fly. This is known as *dynamic scheduling*. It is usually implemented as some kind of load balancing heuristic because the scheduler has only local information about the parallel program at any point in time. The disadvantage of dynamic scheduling is its inadequacy in finding global optimums and the corresponding overhead which occurs because the schedule must be determined while the program is running.

Under the static scheduling branch of the taxonomy given in Figure 9.2, we distinguish between cases where an optimal solution can be achieved and other cases in which the problem becomes computationally infeasible. The most general form of this problem is known to be NP-complete. When an optimal solution is computationally infeasible, suboptimal solutions can be reached using approximations by restricting the model representing the parallel program, or the machine, or both.

Fast heuristics are another way to obtain suboptimal solutions. We usually use our intuition to come up with heuristics that make use of special parameters that affect the system in an indirect way. For example, tasks that heavily communicate with each other should be placed on the same processor or on processors that are close to each other. This might avoid additional communication delay between processors.

In dynamic scheduling, decisions are not made until the tasks are already running. If the work involved in making decisions is distributed among different processors, it is called *physically distributed*. Otherwise, if the scheduling responsibility is assigned to only one processor, it is called *physically non-distributed*.

The physically distributed branch is further classified into cooperative versus non-cooperative techniques. As can be determined from the term cooperative, in this approach the local schedulers at each processor cooperate and work together to come up with a global schedule that is based on the situation in the whole system. On the other hand, in noncooperative systems, individual processors work independently and arrive at decisions that will affect local performance only.

Beneath the cooperative dynamic scheduling branch of the taxonomy tree, we distinguish between optimal and suboptimal solution cases. The same discussion that was presented in the static scheduling case applies here as well.

9.3 AN ALTERNATE SCHEDULING TAXONOMY

The taxonomy tree given in the previous section is by no means a complete description of all scheduling issues. In addition, there are a number of distinguishing characteristics that scheduling systems may have. In this section we cover some of the scheduling classifications that may not fit directly in Figure 9.2.

9.3.1 Single Versus Multiple Application Systems

In this classification, we distinguish between two cases. The first case is when only one application can run at a time, for example, when a single application, consisting of several tasks cooperating and communicating, is run on a hypercube. The goal is to minimize the completion time of that application. In the second case, several parallel applications can run at the same time, for example, different parallel applications may run at the same time in a time-sharing parallel environment like the Sequent Symmetry. The objective here would be to minimize the response time and the average completion time per application.

If the entities are jobs in the traditional batch processing sense of the term, scheduling becomes a load balancing problem where our goal is to be fair to the hardware resources of the system. Normally, processors would exchange information, periodically or on demand, about the load in the system. Jobs can be sent from loaded processing elements to unloaded ones to achieve load balancing in the whole system.

9.3.2 Nonpreemptive Versus Preemptive

With *nonpreemptive scheduling*, a task cannot be interrupted once it has begun execution. It must be allowed to run to completion. In general, *preemptive scheduling* per-

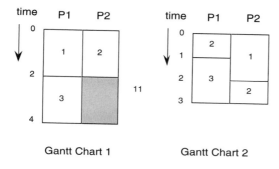

Gantt Chart 1   Gantt Chart 2

Figure 9.3 (a) Nonpreemptive; (b) Preemptive schedules for a system of three independent tasks of execution time 2 scheduled on two identical processors

mits a task to be interrupted and removed from the processor under the assumption that it will eventually receive all the execution time it requires.

Figure 9.3 shows an example illustrating the two kinds of schedules. A task graph consisting of three independent tasks of execution time 2 is to be scheduled on a target machine of two identical processors. A nonpreemptive schedule for the system takes 4 units of time, while a preemptive schedule takes only 3 units of time.

9.3.3 Nonadaptive Versus Adaptive

A *nonadaptive scheduler* is a scheduler that does not change its behavior according to feedback from the system. In other words, it does not modify its basic control mechanism on the basis of the history of the system activity. In contrast to a nonadaptive scheduler, an *adaptive scheduler* changes its scheduling decisions according to the previous and current behavior of the system.

Adaptive schedulers are usually dynamic because they may collect information about the system and make scheduling decisions on the fly. Looking back at the bank analogy given in Chapter 1, if the bank management modifies the policy it uses for assigning customers to tellers according to the current traffic in the bank lobby or due to other factors, then it is considered adaptive scheduling. On the other hand, when the same policy is used all the time regardless of the situation of the bank, it is a nonadaptive system.

9.4 STATIC SCHEDULING

There are four basic categories of algorithms to optimally solve the static scheduling problem: (1) graph-theoretic approach, (2) mathematical programming, (3) solution space enumeration and search, and (4) queueing theory [Chen, Efe, Bokhari, Stone]. We survey the graph-theoretic approach here.

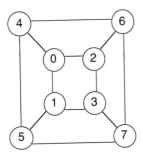

Figure 9.4   Schematic of Target machine

The models we study in this section are deterministic in the sense that all information governing the scheduling decisions is assumed to be known in advance. In particular, the task graph representing the parallel program and the target machine are assumed to be available before the program starts execution.

In what follows, we describe the general model to formulate the scheduling problem. All the problems we study in this chapter can be represented as a special case of the model. We must also mention that loops cannot be represented in parallel program models using this system. In Chapter 10 we give a different model and approach in scheduling parallel program tasks with loops. The model is described by considering the target machine (resources), parallel program (consumers), and performance measures.

9.4.1   Target Machine (Resources)

The target machine can be described as the system $(P, (P_{ij}), (S_i))$ as follows:

1. $P = \{P_1, \ldots, P_m\}$ is a set of processors forming the parallel machine.

2. (P_{ij}) is an $m \times m$ interprocessor connectivity matrix.

3. The speed S_i, $1 \leq i \leq m$, specifies the speed of processor P_i.

The connectivity of the processors can be represented using an undirected graph called the target machine graph. Figure 9.4 shows an example of a target machine consisting of 8 processors ($m = 8$) forming a cube of dimension = 3.

Processors are occasionally referred to simply by their indices (e.g., 1 may be used rather than P_1, especially when target machine nodes are more conveniently labeled with integers).

9.4.2   Parallel Program Tasks (Consumers)

The task system for a given set of resources can be defined as the system $(T, <, (D_{ij}), (A_i), (W_j))$ as follows:

1   $T = \{T_1, \ldots, T_n\}$ is a set of tasks to be executed.

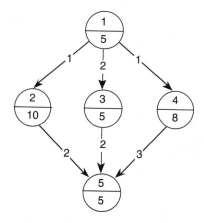

Figure 9.5 Task graph showing node numbers, node execution times, and communication size

2 < is a partial order defined on T which specifies operational precedence constraints. That is, $T_i < T_j$ signifies that T_i must be completed before T_j can begin.

3 (D_{ij}) is an $n \times n$ matrix of communication data, where $D_{ij} > 0$ is the amount of data required to be transmitted from task T_i to task T_j, $1 \le i, j \le n$.

4 (A_i) is an n vector of the amount of computations, where $A_i > 0$ is the number of instructions required to execute in T_i, $1 \le i \le n$.

5 The weights W_i, $1 \le i \le n$, are interpreted as deferral costs or cost rates.

The partial order < is conveniently represented as a directed acyclic graph called a *task graph*. A directed edge (i,j) between two tasks T_i and T_j specifies that T_i must be completed before T_j can begin. Figure 9.5 shows an example of a task graph consisting of 5 nodes ($n = 5$), where each node represents a task. The number shown in the upper portion of each node is the node number, the number in the lower portion of a node i represents the parameter A_i (the amount of computation needed by task T_i), and the number next to an edge (i,j) represents the parameter D_{ij}. For example, $A_1 = 5$, $D_{45} = 3$.

Having the speed of the processors (S) and the amount of computation (A), we can obtain (T_{ij}), which is an $m \times n$ matrix of execution times, where $T_{ij} > 0$ is the time required to execute T_i, $1 \le i \le n$, on processor P_j, $1 \le j \le m$.

9.4.3 Performance Measures

Before discussing performance measures, let us explain the means by which schedules are represented graphically. We use a timing diagram called a Gantt chart to illustrate the allocation of the parallel program tasks onto the target machine processors and their execution order. A *Gantt chart* consists of a list of all processors in the target machine and for each processor a list of all tasks allocated to that processor ordered

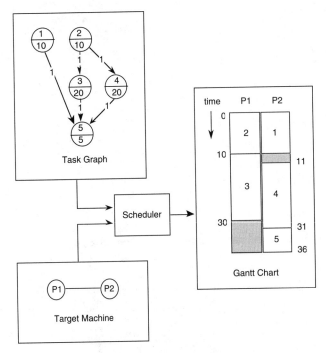

Figure 9.6   A scheduler takes task graph and target machine topologies as inputs, and produces a Gantt chart as output

by their execution time, including task start and finish times. The symbols s_i and f_i denote, respectively, the start and finish times of T_i. When necessary for indicating the dependence on a particular schedule S, the notation $s_i(S)$ and $f_i(S)$ is used. Figure 9.6 shows a scheduling system where the input is a task graph and a target machine description while the output schedule is shown in the form of a Gantt chart. The Gantt chart gives an informal notion of the schedule where the symbols s_i and f_i for all tasks can be easily shown. For example, $s_1 = 0$ and $f_1 = 10$, while $s_4 = 11$ and $f_4 = 31$.

More formally, a schedule can be defined as a suitable mapping that assigns a sequence of one or more disjoint intervals in $(0, \infty)$ to each task such that:

1   Exactly one processor is assigned to each interval.

2   The sum of the intervals is the execution time of the task, taking into account, if necessary, different processing rates on different processors.

3   No two execution intervals of different tasks assigned to the same processor overlap.

4   Precedence constraints are observed.

5   There is no interval in $(0, \max\{f_i\})$ during which no processor is assigned to some task.

For nonpreemptive schedules there is exactly one execution interval for each task.

Now, in light of the description of the scheduling problem, the idea is to find an efficient algorithm for scheduling the tasks on the available processors to optimize some desired performance measure. There are two primary measures of scheduling performance: *schedule length* or *maximum finishing time, $w(S)$*, and *mean weghted finishing time, $w'(S)$* :

$$w(S) = \max \{f_i(S)\}$$

$$w'(S) = \frac{1}{n} \sum_{i=1}^{n} w_i f_i(S)$$

In the rest of this chapter, we will focus on the schedule length or maximum finishing time, $w(S)$.

9.5 OPTIMAL SCHEDULING ALGORITHMS

There are few known polynomial-time scheduling algorithms even when severe restrictions are placed on the task graph representing the program and the parallel processor model. Polynomial algorithms can be obtained in the following two cases: (1) when the task graph is a tree, and (2) when there are only two processors available. In the two cases, all tasks are assumed to have the same execution time.

When the task graph is a tree and all tasks execute in one time unit, Hu [1961] introduced a linear algorithm that uses a level number equal to the length of the longest path from the node to the ending node as a priority number, i.e., tasks are executed level by level from the highest level first.

Coffman and Graham [Coffman] gave an $O(n^2)$ scheduling algorithm similar to Hu's algorithm except that the task scheduling priorities are assigned in such a way that nodes at the same level have different priorities. The algorithm gives an optimal length schedule for an arbitrary graph containing unit-time delay tasks on a 2-processor system. Sethi [1976] gave a less complex algorithm which provides the same schedule in $O(n\, a(n) + e)$, where e is the number of edges in the graph, and $a(n)$ is almost a constant function of n.

9.5.1 Scheduling Tree-Structured Task Graphs

In this section we assume that the task graph is a forest of n tasks and all tasks have the same execution time. There is no loss of generality if we suppose the tasks all have unit execution times. We also assume a target machine of m identical processors. The algorithm given in this section is almost linear for determining a minimal-length nonpreemptive schedule [Hu].

Let the *level* of a node x in a task graph be the maximum number of nodes (including x) on any path from x to a terminal task. In a forest, there is exactly one such path.

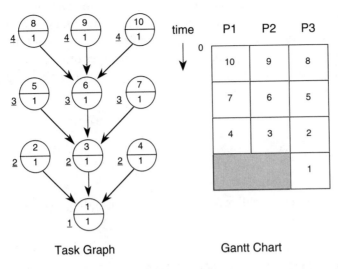

Figure 9.7 **(a) A tree-structured task graph, (b) A schedule for the task graph on three identical processors**

A terminal task is at level 1. Let a task be *ready* when all its predecessors have been executed. The optimal algorithm is described as follows.

Algorithm 9.1

1 The level of each node in the task graph is calculated and used as each node's priority.

2 Whenever a processor becomes available, assign it the unexecuted ready task with the highest priority.

Example 9.1

Consider the problem of scheduling the task graph given in Figure 9.7 on a fully connected target machine of 3 identical processors. Applying algorithm 9.1, we first compute the level at each node. The underlined number next to each node indicates its level. At the beginning, among all the ready tasks (2, 4, 5, 7, 8, 9, 10), tasks 8, 9, and 10 with level 4 are assigned first as shown in the resulting schedule given in Figure 9.7. Following the path from tasks 8, 9, or 10 to the terminal, it can be noticed that regardless of the number of processors available, at least 4 units of time will be required to execute all the tasks in the system.

9.5.2 Arbitrary Task Graphs on Two Processors

There are no known polynomial algorithms for scheduling task graphs, where all tasks have the same execution time, on a fixed number of processors m, if $m > 2$. For $m = 2$ we present an $O(n^2)$ algorithm introduced in Coffman as follows .

As given in the previous section, the highest-level-first strategy was found to be optimal for forests. Since trees are special cases of DAGs (directed acyclic graphs), we expect the level to play a role in scheduling DAGs. Labels from the set $\{1,2,...,n\}$ are assigned to each task in the task graph by the function $L(*)$, as we explain in algorithm 9.2.

Algorithm 9.2

1   Assign 1 to one of the terminal tasks.

2   Let labels 1, 2, ..., $j-1$ be assigned. Let S be the set of unassigned tasks with no unlabeled successors. We next select an element of S to be assigned label j.
For each node x in S define $l(x)$ as follows: Let $y_1, y_2,...,y_k$ be the immediate successors of x. Then $l(x)$ is the decreasing sequence of integers formed by ordering the set $\{L(y_1), L(y_2),..., L(y_k)\}$. Let x be an element of S such that for all x' in S, $l(x) \le l(x')$ (lexicographically). Define $L(x)$ to be j.

3   When all tasks have been labeled, use the list $(T_n, T_{n-1},..., T_1)$, where for all i, $1 \le i \le n$, $L(T_i) = i$, to schedule the tasks.

Since each task is executed for one unit of time, processors 1 and 2 become available at the same time. We assume that processor 1 is scheduled before processor 2.

Example 9.2

To understand the algorithm, let us examine the task graph given in Figure 9.8. The three terminal tasks 15, 16, 17 are assigned the labels 1, 2, 3, respectively. At this point the set S of unassigned tasks with no unlabeled successors becomes $\{12,13,14\}$. Also it can be noticed that $l(12) = \{3,2\}$, $l(13) = \{3\}$, and $l(14) = \{3,1\}$. And since $\{3\} \le \{3,1\}, \le \{3,2\}$ (lexicographically), we assign labels 4, 5, 6 to tasks 13, 14, 12, respectively. The algorithm continues until all tasks are labeled. The underlined number next to each task in Figure 9.8 indicates its label. Task 3 with the highest label gets scheduled first on processor 1, then task 2 on processor 2. After tasks 2 and 3 are done, the only ready tasks are 1 and 11 with labels 15 and 7, respectively. Recall that a task is called ready when all its predecessors have been executed. Since task 4 is the only ready task after executing tasks 3, 2, 1, 11, processor 2 stays idle for 1 unit of time until task 4 is done. The reader is encouraged to try the labeling algorithm on the rest of the nodes in the given task graph. This algorithm is proved to be optimal for the two-processor target machine [Coffman].

9.5.3   Other Work

Finding the optimal schedule length for this type of problem is generally very hard and is an NP-complete problem. The problem is NP-complete even in two simple restricted cases: (1) scheduling unit-time tasks to an arbitrary number of processors, (2) two-processor scheduling with all tasks requiring one or two time units [Coffman].

Kaufman [1974] reported an algorithm similar to Hu's algorithm that works on a tree containing tasks with arbitrary execution time. This algorithm finds a schedule in time bounded by $(1 + (m - 1) T_{long}) / T_{total}$, where m = number of processors,

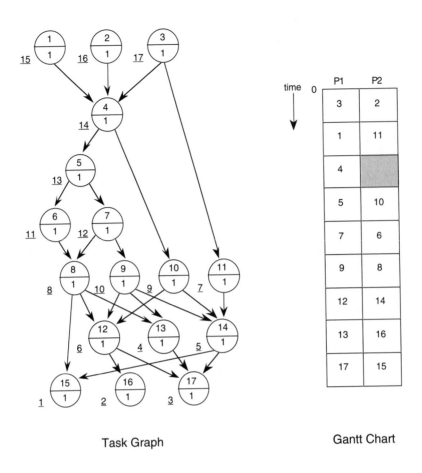

Task Graph

Gantt Chart

Figure 9.8   Task graph and its optimal Gantt chart on two processors

T_{long} = longest task execution time, and T_{total} = summation of all task execution times.

All of the algorithms described above belong to the more general class of HLF-algorithms (highest-level-first), which have also been called CP (critical path), LP (longest path), or LPT (largest processing time) algorithms.

Since no schedule for an arbitrary graph can be shorter than its critical path, the level number or critical path length is the key to successful precedence task scheduling. In fact, experimental studies of simulated task graphs show that very simple HLF algorithms can produce optimal schedules most of the time for unit time tasks (within 90% of optimal for over 700 cases) [Bashir], HLF algorithms yield "near optimal" schedules most of the time for arbitrary time tasks (4.4% away from optimal in 899 of 900 cases). HLF algorithms also provided the best results compared to other scheduling algorithms (847 cases of 900 cases) [Adam]. Bounds on the ratio of HLF algorithm schedules versus optimal schedules are summarized in Table 9.1.

Kohler [1975] suggested a branch-and-bound algorithm to obtain the optimal solution for an arbitrary task graph. The algorithm begins with construction of a searching tree. Then an elimination rule is used to eliminate branches that violate the constraints, and a selection rule is used to select only the most promising branches first. Therefore, only part of the solution space is searched. The algorithm is very general and can be applied to many kinds of scheduling problems. Branch-and-bound guarantees an optimal solution, but the solution space for the precedence-constraint scheduling problem is very large. Therefore, the branch-and-bound algorithm is much slower than HLF algorithms. Also, it is generally difficult to find a good selection and elimination rule.

Precedence	m^*	T^*	Algorithm	Bound
Tree	Ar^*	$=1$	Algorithm 9.1	optimal
Ar	$=2$	$=1$	Algorithm 9.2	optimal
Ar	$=2$	Ar	HLF	4/3
Ar	Ar	Ar	HLF	$2-1/(m-1)$

Table 9.1 HLF algorithms vs. optimal schedules

$^*m$ = number of processors, T = task execution time, Ar = arbitrary (precedence, number of processors, execution times)

9.6 SCHEDULING HEURISTICS

As shown in the previous section, optimal schedules can be obtained in very restricted cases. Even when the target machine is assumed to be fully connected and no communication is assumed between tasks in the task graph, the problem is still NP-complete in some restricted cases, as shown in Table 9.2. The complexity of the problem further increases because of such real-world factors such as: (1) tasks may have different execu-

Task Graph	Task Execution Time	Number of Processors	Complexity
Tree	identical	arbitrary	$O(n)$
arbitrary	identical	2	$O(n^2)$
arbitrary	identical	arbitrary	NP-complete
arbitrary	1 or 2 time units	≥ 2	NP-complete
arbitrary	arbitrary	arbitrary	NP-complete

Table 9.2 Complexity comparison of scheduling problem. Assuming fully connected target machine and no communication

tion times, (2) communication links between tasks may consume a variable amount of communication time, (3) communication links may be themselves shared, thus giving rise to contention for the links, (4) the network topology may influence the schedule due to multiple-hop links, or missing links, and (5) the parallel program may contain loops and branches.

It is well known that linear speedup generally does not occur in a multiprocessor system because adding additional processors to the system also increases interprocessor communication. In order to be more realistic, communication delay needs to be considered in scheduling tasks onto a multiprocessor system. Prastein [1987] proved that by taking communication into consideration, the problem of scheduling an arbitrary precedence program graph onto two processors is NP-complete and scheduling a tree-structured program onto fully connected many processors is also NP-complete.

Because of the computational complexity of optimal solution strategies, a need has arisen for a simplified suboptimal approach to this scheduling problem. Recent research in this area has emphasized heuristic approaches. A heuristic produces an answer in less than exponential time, but does not guarantee an optimal solution. Therefore, the term "near-optimal" means the solutions obtained by a heuristic fall near the optimal solution, "most of the time."

A heuristic is said to be better than another heuristic if solutions fall closer to optimality more often, or if the time taken to obtain a near-optimal solution is less.

Some of the principle difficulties encountered when designing schedulers of the general scheduling problem are presented in the following three subsections. The first two problems are due to communication delay, and the third problem is due to the alteration of critical paths of a task graph.

9.6.1 Parallelism Versus Communication Delay

When there is a communication delay, scheduling must be based on both the communication delay and the point in time when each processor is ready for execution. It is possible for ready tasks with long communication delays to end up assigned to the same processor as their immediate predecessors. For example, let us take a look at Gantt chart A of Figure 9.9. It can be noticed that the start time of task 3 on P_2 is later than its start time on P_1 since the communication delay D_x of task 3 is greater than the execution time of task 2. So task 3 should be assigned to P_1, which has its immediate predecessor. Conversely, as shown on Gantt chart B, if the communication delay D_x is less than the execution time of task 2, task 3 should be assigned to P_2 instead. Hence, adding the communication delay constraint increases the difficulty of arriving at an optimal schedule because the scheduler must examine the start time of each node on each available processor in order to select the best one.

As shown above, it would be a mistake to always increase the amount of parallelism available by simply starting each task as soon as possible. Distributing parallel tasks to as many processors as possible tends to increase the communication delay, which contributes to the overall execution time. In short, there is a trade-off between taking advan-

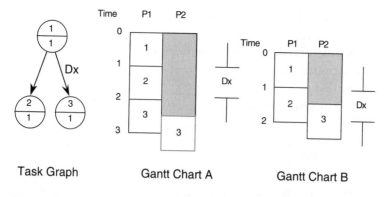

Task Graph   Gantt Chart A   Gantt Chart B

Figure 9.9   **The allocation consideration due to communication delay**

tage of maximal parallelism versus minimizing communication delay. This problem is called the *maxmin problem* for parallel processing.

The task graph in Figure 9.10 demonstrates the dramatic effect of the maxmin problem. If communication delay D_3 between task 1 and task 3 is less than the execution time of task 2, task 3 is assigned to P_2 in order to begin its execution sooner. Because task 2 and task 3 are the immediate predecessors of task 4, and they are assigned to different processors, task 4 cannot avoid the communication delay from one of its immediate predecessors. Thus, the execution time of this task graph is the summation of the execution times of tasks 1, 2, 4, plus communication delay D_x or D_y depending on where task 4 is assigned.

But, what happens if task 4 communication delays are larger than task 3 execution time? Then, assigning task 3 to P_1 will result in a shorter task graph execution time.

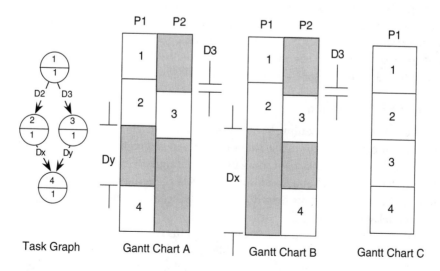

Task Graph   Gantt Chart A   Gantt Chart B   Gantt Chart C

Figure 9.10   **The trade-off between parallelism and communication delay**

This is so even if task 3 finishes its execution later than the previous assignment, as shown in Gantt chart C.

Current communication delay scheduling heuristics try to take advantage of parallelism and reduce communication delay. One solution is to favor the best task start time. Another method solves the maxmin problem by duplicating tasks where necessary to reduce the overall communication delay and maximize parallelism at the same time

9.6.2 Grain Size Problem

Another problem closely related to the maxmin problem is the *grain size problem*. The challenge of this problem is to determine the "best" clustering of tasks in the task graph such that the task graph execution time is minimized. The size of a cluster is altered by adding or removing tasks from the cluster. Such clusters are called *grains*.

If a grain is too big, parallelism is reduced because potentially concurrent tasks are grouped in a cluster and executed sequentially by one processor. If a grain is too small, more overhead in the form of context switching, scheduling time, and communication delay is added to the overall execution time.

The solution to the maxmin problem can be used to solve the grain size problem, since in the grain size problem, there is also a trade-off between parallelism (small grain) and communication (large grain).

For large grain, the order of execution of each small task grouped inside the larger grain is fixed before schedule time, and the order may not be the optimal one. Fixing the order of execution of the small grains too early in the algorithm might result in sequential execution of the whole task graph.

The grain size can be defined by grouping the scheduled tasks obtained from a small grain schedule to form a larger grain schedule. The grouping decision depends on the underlying parallel processor system hardware and software. Usually, the more we can group smaller grains, the shorter the task graph execution time because of the reduction of overhead. For more details about the grain size problem and its solutions, the reader may refer to [Kruatrachue].

9.6.3 Level Alteration

Another important scheduling problem caused by the introduction of nonzero communication delays is due to the alteration of node levels and their impact on critical path calculation. Any heuristic that uses level numbers or critical path length faces this problem. The level of a node is defined as the length of the longest path from the node to the exit node. This length includes all node execution times and all communication delay times along the path.

Node level was first used in scheduling by Hu. Adam et al. showed that among all priority schedulers, level priority schedulers are the best at getting close to the optimal schedule. Unfortunately, the level numbers do not remain constant when commu-

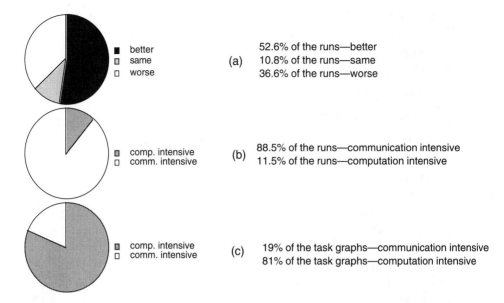

Figure 9.11 **(a)** **Using communication in calculating the level, (b)** **When using communication in calculating, the level is better, (c)** **When using communication in calculating, the level is worse**

nication delays are considered because the level of each node changes as the length of the path leading to the exit node changes. The path length varies depending on communication delay, and the communication delay changes depending on task allocation. Communication delay is zero if tasks are allocated to the same processor, and nonzero if tasks are allocated to different processors. Also, the number of hops between processors makes a difference in computing the communication delay portion of the level.

When the target machine processors are not identical, the execution time portion of the level again becomes hard to obtain because the execution time of a node depends on the speed of the processor that runs that node. We call this the *level number problem* for parallel processor scheduling.

Some heuristics assume identical processors and compute a node's level as the summation of node computation times along the path to the exit node excluding the communication delay. A better approximation of level number may be obtained by iteration: schedule, then calculate node level, schedule,…etc. The time complexity would be tremendously increased and the resulting level number would be only an approximation. Hence, the use of level as a priority for scheduling with communication delay is less accurate than that without communication delay.

We have conducted an experiment to show the effect of using communication delays in calculating the level of a node in a task graph. That is, when computing the level of a node as part of the scheduling heuristic, we add the communication delay to the execution time. The details of the experiment can be found in [El-Rewini

1990]. The results of the experiment suggest that for communication-intensive applications, the scheduler should consider communication delay in the scheduling algorithm's priority; however, for computation-intensive applications, priority scheduling is insensitive to the communication delays of the application. The pie charts given in Figure 9.11(a,b,c) summarize the results.

9.6.4 List Scheduling

In list scheduling each node (task) is assigned a priority, then a list of tasks is constructed in decreasing priority order. Whenever a processor is available, a ready task with the highest priority is selected from the list and assigned to the processor. If more than one task has the same priority, a task is selected randomly

The schedulers in this class differ only in the way that each scheduler assigns priorities to tasks. Priority assignment results in different schedules because tasks are selected in a different order. The comparison between different task priority (level, co-level, random) has been studied by Adam et al., which suggests that the use of level number as a priority is the nearest to optimal. More recent work by Lee et al. [1988] has extended the family of list algorithms to Earliest-Task-First and Earliest-Ready-Task variants. The list scheduling algorithm is given as follows.

Algorithm 9.3

1 The level of each node in the task graph is calculated and used as each node's priority. A priority queue is initialized for ready tasks by inserting every task that has no immediate predecessors. Tasks are sorted according to the level priorities of their tasks, with the highest priority task first.

2 As long as the priority queue is not empty, do the following:
(i) Obtain a task from the front of the queue.
(ii) Select a processor to run the task. A processor is selected in such a way that the task cannot finish on any other processor earlier. The selected task is then allocated to the selected processor.
(iii) When a task finishes execution, the number of reasons that prevent any of its immediate successors from being run (initially equal to the number of its immediate predecessors) is decreased by one. When all the immediate predecessors of a particular task are executed, that successor can be added to the ready queue.

3 Step 2 is repeated until all the task graph nodes are scheduled.

Example 9.3

Consider the task graph shown in Figure 9.12. In this example, we take the approach that excludes communication in calculating the level of each node. The underlined number next to each node gives its level. Initially task 1 is the only ready task because it does not have any predecessors. The table in Figure 9.13 gives the task number, the number of reasons that prevent each task from starting execution which is initialized as the number of immediate predecessors, and the level of each task.

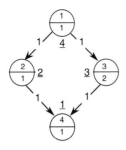

Figure 9.12 An example of a task graph. The underlined number next to each node indicates its level.

Task	#Pr	Level
1	0	4
2	1	2
3	1	3
4	2	1

#Pr : number of immediate predecessors
that are not yet executed

Figure 9.13 The table shows each task, its level, and the number of its immediate predecessors that are not yet executed

Figure 9.14 illustrates the step-by-step execution of the main list scheduler along with the scheduling result in the Gantt chart form, ready queue, and task graph at each scheduling step, given the sample task graph in Figure 9.12 and a target machine consisting of two identical processors. The heuristic used in this example selects the processor that has the earliest start time for each assigned task with consideration to the communication delay. The reader is advised to follow the four steps given in Figure 9.14 to fully understand list scheduling.

9.6.5 Task Duplication

Task duplication heuristics use duplication of tasks to offset communication. The duplication solves the maxmin problem by duplicating the tasks that influence the communication delay. As shown in Figure 9.15, task 1 is duplicated to run on both P_1 and P_2. This duplication decreases the starting time of task 3 on P_2. Thus, task 5 can start execution sooner than if we were to assign tasks 2 and 3 to the same processor. It can be noticed that duplicating task 1 takes advantage of parallelism and reduces communication delay at the same time.

Kruatrachue [1987] introduced a list scheduling heuristic based on the concept of task duplication. The main part of the heuristic is the task duplication process (TDP). The inputs to TDP are the ready task with the highest priority (T_{HP}) and a candidate processor (P_C). TDP calculates the starting time ST of the task T_{HP}, and constructs the so-called duplication task list (DTLST). The duplication task list is a list of duplicated tasks and their starting times on the candidate processor P_C.

TDP begins with the calculation of the message ready time of the task T_{HP}. The message ready time of a task is the time when all the messages to the task have been received by its processor.

TDP also finds the latest immediate predecessor task (LIP) that sends the message that arrives last. Then, if T_{HP}'s starting time is greater than P_C's ready time (there is a communication delay) and the LIP was not assigned to P_C, TDP tries to

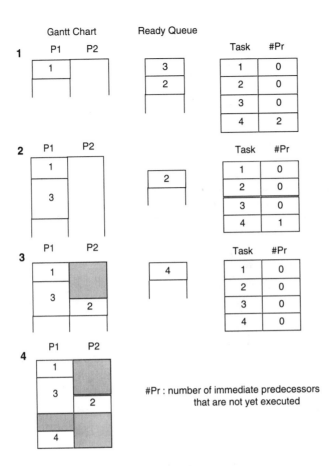

Figure 9.14 Gantt chart construction

minimize the communication delay by copying predecessor(s) of T_{HP} to P_C with the hope that the copy-task will reduce the communication delay.

To copy LIP, there are two cases depending on where LIP is located. First, we define the idle time slot of a processor to be the time interval between the processor's ready time and its assigned task's starting time.

Case 1: LIP is not assigned to P_C.

TDP tries to copy LIP task into the idle time slot of P_C, since the duplication of the LIP may improve the start time of T_{HP}.

Case 2: The LIP has already been duplicated in the idle time slot of P_C.

In order to start the T_{HP} sooner, the LIP has to start execution sooner. Thus, the DTLST is searched to find the task that affects the start time of the LIP task. The search starts with the LIP of the LIP of the T_{HP}. If that task is assigned to some other processor, the search process stops and that task is the search task. Otherwise, the process searches deeper levels until it finds the LIP of the LIP task that is located in some other processor, and that task becomes the search task.

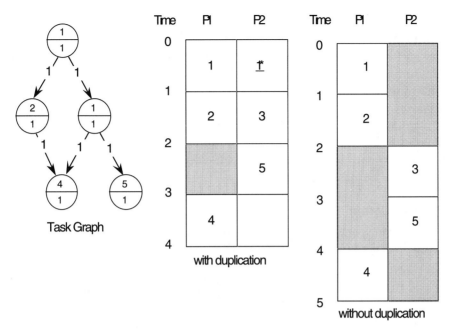

Task Graph

with duplication

without duplication

* underlined number indicates duplicated node

Figure 9.15   Task duplication heuristics

Once the search task is found, it is copied into the idle time slot of the P_C. Then all the duplicated tasks that start after the copied task are removed and recopied due to the duplication of the search task. The reason for recopying is that the start time (and the order in DTLST) of the task located after the copied-search task may change due to the presence of the search task. The recopy may indirectly cause the LIP task starting time to decrease so the T_{HP} can start execution sooner. The duplication process continues until duplication fails or the LIP was already assigned to P_C (no reason to copy).

To copy a task, the starting time of the copied task and the LIP task of the copied task have to be determined first. If the copied task starting time is within the idle time slot and no duplicated task is assigned to that time, then the duplication is successful and the LIP of the copied task is recorded for the purpose of searching as previously described. If the copied task starting time is not in the idle time slot, the LIP task of the copied task has to be duplicated if possible. Otherwise, the copy fails and the duplication process is terminated at that point. If the idle time slot is large enough, TDP will continue to duplicate the predecessors of the T_{HP} in order to make the task start sooner.

9.6.6 Target Machine Interconnection Topology

The mapping heuristic (MH) proposed by El-Rewini [El-Rewini 1990] considers real-world constraints such as the interconnection topology of the target machine. It tries to achieve three goals: (1) to include delays due to contention in communication, (2) to find message passing routes with lower communication delays, and (3) to produce more realistic schedules and timing information. MH keeps contention information in tables and updates them when certain events take place so it can make scheduling decisions based on a current traffic state. The output of MH is the allocation of tasks onto processors and the task execution order that optimizes the completion time of the parallel program.

System Parameters

The following parameters are required to represent the computational and communication costs incurred in a specific parallel processing system.

1 T_{ij}: the execution time of task i when executed on processor j. It reflects the speed of the processors and the size of the tasks and can be computed as follows:

$$T_{ij} = A_i/S_j$$

Here

A_i = the number of instructions to be executed in task i

S_j = the speed of processor j.

2 $C(i_1, i_2, j_1, j_2)$: the communication delay between tasks i_1 and i_2 when they are executed on processing elements j_1 and j_2, respectively. It reflects the target machine performance parameters as well as the size of the data to be transmitted and can be computed as follows:

$$C(i_1, i_2, j_1, j_2) = \left(\frac{D_{i_1 i_2}}{R} + I\right) \times H_{j_1 j_2} + CD_{j_1 j_2}$$

Here

D_{ij} = the size of the data to be sent from task i to j.

R = the transmission rate over the link connecting any two adjacent processors.

I = the time to initiate message passing on the I/O channel.

H_{ij} = number of hops between processing elements i and j.

CD_{ij} = communication delay due to contention when sending data from processors i to j.

It is assumed that the I/O processors are identical and take the same amount of time to initiate a message. It is also assumed that the transmission rate is the same over all of the interconnection network.

3 L_{ij}: the preferred outgoing line to use when sending data from processor i to j.

Mapping Heuristic (MH)

MH is a modified list scheduling technique. It uses the level of each node in the task graph as each node's priority. It breaks ties by selecting the task with the largest number of immediate successors. If this does not break the tie, it selects a task at random.

When a task is ready, a processor is selected to run that task in such a way that the task cannot finish earlier on any other processor. The parameters T and C, which reflect the speed of the processors, interconnection topology, and contention are considered when a processor is selected. The selected task is then allocated to the selected processing element. The following function explains how to compute the finish time of task t on processor p.

function finish_time(t,p)
begin
Let IMP be the set of all immediate predecessors of t.
    if IMP is empty **then**
        finish_time $\leftarrow$ ready_time[P] + T_{tp}
    else
        Let IMP = $\{t_1, t_2, \ldots, t_m\}$
        where t_i is assigned to processor $p[t_i]$.
        Time_message_ready $\leftarrow$ max(ready_time[$p[t_i]$]+ $C(t_i, t, p[t_i], p)$), $1 \leq i \leq m$.
        start_time $\leftarrow$ max(Time_message_ready, ready_time[p])
        finish_time $\leftarrow$ start_time + T_{tp}
end.

When a task is done, the status of the immediate successors of the finished task is modified. So when a task finishes execution, the number of conditions that prevent any of its immediate successors from being run is decreased by one. When the number of conditions associated with a particular successor becomes zero, then that successor node can be scheduled.

Two time delays contribute to the communication delay: (1) the time delay incurred in transmitting data over an empty route, and (2) the queuing delay (contention) due to multiple messages sent through the same route. In order to compute the delay due to contention, for each processor in the system, we maintain a routing table that has contention information indexed by, and containing one entry for, each other processor. This entry contains three parts: (1) the number of hops (H), (2) the preferred outgoing line to use for that destination (L), and (3) the communication delay due to contention (CD).

Initially, we use the shortest path between any two processing elements to determine the number of hops (H) and the preferred outgoing line (L). If we have more

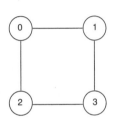

	0			1			2			3		
	H	L	CD	H	L	CD	H	L	CD	H	L	CD
0	0	–	0	1	0	0	1	0	0	2	2	0
1	1	1	0	0	–	0	2	0	0	1	1	0
2	1	2	0	2	3	0	0	–	0	1	2	0
3	2	1	0	1	3	0	1	3	0	0	–	0

Figure 9.16   A target machine with 4 processing elements and their associated tables

than one shortest path, we just pick any one randomly. The delay (CD) is assigned zero. We use H_{ij} to refer to the number of hops between processing elements i,j (could be longer than the shortest path). Also, L_{ij} and CD_{ij} are used similarly.

Figure 9.16 shows a parallel computer system with four processing elements forming a ring (cube) and the initial tables for the four processing elements. For example, the value of L_{12} is 3, as shown from the table associated with processing element 1.

The tables maintained for each processing element are used to obtain the "best" route to send a message and to compute communication delay which guides the selection of the best processor for a certain task.

The tables maintained for each processing element are updated during scheduling so that the decisions made in choosing a route to send a message or selecting a processor to run a task are based on information about the current traffic. We should keep in mind that the more often the tables are updated, the better view of the current traffic we get. However, frequent updating becomes more expensive. There is a trade-off between having a real view of the traffic and the complexity of the update procedure. MH updates the tables when either of the following two events happen during scheduling: Event 1) a task starts sending a message to another task, Event 2) a message arrives at its destination. The first event is important because it keeps communication routes busy during transmission. The second event is important because it frees a route for sending messages by other processing elements in the system.

We perform the update twice for each arc in the task graph. Recall that in a dataflow-like model, each arc is used only once. Not every table is updated, only those tables associated with the processing elements on the routes where traffic status is affected as a result of having one or more messages occupying some (or all) of the channels on those routes. Tables are updated only once. Tables of processing elements on the communication route are updated first (Direct Effect on the Route), then the tables of the neighbors that have been affected and have not been updated yet are updated (Indirect Effect on Neighbors).

Event 1 Update

Suppose that task t_1 on processing element p_1 sends a message to task t_2 on processing element p_2.

Direct Effect on the Route (Event 1): All tables of processing elements on the route from p_1 to p_2 except p_2 are updated. The table associated with processing element p_2 is not updated because the route from p_2 to other processing elements has not been affected. The following procedures explain the update process.

procedure Direct_Effect_on_the_Route_Event_1 (t_1, t_2, p_1, p_2)
    begin
        (* task t_1 on p_1 sends a message to t_2 on p_2 *)
        transmission $\leftarrow (D_{t_1 t_2} / R + I)$.
        Update_Delay (transmission, p_1, p_2, 1, delay)
    end

procedure Update_Delay (transmission, p_1, p_2, event, **var** delay)
    begin
        if $L_{p_1 p_2} = p_2$ **then**
            begin
                case   event = 1 delay $\leftarrow CD_{p_1 p_2}$ + transmission.
                           event = 2 delay $\leftarrow CD_{p_1 p_2}$ - transmission.
                $CD_{p_1 p_2} \leftarrow$ delay
            end
        else
            begin
                Update_Delay (transmission, p_1, $L_{p_1 p_2}$, event, delay$_1$)
                Update_Delay (transmission, $L_{p_1 p_2}$, p_2, event, delay$_2$)
                delay $\leftarrow$ delay$_1$ + delay$_2$
                $CD_{p_1 p_2} \leftarrow$ delay
            end

    end

Consider the target machine given in Figure 9.16. Suppose that task t_1 is assigned to processing element 0 ($p_1 = 0$) and task t_2 is assigned to processing element 3 ($p_2 = 3$), and $D_{t_1 t_2} = 5$. Also assume that $R = 1$ and $I = 0$. Using the previous procedure, tables 0 and 1 are updated as follow:

	0			1		
	H	L	CD	H	L	CD
0	0	–	0	1	0	0
1	1	1	5	0	–	0
2	1	2	0	2	3	0
3	2	1	10	1	3	5

It has an indirect effect on neighbors. The tables of the neighbors of processing elements with updated tables are updated according to the following procedures.

procedure Indirect_Effect_on_Neighbors (p_1, p_2)
    begin
        Let A be the set of all neighbors of p_1.
        $p_{next} \leftarrow L_{p_1 p_2}$
        $A' \leftarrow A - \{p_{next}\}$
        enqueue all elements of A' in Q.
        while Q is not empty **do**
            begin
                dequeue (Q,p) (* get p from the front of Q *)
                if the table associated with p has not been updated yet
                    then
                        begin
                        Let A" be the set of all neighbors of p.
                        Update_Neighbors(A", p).
                        enqueue all elements of A" in Q.
                end
            end
    end

procedure Update_Neighbors (A, p)
    begin
        Let A = $\{a_1, a_2,..., a_b\}$.
        for i := 0 to N-1 **do**
        begin
            $CD_{pi} \leftarrow CD_{pa_k} + CD_{a_k i}$
           $L_{pi} \leftarrow a_k$
           $H_{pi} \leftarrow 1 + H_{a_k i}$
           where $CD_{pa_k} + CD_{a_k i} \leq CD_{pa_j} + CD_{a_j i}$, $1 \leq j \leq b$.
        end
    end

Consider the target machine given in Figure 9.16. As shown earlier, only tables 0 and 1 have been updated after direct effect update. Now we do the indirect effect on the neighbors of processing element 0. It can be noticed that $p_1 = 0$, $p_{next} = 1$, $A = \{1,2\}$, $A' = \{2\}$, and Q has only one element 2. Processing element 2 needs to modify its table according to information from its neighbors, processing elements 0 and 3. The tables associated with the neighbors of processing element 2 (0 and 3) and the new table for 2 are shown below. It can be noticed that $CD_{20} = 0$ and $CD_{23} = 0$. Consider how the new route from 2 to 1 is computed. Processing element 2 knows it can have $CD_{21} = 5$ (5 + 0) if it takes the route passing by 0 or $CD_{21} = 0$ (0 + 0) if it takes the route passing by 3. The best of these two values is 0, of course, so we update the route to go through 3.

	0			3			2		
	H	L	CD	H	L	CD	H	L	CD
0	0	–	0	2	2	0	1	0	0
1	1	1	5	1	1	0	2	3	0
2	1	2	0	1	2	0	0	–	0
3	2	1	10	0	–	0	1	3	0

Event 2 Update

Suppose that the message sent from task t_1 on processing element p_1 to task t_2 on processing elements p_2 has already arrived.

Direct Effect on the Route (Event 1): All the tables of the processing elements on the route from p_1 to p_2 except p_2 are updated according to the following procedure.

procedure Direct_Effect_on_the_Route_Event_2 (t_1, t_2, p_1, p_2)
    begin
    (* a message from t_1 on p_1 to t_2 on p_2 has already arrived*)
    transmission $\leftarrow$ $(D_{t_1 t_2} / R + I)$.
    Update_Delay (transmission, p_1, p_2, 2, delay)
    end

Indirect Effect on Neighbors (Event 2). The tables of the neighbors of processing elements with updated tables are updated according to the same algorithm given earlier for Event 1.

Consider the target machine given in Figure 9.16 after reflecting the direct effect update and the indirect effect on neighbors as shown earlier. Now suppose that task t_2 on processing element 3 has already received its message from task t_1 on processing element 0 and is about to start execution. Now it is time to update the tables according to "Event 2 Update" which produces the original tables given in Figure 9.16 with the only difference in the table associated with processing element 2, the route from 2 to 1 goes through 3 instead of 0.

9.7 EXAMPLE: ATMOSPHERIC SCIENCE APPLICATION

In this section we show the result of scheduling a finite element technique applied to an atmospheric science application on a parallel machine [Judge]. In this application, the Spatial Coherence Method is used to analyze images produced from satellite data to determine cloud cover and cloud free radiances of specific regions. A typical scene of data consists of an array of 256*256 pixel values. Each scene typically

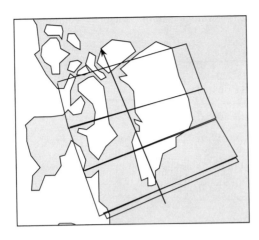

Figure 9.17 Six scenes of satellite data over Greenland

covers an actual 1000 km^2 region (see Figure 9.17). Based on the *Spatial Coherence Method,* the analysis scheme is able to derive an estimate for fractional cloud cover and radiative properties for a fixed scene of data. AVHTST is the first pass of a series of routines which implement this method. AVHTST first takes a scene of data as input, divides it into frames, and calculates local means and standard deviations of 1024 2*2 pixel arrays.

This application was analyzed on a number of parallel computer interconnection networks, but only the schedule for a hypercube interconnection is shown in Figure 9.18.

In Figure 9.18(a), the task nodes are numbered from 1 to 18. Below the task node numbers is the time estimate for executing that node. Next to each arc is a time estimate for the communication delay. While the communication delay was one for this application, the technique accommodates any positive integer delay. It is important to note that this task graph is for only one simple instance of the problem—when we have one scene of data with 2 frames in each direction. The typical scene of data with 4 frames in each direction would have a task graph with 66 nodes (as opposed to only 18 for this example).

Figure 9.18(b) shows the interconnection of 8 processing elements arranged as a hypercube. Notice the number of "hops" from one processor to the next. The number of hops will determine the schedule, along with processing loads, and communication intensity.

Figure 9.18(c) shows the schedule derived by the MH list scheduling heuristic. The labeled dark segments correspond with task execution; the lighter segments correspond with communication delays; and the clear segments mean the processor is idle. The number in each communication segment refers to the source task that is sending a message to the destination task (when a destination task is waiting for more than one source task, the largest message is the only one shown).

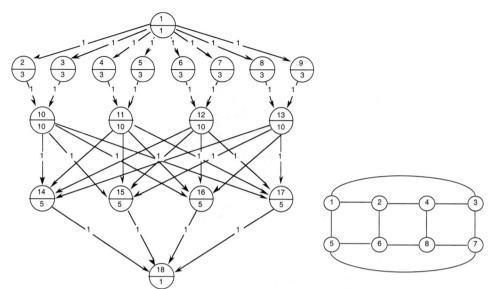

Figure 9.18(a) Program task graph

Figure 9.18(b) Hypercube of dimension 3

In the example, it should be pointed out that the tasks 7, 8, and 9 are delayed in their execution because they are placed on processors that are two hops away from processor 1. This introduces additional communication delay. Tasks on the same processor enjoy zero delays in communication.

9.8   TASK GRAPHER: A PRACTICAL SCHEDULING TOOL

Because we believe that different heuristics apply to different kinds of problems, we are led to the conclusion that the best solutions are obtained in cooperation with a human designer. Task Grapher is a tool to answer "what if..." questions about a parallel program design, and to provide information that can be used to fine-tune a design before it is actually run on a parallel computer.

Task Grapher produces schedules in the form of Gantt charts for a number of scheduling heuristics, performance charts in the form of line and bar graphs, simple animations in the form of a simulation, and critical path analysis.

With Task Grapher, a user can: (1) model a parallel program as a task graph, (2) choose a method of optimization from several scheduling heuristics which will automatically schedule tasks onto processors, (3) choose the topology of the desired target machine or design an arbitrary topology for the parallel processor of interest, and (4) observe anticipated scheduling and performance estimates obtained from the mapping of a task graph onto a target machine.

A parallel program is represented by a task graph as shown in Figure 9.18(a). Each node represents a task—nodes are numbered, and they are assigned an estimate repre-

Processors

Time	1	2	3	4	5	6	7	8
1	1							
2	3	1	1	1	1	1	1	
3		4	5		6			
4				7		8	9	
5	2							
6								
7		6		11	8			
16	10	12			13			
17								
18	12	10	10		10			
19	15							
23		16	17		14			
24								
25	16							
26	18							

Figure 9.18(c)   Gantt chart schedule

senting the execution time for the task. Each arc represents an information flow from one task to another. The arcs are labeled with an estimate of the size of the message transmitted from node to node—this number can be converted into a communication time delay estimate once the performance of the interprocessor communication link is known. Task execution time can vary from node to node, and communication arcs can be labeled with any positive value. However, not all heuristics use this information in computing a schedule. For example, the algorithm proposed by Hu ignores communication delay estimates.

After a task graph is entered, various functions can be performed on it. The main purpose is to compute schedules using one or more heuristics. We want to know which schedule is "best," and we want to ask various "what if..." questions. For example, what is the schedule if we use the algorithm proposed by Hu?

Figure 9.18(c) shows a schedule computed by Task Grapher for the n = 18 node task graph given in Figure 9.18(a). This schedule assumed 8 processors organized as a hypercube as shown in Figure 9.18(b), but the program designer might ask, "what if there were 16 processors?"

Any number of processors can be selected, and a corresponding Gantt chart computed, but a more insightful display is a speedup line graph which compares the

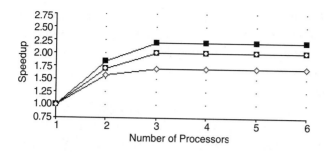

Figure 9.19 Speedup line curve for three different heuristics

expected performance improvement versus the number of processors employed. A speedup chart can be generated by computing schedules while the number of processors is varied from 2 to *n*.

Figure 9.19 shows speedup line graphs for the atmospheric science application. It shows speedups for one or more scheduling heuristic in one line graph. This can be an effective method of resolving "what if..." questions.

9.8.1 Task Grapher Heuristics

Task Grapher incorporates a number of scheduling heuristics that are based on the following basic scheduling algorithm.
Assign task priorities
repeat
    Select a task
    Select a processor to run the task
    Assign the task to the processor
until all tasks are scheduled

Although these algorithms agree in the task selection portion of the basic algorithm (the task with the highest priority is scheduled first), they use different techniques in assigning priorities to tasks and tasks to processors. They also use different assumptions regarding the task graph parameters or the target machine interconnection.

Algorithm 1 (Hu without Communication) [Hu]

Hu presented a linear heuristic scheduler using node level as a scheduling priority. This heuristic constructs an optimal length schedule for a tree-structured task set by assuming task processing time equal to one, and identical processors, see section 9.5.1. This heuristic can also schedule any acyclic task graph in linear time; however, the solution is not optimal. Although his results were very good, the heuristic assumes no communication delay in the parallel processing system.

Algorithm 2 (Hu with Communication) [Kruatrachue]

This algorithm is a modification of algorithm 1 that considers communication. Task selection criterion remains the same as described in algorithm 1. The communication delay is included in computing the start time of a selected task when selecting a processor. The processors containing the assigned node's immediate predecessors are considered first in an attempt to reduce communication delay by placing message source and destination tasks in the same processor.

Algorithm 3 (Equal Node Size) [Yu]

Yu's heuristics are based on Hu's algorithm. Yu's improvements were to consider communication delays when making task assignments, and to use a combinatorial min-max weight matching scheme at each task assignment step. Yu's results were compared with results from Hu's algorithms, and the comparisons were good for large communication delays. However, the results were not significantly different from those of Hu for small communication delays. Also, nodes in the application task graph must have identical size (execution time) and so must the communication delays.

Algorithm 4 (ISH) [Kruatrachue]

The Insertion Scheduling Heuristic (ISH) tries to utilize processor idle time by inserting ready tasks into idle time slots. This added factor complicates the scheduling problem, but offers a more realistic result.

Algorithm 5 (DSH-1) [Kruatrachue]

This heuristic is a based on the task duplication idea. The algorithm duplicates only immediate predecessors, reducing communication delay, before each task is allo-

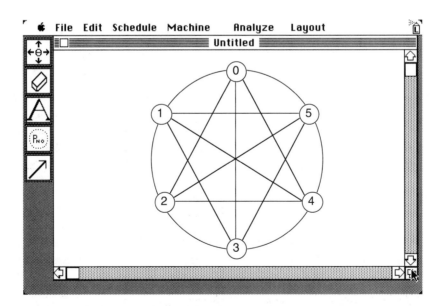

Figure 9.20 Fully connected interprocessor connection topology—any connection topology can be evaluated by entering the topology into this screen

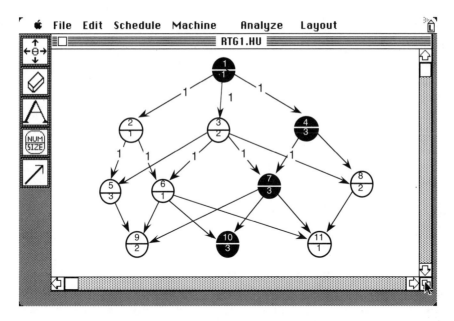

Figure 9.21   The shaded nodes show which tasks lie along the path of greatest execution time

cated. This lowers the time-complexity of the DSH algorithm, but may decrease the quality of the schedule.

Algorithm 6 (DSH-2) [Kruatrachue]

This is a full task duplication algorithm that duplicates all of the ancestor tasks which influence communication delays for each assigned task. It is an $O(n^4)$ algorithm.

Algorithm 7 (MH) [El-Rewini 1990]

This heuristic uses the mapping heuristic given in Section 9.6.6.

9.8.2   Target Machine Topology

The performance of a parallel program represented as a task graph is influenced by the interconnection topology of the parallel processors. Figure 9.20 shows the topology of a fully connected system, but in general, tree, mesh, toroid, and hypercube topologies are of interest and can be automatically generated by the tool. In addition, we would like to ask "what is the effect on expected speedup if the underlying topology is changed?" This question is answered by selecting an alternate topology, or by manually drawing an arbitrary network on the screen and producing a new speed-up line graph.

9.8.3 Critical Path Analysis

Feedback from Task Grapher is used to improve the performance of a parallel program design. A variety of performance measures can be used to discover what hinders greater performance. But the feature of greatest interest to a designer will be the path of greatest delay, e.g., the critical path through the task graph.

A critical path in a task graph is a path from the beginning node to the terminating node, which represents the longest execution delay. This is the portion of the program containing the greatest opportunity for improvement. Figure 9.21 shows how Task Grapher displays a critical path. The tasks and arcs along this path are candidates for tuning.

9.8.4 Other Visual Outputs from Task Grapher

In addition to the displays given above, Task Grapher can display bar charts showing the percentage of total processing time performed by each of the processors and the average efficiency of parallel systems of different size. The efficiency is defined as the speedup achieved by the parallel machine divided by the number of processors. The utilization chart shown in Figure 9.22 can be used to study processor load balance. Figure 9.23 shows the bar chart produced by Task Grapher to study the effect of using target machines with different numbers of processors on the efficiency.

Greater insight can be obtained by watching a parallel program execute dynamically. Task Grapher incorporates a design simulator which shows the dynamic behavior of the parallel program design. This is done by animation of the topology screen.

The animation feature gives immediate feedback and insight into the dynamic behavior of parallel programs. Idleness, congestion, and other measures of "goodness"

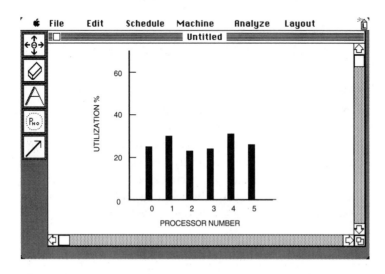

Figure 9.22 Processor utilization chart of a target machine with six processors

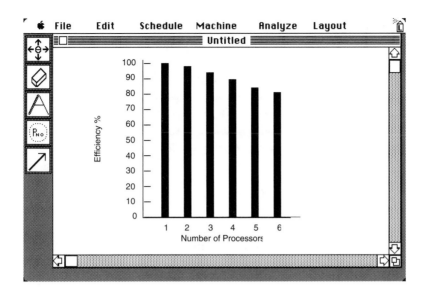

Figure 9.23 Average efficiency chart produced by task grapher

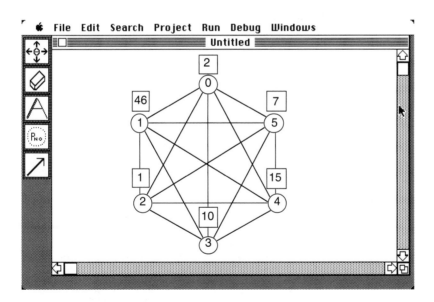

Figure 9.24 Dynamic activity display of a task graph on 6 processors forming a fully connected machine. At the time of the snap shot tasks 1, 2, 7, 10, 15, and 46 were assigned to processors 2, 0, 5, 3, 4, and 1, respectively

become vividly obvious after only a few minutes of using Task Grapher. These observations do not always support intuition, and lead to a new understanding of parallel programming.

Figure 9.24 shows a snapshot of the dynamic activity display. Tasks are dynamically assigned to processors as execution of the parallel program is simulated over time. The number of the node that is currently executing on each processor is displayed in a box above each processor node. When the task terminates, it is replaced by the next task to execute, or else the processor goes idle.

PROBLEMS FOR DISCUSSION AND SOLUTION

1 Consider the task graph of Figure 9.7(a). What is the minimum number of processors required to execute all tasks in 4 units of time? Devise a Gantt chart showing a schedule for the same task graph on a fully connected target machine of 4 identical processors.

2 Find the time complexity of the task duplication algorithm in Section 9.6.5.

3 Conduct a thorough comparison between static and dynamic scheduling. Show some cases where one approach may perform better than the other.

4 Suggest a model for representing conditional branching (IF statements) in the task graph. Develop a static scheduling algorithm that can handle your new task graph with conditional branching.

5 Prove that algorithm 9.2 produces an optimal schedule for a two-processor target machine.

6 Using the task duplication idea presented in Section 9.6.5, devise a Gantt chart schedule for the task graph given in Figure 9.18(a) when the communication on all arcs is 10 and the target machine has 4 processors.

7 Repeat problem 6 using the mapping heuristic (MH) when the target machine is:
(a) two-dimensional hypercube,
(b) mesh-connected machine with 9 processors.

8 All the task graphs we studied in Chapter 9 are acyclic ones. How can we represent loops in the task graph? How do loops affect the complexity of the problem? Can you suggest a static scheduling strategy that can handle loops in the task graph?

9 Show how the visual outputs from the Task Grapher can help the parallel program designer to produce better programs. Study the critical path analysis, speedup curves, processor utilization, and efficiency chart.

References

Adam, T., Chandy, K., and Dickson, J. A., "Comparison of List Schedulers for Parallel Processing Systems," *Comm. ACM,* Volume 17, pp. 685 – 690, December 1974.

Bashir, A., Susarla, and Karavan, K., "A Statistical Study of a Task Scheduling Algorithm," *IEEE Transaction Comput.,* Volume C–32, No. 8, pp. 774 – 777, August 1983.

Bokhari, S., "A Shortest Tree Algorithm for Optimal Assignments Across Space and Time in Distributed Processor System," *IEEE Transaction on Software Engineering,* Volume SE–7, No. 6, November 1981.

Bokhari, S., "On the Mapping Problem," *IEEE Transactions on Computers,* C–30, 3, pp. 207 – 214, 1981.

Chen, N., and Liu, C., "On a Class of Scheduling Algorithm for Multiprocessing Systems, *Proceedings 1974 Segamore Computer Conference on Parallel Processing,* T. Feng, ed., Springer: Berlin, pp. 1 – 16, 1095

Coffman, E., *Computer and Job-Shop Scheduling Theory,* Wiley, New York, 1976.

Efe, K., "Heuristic Models of Task Assignment Scheduling in Distributed Systems," *IEEE Computer,* pp. 50 – 56, June 1982.

El-Rewini, H., and Lewis, T. G., "Scheduling Parallel Program Tasks Onto Arbitrary Target Machines," *Journal of Parallel and Distributed Computing,* June 1990.

El-Rewini, H., "Task Partitioning and Scheduling on Arbitrary Parallel Processing Systems," *Ph.D. Thesis,* Department of Computer Science, Oregon State University, 1990.

Hu, T., "Parallel Sequencing and Assembly Line Problems," *Operation Research,* Volume 9, pp. 841 – 848, 1961.

Judge, D., and Rudd, W., "A Test Case for the Parallel Programming Support Environment: Parallelizing the Analysis of Satellite Imagery Data," *Tech. Report 89–80–2,* Department of Computer Science, Oregon State University, 1989.

Kaufman, M. T., "An Almost-Optimal Algorithm for the Assembly Line Scheduling Problem," *IEEE Transaction Comput.,* Volume C-23, No. 11, pp. 1169 – 1174, November 1974.

Kohler, W. H., "A Preliminary Evaluation of the Critical Path Method for Scheduling Tasks on Multiprocessor Systems," *IEEE Transaction Comput.,* Volume C-15, No. 12, pp. 1235 – 1238, December 1975.

Kruatrachue, B., "Static Task Scheduling and Grain Packing in Parallel Processing Systems," *Ph.D. Thesis,* Department of Computer Science, Oregon State University, 1987.

Lee C. Y., Hwang, J. J., Chow, Y. C., and Anger, F. D., "Multiprocessor Scheduling with Interprocessor Communication Delays," *Operations Research Letters,* 7, 3, pp. 141 – 147, 1988.

Prastein, M., "Precedence-Constrained Scheduling with Minimum Time and Communication," *M.S. Thesis,* University of Illinois at Urbana-Champaign, 1987.

Sethi, R., "Scheduling Graphs on Two Processors," *SIAM J. Comput.,* Volume 5, No. 1, pp. 73 – 82, March 1976.

Stone, H., and Bokhari, S., "Control of Distributed Processes," *IEEE Computer,* pp. 85 – 93, July 1987.

Stone, H., "Multiprocessor Scheduling with the Aid of Network Flow Algorithms," *IEEE Transaction Software Eng.,* pp. 85 – 93, January 1977.

Ullman, J., "NP-Complete Scheduling Problems," *Journal of Computer and System Sciences,* Volume 10, pp. 384 – 393, 1975.

Yu, W. H., "LU Decomposition on a Multiprocessing System with Communication Delay, *Ph.D. Thesis,* Department of Electrical Engineering and Computer Sciences, University of California, Berkeley, 1984.

Chapter 10

Loop Scheduling

Loops are considered one of the largest sources of parallelism in parallel programming. Loops can be parallelized by assigning different loop iterations to different processors. Also, different tasks within the same iteration may be executed in parallel. The question is how to schedule both loop iterations and tasks in order to improve overall performance.

The factors to be considered in loop scheduling are *data dependencies* between loop iterations, *processor load balancing,* and the *overhead* due to *synchronization* and communication between tasks. These are the subjects of this chapter.

If there is no data dependency between tasks in different iterations, the iterations are completely independent and can be scheduled to run in parallel. However, they must be distributed evenly between system processors to maintain a satisfactory level of *load balancing* between system processors.

Communication between processors may be necessary if a data dependency relation exists between two loop iterations and the iterations are placed on separate processors. In this case, the iterations must be synchronized. Synchronization can degrade overall performance.

What about parallelism within each iteration? If we assign all tasks in one iteration to the same processor, the parallelism that might exist within loop iterations is not exploited. A loop scheduling policy should consider the parallelism that might exist between different loop iterations and within each iteration with minimum communication delay.

In this chapter, we give a brief introduction to data dependence in loops, which will be discussed again in more detail in Chapter 11. We then discuss scheduling loop iterations using static and dynamic methods. A load balancing technique called *loop spreading* evenly distributes parallel tasks on multiple processors when the times to execute the iterations of the loop are all equivalent.

Then, we introduce a solution to the problem of scheduling nested loops on parallel processors. This solution is based on loop unrolling and allows several iterations of a set of loops as well as tasks within the same iteration to overlap in execution in a way that minimizes loop completion time. This technique is extended to cover the case where the loop iterations consume different amounts of time, depending on the iteration number.

We highly recommend that the reader study the papers listed here for details on the performance of the techniques described, as space does not permit a full discussion.

10.1 DATA DEPENDENCE IN LOOPS

Independent loops in which no iteration depends on data passed from any other iteration, are perfect for parallel execution. If the iterations of a loop can be executed in random order and still produce the correct result, it is an independent loop.

But loops are rarely independent. *Dependent loops*, in which the dependency involves all the statements in the loop, must execute serially on any machine due to dependency. When the dependency does not involve all the statements in the loop, partial overlapping, or *pipelining* of successive iterations may be possible during execution.

Data dependence is a consequence of the flow of data in a program. A task that uses a variable in an expression is data dependent on the task which computes the value of that variable. Such a dependence between tasks forming a program is a kind of *precedence relation*. If task T_w is data-dependent on task T_v, then execution of task T_v must precede execution of task T_w.

Data dependence in loops can be further classified as *loop-carried* and *loop-independent* data dependence. When some tasks are contained in n nested loops, we can refer to separate instances of their execution using an *iteration vector* [Wolfe]. A vector $I = <i_1, i_2, ..., i_n>$ is called an iteration vector if the loop body is executed in the period when the jth level loop is in the i_jth iteration, $1 \le j \le n$. Simply, an iteration vector holds the values of the loop control variables of the n nested loops. We use $T(I)$ to denote the execution of task T during the iteration $I = <i_1, i_2, ..., i_n>$.

We define the *distance vector* for each dependence between two tasks. Suppose that T_v and T_w are two tasks enclosed in n nested loops and $T_w(I_w)$ is data dependent on $T_v(I_v)$, then the distance vector for this dependence is $I_d = I_w - I_v$. Task T_w is *loop-carried data dependent* on task T_v iff $I_w \ne I_v$, which means that the distance vector elements are not all zeros. Otherwise the dependence is called *loop-independent* (the distance vector elements are all zeros). Furthermore, T_w and T_v have level j loop-carried data dependence iff I_w and I_v agree in the first $j - 1$ elements.

10.2 SCHEDULING LOOP ITERATIONS

Loops can be parallelized by assigning different iterations of a loop to different processors. A loop at level j is completely parallelizable if the loop body does not have any loop-carried data dependencies at level j. A parallelizable loop of the form (*I*) can be parallelized using the parallel construct of form (*II*).

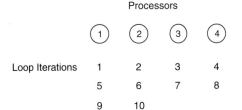

Processors

Loop Iterations

Figure 10.1   Static loop scheduling for 10 iterations on 4 processors

```
[I]   for i := 1 to N do      [II]   par i := 1 to N do
         s(i);                          s(i);
      endfor;                        endpar;
```

The parallel construct **par** uses N processes to execute the N iterations in parallel. To reduce the overhead caused by the *minimax problem*, most systems use fewer than N processors even though there may be $P > N$ processors in the system.

Static scheduling may apply when the loop iterations take roughly the same amount of time, and we know in advance how many iterations are required. Dynamic scheduling adjusts the schedule during execution, so we use it whenever it is uncertain how many iterations to expect, or the iterations take different amounts of time, due to a branch inside the loop.

10.2.1   Static Scheduling

Static or dynamic scheduling techniques can be used to schedule the N processes on P processors in some optimal way. Chapter 9 surveys the variety of scheduling techniques that may apply. We give details on how to adapt static scheduling to loop iteration scheduling in what follows.

Static scheduling is frequently used when loop iterations take roughly the same amount of execution time. In static scheduling, the N iterations are divided into $\lceil N/P \rceil$ *rounds*. In each round except the last one, P iterations are executed in parallel. In the last round (N mod P) iterations are executed in parallel. The parallel code using static scheduling for loop (I) is given as follows.

```
par g := 1 to P do
     for i:= g to N step P do
        s(i);
     endfor;
endpar;
```

Here, each processor executes code segments that are P iterations apart. Figure 10.1 illustrates how loop iterations are assigned to the processors, when $N = 10$ and $P = 4$.

Another way to schedule loop iterations statically is to assign $\lceil N/P \rceil$ iterations to each of the first (N mod P) processors. Each of the remaining ($P - N$ mod P) processors executes $\lfloor N/P \rfloor$ iterations. In this method, each processor executes a number of

Processors

Loop Iterations

	1	4	7	9
	2	5	8	10
	3	6		

Figure 10.2 Another static loop scheduling method for 10 iterations on 4 processors

adjacent iterations. Figure 10.2 shows this method when $N = 10$ and $P = 4$. The parallel code for loop (I) using this method is given as follows.

```
shares := (N+P-1) div P;
B := N mod P;
par g := 1 to P do
      if g <= B then
         for j:=1 to shares do
            i := (g-1)*shares + j
            s(i);
         endfor;
      else
         S := shares -1;
         for j:=1 to S do
            i := B* shares + (g-B-1)*S + j
            s(i);
         endfor;
      endif;
endpar;
```

Static scheduling may perform unacceptably when the loop iterations are of varying size, because the load on the processors might not be well balanced. This is one reason to use dynamic scheduling.

10.2.2 Dynamic Scheduling

In dynamic scheduling, processors take iterations from a shared *queue* of waiting iterations, they run the iteration as a task, and continue to schedule themselves in this manner until all iterations have been processed. Iterations are taken from the front of the shared queue, in FIFO (first-in-first-out) order (see Figure 10.3).

The parallel code for loop (I) using dynamic scheduling is given as follows.

```
par g := 1 to P do
      i := TopOfQueue();
      while NOT QueueEmpty() do
```

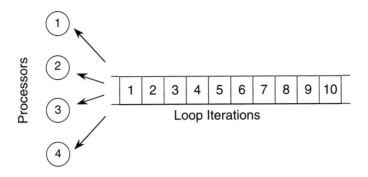

Figure 10.3 Dynamic scheduling (4 processors and 10 loop iterations)

```
        s(i);
      i := TopOfQueue();
    endwhile;
endpar;
```

Although this technique balances the load between processors, maintaining the shared queue introduces a decrease in performance due to overhead.

10.3 LOOP SPREADING

Balancing the distribution of iterations across all processors is a challenging requirement because of the mismatch between the number of iterations and the number of processors. *Loop spreading* is a technique for smoothing out the load across all processors even when there is a mismatch.

Suppose the number of processors P is less than the number of iterations N, and there is no data dependence across iterations. The loop can be executed in $\lceil N/P \rceil$ evenly balanced rounds except for the last round, which executes (N mod P) tasks. In many cases, all but one processor is idle in the last round, which causes a significant drop in performance. This performance drop becomes increasingly detrimental as the number of processors increases.

Figure 10.4 shows speedup of the parallel decomposed *simplex algorithm* using 8 processors [Wu]. Notice how speedup drops from over 6 to around 4 when the number of iterations changes from 8 to 9. The reason for the drop is that the parallel loop of 9 iterations must be executed in two rounds when using 8 processors. The second round uses only 1 processor, leaving the other 7 idle.

This phenomenon is not peculiar to the simplex algorithm. The usual way to execute a loop in parallel is to let each processor execute one iteration, and if more iterations remain, to have each processor execute one more iteration, and so on. When running a parallel loop that has N iterations on P processors, the formula for

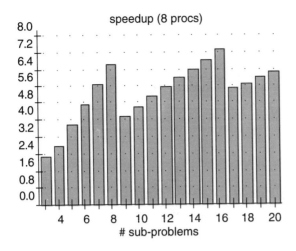

Figure 10.4 **Effect of processor load balance on performance of a parallel simplex algorithm using 8 processors**

speedup is $S(N) = N/\lceil N/P \rceil$. Figure 10.5 shows $S(N)$ when N changes from 1 to 30 for $P = 5$, 10, and 20. In this figure, we see that not only does the performance drop when executing parallel loops, but also the performance drop increases as the number of processors increases.

10.3.1 What is Loop Spreading?

Loop spreading is a technique introduced by Wu and Lewis [Wu; Wu and Lewis] to automatically restructure parallel loops so as to balance parallel tasks on multiple

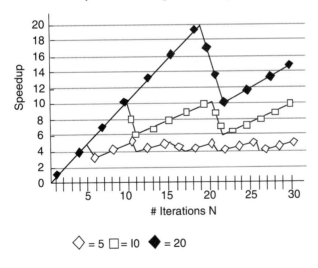

Figure 10.5 **Effect of processor load balance on parallel loops**

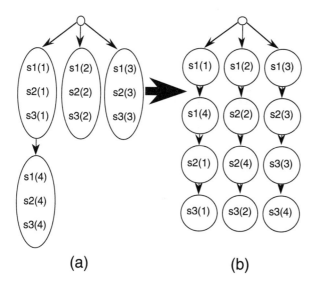

Figure 10.6 (a) Unbalance execution, (b) Balance execution

processors. A *spread loop* runs at least as fast as the nonspread loop even when $N \bmod P$ = 0, and shows no performance drop when the number of iterations changes. To describe loop spreading consider the following loop:

```
par i:=1 to 4 do
      s1(i); s2(i); s3(i);
endpar;
```

Assume that each task $s_j(i)$, $1 \le j \le 3$, $1 \le i \le 4$, takes T time units to execute on a single processor. We also assume $P = 3$ processors are used to run the loop in parallel.

At least one processor needs to execute two iterations of this loop so the total execution time will be $6T$. This execution is illustrated in Figure 10.6(a). However, if we spread $s_1(4)$, $s_2(4)$, and $s_3(4)$ to different processors, as shown in Figure 10.6(b), the total execution time becomes only $4T$ time units, and the restructuring leads to a significant performance improvement.

In the remainder of this section we give algorithms for loop spreading in two cases: (1) when the statements inside a loop are independent, and (2) when the statements are dependent. We also give results of performance analysis studies using the loop spreading technique.

10.3.2 Algorithm for Independent Substatements

Assume statements $s_1(i)$, $s_2(i)$, ..., $s_k(i)$ in Loop LI are independent and each takes T units of time to execute.

Loop LI:

```
par i:=1 to N do
      s1(i); ... sk(i);
```

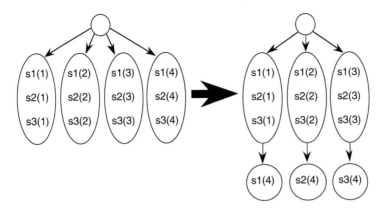

Figure 10.7 Loop spreading for independent substatements

```
endpar;
```

The first $(N - M)$ iterations, where $M = N$ mod P, can be evenly distributed on P processors, and we only need to spread the remaining M iterations. This approach is shown in the code of Loop LII. Figure 10.7 illustrates the technique when $N = 4$ and $P = 3$.

Loop LII:

```
par g := 1 to P do
     M := N mod P;
     U := N - M;
     for i:=1 to U step P do
        s1(i);s2(i), ..., sk(i);
     endfor;
     for i:=g to M*K step P do
        j := (i-1) DIV M + 1;
        ii := U + (i-1) MOD M + 1;
        case j of
           1:  s1(ii);
           2:  s2(ii);
           .....
           k:  sk(ii);
        endcase;
     endfor;
endpar;
```

To reduce the overhead of loop spreading, some division and multiplication operations in Loop LII can be replaced by iterative additions and subtractions. Statements like $(i - 1)$ DIV $M + 1$ or $(i - 1)$ mod $M + 1$, performed in each iteration, are replaced by one or a few additions or subtractions in each iteration, as shown in Loop LIII.

Loop LIII:

```
par g := 1 to P do
```

```
    M := N mod P;
    U := N - M;
    for i:=1 to U step P do
        s1(i);s2(i); ... ,sk(i);
    endfor;
    a := g; j := 1;
    for i:=g to M*K step P do
        while a > M do
            a := a - M; j := j + 1;
        endwhile;
        ii := a + U; a := a + P;
        case j of
            1:  s1(ii);
            2:  s2(ii);
            .....
            k:  sk(ii);
        endcase;
    endfor;
endpar;
```

10.3.3 Algorithm for Dependent Substatements

We next consider the case when the k substatements $s_1(i)$, $s_2(i)$, ..., $s_k(i)$ in Loop LI are dependent. First assume that $s_1(i)$, ...,$s_k(i)$ are *totally dependent,* meaning that $s_{j+1}(i)$ depends on $s_j(i)$ for $j = 1$, ..., $k-1$. Later we extend the result to partially dependent cases.

When $s_1(i)$, ..., $s_k(i)$ are dependent, the spreading algorithm discussed in Section 10.3.2 needs modification, or else inconsistent results may be produced by the spread loop. For example, consider the loop LI when $P = 3$ and $N = 4$. Assume $s_3(i)$ uses the result of $s_2(i)$ and $s_2(i)$ depends on $s_1(i)$. If we use the scheme in Loop LIII , we get the situation shown in Figure 10.8.

Depending on the relative speed of the processors, $s_1(4)$ can finish either before or after $s_2(4)$ starts. If $s_1(4)$ finishes after $s_2(4)$ starts, $s_2(4)$ will be unable to use a result from $s_1(4)$, and the result will be incorrect. Without a mechanism to enforce the ordering in which $s_1(4)$ finishes before $s_2(4)$ starts, the only way to guarantee a correct result is to let $s_1(4)$ and $s_2(4)$ run on a single processor, or to synchronize the execution of these tasks on separate processors.

SYNC/WAIT primitives [Wolfe; Wu and Lewis] can be used to enforce sequential execution when dependent statements are executed on multiple processors. SYNC(i, j) is used to indicate that statement $s_j(i)$ has finished execution, and WAIT(i, j) is used to force a statement that is dependent on statement $s_j(i)$ to delay execution until statement $s_j(i)$ has finished.

As long as proper SYNC/WAITs are used, loop spreading is a safe way to produce correct results. However, we cannot simply insert SYNC/WAITs in Loop LIII to achieve the time saving of loop spreading while conserving data dependence. This

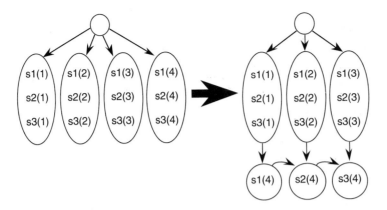

Figure 10.8 Inconsistent loop spreading with dependent substatements

will become clear after we prove Theorem 10.1. Our objective is to improve the total execution time as much as possible through loop spreading while keeping the number of SYNC/WAITs needed to conserve data dependence at a minimum.

Theorem 10.1.

If $N < P$ and $s_1(i), s_2(i), \ldots, s_k(i)$ are totally data dependent, loop spreading can not improve performance over Loop LI.

Proof. As $s_{j+1}(i)$ must run after $s_j(i)$ for $j = 1, \ldots, k-1$, at least KT time units are needed to run the loop. KT is also the time needed by Loop LI when $N < P$. (Q.E.D.)

In Loop LIII, we only spread the last $N \bmod P$ iterations of Loop LI. As $(N \bmod P) < P$, it is obvious from Theorem 10.1 that Loop LIII cannot improve performance over Loop LI by inserting SYNC/WAITs.

Theorem 10.2.

If $N \geq P$, we can spread the N iterations of Loop LI so that the total execution time of the spread loop is minimized.

Proof. Assume $q = (N \bmod P)$ and $m_j = (j*N) \bmod P$. First, $s_1(1), \ldots, s_1(N)$ are placed on the P processors so that $s_1(i)$, $1 \leq i \leq P$, are placed on processor i in the first round $\ldots, s_1((q-1)*P + i)$, $1 \leq i \leq P$, are placed on processor i in the qth round, and $s_1(q*P + i)$, $1 < i \leq m_1$ are placed on processor i in the $(q + 1)$th round. In general, assume $s_j(1)$, $\ldots, s_j(N)$ have been placed in $\lceil j*N/P \rceil *P$ rounds and the last round has only used the first m_j processors. We assign $s_{j+1}(1), \ldots, s_{j+1}(P - m_j)$ to the remaining processors in that round, $s_{j+1}(P - m_j + 1)$, $s_{j+1}(P - m_j + 2), \ldots, s_{j+1}(P - m_j + P)$ to the next round, $\ldots$, and so on.

An example of this spreading of Loop LI is shown in Figure 10.9, where $N = 8$, $k = 3$, and $P = 5$.

From the above arrangement, we can observe the following:

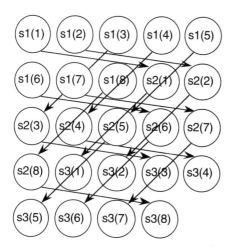

Figure 10.9 Spreading dependent substatements

1 $s_j(i)$ must be at least one round before $s_{j+1}(i)$. This is because $s_j(i)$ is executed in round r_j, where

$$\begin{aligned}
r_j &= \lceil ((j-1)^*N + i)/P \rceil \\
&= \lceil ((j-1)^*(N \bmod P + q^*P) + i)/P \rceil \\
&= (j-1) * q + \lceil (j-1)^*(N \bmod P) + i)/P \rceil
\end{aligned}$$

and $s_{j+1}(i)$ is executed in round r_{j+1}, where

$$\begin{aligned}
r_{j+1} &= \lceil (j^*N + i)/P \rceil \\
&= \lceil (j^*(N \bmod P + P) + i)/P \rceil \\
&= j * q + \lceil (j^*(N \bmod P) + i)/P \rceil.
\end{aligned}$$

It can also be noticed that $r_{j+1} - r_j = q + \lceil (j^*(N \bmod P) + i)/P \rceil - \lceil (j-1)^*(N \bmod P) + i)/P \rceil \ge q$. Since $N \ge P$, we know that $r_{j+1} - r_j \ge q \ge 1$.

2 The data dependence relation can be preserved by issuing SYNC(i, j) after every statement $s_j(i)$, and issuing WAIT(i, j) before every $s_{j+1}(i)$, $j = 1, ..., k-1$.

From point (1) we know that $s_{j+1}(i)$ is in a later round than $s_j(i)$. This implies that when the WAIT(i, j) from $s_{j+1}(i)$ is issued, the corresponding SYNC(i, j) from $s_j(i)$ will have already been issued (remember, we assume that all $s_j(i)$ are of equal size). Since the arrangement above leaves no unused processor in the first $\lfloor K^*N/P \rfloor$ rounds and no actual waiting takes place, the total execution time of the loop is $\lceil K^*N/P \rceil^*T$. (Q.E.D.)

Theorem 10.3.

When using the arrangement of Theorem 10.2 to spread Loop LI to achieve optimal time saving, we need $N^*(k-1)$ SYNC/WAITs whenever $N \bmod P \ne 0$.

Proof. With the arrangement of Theorem 10.2, it is not difficult to see that $s_j(i)$ is placed on processor $p(s_j(i)) = ((j-1)*N + i - 1) \bmod P + 1$, and $s_{j+1}(i)$ is on processor $p(s_{j+1}(i)) = (j*N + i - 1) \bmod P + 1$. It can be also seen that $p(s_j(i)) - p(s_{j+1}(i)) = N \bmod P$. Since $N \bmod P \neq 0$, we know $p(s_j(i)) - p(s_{j+1}(i)) \neq 0$, meaning that $s_j(i)$ and $s_{j+1}(i)$ run on different processors. So, all statements $s_j(i)$ need SYNCs and all statements $s_{j+1}(i)$ need WAITs, for $j = 1, \ldots, k-1$, $i = 1, \ldots, N$, resulting in a total of $N*(k-1)$ SYNC/WAITs. (Q.E.D.)

The above theorems state that we can always achieve optimal time saving through loop spreading, as long as $N > P$, using $N*(k-1)$ SYNC/WAITs. This suggests that, for any $N > P$, we can always separate the N iterations into two parts: iteration 1 to iteration U, and iteration $U+1$ to iteration N, where the value of U is chosen such that U is a multiple of P and minimizes $(N - U) > P$. Once we find U, we can evenly execute the first U iterations without using SYNC/WAITs and spread the remaining $N - U$ iterations using our method. Obviously, $U = N - M$, where $M = P + N \bmod P$. So, for any given N, we only need to spread the last $P + N \bmod P$ iterations. We code the spreading scheme in Theorem 10.2 with this modification in Loop LIV.

Loop LIV:

```
par g := 1 to P do
    if N <= P then M := 0
    else M := N MOD P + P;
    U := N - M;
    for i:=g to U step P do
        s1(i);s2(i),....,sk(i);
    endfor;
    for ij := g to M*K step P do
        i := (ij-1) MOD M + 1;
        j := (ij-1) DIV M + 1;
        case j of
            1:  s1(i + U); SYNC(1,i);
            2: WAIT(1,i);s2(i+U); SYNC(2,i);
            .....
            K:  WAIT(k-1,i); sk(i + U)
        endcase
    endfor;
endpar;
```

If $s_1(i)$, $s_2(i)$, ..., $s_k(i)$ in Loop LI are only partly dependent, then we can adapt the strategy in Theorem 10.2 with less than $(P + N \bmod P) * (k - 1)$ SYNC/WAITs to conserve data dependence. First, only the substatements in the last $(P + N \bmod P)$ iterations need SYNC/WAITs. We can use the following guidelines to issue SYNCs and WAITs:

1 Transitive dependence can be ignored. This guarantees that the total number of SYNC/WAITs for partially dependent $s_1(i)$, $s_2(i)$, ..., $s_k(i)$ will be no more than that for totally ordered $s_1(i)$, $s_2(i)$, ..., $s_k(i)$.

2 Only one SYNC is needed for multiple dependence from the same source statement.

3 If $s_j(i)$ depends on d $(0 \le d \le k - 1)$ statements, it should issue d WAITs before starting execution. Since d can be zero, if $s_j(i)$ is not dependent on any other $s_j(i)$, it does not need to issue a WAIT operation.

10.3.4 Performance Analysis

The speedup expected from scheduling parallel loops using loop spreading is calculated as follows:

$$SP = \frac{N*K}{\lceil N*(K/P) \rceil}, \begin{cases} K \ge 1 \text{ and no spreading when } K = 1 \\ N \ge 1 \text{ if independent substatements} \\ N \ge P \text{ if dependent substatements} \end{cases}$$

The effectiveness of loop spreading depends on (1) the value of k, with the optimal k being $\min(k \mid (N*k) \bmod P = 0)$, and (2) whether or not the loop body can be broken into k substatements that take similar amounts of time to execute. Since N is usually unknown, $k = P$ is the obvious choice, and it is recommended that K be in the range of $P/2$ to P, depending on which k results in evenly divided substatements.

Figure 10.10 describes the performance for $P = 10$, $k = P/2$, $k = P - 1$, and $k = P$. It is clear that loop spreading effectively removes the performance drop-off.

Note that although the improvement due to loop spreading decreases as N increases, the spreading schemes spread only the last $N \bmod P$ iterations, and for this part of the loop the performance improvement through loop spreading is significant.

We finally show the experimental results of applying loop spreading in Loop LIII to matrix multiplication [Wu and Lewis]. The algorithm with loop spreading to calculate the product of two matrices X and Y of size $N*k$ is as follows.

```
par g := 1 to P do
    M := N mod P; U := N - M;
    for i:=g to U step P do
        for j:=1 to K do
            Z[i,j] := innerProd(X[i],Y[j]);
        endfor;
    endfor;
    a := g; j := 1;
    for i:=g to M*K step P do
        while a > M DO
            a := a - M; j := j + 1;
        endwhile;
        ii := a + U; a := a + P;
        Z[ii,j] := innerProd(X[ii],Y[j]);
    endfor;
endpar;
```

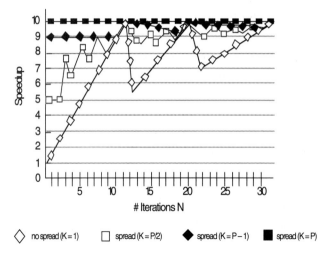

Figure 10.10 Performance of spreading

The speedup of the parallel matrix multiplication algorithm was measured with/without loop spreading over the sequential algorithm on 7 and 8 processors. The algorithm with loop spreading shows stable speedup increases as the input size increases, regardless of whether or not N is a multiple of P (see Figure 10.11). Furthermore, for almost all N, the spread loop shows a speedup at least as great as the non-spread loop.

10.4 LOOP UNROLLING

In this section we introduce a solution to the problem of scheduling parallel program tasks that are enclosed in a set of nested loops on distributed-memory parallel computers. We approach this problem using the well-known loop unrolling technique borrowed from compiler construction technology.

Loop unrolling is the process of replacing the iterations of a loop with noniterated straight-line code. The basic idea is to unroll the loop in order to uncover loop-carried dependencies which may allow several iterations to overlap in execution. For example, the loop

```
For i: = 3 to 6 do
   A[i]: = A[i - 1] + A[i - 2];
```

is unrolled to

```
A[3]: = A[2] + A[1]
A[4]: = A[3] + A[2]
A[5]: = A[4] + A[3]
A[6]: = A[5] + A[4]
```

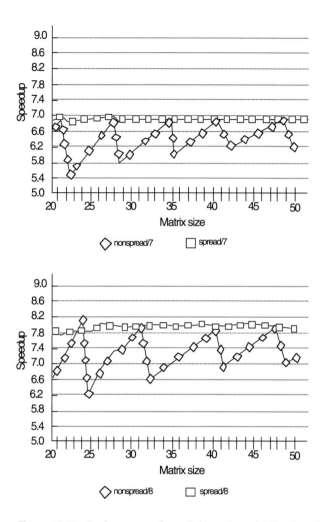

Figure 10.11 **Performance of parallel matrix multiplication algorithm with loop spreading**

Unrolling reveals independent iterations which we can group together in a manner that allows some parallelism. The resulting groups can be scheduled to take advantage of the limited parallelism. This is the problem of scheduling loops using loop unrolling.

We start by giving the following definitions:

Upper Bound Vector. The upper bound vector for n nested loops is $<b_1, b_2, ..., b_n>$, where b_i is the upper bound of the loop at the ith level (notice that the outermost loop is at the first level and the innermost loop is at the nth level).

Unrolling Vector. The unrolling vector $= <u_1, u_2, ..., u_n>$, gives the ith loop that is unrolled u_i times.

Dependency Ordered Pair. We define a dependency ordered pair between two tasks $T_w(I_w)$ and $T_v(I_v)$ as (I_d, D) where I_d is the distance vector $I_d = I_w - I_v$ and D is the size of the message that T_w receives from T_v. Task T_w can have more than one data dependency ordered pair from task T_v. This multi-dependence between T_v and T_w can be represented using a dependency set.

Dependency Set. The dependency set between two tasks is the set of all dependency ordered pairs between those tasks.

10.4.1 Dependence Representation

The loop-independent data dependences between tasks can be easily represented using directed edges in task graphs. However, *loop-carried data dependences* are difficult to represent in task graphs since they express dependences between tasks in different loop iterations. In this section we introduce a *dependency matrix* (*DM*) to represent loop-independent as well as loop-carried data dependences between tasks that are enclosed in a set of nested loops.

Dependency Matrix (DM)

Suppose V is the set of tasks enclosed in n nested loops, where $k = |V|$. Loop-carried and loop-independent data dependence among the tasks in V can be represented using a $k \times k$ matrix, called the *Dependency Matrix* (*DM*). $DM[i, j]$ represents the dependency set between tasks v_j and v_i, where $v_j, v_i \in V$. A Φ entry in $DM[i, j]$ means that there is no dependence between v_j and v_i.

Example

Consider the code segment for two tasks a and b that are enclosed in 2 nested loops, as shown below.

```
for i := 1 to n do
    for j:= 1 to m do
        a: A[i,j] := F1(D[i-1,j],A[i-1,j-1])
           C[i,j] := const1
           D[i,j] := const2
        b: B[i,j] := F2 (C[i,j],B[i-1,j])
    endfor;
endfor;
```

In this example, we assume that each element of arrays A, B, C, and D takes 10, 12, 20, and 5 units of storage, respectively. Since there is no data dependence from b to a, $DM[a, b] = \Phi$. That is, b does not compute anything that a uses.

Task a during iteration $<i, j>$ uses $D[i-1, j]$, which is computed by task a during iteration $<i-1, j>$, and $A[i-1, j-1]$, which is computed by task a during iteration $<i-1, j-1>$. Since the size of an element in D is 5 units of data, and the size of an element in A is 10 units of data, $DM[a, a] = \{(<1, 0>, 5), (<1, 1>, 10)\}$.

Task b during iteration $<i, j>$ uses $C[i, j]$, which is computed by task a during the same iteration $<i, j>$. And since the size of an element in C is 20 units of data, $DM[b, a] = \{(<0, 0>, 20)\}$. Task b also uses $B[i–1, j]$, which is computed by task b during iteration $<i – 1, j>$ and since the size of an element in B is 12 units of data, $DM[b, b] = \{(<1, 0>, 12)\}$. Figure 10.12 shows the complete DM for the two tasks a and b.

$DM[a, a] = \{(<1, 0>, 5), (<1, 1>, 10)\}$ means that an instance of task a, during iteration $<i, j>$, is data dependent on instances of itself during iterations $<i – 1, j>$ and $<i – 1, j – 1>$ and the data sizes are 5 and 10 bytes, respectively; $DM[a, b] = \Phi$ means that there is no data dependence from b to a; $DM[b, a] = \{(<0, 0>, 20)\}$ means that b is data dependent on a during the same iteration and the data size is 20 bytes (notice that this is a loop-independent data dependence); and finally, $DM[b, b] = \{(<1, 0>, 12)\}$ means that an instance of task b, during iteration $<i, j>$, is data dependent on an instance of itself during iteration $<i – 1, j>$ and the data size is 12 bytes.

$$
\begin{array}{c@{}c}
& \quad\text{a} \qquad\qquad\qquad\qquad\qquad \text{b} \\
\begin{array}{c} \text{a} \\ \text{b} \end{array} &
\left(
\begin{array}{cc}
\{ (\langle 1, 0\rangle, 5), (\langle 1, 1\rangle, 10) \} & \Phi \\
\{ (\langle 0, 0\rangle, 20) \} & \{ (\langle 1, 0\rangle, 12) \}
\end{array}
\right)
\end{array}
$$

Figure 10.12   DM for two tasks a and b enclosed in two nested loops

10.4.2   The Unrolling Process

When a single loop, with upper bound b, is unrolled u times, $u + 1$ copies of the body are replicated, the loop control variable is adjusted for each copy, and the step value of the loop is multiplied by $u + 1$. Similarly, when a set of n nested loops, with upper bound vector $= <b_1, b_2, ..., b_n>$, is unrolled using unrolling vector $= <u_1, u_2, ..., u_n>$,

$$\prod_{i=1}^{n} (u_i + 1)$$ copies of the body are replicated, the loop control variables are adjusted

for each copy, and the step value of the ith loop is multiplied by $u_i + 1$.

For each $v_j \in V$, where V is the set of tasks in the pre-unrolling loop, there are

$$\prod_{i=1}^{n} (u_i + 1)$$ tasks: $v_j^{y_1, y_2, ..., y_n}$, $(0 \le y_i \le u_i, 1 \le i \le n)$ in the unrolleed loop.

Figure 10.13 shows an example of loop unrolling when 2 nested loops are used. Consider the nested loops given in (a), where the body of the loop has only one task, v. (b) shows the loop resulting from unrolling the innermost loop once ($u = < 0, 1>$) and the resulting tasks v^{00} and v^{01}. Similarly, (c) shows the loop resulting from unrolling the outermost loop once ($u = <1, 0>$) and the resulting tasks v^{00} and v^{10}. Finally, (d) shows the loop resulting from unrolling both loops once each ($u = <1, 1>$) and the resulting tasks v^{00}, v^{01}, v^{10}, and v^{11}. In this example, the loop upper bounds are assumed, for simplicity, to be multiples of two.

```
for i := 1 to 2*n₁ do
      for j := 1 to 2*n₂ do
v          T(i,j);
      endfor
endfor
```
(a)

```
for i := 1 to 2*n₁ do
      for j := 1 to 2*n₂ step 2 do
v⁰⁰          T(i,j);
v⁰¹          T(i,j+1);
      endfor
endfor
```
(b)

```
for i := 1 to 2*n₁ step 2 do
      for j := 1 to 2*n₂ do
v⁰⁰          T(i,j);
v¹⁰          T(i+1,j)
      endfor
endfor
```
(c)

```
for i := 1 to 2*n₁ step 2 do
      for j := 1 to 2*n₂ step 2 do
v⁰⁰          T(i,j);
v⁰¹          T(i,j+1);
v¹⁰          T(i+1,j);
v¹¹          T(i+1,j+1);
      endfor
endfor
```
(d)

Figure 10.13 (a) Original loop, (b) Innermost loop is unrolled once (u = <0,1>), (c) Outermost loop is unrolled once (u = <1,0>), (d) Both loops are unrolled once each (u = <1,1>)

10.4.3 Scheduling Unrolled Loops

We define the task graph $G_0 = (V, E)$ that represents the body of a pre-unrolled loop, where V is the original set of tasks and E is the set of loop-independent data dependency edges given in the dependency matrix DM. Thus, the loop-carried data dependences are ignored in G_0 and the pre-unrolled graph is simply scheduled by executing the iterations one after another without any overlap between iterations.

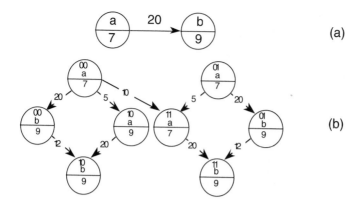

Figure 10.14 (a) G_0, (b) G_u (u = <1,1>) for the loop represented by *DM* given in Figure 10.12

In order to consider the loop-carried dependences in a task graph, we define the task graph $G_u = (V', E')$ that represents the body of an unrolled loop using $u = <u_1, u_2, ..., u_n>$ as unrolling vector, where V' is the set of all tasks generated in the unrolled loop and E' is the set of edges that represent loop-independent and loop-carried data dependence generated from *DM*. Scheduling the unrolled graph, G_u allows different iterations of the loop to overlap in execution. For example, the task graphs G_0 and G_u, when $u = <1, 1>$, for the *DM* given in Figure 10.12 are shown in Figures 10.14(a) and 10.14(b), respectively. The upper portion of each node contains the task title, while the lower portion contains the task size which is the computation time for the task's execution (we assume that the sizes of tasks a and b are 7 and 9, respectively). The number next to an edge represents the message size to be passed through that edge.

The basic idea is to unroll the loop using some iteration vector to allow dependencies between different iterations to appear in the task graph G_u. The task graph is then scheduled on a given target machine using one of the scheduling techniques described in Chapter 9.

We give two examples to show how loop unrolling minimizes loop execution time. The examples also show the change in the loop execution time that results from using different loop unrolling vectors. In both examples we assume that the communication time between any two tasks running on the same processor is negligible. We also assume that the processing speed and the transfer rate in the target machine are always equal to one (this allows us to deal with the message size and the task size as units of time).

Example

Consider the *DM* in Figure 10.15. Assume that tasks a and b, which are enclosed in a single loop ($n = 1$), have task size = 15. The pre-unrolled task graph

G_0 is given in Figure 10.16(a), which shows that there is no loop-independent data dependence between the two tasks. This means that within one iteration, tasks a and b can run totally in parallel. Let's assume (just for the sake of discussion) that the upper bound of the loop is known to be 4. In the case when we have only one processor, tasks a and b run sequentially in any order (we assume that task a executes first) and this process is repeated 4 times with execution time totaling 120 units of time, as shown in Figure 10.16(b).

$$
\begin{array}{c}
\quad\quad\quad a \quad\quad\quad\quad\quad\quad b \\
\begin{array}{c} a \\ b \end{array}
\left(
\begin{array}{cc}
\Phi & \{\,(\langle 1 \rangle,\, 10)\,\} \\
\{\,(\langle 1 \rangle,\, 10)\,\} & \Phi
\end{array}
\right)
\end{array}
$$

Figure 10.15 *DM* two tasks a and b enclosed in a single loop

Now suppose we exploit only the parallelism within each iteration and neglect the parallelism that might take place if we unroll the loop. We run tasks a and b concurrently on processors p_1 and p_2, respectively, so each iteration takes only 15 units of time. Since task a during iteration $<i>$ receives data from task b during iterations $<i-1>$, and task b during iteration $<i>$ receives data from task a during iteration $<i-1>$, and since tasks a and b are scheduled on different pro-

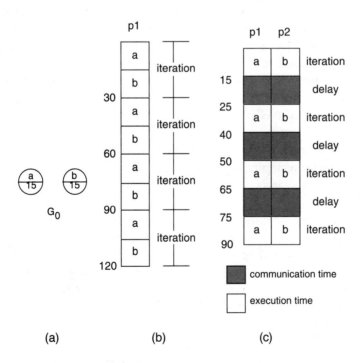

Figure 10.16 (a) Task graph G_0, (b) and (c) Gantt charts result from scheduling four iterations of the loop on one and two processing elements, respectively

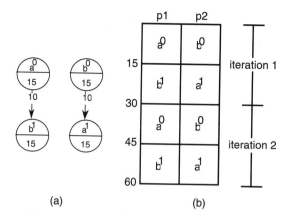

Figure 10.17 (a) Task graph G_u, $u = <1>$; (b) Gantt chart results from scheduling two iterations of the unrolled loop on two processing elements

cessors, a new iteration has to wait 10 units of time before starting execution. Figure 10.16(c) shows that each iteration takes 15 units of time; however, due to the communication delay, a new iteration can be initialized every 25 units of time and the 4 iterations take 90 units of time.

Figure 10.17(a) shows the task graph G_u when the loop is unrolled once ($u = <1>$). It is easily noticed that scheduling tasks a^0 and b^1 together on one processor and tasks b^0 and a^1 on the other is the best way to schedule task graph G_u on two processors. Now we are able to initialize a new iteration every 30 units of time without having to wait for any communication and the total execution time is only 60 units of time, as shown in Figure 10.17(b).

By exploiting the parallelism without unrolling, we get speedup $= 1\frac{1}{3}$;

however, after unrolling the loop once, speedup = 2. It is not always the case that we have zero communication delay between iterations because the delay depends on the way we assign the tasks to the available processing elements.

Example

In the case of nested loops, the performance might differ depending on which loop is unrolled. Figure 10.18 shows the DM for tasks a and b enclosed in 2 nested loops. In this example, we assume that the upper bound vector $b = <2, 4>$ and the size of tasks a and b is 10. Figures 10.19(a), (b), (c) show the original loop, the loop after unrolling the outermost loop once, and the loop after unrolling the innermost loop once.

Figure 10.20(a) shows the task graph G_u, when the outermost loop is unrolled once ($u = <1, 0>$). The Gantt chart given in Figure 10.20(b) shows that a new iteration has to wait 10 units of time because task a (b) during iteration (i, j) receives data from task b (a) during iteration $(i, j-1)$ and they are located on different processors. That leads to total execution time equal to 110 units of time. On the other hand, when the innermost loop is unrolled once, no delay is needed and the total execution time is 80 units of time. Figure 10.21(a) shows the task graph G_u when the innermost loop is unrolled once (u = <0, 1>), and the Gantt chart is given in Figure 10.21(b).

$$
\begin{array}{c}
\quad\quad\quad\quad\text{a} \quad\quad\quad\quad\quad\quad\quad\quad\quad\quad \text{b} \\
\begin{array}{c} \text{a} \\ \text{b} \end{array}
\left(
\begin{array}{cc}
\Phi & \{\,(\langle 1, 0\rangle, 5),\ (\langle 0, 1\rangle, 20)\,\} \\
\{\,(\langle 1, 0\rangle, 5),\ (\langle 0, 1\rangle, 20)\,\} & \Phi
\end{array}
\right)
\end{array}
$$

Figure 10.18 Two tasks a and b enclosed in two nested loops represented using DM and TS

10.4.4 Loop Unrolling Optimization Problem

Now we need to answer the following questions: How many times should a loop be unrolled to speed up its execution, and how should the tasks forming the body of the loop be scheduled onto a given arbitrary target machine? Our goal is to find the vector u = <u_1, u_2, ..., u_n> and schedule the tasks in the task graph G_u on a given parallel system such that the loop total execution time is minimized. This problem is an example of *combinatorial minimization*. The space over which the function is defined is n-dimensional discrete but very large, so it cannot be explored exhaustively.

One way of dealing with this *optimization problem* is to start with some initial solution and go greedily for the quick nearby solution. That is, from the starting point, we go immediately downhill as far as we can go. This approach leads to a local, but not necessarily a global, optimum. An example of this technique is *Local Neighborhood Search* [Peir]. *Simulated annealing* is a probabilistic modification of traditional neighborhood search techniques [Peir].

To make use of the local neighborhood or the simulated annealing methods, we must provide a description of possible system configurations, a generator of changes

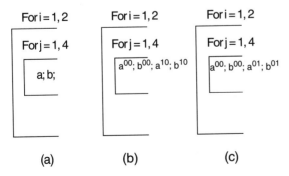

Figure 10.19   (a) Original loop, (b) The loop after unrolling the outermost loop once, (c) The loop after unrolling the innermost loop once

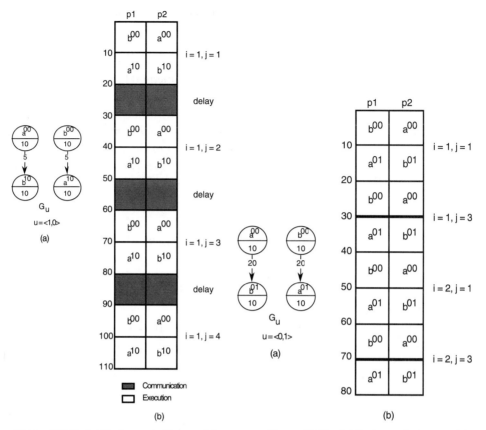

Figure 10.20 (a) Task graph G_u, $u=<1,0>$, (b) The schedule after unrolling the outermost loop once

Figure 10.21 (a) Task graph G_u, $u=<0,1>$, (b) The schedule after unrolling the innermost loop once

in the configuration, and an objective function whose minimization is the goal of the procedure. The unrolling vector is used as system configuration which is updated to generate new system configurations. If the upper bound vector is known when the schedule is generated, a complete unrolling might be done to generate the task graph G_u for scheduling. If the nested loops are too large to unroll completely, then an exact formula for the time to execute the outermost loop is used as an objective function. If the upper bound vector is not known when the schedule is generated but is known before the loop begins execution, another formula that does not contain the loop upper bounds is needed to reflect the effect of using different values of the unrolling vector.

The *loop unrolling optimization problem* can be formalized as follows:

1 *Configuration:* A configuration is a vector $u = <u_1, u_2, \ldots, u_n>$, where $u_i \geq 0$, $1 \leq i \leq n$.

2 *Update:* An update is of two types: (a) An i is chosen randomly in the range $(1,$

n), then u_i is changed according to some policy; or (b) some u_i's (chosen randomly) are selected for change, $1 \leq i \leq n$.

3 *Objective Function (E):* The total loop execution time.

4 *Schedule:* The local neighborhood search method keeps trying until some terminating condition occurs. In the simulated annealing method, we choose a starting value for the temperature parameter T greater than the largest ΔE. We proceed downward in multiplicative steps each amounting to some decrease in T. We hold each new value of T constant for some number of changes in the unrolling vector, or for some number of successful moves, whichever comes first. When the effort to reduce E further becomes sufficiently discouraging, we stop.

10.4.5 The Objective Function

We now turn to the completion time of the body of a loop and the communication delay between different iterations. We discuss the objective function used in the local neighborhood search and the simulated annealing methods. In all cases, we assume that the amount of computation needed by each task in the loop is known beforehand.

Our goal is to minimize the total execution time of the loop. The completion time of the tasks forming the body of the loop as well as the communication delay among different iterations in the unrolled loop play an important role in computing the total execution time of a loop.

Given a DM that represents data dependence between tasks enclosed in a set of n nested loops with an upper bound vector $b = <b_1, b_2, \ldots, b_n>$, we assume that the loop is unrolled using $u = <u_1, u_2, \ldots, u_n>$. Recall that G_u is a task graph that represents the body of an unrolled loop. We define the following:

$\tau_{u,i}$ is the time to execute the loop at level i. Notice that $\tau_{u,n+1}$ is the time to execute G_u only once, and that $\tau_{u,1}$ is the time to execute the outermost loop (the whole thing).

$\lambda_{u,i}$ is the communication delay between any two consecutive iterations of a loop at level i. Notice that $\lambda_{u,i} = 0$ when $u_i = b_i - 1$ because when we unroll a loop at the ith level $b_i - 1$ times, we generate all the instances of that loop.

Given an unrolling vector u, and dependence matrix DM, we show how to obtain the parameters $\tau_{u,n+1}$ and $\lambda_{u,i}$, $1 < i \leq n$.

The task graph G_u can be scheduled using one of the techniques covered in chapter 9. From the Gantt chart produced by the scheduling algorithm, we obtain $\tau_{u,n+1}$ (the time to run the tasks represented by the task graph G_u). The communication delay between any two consecutive iterations of a loop at level k ($\lambda_{u,i}$, $1 \leq i < n$) can also be figured out from the Gantt chart and the task graph G_u as the maximum time that a task has to wait until it receives a message from a task scheduled in some previous iteration.

When the upper bound vector is unknown before execution time, it becomes impossible to find $\lambda_{u,i}$, $1 \le i < n$. However, we can always obtain the worst case communication delay by considering only one iteration for all levels greater than i (enclosed in a loop at level i).

10.4.6 Completion Time Formulas

Given a DM that represents data dependence between tasks enclosed in a set of n nested loops with an upper bound vector $b = <b_1, b_2, \ldots, b_n>$ and an unrolling vector $u = <u_1, u_2, \ldots, u_n>$, the time to execute the nested loop is obtained as follows.

$$\tau_{u,1} = \left\lceil \frac{b_1}{u_1 + 1} \right\rceil (\tau_{u,2} + \lambda_{u,1}) - \lambda_{u,1} - \left(\left\lceil \frac{b_1}{u_1 + 1} \right\rceil - \frac{b_1}{u_1 + 1} \right) \tau_{u,2} \qquad (1)$$

Changing the unrolling vector u might change loop execution time. The best value of the unrolling vector is the one that gives the shortest loop execution time. When the upper bound vector b is known before execution time, formula (1) gives the completion time.

Different values of the unrolling vector u are tried in order to find the shortest completion time. When the upper bound vector b is not known, another formula that does not contain b is needed to compare the effect of using different values of the unrolling vector.

Formula (1) is bounded as:

$$\tau_{u,1} \le \left\lceil \frac{b_1}{u_1 + 1} \right\rceil (\tau_{u,2} + \lambda_{u,1}) \qquad (2)$$

$\tau_{u,1}$ is approximated as:

$$\tau_{u,1} \approx \frac{b_1}{u_1 + 1} (\tau_{u,2} + \lambda_{u,1}) \qquad (3)$$

The time to execute a loop at level i is approximated as follows.

$$\tau_{u,i} \approx \frac{b_i}{u_i + 1} (\tau_{u,i+1} + \lambda_{u,i}), 1 \le i \le n \qquad (4)$$

Using formula (4), the time to execute the outermost loop is obtained as follows:

$$\tau_{u,1} \approx \frac{b_1}{u_1 + 1} \left(\frac{b_2}{u_2 + 1} \left(\frac{b_3}{u_3 + 1} \left(\cdots \left(\frac{b_n}{u_n + 1} (\tau_{u,n+1} + \lambda_{u,n}) + \ldots \right) \right) \right) \right)$$

$$+\lambda_{u,3}) +\lambda_{u,2}) +\lambda_{u,1}) \tag{5}$$

$$\approx \prod_{i=1}^{n} \frac{b_i}{u_i+1}(\tau_{u,n+1}+\lambda_{u,n}) + \prod_{i=1}^{n-1} \frac{b_i}{u_i+1}\lambda_{u,n-1} + \dots$$

$$+ \prod_{i=1}^{2} \frac{b_i}{u_i+1}\lambda_{u,2} + \frac{b_1}{u_1+1}\lambda_{u,1} \tag{6}$$

(When $<u_1, u_2, \dots, u_n> = <b_1-1, b_2-1, \dots, b_n-1>$, $\lambda_{u,i}=0$, $1 \le i \le n$ and $\tau_{u,1} \approx \tau_{u,n+1}$).

Since $1 \le u_i < b_i$, then $\dfrac{b_i}{u_i+1} \ge 1$, $1 \le i \le n$, $\tau_{u,1}$ is bounded by:

$$\tag{7}$$

$$\left(\prod_{i=1}^{n} \frac{b_i}{u_i+1}\right)\left(\tau_{u,n+1} + \sum_{i=1}^{n} \lambda_{u,i}\right)$$

Notice that when $n = 1$ (single loop), the two formulas (6) and (7) are identical, which means:

$$\tau_{u,1} = \frac{b_1}{u_1+1}(\tau_{u,2}+\lambda_{u,1}) \tag{8}$$

The execution time as given in formula (7) is a suitable objective function. However, since the upper bound vector b is usually not given before execution time and since $\prod_{i=1}^{n} b_i$ does not change during the optimization search, the objective function can be given as:

$$E = \left(\prod_{i=1}^{n} \frac{1}{u_i+1}\right)\left(\tau_{u,n+1} + \sum_{i=1}^{n} \lambda_{u,i}\right) \tag{9}$$

10.5 SUMMARY

Balanced loops can be scheduled using classical techniques described in the next chapter, or the more efficient loop spreading technique described here. Iterations must all take the same amount of time for these solutions to apply. For unbalanced loops, the scheduling technique must be modified.

The dependency matrix DM is a new way to express loop-carried data dependences between iterative tasks that are not balanced in the sense that they take the same amount of time to execute each iteration. DM makes it possible to schedule unrolled loops onto arbitrary machines in a pattern that minimizes the completion time. The scheduler considers communication delays between tasks on different processors, which makes this method particularly useful for loop unrolling on distributed-memory machines.

The designer can use either local neighborhood search or simulated annealing methods to find:

1 The best unrolling vector for a particular set of tasks when they run on a particular machine, and

2 The Gantt chart that indicates the allocation and the order of the tasks in the unrolled loop on the available processing elements.

We recommend that both methods be tried since their performance differs from one application to another and from one target machine to another. We believe that finding the best unrolling vector and the best schedule should be achieved through iterative interaction between the parallel program designer and an automated loop unrolling tool.

Additional research is needed to incorporate other factors such as network contention for physical links, message-passing initiation time in the target machine, and software considerations such as program branches. These remain research topics at the time of this writing.

PROBLEMS FOR DISCUSSION AND SOLUTION

1   Show the task graph and the dependency matrix (DM) for the following:

(a)
```
for i := 1 to 100 do
  for j := 1 to 100 do
     T:                      x [i,j] := comp (x [i+2 ,j-3]);
  endfor;
end;
```

(b)
```
for i := 1 to 100 do
T1:a[i] = b[i] + c[i];
T2:d[i] = a[i] / e[i];
T3:e[i+1]) = SQRT (d[i] + d[i+1]);
T4:f[i] = f[i-1] / d[i];
endfor;
```

(c)
```
for i := 1 to 100 do
   for j := 1 to 100 do
     T1: x [i,j] := 2 * x [i+2 ,j-3];
     T2: y [i,j] := (y[i,j-1] + y[i,j+1] + y[i-1,j] + y[i+1,j]) / 4;
     T3: z [i,j] := (x [i,j] + y[i,j]) * z[i-1,j-1];
   endfor;
endfor;
```

2 What are the implications of having negative values in a distance vector of a dependence relation between two tasks (statements)?

3 Indicate some cases in which:
(a) loop static scheduling is better than dynamic scheduling,
(b) loop dynamic scheduling is better than static scheduling,
(c) both scheduling techniques perform almost the same.

4 Give guidelines that a program designer should follow in order to reduce the number of synchronization operations in a parallel program. Give an example in which a sequential version of a program performs better than a parallel version with synchronization code.

5 Show an example in which loop unrolling will not help in exploiting parallelism between different loop iterations.

6 Conduct a thorough comparison of all the techniques covered in this chapter in the following ways:
(a) applicability to real world problems,
(b) associated overhead,
(c) suitability for use in both shared-memory and distributed-memory systems.

References

Abu-Sufah, W., "Improving the Performance of Virtual Memory Computers," *Ph.D. Thesis,* Department of Computer Science, University of Illinois at Urbana-Champaign, 1978.

Allen, R., Callahan, D., and Kennedy, K., "Automatic Decomposition of Scientific Programs for Parallel Execution," *Proceedings of the 14th Annual ACM Symp. on Priniciples of Programming Languages,* pp. 63 – 76, January 1987.

Allen, R., and Kennedy, K., "A Parallel Programming Environment," *IEEE Software,* Volume 2, No. 4, pp. 21 – 29, July 1985.

Cytron, R., "Limited Processor Scheduling of Doacross Loops," *Proceedings of ICPP 87,* pp. 226 – 234, 1987.

El-Rewini, H., and Lewis, T., "Schedule-Driven Loop Unrolling for Parallel Processors," *Proceedings of the 24th Hawaii International Conference on System Sciences,* Kailua-Kona, Hawaii, January 8 – 11, 1991.

Fisher, J. A., "Trace Scheduling: A Technique for Global Microcode Compaction," *IEEE Transaction on Computers,* Volume C–30, No. 7, July 1981.

Hwang, K., and Briggs, F., "Computer Architecture and Parallel Processing," McGraw-Hill, 1984.

Muraoka, Y., "Parallelism Exposure and Exploitation in Programs," *Ph.D. Thesis,* Department of Computer Science, University of Illinois at Urbana-Champaign, 1971.

Padua-Haiek, D., "Multiprocessors: Discussion of Some Theoretical and Paractical Problems," *Ph.D. Thesis,* University of Illinois, Urbana, 1980.

Peir, J., and Gajski, D., "Minimum Distance: A Method for Partitioning Recurrences for Multiprocessors," *Proceedings of ICPP 87,* pp. 217 – 225, 1987.

Press, W., Flannery, B., Teukolsky, S., and Vetterling, W., *Numerical Recipes,* Cambridge University Press, 1986.

Wolfe, M., "Optimizing Supercompilers for Supercomputers," *Research Monographs in Parallel and Distributed Computing,* The MIT Press, 1989.

Wu, Y., "Parallel Decomposed Simplex Algorithms and Loop Spreading," *Ph. D. Thesis,* Department of Computer Science, Oregon State University, 1988.

Wu, Y., and Lewis, T., "Implementation of Synchronization Primitives for Loop Spreading," *Technical Report,* Departmentof Computer Science, Oregon State University, 1988.

Zaky, A., and Sadayappan, P., "Optimal Static Scheduling of Sequential Loops on Multiprocessors," *Technical Report* (OSU-CISRC-12/88-TR42), Department of Computer and Information Science, The Ohio State University, 1988.

PROBLEMS FOR DISCUSSION AND SOLUTION

Chapter 11
Parallelizing Serial Programs

The investment in traditional serial software is so enormous that it will be many years before parallel software dominates. The question is how to run these serial programs on parallel computers. One obvious answer is to develop compilers that convert serial programs into parallel equivalents that run on parallel computers.

Automatic conversion of serial programs into parallel programs is a difficult problem that has been studied for decades. The basic theory is based on data dependency analysis, which we have not yet formalized in this book. Therefore, formalization of the various forms of data dependency is the first topic discussed. We learn that there are three fundamental kinds of dependency: (1) flow dependency, (2) anti-dependency, and (3) output dependency.

We employ dependency analysis as a tool to partition a serial program into blocks of code that contain well-defined dependencies. These blocks may be converted into independent tasks, scheduled onto one or more parallel processors, and run as a parallel program. Simple as this seems, the problem becomes difficult when the blocks are control structures such as loops, branches, and procedures. Loops are especially difficult to analyze, and yet they possess the greatest amount of potential parallelism.

Finding and utilizing *loop parallelism* is clearly crucial in achieving high performance. If we can replace serial execution of each loop iteration with execution of all loop iterations in parallel, the speedup can be as great as the maximum number of loop iterations. Thus, a loop that takes N time units to iterate on one processor might execute in one time unit on N processors.

While we are interested in the parallelism in all parts of a serial program, the potential for speedup in loops is so great that we focus all our attention on this problem. We discuss compiler techniques for extracting parallelism from serial loops and transformation techniques that reconstruct them into a parallel equivalent.

This problem is approached in three steps: (1) we must develop tests for data dependence to determine if parallelization is possible, then (2) we optimize to enhance the availability of parallelism, and finally (3) we generate code for shared-memory and/or distributed-memory parallel systems.

The purpose of dependence analysis is to prove the absence of data dependence. There are two basic forms of dependence analysis: exact and inexact. Exact dependence requires exact knowledge of both dependence direction and distance. This is the best case, but unfortunately, it is also difficult or sometimes impossible to compute.

Inexact dependence requires knowledge only of dependence direction. However, inexact analysis cannot guarantee independence, so we must resort to worst-case assumptions when using it.

After the dependence test reveals potential parallelism, parallel optimization transformations are tried in an attempt to coax more parallelism from the loop. The most common transformations are vectorization, fusion, coalescing, distribution, interchange, node splitting, shrinking, unrolling, and skewing.

These transformations are applied independently and in an arbitrary order. They are highly unrelated to each other in the sense that the end result is the same independent of the order in which they were applied. Unfortunately, it is frequently the case that the order of application is significant. Thus, if we apply the same set of n transformations to the same program $n!$ different ways, we will get $n!$ semantically equivalent programs. Due to the differences in their syntax, these programs will contain varying amounts of parallelism, resulting in possibly different performance on the same machine. The best order of application is known for only a few special cases [Polychronopoulos 1988b]. In general, finding the best order to apply the transformations is an open research problem.

Another open research problem is that of mapping the parallel loop iterations onto the processors in some optimal pattern. We give recommendations for how to map iterations to shared-memory and distributed-memory machines. One method was described in Chapter 10, but we list the research problems that remain to be solved before loop scheduling has a general solution.

11.1 LOOP PARALLELIZATION TECHNIQUES

The problem to be solved is that of automatically converting a serial program into a parallel program equivalent. It is hoped that the converted parallel version will run much faster on the parallel computer than the serial program runs on a serial computer. The success of automatic parallelization depends on two factors: (1) how accurately and efficiently we can compute data dependence, and (2) how we restructure the program so that maximum parallelism is discovered while retaining the semantics of the program.

Serial program loops and branches offer the greatest resistance to automatic parallelization. Branches are the most difficult to analyze and they contain less potential for speedup than loops. As a consequence, loop parallelization is the most fully developed technology. In fact, at least two decades of research have been focused on parallelization of loops.

This intensive research effort resulted in a long list of techniques based on a three-step process: (1) test for data dependence, (2) restructure the loop into a form that has more parallelism, and (3) schedule the parallel iterations onto parallel processors in a pattern that reduces the elapsed execution time as much as possible.

More specifically, we want to develop techniques in this chapter to automate the following steps:

1 Perform one of several data dependence tests to detect potential parallelism;

2 Restructure the loop into one of several forms: DOALL, DOACROSS, or DOSEQ, and optimize this form to obtain the greatest degree of parallelism; and

3 Generate parallel code for a particular parallel computer by scheduling the iterations on specific processors, and then synthesizing either locks (shared memory) or messages (distributed memory).

The question of loop parallelization is more difficult than it may at first appear due to the often convoluted nature of dependencies found in loops. As a consequence, it is not readily apparent which techniques apply to each of the steps listed above. Therefore, we summarize the techniques, where each applies, and list some of the specific tests to be studied in Table 11.1. We study how the items in Table 11.1 relate to restructuring transformations presented later in this chapter.

Table 11.1 lists four kinds of representations of data dependence and where each is most useful [Kennedy 1981, Padua et al. 1980]. For example, the dependence graph is a general representation that works best for loop distribution and node splitting. The iteration space notation is suited to nested loops that are analyzed with an exact, GCD, or bounds test. These lead to loop coalescing, shrinking, and skewing.

The reader should consult Table 11.1 periodically as she or he reads this chapter.

Dependence notation	What it is for	Dependence test (Parallelization)	Restructuring (Optimization)
Dependence graph	General	General	Loop distribution Node splitting
Iteration space	Nested loop	Exact test GCD test Bounds test	Loop coalescing Loop shrinking Loop skewing
Distance vector	Nested loop	DOACROSS test	Loop skewing
Direction vector	Nested loop	Direction vector test	Loop fusion Loop distribution Loop interchange

Table 11.1 Different representations of data dependence and their usages

11.2 FORMAL DEFINITION OF DATA DEPENDENCE

The essence of data dependence analysis is to determine whether two memory references are to the same location such that one has to follow the other in order to guarantee correct computation. Thus, *data dependence* is a partial order or precedence relation on the statements of a program. Statement T depends on statement S, denoted $S \delta T$, if there exists an instance S' of S, an instance T' of T, and a memory location M, such that

1 both S' and T' reference M, and at least one reference is a writer;

2 in sequential execution of the program, S' is executed before T'; and

3 in the same execution, M is not written between the time S' finishes and the time T' starts.

Thus, there are three types of dependence based on the references to M:

Flow(δ^f) dependences: $S \delta^f T$ if S' writes M and then T' reads M

Anti(δ^a) dependences: $S \delta^a T$ if S' reads M and then T' writes M

Output(δ^o) dependences: $S \delta^o T$ if S' writes M and then T' writes M again.

A statement T is *indirectly dependent* on statement S if there are statements $S_1, \ldots, S_n$ such that $S \delta S_1, \ldots, S_n \delta T$.

For a dependence to exist in an array, we must have two values of the index of the array, I_1 and I_2, such that $1 \le I_1 \le I_2 \le N$ and $I_1 + K = I_2$ where K is the *dependence distance*. If $K \le N$ then a dependence may exist. However, if $K > N$, no dependence exists. Usually, K is known but N is not, and so N is assumed to be some large integer.

11.2.1 Input and Output Set

Normally, data dependence is defined with respect to the set of variables that are used and modified by a statement, denoted by the *IN set* and *OUT set* respectively. An *input set* $\text{IN}(S_i)$ is a set of input items of statement S_i whose values are fetched in statement S_i. An *output set* $\text{OUT}(S_i)$ is a set of output items of statement S_i, whose values are changed in statement S_i.

11.2.2 Execution Order

Execution order is denoted by the symbol "Θ", $S_i \Theta S_j$ means statement S_i can be executed before statement S_j.

If S_i is enclosed in d-nested loops with indexes $I_1, I_2, \ldots, I_d$, then we write $S_i [i_1, i_2, \ldots, i_d]$ to refer to the instance of S_i during the particular iteration step when $I_1 = i_1, \ldots, I_d = i_d$. If both S_i and S_j are enclosed in d-nested loops with indexes $I_1, I_2, \ldots, I_d$, we write $S_i [i_1, i_2, \ldots, i_d] \Theta S_j [j_1, j_2, \ldots, j_d]$, if $S_i [i_1, i_2, \ldots, i_d]$ can be executed before $S_j [j_1, j_2, \ldots, j_d]$.

Example

```
L₁:DO I = 1, 5
L₂:    DO J = 1, 4
S₁:        A(I,J) = B(I,J) + C(I,J)
S₂:        B(I,J+1) = A(I,J) + B(I,J)
        ENDDO
    ENDDO
```

The execution order of this example is:

1. $S_1[i', i'] \Theta S_2[i'', i'']$

   whenever $i' < i''$ or both $i' = i''$ and $j' \leq j''$

   e.g., $S_1[1, 1] \Theta S_2[1, 1]$

2. $S_2[i'', j''] \Theta S_1[i', j']$

   whenever $i'' < i'$ or both $i'' = i'$ and $j'' < j'$

   e.g., $S_2[2, 3] \Theta S_1[3, 1]$

Computing the exact dependence relations can be very time-consuming or even impossible. So, we approximate the data dependence relations using IN/OUT sets and execution order.

If $S_1 \delta^f S_2$ then $S_1 \Theta S_2$ and $\text{OUT}(S_1) \cap \text{IN}(S_2) \neq 0$.

If $S_1 \delta^a S_2$ then $S_1 \Theta S_2$ and $\text{IN}(S_1) \cap \text{OUT}(S_2) \neq 0$.

If $S_1 \delta^o S_2$ then $S_1 \Theta S_2$ and $\text{OUT}(S_1) \cap \text{OUT}(S_2) \neq 0$.

The converse conditions are not true, but testing for execution order and set intersection is conservative. No dependence relations will be missed using this approximation.

Example

```
S1 : A = B + D
S2 : C = A * 3
S3 : A = A + C
S4 : E = A / 2
```

In this example, even though $S_1 \Theta S_4$ and $\text{OUT}(S_1) \cap \text{IN}(S_4) \neq 0$, there is no $S_1 \delta^f S_4$ relation, because S_4 cannot use the value of A computed in S_1, and S_3 recomputes A, hence S_4 will always use the value of A from S_3.

11.3 REPRESENTATIONS OF DATA DEPENDENCE

Table 11.1 lists four notations for representing data dependence. These are used by various dependence tests to detect potential parallelism by noting the absence of certain kinds of data dependencies. The most general notation is the dependence graph.

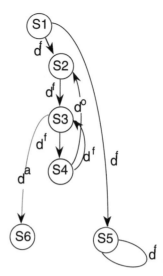

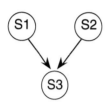

Figure 11.1 Data dependence graph is a precedence graph where nodes are statements and arcs are dependencies

Figure 11.2 Data dependence graph for a looping program

11.3.1 Dependence Graph

A *dependence graph* is a directed graph $G(V, E)$ where V is a set of nodes $V = \{S_1, S_2, ..., S_n\}$ corresponding to statement(s) in a program, E is a set of arcs $E = \{e_{ij} = (S_i, S_j) \mid S_i, S_j \in V\}$ representing data dependences between statement(s).

A *dependence cycle* is a sequence of dependencies initially starting with a node S and eventually returning to the starting node S. This makes the dependence graph cyclic.

Dependence graphs are also precedence graphs with the properties discussed in earlier chapters (see Figure 11.1). An arc from node S_1 to node S_3 in the graph means that statement S_1 must precede statement S_3 because S_3 depends on S_1 for a result. Typically each arc is labeled with δ^f, δ^a, or δ^o indicating which kind of dependency exists.

Example

Draw the data dependence relations and the data dependence graph for the following program (see Figure 11.2).

```
S₁:x = y +1
L₁:DO I = 2,30
S₂:   C(I) = x + B(I)
S₃:   A(I) = C(I - 1) + z
S₄:   C(I+1) = B(I) * A(I)
L₂:   DO J = 2, 50
S₅:     F(I,J) = F(I,J - 1) + x
```

```
         ENDDO
      ENDDO
   S6:z = y + 3
```

Data dependence relations in the graph of Figure 11.2:

$$S_1 \, \delta^f \, S_2 \qquad S_1 \, \delta^f \, S_5 \qquad S_2 \, \delta^f \, S_3 \qquad S_3 \, \delta^f \, S_4$$

$$S_4 \, \delta^f \, S_3 \qquad S_5 \, \delta^f \, S_5 \qquad S_3 \, \delta^a \, S_6 \qquad S_4 \, \delta^o \, S_2$$

11.3.2 Dependence Distance and Distance Vector

The greatest opportunity for parallelism is in converting nested loops. But, to understand the dependencies in nested loops, we need to define a measure of distance between the source and sink statements involved in a dependence relation.

Suppose a statement S is in a nested loop L. Let the first instance of S occur when the loop index is I_1, and the second instance occur when the index is I_2, where iteration I_1 is the source of a dependence and I_2 is the sink of the dependence relation. The *distance vector* is $I_1 - I_2$ for this dependence [Banerjee 1988b].

If the distance vector is the same for all dependencies of the loop, we say it has a *constant dependence distance*, otherwise it has a *variable dependence distance*.

Example
```
   L1:DO I = 1, 5
   L2:   DO J = 1,4
   S1:      A(I,J) = B(I,J) + C(I,J)
   S2:      B(I,J + 1) = A(I,J) + B(I,J)
         ENDDO
      ENDDO
```

The distances are 0 and 1 for the I and J loops, respectively. In this example, the distances are small constants, but in more complex cases, the distances may be difficult to compute. In such cases, we must use only the direction of the distance vector to make an inexact test of dependence.

Distance vectors are used in making exact tests of dependence, while direction vectors are used to make inexact tests. Both distance and direction have meaning in a graphical sense, when displayed in an iteration space graph.

11.3.3 Iteration Space Graph

The *iteration space* of a d-nested loop is defined as a d-dimensional discrete Cartesian space where each axis of the iteration space corresponds to a loop counter. Each point in the space represents the execution of all the statements in one iteration of the loop. Figure 11.3 shows an iteration space for the following nested loop.

Example
```
      DO I = 1, 4
         DO J = I, 4
            A(I, J) = A(I, J) + B(I, J)
```

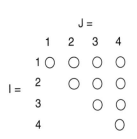

Figure 11.3 Iteration space of the nested loop

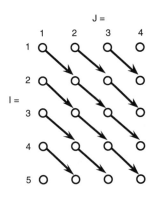

Figure 11.4 Iteration space graph with data dependence arrows

```
        ENDDO
    ENDDO
```

The lower bound of the inner loop is a simple function of the outer loop index. This means that only the lower diagonal portion of the iteration space is covered by the loop indexes.

Iteration space dependence graphs are used to represent the dependence relations in nested loops. The iteration space dependence graph shows these dependencies with an arrow drawn from the point corresponding to iteration $i = (i_1, i_2, ..., i_d)$ to the point corresponding to iteration $j = (j_1, j_2, ..., j_d)$ whenever there exist statements S_i and S_j in the loop such that $S_i[i] \, \delta \, S_j[j]$, for each pair of iterations $i \neq j$.

Example

```
DO I = 1, 5
    DO J = 1, 4
        X(I + 1, J + 1) = X(I, J) + Y(I, J)
    ENDDO
ENDDO
```

The iteration space dependence graph is shown in Figure 11.4.

As a convention, we will draw the iteration space graph as follows. The innermost loop index will be drawn horizontally, left to right. The outermost loop will be drawn vertically, from top to bottom of the diagram. Typically, we designate the innermost loop index as *J*, and the outer loop index as *I*.

11.3.4 Direction Vectors

The distance vector described previously is used to perform an exact test of dependence. *Exact testing* is the best that we can do; but it is often difficult or impossible to calculate an exact dependence. Therefore, *inexact tests* are performed to approximate dependence. Inexact testing uses direction instead of distance to detect possibilities of dependence. For this reason, we need a data dependence direction.

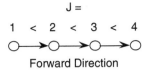

J =

1 < 2 < 3 < 4

Forward Direction

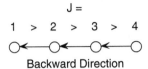

J =

1 > 2 > 3 > 4

Backward Direction

Figure 11.5   Forward direction is designated < and backward direction is designated >, when a dependence vector points along any dimension of the iteration space

Informally, *data dependence direction* is the direction of the data dependence within an iteration space. In terms of the iteration space, a forward direction always points toward higher indexes along at least one dimension, and a backward direction always points toward a lower index value (see Figure 11.5). The direction vectors of Figure 11.4 are forward because the arrows point toward higher numbered iterations.

We use a shorthand notation to designate a variety of dependence directions:

<   means the dependence crosses an iteration boundary $(i \rightarrow i + 1)$ forward.

=   means the dependence does not cross an iteration boundary.

>   means the dependence crosses an iteration boundary $(i \rightarrow i - 1)$ backward.

ø   means the iteration is unknown and so the data direction vector is simply a description of the direction of the dependence in each dimension.

In some cases, distances are clumsy to find and represent. Therefore, we are forced to use direction only. The sign of the distance is positive for a forward distance, negative for a backward direction, and distance zero otherwise.

11.4   OTHER DEPENDENCES

Here we give a brief description of some other types of dependence. For more discussion, refer to [Allen et al.; Burke; Callahan et al.].

11.4.1   Control Dependence

Control and data dependence decide dependence relations in both serial and parallel programs. But in parallel programs, data dependence determines execution order of the statements, while control dependence determines the set of possible execution paths. More specifically, a statement S_2 is *control dependent* on statement S_1 if the execution of S_1 determines whether statement S_2 is to be executed. A typical example is a conditional statement. The value of the condition decides whether the statements in a branch are performed.

Control dependence imposes an order on the execution of statements and thus is an important factor in restructuring, but data and control dependence can be treated uniformly by using the *If-conversion technique* introduced by Allen and Kennedy [Allen et al. January 1983]. We do not pursue this technique here.

11.4.2 Interprocedural Dependence

A more important type of dependence is *interprocedural dependence*. When a procedure or function call appears in a loop, most compilers assume that the loop must be executed serially. Analysis of the effects of the procedure and function call, including which parameters are changed and what global variables are used or changed, determines whether the procedure call prevents parallel code from being generated.

An alternative method for handling procedure and function calls is to expand the procedure or function in-line. This makes possible the application of some transformations that simultaneously manipulate code in the calling and called routines. However, in-line expansion should be done with care to avoid an undue increase in the time required for compilation [Burke; Callahan et al.]. We do not pursue these techniques here.

11.5 DATA DEPENDENCE TESTS

Step 1 of automatic parallelization is to perform a dependence test to detect potential for parallelization (see Table 11.1). Many algorithms have been proposed for data dependence testing [Banerjee 1988b; Allen et al. January 1983; Allen October 1987; Li 1989; Wolfe 1989]. We describe only a handful of the most useful algorithms.

The result of using a dependence test algorithm is said to be *definite* if the algorithm either determines data dependence or determines data independence (*exact test*). If the algorithm can neither determine data dependence nor data independence, the result is said to be *indefinite* (*inexact test*).

Unfortunately, it is not possible to obtain definite results efficiently in the general case. For example, to achieve accurate test results for complicated array references requires linear programming, and is not generally practical [Li 1990, 1989]. Finding practical algorithms for data dependence analysis remains a research topic.

Normally, practical algorithms try to detect data dependence based on some weaker sufficient conditions. If those conditions are not met, we assume there is data dependence and abandon certain possible parallelizations. These practical algorithms are the subject of this section.

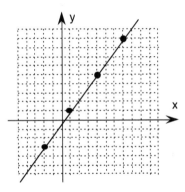

Figure 11.6 Integer solutions to 4x – 3y = 1

11.5.1 Diophantine Analysis

We begin by analyzing the dependencies in an iteration space graph. Since the iteration space is associated with integers, we must find integer solutions to equations defining the dependencies. Therefore, greatest-common-divisor, GCD, and linear *Diophantine equations* are used [Banerjee 1988b].

Let a and b be integer numbers ($b \neq 0$). We say that b divides a, denoted by $a|b$, if and only if there is an integer x such that $a = bx$. The greatest common divisor of $n \geq 1$ integer numbers, $i_1, \ldots, i_n$ which are not all 0, is defined as $GCD(i_1, \ldots, i_n) = \max\{b: i_j \mid b \text{ for all } j \in [1:n]\}$. For example, $GCD(24, 18) = 6$ and $GCD(57, 33, 24) = 3$.

A *linear Diophantine equation* is of the form $\sum\limits_{i=1}^{n} a_i x_i = c$, where $n \geq 1$, c, a_i are integers for all i, not all a_i are equal to 0, and the x_i are integer variables. A Diophantine equation has a solution if and only if $GCD(a_1, \ldots, a_n) \mid c$. Furthermore, GCD gives the minimum number of solutions that exist.

Example

> Does 4x – 3y = 1 have an integer solution? Yes, there is at least one solution to this Diophantine equation because $GCD(-3, 4) = 1$, and $1 \mid 1$.

Diophantine equations also have a geometric interpretation, which is illustrated for 3y = 4x – 1 in Figure 11.6. The straight line representing this equation goes through only those points of the two-dimensional integer space shown for which x and y are solutions. In the illustration, this is the case for the points $\{x, y\} = \{-2, -3\}$ $\{1, 1\}$ $\{4, 5\}$ $\{7, 9\}$. The additional solutions are obviously given by linear extrapolation with multiples of the difference $\{4, 5\} - \{1, 1\} = \{3, 4\}$.

Techniques for finding solutions to general Diophantine equations can be found in the references. We give a working heuristic for the two-dimensional case, as follows.

Solutions to $ax + by = c$:

$$x = \frac{-bt}{GCD(a, b)} + \text{"some multiple of } c\text{,"}$$

$$y = \frac{at}{GCD(a, b)} + \text{"some other multiple of } c\text{,"}$$

$t = 0, 1, 2\dots$.

Finding the multiples of c is usually a trial-and-error process, and t is any integer value.

Example

Solve $2x - 3y = 198$ for x, y. Since $a = 2$, $b = (-3)$, and $c = 198$, the formula yields a trial solution of:

$GCD(2, -3) = 1$

$x = 3t + \text{"some multiple of 198,"}$

$y = 2t + \text{"some other multiple of 198."}$

Trying "some multiple of 198" equal to $2(198) = 396$, and "some other multiple of 198" equal to $1(198) = 198$ gives solutions as:

$x = 3t + 396$

$y = 2t + 198$

Thus, for $t = 0, 1, \dots$ we get:

$x = 396, 399, \dots$

$y = 198, 200, \dots$

Solutions to two-dimensional Diophantine equations are especially useful for finding dependence in 2-nested loops, where each axis in the solution space corresponds to the iterations in a 2-dimensional iteration space. The solution is used to perform an exact test of dependence, as illustrated in the next section.

11.5.2 Exact Test

When a multidimensional array is accessed in a nested loop, the *exact test* is a matter of solving a system of Diophantine equations. The solution gives us the point in the loop where a data dependence exists due to indexing of arrays. If no solution exists, there is no dependence.

Example

Use Diophantine analysis to test the following loop for data dependence:

```
    DO i = 1, 101
S1:    A(2*i) = ...
S2:    ... = A(3*i + 198)
    ENDDO
```

Diophantine equation: $2x = 3y + 198$ where $1 \leq x, y \leq 101$

General solution: $x = 3t + 396, y = 2t + 198$

The constraints on x and y became constraints on t:

$1 \leq 3t + 396 \leq 101$ thus $-131 \leq t \leq -99$,

$1 \leq 2t + 198 \leq 101$ thus $-98 \leq t \leq -49$.

Because $t \leq -99$ contradicts $-98 \leq t$, the Diophantine equation does not have a solution that satisfies the given constraints. Therefore, the pair of references are not data dependent.

Subscripts must be linear in the loop index variables and there can be no other symbolic terms. The general solution of a Diophantine equation can be formulated explicitly as linear functions of some parameters. Given a Diophantine equation $f(i_1, i_2, \ldots, i_n) = c$, its general solution is $i = At + c$ where A is an $n*(n-1)$ integer matrix, and c is an integer vector. There are classical procedures to find the general solution.

If a Diophantine equation has two variables, its general solution is easy to find. Moreover, the solution will only have one parameter, and all constraints on the variables of the equation can be rewritten as constraints on this single parameter. It is straightforward to check whether there are particular values of the parameter that fit all the constraints. An exact data dependence test (Single Index Exact Test) can be efficiently performed on a pair of single-dimensional array references provided the subscript of each reference has only one loop index, since the Diophantine equation for this pair has only two variables.

11.5.3 Inexact Tests

Solving a system of Diophantine equations with arbitrarily many variables is in general too computationally expensive to be applicable to real programs. If a subscript equation contains more than two unknowns, its general solution will contain more than one parameter and the consistency check becomes substantially more difficult. No efficient method is known. Methods weaker than an exact test have to be tried. In this subsection, some inexact test algorithms are discussed.

GCD Test

Statement S with $f(i) = a_0 + a_1 i$ and $g(i) = b_0 + b_1 i$ depends on itself if and only if $GCD(a_1, b_1 i) \mid b_0 - a_0$.

Example

Test for dependences between S_1 and S_2 in the following loop:

```
    DO i = ...
       DO j = ...
S1:       A(2*i + 2*j +101) = ...
S2:       ... = A(2*i -2*j)
       ENDDO
    ENDDO
```

The Diophantine equation is $2i_1 + 2j_1 - 2i_2 + 2j_2 + 101 = 0$. The GCD of its coefficients is 2, and 2 does not divide 101. Therefore, the equation does not have solutions and there is no data dependence between the two references.

Note that the GCD test ignores the region in iteration space associated with the dependence. Thus, it may indicate a dependence when in fact there is none. That is, GCD analysis only yields a necessary condition for dependence, but not a sufficient condition. This subtle difference is illustrated in the next example.

Example

Test for dependences between S_1 and S_2 in the following nested loop:

```
L1:DO I = 0,10
L2:   DO J = 0,10
S1:      A(2*I + J) = ...
S2       ... = A(- I + 2*J - 21)
            ...
         ENDDO
      ENDDO
```

The Diophantine equation is $2i_1 + i_2 + j_1 - 2j_2 + 21 = 0$. The GCD test says there is a solution, but there is no solution to the Diophantine equation in the region covered by the loop indexes: $0 \le i_1, i_2, j_1, j_2 \le 10$. This observation leads to another inexact test, called the bounds test.

Bounds Test

In some cases we do not need to solve the linear Diophantine equation if the solution exceeds limits of the loop indexes. This so-called *bounds test* treats the Diophantine equation as a real-valued equation whose domain is a convex set defined by a bounded constant loop and dependence directions. The equation has real-valued solutions over the given domain if and only if the minimum of the left-hand side is no greater than zero and the maximum is no less than zero [Li 1990].

Example

Test for dependence between S_1 and S_2 in the following bounded loops:

```
L1:DO i = 1, 30
L2:   DO j = 1, 30
S1:      A(200 - i) = ...
S2:      ... = A(i + j)
      ENDDO
```

ENDDO

The Diophantine equation is $i_1 + i_2 + j_1 - 200 = 0$. The solutions are treated as real-valued functions on the domain of $1 \leq i_1, i_2, j_1 \leq 30$. The left-hand side of the equation has its maximum at -110. This lies outside the indexes, so the equation has no solutions and there is no data dependence between the two array references.

Banerjee's Inequality Test

A bounds test analysis is useful only if there is a fast way to find the maximum and minimum on a region. Banerjee provides a fast way to do this [Allen October 1987; Banerjee 1988a, 1988b].

If $f(x) = a_0 + a_1 x$ and $g(y) = b_0 + b_1 y$, then

$$\max(f(x) - g(y)) = a_0 + a_1 - b_0 + 2b_1 + (a_1{}^+ - b_1)^+(N - 2)$$

$$\min(f(x) - g(y)) = a_0 + a_1 - b_0 + 2b_1 - (a_1{}^- - b_1)^+(N - 2)$$

where the superscript notation is defined as follows. If t denotes a real number, then the positive part t^+ and the negative part t^- of t are defined as

$$t^+ = \begin{cases} t, & t \geq 0 \\ 0, & t < 0 \end{cases}$$

$$t^- = \begin{cases} -t, & t \leq 0 \\ 0, & t > 0 \end{cases}$$

Thus $t^+ \geq 0$, $t^- \geq 0$ and $t = t^+ - t^-$. Banerjee's inequality test is :

$$-b_1 - (a_1{}^- + b_1)^+(N - 2) \leq b_0 + b_1 - a_0 - a_1 \leq -b_1 + (a_1{}^+ - b_1)^+(N - 2)$$

Note that this test, like the GCD test, yields only a sufficient condition.

11.5.4 Dependence Direction Vector Test

In general, we want to test both $S_i \, \delta \, S_j$ and $S_j \, \delta \, S_i$ to determine whether, and under what conditions, arrays accessed by the two references *intersect*. Intersection occurs when subscripts are simultaneously equal. The conditions of intersection are a direction vector $(\psi_1, \psi_2, ..., \psi_d)$ relating the indexes:

$I_1 \, \psi_1 \, J_1$

$I_2 \, \psi_2 \, J_2$

...

$I_d \, \psi_d \, J_f$

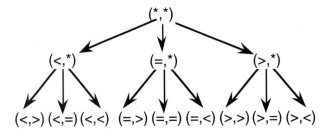

Figure 11.7 Direction hierarchy for two loops

The *direction vector test* looks for intersections with a direction vector. If independence can be proven with this direction vector, then the regions accessed by the two references are disjoint. If independence is not proven, then one direction vector element is redefined as "<", "=", or ">", depending on its direction.

Direction vector testing is done on a hierarchy of direction vectors. The hierarchy for two loops is shown in Figure 11.7. If independence can be proven at any point in the hierarchy, the direction vectors beneath it need not be tested [Wolfe 1987].

The GCD test may conclude that there are dependencies somewhere in iteration space, but not necessarily in the region of the iteration space we are interested in. The direction vector test is used to find data independencies that GCD cannot find. It does this by considering constraints on the search space.

This test can be more difficult to apply than GCD, but it is less computationally expensive than solving the Diophantine equations. The direction vector test is more accurate than GCD when a loop has no dependence relations but the subscripts lie outside of the iteration space.

Example

The following loop has no dependence among its iterations, but the iteration space is contained within a 10 by 10 region while the subscripts of A are outside of this region.

```
DO I = 1, 10
  DO J =1, 10
    A(10*I +J) =
    ....     = A(10*I +J - 1)
  ENDDO
ENDDO
```

The iteration space is defined for $(I, J) = (1{:}10, 1{:}10)$, but the subscripts of A range over $(11{:}110)$ and $(10{:}109)$. GCD says there is a dependence, because $GCD(10, 1) = 1$. In fact, there is no dependence in the region of iteration space that we are concerned with.

11.6 PARALLEL LOOP NOTATION

Step 2 of Table 11.1 requires that we rewrite the serial loop into one of three parallel forms, depending on the kinds of dependencies revealed in step 1. The parallel forms DOALL, DOACROSS, and DOSEQ were proposed by Banerjee [1988b] to simplify the problem of loop analysis. We adopt Benerjee's model adding FORTRAN-like notation to represent vector parallelism in array operations.

1 DOALL is a loop that allows total parallel execution. That is, all iterations of the loop body are allowed to run simultaneously.

2 DOACROSS is a loop that allows partial overlap of successive iterations during execution. That is, DOACROSS is a kind of vector *pipeline* control structure that overlaps loop iterations as if they were executed in different stages of a pipeline.

3 DOSEQ is a serial DO LOOP without parallelism.

DOACROSS is the most complex parallel loop [Cytron (1986)], because it implements a pipeline of synchronized iterations. If all iterations are independent, then a DOACROSS reduces to a DOALL loop. At the other extreme, all iterations of a DOACROSS may depend on previous iterations, in which case the DOACROSS reduces to a DOSEQ loop. DOACROSS can be either very difficult to handle or very easy to convert to DOALL using the loop skewing technique discussed below. A detailed discussion of DOACROSS is beyond the scope of this book. Interested readers should read [Cytron 1986].

Example

Some nested loops studied earlier are rewritten in our FORTRAN-like notation as follows.

```
L1:DOSEQ I = 2, N           {Each iteration is done serially}
L2:   DOALL J = 2, M        {Do this part in parallel}
S1:      A(I,J) = A(I-1, J) +1 {All iterations are independent}
      ENDDO
   ENDDO
```

Now, contrast this loop with its loop-interchanged equivalent below.

```
L2:DOALL J = 2, M           {All iterations in parallel}
L1:   DOSEQ I = 2, N        {Serial task inside each iteration}
S1:      A(I,J) = A(I-1, J) +1
      ENDDO
   ENDDO
```

11.6.1 Vectorization

Vectorization is a transformation of a loop to a sequence of *vector statements*. A vector statement is executed as though all results on the left side of an assignment statement are simultaneously stored.

A vector statement is a restricted form of a DOALL loop in the sense that all vectorizable loops can be converted into DOALL loops. The reverse is not always true. The vector statement

```
A[1:N] = B[1:N] * C[1:N]
```

is functionally equivalent to the loop

```
DOALL I=1,N
    A(I) = B(I) * C(I)
ENDDO
```

11.6.2 Normalization

Some transformations are most easily defined when the syntax of loops is in a restricted form called a *normalized loop*. A loop is normalized if and only if its loop counter is initialized to 1 and its step value is also unity. Thus, DO $I = 1$, N, 1 is normalized, but DO $I = 2$, N, 3 is not.

Many transformation techniques have been developed for the normalized loop. Also some parallelism detection and data dependence testing algorithms are made easier if the loop is normalized. Fortunately, every FORTRAN-like DO loop can be normalized [Allen October 1987; Kuck et al.; Wolfe 1989].

11.6.3 Nested Loops

A nested loop L of *length* m is a sequence of m loops $L = (L_1, L_2, ..., L_m)$ such that L_k contains L_{k+1}, and there is no third loop contained in L_k that also contains L_{k+1} ($1 \le k \le m-1$). The index, lower-bound, and upper-bound of L are three m-vectors l, p, and q, respectively, defined by $l = (l_1, l_2, ..., l_m)$, $p = (p_1, p_2, ..., p_m)$, $q = (q_1, q_2, ..., q_m)$. The nest is *perfect* if and only if the body of L_k is just L_{k+1} ($1 \le k \le m-1$).

A loop is *one-way nested* if there is one loop at each nest level. $L = (L_1, L_2, ..., L_m)$ denotes a one-way nested loop with nest depth m, where L_i ($i = 1, ..., m$) is the number of iterations of the loop at the m-th level [Polychronopoulos 1988a, 1987]. A loop is *multi-way nested* if there are two or more loops at the same nest level [Polychronopoulos 1988a, 1987; Girkar and Polychronopoulos 1988]. Nested loops may contain combinations of DOALL, DOACROSS, and DOSEQ.

Example

The following loop is perfectly nested because the body of L_1 is L_2, only.

```
L1:DO I = 1, N
L2:   DO J = 2, M
S1:      T(I) = T(I) +1
S2:      A(I,J) = B(I,J) + A(I, J-1) *T(I)
      ENDDO
   ENDDO
```

The following loop is not perfectly nested because S_1 is part of the body of L_1.

```
L1:DO I = 1, N
S1:   T(I) = T(I) +1
```

```
L2:    DO J = 2, M
S2:      A(I,J) = B(I,J) + A(I, J-1) *T(I)
       ENDDO
     ENDDO
```

11.7 PARALLELIZATION OPTIMIZATION TECHNIQUES

Step 2 of our approach to automatic parallelization includes an optimization phase, where we attempt to gain greater parallelism by restructuring (see Table 11.1). There are numerous transformations for parallelization optimization. We list only the most widely used transformations. For some, we provide conditions for legal transformation using the data dependence relations. For further discussion, refer to [Callahan; Allen October 1987].

These transformations are applied independently and in an arbitrary order. Unfortunately, it is frequently the case that the order of application is significant. Thus, if we apply the same set of n transformations to the same program $n!$ different ways, we will get $n!$ semantically equivalent programs. Due to the differences in their syntax, these programs will contain varying amounts of parallelism, resulting in possibly different performance on the same machine. The best order of application is known for only a few special cases [Polychronopoulos 1988b]. In general, finding the best order to apply the transformations is an open research problem.

11.7.1 Loop Fusion (*Loop Jamming*)

Loop fusion selectively merges two loops into a single loop. It was originally developed for vector machine compilers to recognize vectorization in FORTRAN loops. But in parallel compilers, it is used to decrease the overhead of parallel loops [Wolfe 1987].

Example
The following disjoint loops are fused into one loop by noting that they are identical in every respect except for different names of index variables.

```
L1:DOALL I = 1, N
S1:   D(I) = E(I) + F(I) + X(I)
   ENDDO
L2:DOALL J = 1,N
S2:   E(J) = D(I) * F(I)
   ENDDO
```

Fused loop:

```
L1:DOALL I = 1, N
S1:   D(I) = E(I) + F(I) + X (I)
S2:   E(J) = D(I) *F(I)
   ENDDO
```

If there are no downward data dependence relations with backward directions, then two loops can be fused.

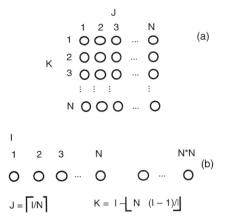

$$J = \lceil I/N \rceil \qquad K = I - \lfloor N \; (I-1)/I \rfloor$$

Figure 11.8 Loop coalescing (a) Before coalescing; nested iteration space, (b) After coalescing; un-nested iteration space

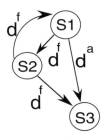

Figure 11.9 Data dependence graph for the example

11.7.2 Loop Coalescing

Loop coalescing transforms several types of nested parallel loops into a single loop. This transformation makes the loop scheduling problem simple and reduces the process creation overhead for some systems.

Coalescing is achieved through a universal index mapping that linearizes multi-dimensional iteration spaces [Polychronopoulos 1987]. Thus, a two-dimensional iteration space is converted into a one-dimensional iteration space (see Figure 11.8).

Example

```
DOALL J = 1,N
   DOALL K = 1,N
      A(J,K) = ...
   ENDDO
ENDDO
```

After loop coalescing:

```
DOALL I = 1, N*N
   A(ceil(I/N)), I-N(bottom(I-1)/N) = ...
ENDDO
```

11.7.3 Loop Distribution

Loop distribution distributes a loop around each statement in its body, or around code modules inside the loop. This is useful for transforming multiway nested loops into one-way nested loops. Vectorization is one form of loop distribution transformation.

In general, loop distribution around two statements S_i and S_j is legal if there is no data dependence between S_i and S_j or if there are data dependences in only one direction.

This example shows how to use loop distribution for parallelization.

```
      DOSEQ I = 1, N
S1:      A(I+1) = B(I-1) + C(I)
S2:      B(I) = A(I) * K
S3:      C(I) = B(I) - 1
      ENDDO
```

Data dependence relations (see Figure 11.9) are:

$$S_1 \; \delta^f \; S_2$$

$$S_2 \; \delta^f \; S_1$$

$$S_1 \; \delta^a \; S_3$$

$$S_2 \; \delta^f \; S_3$$

The whole loop cannot be parallelized, but after loop distribution parts of it can be parallelized.

```
      DOSEQ I = 1, N
S1:   A(I+1)=B(I-1)+C(I)
S2:   B(I) = A(I) * K
   ENDDO
   DOALL I = 1, N
S3:C(I) = B(I) - 1
   ENDDO
```

11.7.4 Loop Interchange

Loop interchange permutes a pair of nested loops so that the outer loop becomes the inner loop and vice versa [Wolfe 1989]. It can be applied repeatedly to interchange more than two loops in a set of nested loops.

When loops are nested, vectorization is possible only for the innermost loop. Loop interchange is used in such cases to bring the vectorizable loop to the innermost position [Polychronopoulos et al.].

On the other hand, when using it for parallelization, we bring the parallelizable loop to the outermost position to achieve maximum parallelism.

Example

```
   L1:DOALL I = 2, N
   L2:   DOSEQ J = 2, M
   S1:      A(I,J) = A(I,J-1) +1
         ENDDO
      ENDDO
```

This loop is not vectorizable since the innermost loop must be executed serially. But the outermost loop is. Interchanging makes vectorization possible as follows.

After loop interchanging:

```
L1:DOSEQ J = 2, N
L2:    DOALL I = 2, M
S1:       A(I,J) = A(I,J-1) +1
       ENDDO
    ENDDO
```

After vectorization:

```
L2:DOSEQ J = 1, M
S1:    A(1:N,J) = A(1:N,J-1) +1
    ENDDO
```

Loop interchange may be used to achieve maximum parallelism instead of vectorization. Consider the following example where the interchange is reversed.

Example

```
L1:DOSEQ I = 2, N
L2:    DOALL J = 1, N
S1:       A(I,J) = A(I-1,J) +B(I)
       ENDDO
    ENDDO
```

After loop interchanging:

```
L2:DOALL J = 1, N
L1:    DOSEQ I = 2, N
S1:       A(I,J) = A(I-1,J) +B(I)
       ENDDO
    ENDDO
```

Loop interchange may achieve maximum parallelism, but interchange is not always possible. In general, two perfectly nested loops can be interchanged if there is no data dependence on a $(<, >)$ direction vector [Allen; Wolfe 1989]. But the reverse is not always true.

Example

```
DOALL I = 2, N
    DOSEQ J = 2, N
S1:    A(I,J) = (A(I,J-1) +A(I,J+1))/2
    ENDDO
ENDDO
```

The dependences are $S_1 \delta^f_{(<, =)} S_1$ and $S_1 \delta^a_{(=, <)} S_1$. There is no $(<,>)$ dependence direction vector so the loops are interchangeable.

After loop interchange:

```
DOSEQ J = 2, N
    DOALL I = 2,N
S1:    A(I,J) = (A(I,J-1) + A(I,J+1))/2
    ENDDO
ENDDO
```

The dependence now is $S_1 \delta^f_{(<,=)} S_1$ and $S_1 \delta^a_{(<,=)} S_1$

A serious weakness of this technique is that there is no unique way to determine the best interchange.

11.7.5 Node Splitting

Loop parallelization is not possible when the statements in the loop body are involved in a *dependence cycle*. There are cases, however, where a dependence cycle can be broken, resulting in parallelization. Usually this transformation is followed by loop distribution.

Example

```
L1:DOSEQ I = 1, N
S1:    A(I) = B(I) + C(I)
S2:    D(I) = A(I-1)* A(I+1)
    ENDDO
```

We eliminate the cycle by splitting the node using renaming, which causes *anti-dependence.*

After breaking the cycle with a temporary array, TEMP:

```
L1:DOSEQ I = 1, N
S1:    A(I) = B(I) + C(I)
S3:    TEMP(I) = A(I+1)
S2:    D(I) = A(I-1)*TEMP(I)
    ENDDO
```

After statements reordering:

```
L1:DOSEQ I = 1, N
S3:    TEMP(I) = A(I+1)
S1:    A(I) = B(I) + C(I)
S2:    D(I) = A(I-1)*TEMP(I)
    ENDDO
```

After loop distribution:

```
L1:DOALL I = 1, N
S3:    TEMP(I) = A(I+1)
    ENDDO
L1:DOALL I = 1, N
S1:    A(I) = B(I) + C(I)
    ENDDO
L1:DOALL I = 1, N
S2:    D(I) = A(I-1)*TEMP(I)
    ENDDO
```

Data dependence graphs for these are left as exercises.

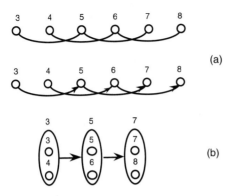

Figure 11.10   Iteration spaces (a) before loop shrinking; (b) after loop shrinking

11.7.6   Loop Shrinking

When all dependences in a cycle are flow dependent, node splitting cannot help. Depending on the distance of each dependence, however, we may parallelize some parts of these loops using *loop shrinking* [Polychronopoulos et al., 1988a].

Example

```
L1:DOSEQ I = 3,N
S1:    A(I) = B(I-2) -1
S2:    B(I) = A(I-3)* k
    ENDDO
```

After shrinking :

```
L1:DOSEQ J = 3, N, 2
      DOALL I = J, J+1
S1:      A(I) = B(I-2) -1
S2:      B(I) = A(I-3)*k
      ENDDO
   ENDDO
```

The iteration space graph for before and after shrinking of the example is shown in Figure 11.10. In this example, the length of the loop is shrunk by one half.

11.7.7   Loop Unrolling

Simple *loop unrolling* was used in Chapter 10 to illustrate how to schedule loops. Recall that loop unrolling restructures a loop by writing the iterations as straight-line code segments. That is, it makes one or more copies of the loop body.

Loop unrolling is done by peeling off iterations at the beginning, middle, or end of the loop [Polychronopoulos 1988a; Padua December 1986].

Example

Remove the first iteration from the loop:

```
     J = N
     DOSEQ I = 1,N
        A(I) = (B(I) +B(J))/2
        J=I
     ENDDO
```

After unrolling the first iteration of the loop:

```
     A(1) =(B(1) +B(N))/2
     DOSEQ I = 2,N
        A(I) = (B(I) +B(I-1))/2
     ENDDO
```

Example

Remove iterations from the end of the loop by increasing the stride:

```
     DOSEQ J = 1,N,K
        DOSEQ I= J, MIN(J+K,N)
           A(I) = B(I) + C(I)
        ENDDO
     ENDDO
```

If the relationship of N and M in the function call MIN(M, N) is known, this function call can be eliminated by peeling off the last iteration of the loop. MIN(J + K, N) will be executed TRUNC(N/K) times, which is unnecessary.

```
     N1 = TRUNC(N/K)
     N2 = N1*K
     N3 = N-N2
     DOSEQ J = 1,N2,K
        DOSEQ I = J,J+K
           A(I) = B(I)+C(I)
        ENDDO
     ENDDO
     DOSEQ I = N3+1, N
        A(I) = B(I) +C(I)
     ENDDO
```

In general, loop unrolling replicates the body of the loop inside the loop for K successive values of the loop index and increments the loop stride by K–1. This has the effect of reducing the overhead of performing loop control testing.

Example
```
L1:DOSEQ I = 1, 100
S1:    A(I) = B(I+2)*C(I-1)
          ENDDO
```

After loop unrolling:

```
L1:DOSEQ I = 1, 99, 2
S1:    A(I) = B(I+2)*C(I-1)
S1:    A(I+1) = B(I+3)*C(I)
          ENDDO
```

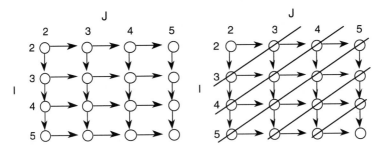

Figure 11.11 Iteration space containing a diagonal wave front

11.7.8 Loop Skewing

Loop skewing extracts parallelism from multiple nested loops in many cases where parallelism cannot be found in any single loop [Wolfe 1986].

Example
```
DOSEQ I = 2, N-1
  DOSEQ J = 2, N-1
    A(I,J) = (A(I+1, J)+A(I-1,J)+A(I, J+1)+ A(I, J-1))/4
  ENDDO
ENDDO
```

Neither the J loop nor the I loop can be parallelized. But if we examine the iteration space graph shown in Figure 11.11, we notice a *wave front* along the diagonal. The iterations along the diagonal can be done in parallel.

In general, the wavefront method depends on finding the angle of the wavefront through the iteration space. But, this method only works with simple subscript expressions and is not integrated with other well-known data dependence tests for parallelism detection.

Loop skewing shifts the index set of the original loop, creating a rhomboid iteration space out of what was a square (see Figure 11.12). The corresponding restructured code is given below.

```
DOALL I = 2, N-1
  DO J = I+2, I+N-1
    A(I,J-1) = (A(I+1, J-I)+A(I-1,J-I)+A(I, J+1-I)+ A(I, J-1-I))/4
  ENDDO
ENDDO
```

11.8 CODE GENERATION

Once parallelism is found and optimization is completed, the blocks of dependent code must be packaged into tasks, and the tasks must be scheduled to run on the target machine. This is the final step in our 3-step process. Unfortunately, methods for achieving this step vary according to the architectural features of the target machine.

At one extreme is the simplicity of global data in a shared-memory machine, and at the other extreme is the complexity of message-passing and *data partitioning* required in a distributed-memory machine.

The primary concern with shared-memory machines is the high cost of process initiation, which we must pay each time a task is started. The analog of this cost is the high cost of message-passing in distributed-memory machines. Here, we strive to reduce the communication overhead while maximizing the parallelism. Both kinds of machines require the code generator to solve the *minmax problem* of parallel programming.

11.8.1 Parallelizing Shared-Memory Program Loops

Code generation for shared-memory systems is not very difficult once dependence analysis and transformations have been performed. The compiler merely needs to insert synchronization statements in the appropriate places. For details, the interested reader should read the numerous works of Allen and Kennedy.

A variety of scheduling techniques can be used to minimize process initiation overhead, while maximizing the parallelism. These have been discussed in previous chapters.

11.8.2 Parallelization for Distributed-Memory System

In the last few years research attention has been focused on developing parallel compilers for shared-memory parallel systems. Reasonable performance results have been achieved, but research on parallel compilers for distributed-memory systems is still in its infancy [Lee 1990; Paalvast et al. 1990; Reed et al. 1987].

The concept of parallelization for distributed-memory systems is significantly different from that of shared-memory systems, because of (1) data partitioning — data must be explicitly distributed to each processor, and (2) communication —*message passing* must be specified explicitly. This is the so-called *distribution problem* of distributed-memory machines.

Data partitioning influences the subsequent communication overhead, which in turn has remarkable influence on the speed of the parallel program. The problem of

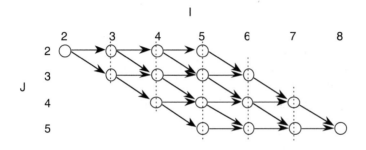

Figure 11.12 Skewed iteration space is a rhomboid

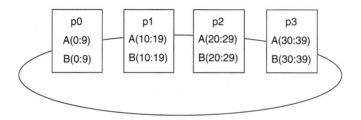

Figure 11.13   Ring-connected distributed-memory system with 4 nodes

determining an optimal partition with regard to the *minimax problem* is intractable and no adequate near-optimal methods are known thus far [Colin et al.].

Even if we assume that data partitioning is done by some unknown means, we must somehow find the appropriate message-passing patterns [Ikudome et al.]. That is, we must set up a logical network topology that best suits the application program, and then map this to the hardware network IN (Interconnection Network). This is the second major open research problem facing distributed-memory compiler writers.

11.8.3   Distribution Patterns

A *communication point* is a statement in a task that performs a message-passing operation such as a SEND or RECEIVE. A pattern of communication is established by inserting communication points in each parallel task. In this subsection we discuss some methods of identifying and inserting communication points in parallel loops.

For simplicity, assume the application is suited to a logical topology that is a *ring*. The ring is used to illustrate three distribution patterns common to most loops: (1) *simple distribution* (2) *prefetching*, and (3) *interleaving*.

Example

Suppose we want to distribute two arrays, $A(40)$ and $B(40)$ throughout a ring as shown in Figure 11.13. For simplicity, we assume a simple ring-connected distributed-memory machine with 4 nodes. The goal is to distribute the two arrays to the 4 processors in a pattern that minimizes the message-passing delay and overhead. Figure 11.13 shows the end-result of the distribution, but it does not show how the arrays got to each processing node in the ring.

Simple Distribution

Simple distribution is used when the iterations of a loop are independent and the data are evenly distributed across all processors. In the previous example, each of the 4 processors is allocated exactly 1/4 of the elements in arrays A and B. Thus, processor p_0 receives elements 0:9, p_1 receives elements 10:19, and so forth.

Example

```
DOALL I = 0, N-1
   A(I)=A(I)+B(I)
ENDDO
```

Assuming $N = 40$, 4 processor nodes, and equal distribution of A and B, the compiler must generate parallelized code that is equivalent to:

```
DOSEQ I = 1, 4                 {4 processor nodes}
   PL = 10*(I-1)               {Lower index = 0, 10, 20, 30}
   PU = 10*I - 1               {Upper index = 9, 19, 29, 39}
   SEND(A(PL:PU), B(PL:PU), I) {Processor I gets a chunk}
ENDDO
{Now, each of the 4 nodes do identical loops on different chunks...}
RECEIVE(A(0:9), B(0:9))        {These are different A(10), B(10)'s}
DOSEQ I = 0,9                  {Grain size equals 40/4 }
   A(I) = A(I) + B(I)          {4 of these are going on in parallel}
ENDDO
```

This distribution pattern is relatively simple, but it hides the inefficiencies that may result if it is applied blindly. For example, each processor must wait until it receives 1/4 of A and B. The selected elements of A and B are sequentially dispensed from p_0, and may take more time to send than to process!

After the loop computes the sum, and replaces each element of A with $A + B$, the resulting values of A must be collected on one or more of the processors. This is not shown in the example, but it takes time, reducing the overall benefit of parallelism.

Prefetching

The previous example performed simple distribution, using a simple pattern. What happens when the distribution pattern is more elaborate? Consider the following example where the application requires communication between neighbors. A simple average is computed by summing adjacent elements of B.

Example

```
DOALL I = 1, N-2
   A(I) = 0.5 * (B(I-1)+B(I+1))
ENDDO
```

Assume the data are partitioned and distributed evenly across all 4 processors as before. Then, processor p_0 averages elements $B(0:9)$, p_1 averages $B(10:19)$, p_2 averages $B(20:29)$, .and p_3 averages $B(30:39)$. The averages are stored in $p_0:A(1:9)$, $p_1:A(10:19)$, $p_3:A(20:29)$, and $p_3:A(30:38)$, respectively.

Simple distribution fails to distribute all of the data needed at each processor, however, due to end conditions. Note that processor p_0 needs $B(10)$ from processor p_1; p_1 needs $B(9)$ from p_0, etc. That is, the array references overlap, leading to a flurry of swaps during the processing. We see this pattern of swaps emerge if we modify the previous solution to fit this problem as follows.

```
DOSEQ I = 1, 4                 {4 processor nodes}
   PL = 10*(I-1)               {Lower index = 0, 10, 20, 30}
   PU = 10*I - 1               {Upper index = 9, 19, 29, 39}
   SEND(A(PL:PU), B(PL:PU), I) {Processor I gets a chunk}
ENDDO
```

```
{Processors are numbered, 0,1,2,3. Variable ME=Processor Id}
{On ME.....}
DIMENSION A(1:10), B(0:10)      {Extra elements used to hold overlaps}
RECEIVE(A(0:9), B(0:9))         {These are different A, B's}
DOSEQ I = 1, 9                  {Grain size equals 40/4}
    IF (ME=0) THEN
           SEND(B(9), ME+1) {Swap with p1...}
           RECEIVE (B(10), ME+1)
    IF (ME=3) THEN
      SEND (B(1), ME-1)
      RECEIVE(B(0), ME-1) {Swap with p2...}
    IF ((ME=1) .OR. (ME=2)) THEN   {All other processors, Swap}
      SEND (B(1), ME-1)
      SEND (B(9), ME+1)
      RECEIVE(B(10), ME+1)
      RECEIVE(B(0),  ME-1)
    A(I) = B(I-1) + B(I+1)
ENDDO
```

Clearly, these SEND/RECEIVE operations in the middle of each loop introduce a delay, and add to processing overhead. Because they are not dependent on the loop counter, they can immediately be moved out of the loop, and combined with the initial RECEIVE message. That is, they can be prefetched, once we know their pattern of communication.

In addition, we can take advantage of the ring topology of the logical network in the prefetching phase. If memory is large enough, we send all of B to processor p_0. Then we send all but $B(0:8)$ to p_1, p_1 sends all but its $B(0:8)$ to p_2, and p_2 sends all but its $B(0:8)$ to p_3. Each processor ends up with its overlapping duplicates plus its unique elements of each array.

Ring communication parallelizes the message-passing operations as well as the loop processing operations, yielding a higher degree of performance. The code to do prefetching across a ring is left as an exercise for the reader (see Problem 8).

Interleaving

In some applications the distribution pattern is a *broadcast* to all processors as illustrated in the next example. This example is similar to the previous examples except each element of A contains the sum of N elements of B. While not a very interesting application, the resulting loop is challenging from the point of view of distribution patterns.

Example
```
DOALL I = 0,N-1
   DOSEQ J = 0,N-1
      A(I) = A(I) + B(J)
   ENDDO
ENDDO
```

In this example, each processor needs the entire vector B. Every processor might prefetch the whole vector B into local memory before entering the parallel loop, but this assumes all processors have enough memory to hold copies of B. To get around the high demand for memory, the compiler can generate code to interleave the broadcasts with the computation.

The broadcasts constitute overhead that can be overlapped with the computation if asynchronous communication is supported by the hardware. We might send a block of B to all processors, let them compute a partial total, discard the block of B's, and wait to receive another block. Each processor receives a subsequent block, continues to sum, and then discards the block and so forth, until all elements of B have been sent, totaled, and discarded.

11.9 PARALLELIZING TOOLS

There have been many attempts to construct a parallelizing compiler that creates parallel code or automatically extracts parallelism out of existing serial programs. Examples of automatic parallelizing compilers are Parafrase–2, PFC$^+$, and SUPERB [Zima; Polychronopoulos et al.; Allen; Allen et al.].

Fully automatic analysis of complete programs is still not possible. But semi-automatic restructuring tools have been constructed to interactively perform dependence analysis and help a programmer identify parallelism and perform the necessary transformations. Examples are FORGE(MIMDizer) from Pacific Sierra, PTOOL(Rice University), and ParaScope [Allen et al.; Polychronopoulos et al.].

PROBLEMS FOR DISCUSSION AND SOLUTION

1 Discuss which representations of data dependence are better and under what conditions: task graph, iteration space, flow dependence, dependence direction.

2 Draw the iteration space graph for the following program.

```
    DO I = 1, 3
S1:  A(I) = B(I)
     DO J = 1,2
S2:     C(I,J) = A(I) + B(J)
     ENDDO
    ENDDO
```

3 Draw the iteration space graph and find the direction vector for the following loop.

```
L1:DO I1 = 1, 10
L2:  DO I2 = 2,20
S1:     A(I1,I2) = B(I1,I2-1) + C(I1,I2)
S2:     B(I1,I2) = A(I1,I2) + B(I1,I2)
```

```
        ENDDO
    ENDDO
```

4 Consider the following program and find the data dependence relations between S_1 and S_2. Transform this program into a parallel equivalent.

```
L₁:DO I1 = 1, 10
L₂:    DO I2 = 1, 4
L₃:      DO J = 1, 10
S₁:          A(I1,I2+1,J) = B(I1,I2,J) *D(I1,I2,J)
S₂:          B(I1+1,I2,K) = A(I1,I2,K+1) + C(I1,I2,K)
          ENDDO
        ENDDO
    ENDDO
```

5 Find the dependence relations for the following loop. Can this loop be converted into a parallel equivalent? If so, give the restructured version.

```
L₁:DO I = 1,N
L₂:    DO J = 2,N
S1:      A(I,J) = A(I, J-1) + B(I,J)
S2:      C(I,J) = A(I,J)+D(I+1,J)
S3:      D(I,J) = 0.1
        ENDDO
      ENDDO
```

6 Vectorize the following loop. (Hint: No dependence cycle)

```
L₁:DO I =1,N
S1:    A(I) = B(I)
S2:    C(I) = A(I) + B(I)
S3:    E(I) = C(I+1)
    ENDDO
```

7 Consider the following loop.

```
L₁:DO I = 2, N
S1:    A(I) = B(I)
S2:    C(I) = A(I) + B(I-1)
S3:    E(I) = C(I+1)
S4:    B(I) = C(I)+2
    ENDDO
```

(a) Draw its data dependence graph. (b) Vectorize all statements.

8 Give the code for ring communication in the example given in Section 11.8.3.

9 Explain why communication is necessary for loops that run on distributed-memory parallel computers.

10 Discuss why distributed-memory parallel computers are more difficult to program than shared-memory parallel computers.

11 Discuss why a parallel compiler is more difficult to build than a serial compiler.

References

Allen, J. R., and Kennedy, K., "PFC: A Program to Convert Fortran to Parallel Form," *Proceedings of the IBM Conference on Parallel Computers and Scientific Computations*, 1982.

Allen, J. R, and Kennedy, K., "Automatic Translation of Fortran Programs to Vector Form," *ACM Transaction on Programming Languagres and System*, October 1987.

Allen, J. R., et al., "Conversion of Control Dependence to Data Dependence," *Proceedings of Tenth Annual ACM Symposium on Principles of Programming Languages*, Austin, Texas, January 1983.

Allen, J. R., et al., "PTOOL: A Semi-Automatic Parallel Programming Assistant," *Proceedings of the 1986 International Conference on Parallel Processing*, 1986.

Banerjee, U., "An Introduction to a Formal Theory of Dependence Analysis," *Journal of Supercomputing* **2**, 1988a.

Banerjee, U., *Dependence Analysis for Supercomputing*, Kluwer Academic Publishesr, Boston, Mass., 1988b.

Burke, M., and Cytron, R., "Interprocedural Dependence Analysis and Parallelization," *Proceedings of the SIGPLAN 86 Symposium on Compiler Construction*.

Callahan, D., et al., "Interprocedural Constant Propagation," *Proceedings of the SIGPLAN 86 Symposium on Compiler Construction*, 1986.

Callahan, D., Cocke, J., Kennedy, K., "Compiling Programs for Distributed-Memory Multiprocessors," *Journal of Supercomputing*, October 1988.

Colin, J. Y., et al., "Allocating Tasks on a Virtual Distributed System," *Proceedings of International Conference on Supercomputing*, 1988.

Cytron, R., "Doacross: Beyond Vectorization for Multiprocessors," *Proceedings of the 1986 International Conference on Parallel Processing*, 1986.

Cytron, R., "Limited Processor Scheduling of Doacross Loops," *Proceedings of the 1987 International Conference on Parallel Processing*, 1986.

Girkar, M., Polychronopoulos, C., "Compiling Issues for Supercomputers," *Supercomputing*, 1988.

Ikudome K., et al., "An Automatic and Symbolic Parallelization System for Distributed Memory Parallel Computers," *DMCC*, 1990.

Kennedy, K., "A Survey of Data-flow Analysis Techniques," *Program Flow Analysis: Theory and Applications*, Much and Jones, Eds., Prentice Hall, Englewood Clifs, N.J., 1981.

Kuck, D. J., et al., "Dependence Graphs and Compiler Optimization," *SIGACT-SIGPLAN Symposium on Principles of Programming Languages*, January 1981.

Lee, F., "Partitioning of Regular Computation on Multiprocessor Systems," *Journal of Parallel and Distributed Computing* **9**, 1990.

Li, Z., Yew, P. C., Zhu, C. Q., "Data Dependence Analysis on Multidimensional

Array References," *ACM International Conference on Supercomputing,* July 1989.

Li, Z., Yew, P. C., "Some Results on Exact Data Dependence Analysis," *Languages and Compilers for Parallel Computing, Research Monographs in Parallel and Distributed Computing,* MIT Press, Cambridge, Mass., pp. 374 – 401, 1990.

Paalvast, E. M., van Gemund, A. J., "A Method for Parallel Program Generation with an Application to the Booster Language," *Proceedings of the 1990 International Conference on Parallel Processing.*

Padua, D. A., Kuck, D. J., Lawrie, D. H., "High-speed Multiprocessors and Compilation Techniques," *IEEE Trans. Comput.,* Volume C–24, No. 9, pp. 763 – 776, September 1980.

Padua, D. A., Wolfe, M., "Advanced Compiler Optimizations for Supercomputers," *Communications of the ACM,* December 1986.

Polychronopoulos, C. D., "Loop Coalescing: A Compiler Transformation for Parallel Machine," *Proceedings of the 1987 International Conference on Parallel Processing,* 1987.

Polychronopoulos, C. D., *Parallel Programming and Compilers,* Kluwer Academic Publishers, Boston, Mass., 1988a.

Polychronopoulos, C. D., "Toward Auto-scheduling Compilers," *The Journal of Supercomputing,* 1988b.

Polychronopoulos, C. D., et al., "The Structure of Parafase–2: An Advanced Parallelizing Compiler for C and Fortran," *Languages and Compilers for Parallel Computing, Research Monographs in Parallel and Distributed Computing,* MIT Press, Cambridge, Mass., 1990.

Reed, D. A., Adams, L. M., Patrick, M. L., "Stencils and Problem Partitionings: Their Influence on the Performance of Multiple Processor System," *IEEE Trans. Comput.,* C–36, 7, July 1987.

Wolfe, M., "Loop Skewing: The Wavefront Method Revisited," *International Journal of Parallel Programming,* **15**, No. 4, 1986.

Wolfe, M., "Optimizing Supercompilers for Supercomputers," *Research Monographs in Parallel and Distributed Computing,* MIT Press, Cambridge, Mass., 1989.

Wolfe, M., Banerjee, U., "Data Dependence and Its Application to Parallel Processing," *International Journal of Parallel Programming* **16**, 2, April 1987.

Zima, H. P., Bast, H. J., and Gerndt, M., "SUPERB: A Tool for Semi-autor MIMD/SIMD Parallelization," *Parallel Computing* **6**, NorHolland, pp. 1 – 18, 1988.

Chapter 12

Parallel Programming Support Environments

A *parallel programming support environment* is a coordinated collection of tools for automating part or all of the steps in writing a parallel program. We have seen examples of parallel programming tools in earlier chapters. For example, *CASE* (Computer-Aided Software Engineering) tools for design were described in Chapter 8, and examples of tools for scheduling task graphs have appeared throughout this book.

In this chapter, we look at environments that cover part or all of the steps of the programming life cycle—called phases—of designing, coding, testing and debugging, tuning and improving the performance, and restructuring serial programs into software designed to run on parallel computers.

The beginning of this chapter is devoted to surveying a sample of the environments that existed circa 1990. The emphasis is on coding tools and, in general, existing tools address only part of the entire life cycle.

The second half of the chapter looks more closely at full life cycle environments—those that attempt to cover all of the phases of parallel programming.

A variety of environments and tools have been proposed, prototypes constructed, and a few commercially available systems marketed to parallel programmers. For the most part, this is a field in its infancy, characterized by duplication of effort, a high degree of variability, and target machine-dependency.

12.1 PARALLEL CASE

We have used a variety of tools throughout this book to illustrate many concepts of parallelism. When integrated into a programming environment, such tools become part of *parallel CASE*—computer-aided software engineering for parallel programming. Many of these ideas, and their realization as useful tools, can be summarized in this final chapter by surveying the most prominent of these tools.

Parallel programming environments and their parallel CASE tools can be characterized by the *phase* of development in which they are most useful, the programming paradigm they employ, the workstation or platform on which they run, and the target machine for which they produce software. Roughly speaking, they will use either a shared-memory versus distributed-memory paradigm. Most are implemented for UNIX-based workstations and often use X-Windows to provide a graphical user interface. Some are meant to be portable, while others are designed for a specific parallel computer. All share the common goal of reducing the time and effort needed to write a parallel program.

Table 12.1 summarizes many of the environments that were either in use or proposed circa 1990. The phase information defines the major utility of an environment; the paradigm information tells what style of parallel programming was in the creator's mind when the environment was made; and the remaining information describes what machine the environment runs on, and what machine it is designed to produce software for. Under the name of each environment is the name of the principal author or researcher responsible for the work, along with the sponsoring organization.

Name	Paradigm	Platform	Target	Phase
1. ASPAR/EXPRESS Ikudome; Fox et al. Parasoft Corp.,1990	D	U, X T + G	C, Fortran	Code, Debug, Restructure
2. BUILD/SCHEDULE Dongarra et al. Argonne Nat'l Labs, 1987	S	U, Sun T + G	Alliant FX–8	Code
3. CODE/ROPE Browne et al. Univ. TX-Austin, 1988	S, D	U, X G + T	Portable, Fortran, C, SCHEDULE, and Ada™	Design, Code, Restructure
4. FAUST Guarna et al. University of Illinois	S	U, X T + G	Cedar, Alliant, C, Fortran	Code, Debug, Perform
5. GCDL Francioni et al. Mich. Tech., 1990	D	N/A	N/A	Debug
6. HIGHLAND Meyer Univ. Missouri–Rolla, 1989	D	U, X G + T	Networked Workstations w/Sockets	Design

TABLE 12.1 Parallel programming support environments circa 1990

Name	Paradigm	Platform	Target	Phase
7. HYPERTOOL Wu & Gajski Yale University, 1990	D	U, Sun T	iPSC/2 C	Code, Scheduling, Perform
8. MIMDizer Williamson Pacific-Sierra Research Corp., 1991	S	U, X T	Fortran77	Code
9. NOVIS Glinert Rensselaer Polytechnic, 1990	Systolic- Array	U, X G + T	Message- Passing	Debug, Perform
10. PICL/ParaGraph M. Heath et al. Oakridge Nat'l Labs, 1990	D T+G	U,X	Intel iPSC/2 iPSC/860, nCUBE	Code
11. PIE Segall Carnegie-Mellon Univ., 1990	S	U, X T + G	Encore, Warp, C, Ada, Fortran	Code, Debug
12. POKER Snyder Univ. Washington, 1984	D	X, U G + T	Custom VLSI	Design, Code
13. PPSE Lewis et al., OACIS, Oregon State Univ., 1988	S, D	Macintosh G + T	Sequent, iPSC, Portable via... C-LINDA & Strand	Design, Schedule, Code, Perform, Restructure
14. R^n/PTOOL Kennedy et al. Rice University, 1987	Vector S	U, X T	IBM 3090, Fortran77	Code, Debug, Restructure
15. Start/Pat Appelby & McDowell Georgia Tech/UC-Santa Cruz , 1989	S	U, X T + G	Fortran77 Portable	Code, Debug, Restructure

TABLE 12.1   Parallel programming support environments circa 1990

Legend for Table 12.1:

S = shared-memory, D = distributed memory architecture

U = UNIX, X = X-Windows, T = text, and G = graphics

T+G = predominantly text with graphics, G+T = predominantly graphics

Design = design phase addressed

Code = coding phase addressed

Debug = debugging phase addressed

Perform = performance monitoring and analysis

Schedule = static or dynamic scheduling tool provided

Restructure = source-to-source restructuring provided

The reader should consult the references for a complete description of each environment described here. In the following sections, we merely survey a small sampling of these environments.

The first environment discussed is an example of a coding phase environment where the tools are predominantly focused on writing textual source code after the design has been done. The goal of such environments is to reduce the coding effort, and to achieve portability, where possible.

12.1.1 ASPAR/EXPRESS

EXPRESS is a collection of routine calls that form a toolbox for writing distributed-memory parallel programs. The toolbox routines are used as built-in functions to distribute data among processors and coordinate processors during parallel program execution. In a very general sense, these routines perform data distribution and synchronization mechanisms related to the data-parallel paradigm.

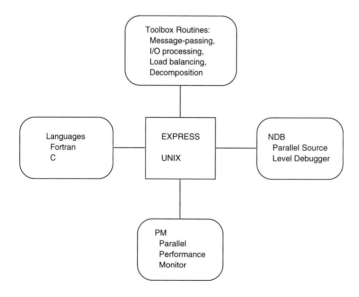

Figure 12.1   General structure of EXPRESS

ParaSoft Corporation of Mission Viejo, California calls these toolbox routines an *operating environment* which runs under UNIX. The routines are called from within standard C and Fortran source code programs.

The advantage of a hardware vendor-independent supplied toolbox is the potential portability across a number of parallel computers. EXPRESS has been implemented on Intel, Mark III, nCUBE, and Transputer-based machines. A parallel program written for one machine will run on any other machine that has the EXPRESS toolbox implemented on it.

A major disadvantage of the EXPRESS approach is the need for programmers to learn a number of exotic toolbox routines. These routines are often complex and esoteric in their operation, and often obscure the parallelism. The second pressing concern with EXPRESS is its lack of true portability. Programs are only portable to the machines that have EXPRESS support. Finally, it is not always possible to achieve high performance because the programmer has little control over placement of tasks on processors.

The toolbox, and a number of tools that provide assistance to the programmer are shown in Figure 12.1. The decomposition tools listed in the toolbox are source code restructuring tools for distributing arrays across multiple processors. A brief description of the tools:

1 Low-level message passing e.g., send/receive

2 High-level message passing, e.g., broadcast, sum/avg/min/max

3 Semi-automatic domain decomposition library for mapping data onto processors

4 Transparent I/O allows any processor to perform input/output

5 Parallel graphics for drawing on any graphics device, from any processor

6 NDB source level debugger

7 PM with graphical display of activity (Gantt charts)

The toolbox routines consist of a collection of commands of the form:
<command> (<Buffer>, <Length>, <Node>, <Type>)

where <command> is one of the approximately 75 routine names supported by EXPRESS, and are usually of the form ex<name> indicating they are EXPRESS routines, e.g., excombine.

<Buffer> is a pointer to data that is to be sent to another task, or received.
<Length> is the number of bytes of data to be moved.
<Type> is the type of message to be sent/received.

In addition, three I/O mode routines are needed to write almost any EXPRESS program: fsingl(fp), fmulti(fp), and fasync(fp):

fsingl(fp): One processor does all of the I/O and passes the results on to all other processors. For example, if an input value is used by all processors, it is not necessary for the value to be read N times. One processor can read the value and make N copies which are passed on to each of the N processors.

fmulti(fp): All processors participate in the I/O but in order of increasing processor number. Each processor puts data in a buffer that must be explicitly flushed. Then, when the I/O is actually performed, it appears in order by increasing processor number.

fasync(fp): All processors run independently and randomly do I/O. Used to report errors as they happen on any processor, this mode allows I/O to occur on all processors at any time.

Vector Multiply Example

As a simple example of the EXPRESS toolbox routines, suppose we want to multiply an $N = 100$ row by $M = 100$ column matrix A times an $M = 100$ element vector X. The idea is to use 100 processors to speed up this calculation. The approach is simple SIMD with data partitioning and lockstep tasks performing identical inner products on different data.

The data will be decomposed and distributed to the 100 processors by placing one row of A along with a complete copy of X on each processor. Because X is to be placed on all processors, we use the fsingl() mode of I/O to place duplicates throughout the parallel computer. Then, we use the fmulti() mode to place one row each of A on the processors.

The sample code assumes MAXVEC = 100, but this can be changed. Also, we have made other simplifying assumptions in order to focus on EXPRESS rather than the algorithm. For example, only one row of A needs to be in local memory at a time—just long enough to compute the inner product. This means the matrix is stored in one vector per processor, and taken together, all 100 rows are stored across 100 processors.

```
#include "express.h"                    /* include the toolbox */
#include <stdio.h>
#define MAXVEC  100                   /* 100 elements    */
struct nodenv  environment;           /* necessary evil; environment */
float X[MAXVEC],                       /* the vector....           */
      A[MAXVEC],                       /* the matrix.....          */
        product;                       /* ... inner product        */
main()
{  int i, size;                          /* working values        */
   exparam(&environment);             /* get EXPRESS env       */
   size = MAXVEC;                      /* this can be generalized  */

   fsingl(stdin);                       /* copy X to all procs    */
   for(i=0; i<size; i++) scanf("%f", &X[i]);
```

```
/* Prompt for A, one row at a time */
    printf("Enter %d Numbers Into A\n", environment.nprocs * size);
    fmulti(stdin);          /* fan-out the rows as they come in */
    for(i=0; i<size; i++) scanf("%f", &A[i]);
    /* Now, a row is in a processor, so do the calculation in SIMD fashion */
    product = 0.0;                          /* there are 100 of these     */
    for(i=0; i<size; i++){
       product += A[i]*X[i];                /* 100 inner products at once   */
    }
    fmulti(stdout);         /* output is switched to "fan-in" */
    printf("Processor # %d, Product = %f\n", environment.procnum, product);
    fflush(stdout);
  exit(0);
}
```

Summation Example

The previous example illustrates a simple fan-out of parallel tasks commonly found in the SIMD paradigm. Typical divide-and-conquer algorithms require tree-like task structures, which are provided by other kinds of EXPRESS toolbox routines. For example, excombine(), exconcat(), exbroadcast(), and exchange() are EXPRESS routines for broadcasting, combining, exchanging, and concatenating data across processors.

In the following example, we use excombine() to collect partial sums from a one-level tree of tasks. This code can be generalized for the case when the tree is more than one level deep. The excombine routine used below has 7 parameters:

&partial = a pointer to a buffer containing the partial sums to be combined

add = a pointer to the add() function which is to perform the summation

sizeof(partial) = the size of partial

1 = number of items to be combined

ALLNODES = number of processors participating in summation

lprocs=0=list of processors used in the excombine, not used with ALLNODES

&etype = pointer to message type, any number between 0 and 16383

```
#include "express.h"                        /* include the toolbox */
#include <stdio.h>
struct nodenv  environment;                 /* necessary evil; environment */
main()
{   int partial,                            /* partial sum returned by each task */
        add(),                              /* summation routine at each task
*/
    etype = 100;                            /* EXPRESS needs to number messages */
```

```
        exparam(&environment);                    /* get EXPRESS env    */
        /* fsingl() is default mode, so the following works on one "master" */
        printf("Enter %d Numbers To Be Summed\n," environment.nprocs);
        /* put one number on each of the nprocs processors  */
        fmulti(stdin);
        scanf("%d", &partial);                 /* SIMD tasks, again. */
        /* Now do summations by combining partials... */
        excombine(&partial, add, sizeof(partial), 1, ALLNODES (int *)0, &etype);
        exit(0);
}
int add(a, b, size)             /* the excombine routine */
int *a, *b, size;               /* global partial is destroyed.... */
{*a += *b;                      /* ... by writing new sum over old sum */
    return(0);
}
```

12.1.2 Semi-Automatic Restructuring in ASPAR

Perhaps the most notable feature of ASPAR (Automatic and Symbolic Parallelization System) is its ability to restructure a C source program in a manner that distributes vectors and arrays to multiple processors. The tool is semi-automatic, because it requires some human assistance for difficult cases.

ASPAR is based on EXPRESS, and uses excombine(), exconcat(), and other routines from the EXPRESS toolbox. In addition, ASPAR adds its own toolbox routines, designated in the following examples by the prefix AS_. We illustrate a number of loop structures which ASPAR is capable of restructuring to show the power of the EXPRESS and AS_ routines.

A C source code program is parallelized in 5 steps as shown in Figure 12.2. The preprocessor step is the normal C preprocessor for removing inline macros from the source code (#defines are converted). The parser creates a parse tree of the C source code; the pre-analyzer creates an A-list (Atom-list) which identifies and records all dataflow dependencies in the program; the analyzer extracts parallelism from the A-list; and the translator rewrites the C source into a parallel form. The output from ASPAR is a parallel EXPRESS C program that uses message passing to communicate among parallel tasks.

Loop Parallelization and Data Distribution

The greatest benefits are obtained by distributing loop iterations across processors and making the data available only on the processors that need it. The ASPAR translator can do much of this automatically, given the EXPRESS toolbox and a routine called AS_set_ranges() that computes AS_cnt[]—a vector of loop upper limits which indicate the range of each loop on each processor.

ASPAR converts four general types of loops as shown in the following. First, the simplest case.

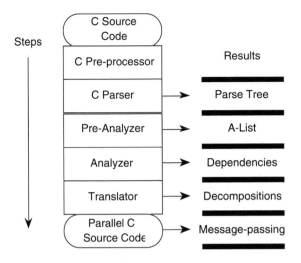

Steps

- C Source Code
- C Pre-processor
- C Parser → Parse Tree
- Pre-Analyzer → A-List
- Analyzer → Dependencies
- Translator → Decompositions
- Parallel C Source Code → Message-passing

Results

Figure 12.2 ASPAR converts serial C into parallel EXPRESS C

No communication:

```
for(i=1;i<=N;i++){X[i] = Y[i+1] - Y[i];}
```

Clearly, each iteration can be done in parallel with all other iterations. The only information needed is the upper limit on groups of iterations when the number of processors is less than the number of iterations. For example, if the loop repeats 1,000 times and there are only 100 processors, then 10 iterations must be scheduled on each processor. AS_cnt[] = 10 and the loop on each processor becomes:

```
AS_set_ranges(0, N, 1, 0);
for(i=1; i<=AS_cnt[0]; i++) {X[i] = Y[i+1] - Y[i];}
```

Combined data:

```
partial = 0.0;
for(i=0; i<=N; i++) {partial += (A[i] * X[ i ]);}
```

This is similar to the earlier summation example. Using the EXPRESS excombine() routine, this becomes the following.

```
partial = 0.0;
AS_set_ranges(0, N-1, 0, 1);
for(i=0; i<AS_cnt[0]1 i++) {partial += (A[i] * X[ i ]);}
excombine(&partial, add, ALLNODES (int *)0, &etype);
```

Concatenated data:

```
for(i=0;i<N;i++) {X[i] = A[i];}
```

The difficulty here is that we may not be able to distribute X across all processors because it is dynamic. That is, portions of X have yet to be computed, and until all array elements have values, it makes no sense to distribute them. If this loop is distrib-

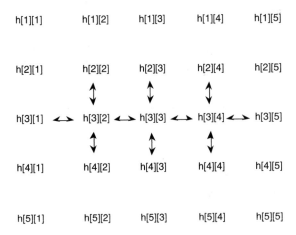

Figure 12.3 Exchange pattern in NEWS stencil. Each value is exchanged with its neighbor, a new value is computed, and the process repeats

uted to where *A* is, then we may have to also distribute elements of *X* from the local processor to other processors. The values of *X* can be concatenated to their neighbors in other processors using the exconcat() routine.

```
AS_set_ranges(0, N-1, 0, 1);
for(i=0;i<AS_cnt[0];i++) {X[i + AS_ofst[0]] = A[i];}
AS_size[0] = sizeof(double) * AS_cnt[0];
exconcat(&X[AS_ofst[0]], X, AS_size[0]);
```

The AS_size and AS_ofst values hold the size and offset values needed to properly concatenate the elements of *X*. The effect of these place keepers is to update elements that are outside of the "reach" of the local processor. But the programmer must be careful that race conditions do not creep into the result!

Exchanged data:
The classical SOR algorithm using a NEWS (North-East-West-South) neighbors *stencil* requires exchanged data as follows.

```
for(j=2; j<= N-1; j++){
  for(k=2; k<=M-1; k++){
    h[k][j] = (h[k][j+1] + h[k][j-1] + h[k+1][j] + h[k-1][j]) / 4.0
  }
}
```

Each processor reads the value of adjacent h[][]'s, thus values are exchanged. For example, assuming there are enough processors so that only one h[][] is located on each processor, we get the exchanges partially shown in Figure 12.3. The value at h[3][2] is exchanged with its neighbors NEW S = h[2][2], h[3][3], h[4][2], h[3][1] values; h[3][3] is exchanged with h[2][3], h[3][4], h[4][3], h[3][2]; h[3][4] is exchanged with h[2][4], h[3][5], h[4][4], h[3][3], and so forth.

Rewriting the nested loops above in ASPAR form, we get the following:

```
/* Establish the offsets in the NEWS pattern.... */
exvchange(&h[1][2], AS_num[1], LEFT,              /* East-West   */
          &h[AS_cnt[0][2], AS_num[1], RIGHT);
exvchange(&h[AS_cnt[0]+1][2], AS_num[1], RIGHT,
          &h[2][2], AS_num[1], LEFT);
exvchange(&h[2][1], AS_num[0], DOWN,              /* North-South */
          &h[2][AS_cnt[1]], AS_num[0], UP);
exvchange(&h[2][AS_cnt[1]+1], AS_num[0], UP,
          &h[2][2], AS_num[0], DOWN);
/*... then use these patterns in each processor  */
AS_set_ranges(1, N-1, 2, 0);                  /* Compute AS_cnt[1]   */
for(j=2; j<= AS_cnt[1]; j++){
  AS_set_ranges(0, M-1, 2, 0);                /* Compute AS_cnt[0]   */
  for(k=2; k<=AS_cnt[0]; k++){
    h[k][j] = (h[k][j+1] + h[k][j-1] + h[k+1][j] + h[k-1][j]) / 4.0
  }
}
```

12.2   OTHER TOOLBOX SYSTEMS

ASPAR/EXPRESS is a kind of toolbox support system because it provides a collection of "toolbox" routines that can be used by a Fortran or C programmer to access parallelism in the hardware. Unlike full programming environments, toolbox systems lack design or debugging tools. Many other programming toolboxes have been suggested, but perhaps the most widely used are SCHEDULE, PICL, and LINDA.

SCHEDULE and PICL have been developed by researchers at two national laboratories which distribute the code free of charge. This generosity has made them widely available and nearly standard among researchers. LINDA is not freely available, but because of its portable nature, it too is widely available.

SCHEDULE is a Fotran toolkit for vector machines. PICL is in both Fortran and C for UNIX machines and supports distributed memory (message-passing) computers such as the nCUBE and iPSC/2. C-LINDA is a C language version of LINDA which is available on both shared-memory and distributed-memory computers.

12.2.1   SCHEDULE/BUILD

Jack Dongarra's SCHEDULE was one of the first text-based toolbox systems for scientific and parallel computing. It is a library of Fortran subroutines, implemented on a number of parallel computers, that provide primitives for parallel programming. These primitives are analogous to the ASPAR/EXPRESS primitives described above. Task spawning, for example, is provided as a SCHEDULE routine.

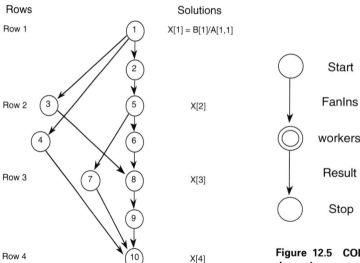

Rows

Row 1

Solutions

X[1] = B[1]/A[1,1]

Row 2

X[2]

Row 3

X[3]

Row 4

X[4]

Figure 12.4   Task graph of forward substitution solution to *AX* = B, *N* = 4

Start

FanIns

workers

Result

Stop

Figure 12.5   CODE computation as a dependency graph. Circled bubbles indicate replication of computational units. This is an example of a simple supervisor/workers computation.

The SCHEDULE routines will not be repeated here as they can be obtained from netlib@mcs.anl.gov by mailing "send sched." We are more interested in the BUILD tool for composing applications that use SCHEDULE.

BUILD is a graphical editor for drawing a task graph representing the program's execution on the screen of a workstation. The task graph contains nodes and arcs; nodes are equated with Fortran subroutine calls, and arcs are equated with control flow. A regular node represents a subroutine call, and a loop node represents a repeated subroutine call.

When used in combination, the BUILD/SCHEDULE system is an automated tool for turning task graphs into programs.

Figure 12.4 contains the BUILD task graph for solution to $AX = B$, when A is a 4 × 4 lower triangular matrix. The program uses forward substitution of X_1 to get X_2; X_1 and X_2 to get X_3, and so on. The tasks are numbered from 1 to 10 indicating the ten steps of forward substitution taken to solve for the four unknowns.

A trace facility has been added to SCHEDULE that produces a postmortem trace of the running program. Trace leaves a file behind which can be played back to observe the execution of the application. The task graph then becomes an execution graph, showing parallelism as a fan-out of tasks.

The BUILD system is very limited, permitting only one level of task graph display. As of this writing, work is continuing on BUILD/SCHEDULE to increase its expressiveness and range of application. Like ASPAR/EXPRESS, its utility hinges on the widespread acceptance of the SCHEDULE library.

12.2.2 PICL/ParaGraph

PICL (Portable Instrumented Communication Library) is a more recent toolbox system for the message-passing paradigm of parallel programming. PICL routines perform rudimentary SEND/RECEIVE operations common to most distributed-memory machines. They also leave a trace of their execution in the form of a trace file which can be read by ParaGraph to produce a postmortem display of what the parallel program did during execution. ParaGraph can replay the program's execution in the form of 22 animated displays. This is a valuable tool for debugging and tuning an application.

PICL contains both low-level and high-level routines for message passing. The low-level routines and a brief description of their behavior is given below.

check0(checking): Disable parameter checking if checking = 0, otherwise enable checking.

clock0(): Return local clock time in seconds.

close0(release): Disable interprocessor communication.

load0(*file, node): Load a program on a processor. If node = −1, load program on all processors.

message0(*numproc, *me, *host): Print short message on host processor.

open0(*numproc, *me, *host): Allocate numproc processors, enable communication, and return the ID number.

probe0(msgtype): Return 1 if a message of msgtype has arrived.

recv0(*buf, bytes, msgtype): Receive message of size bytes, type msgtype, and puts it into buf.

recvinfo0(*bytes, *msgtype, *source): Returns information on most recent recv0() or probe0() call.

send0(*buf, bytes, msgtype, dest): Send message of length bytes to processor numbered dest.

synch0(): Barrier synchronization of all processors. All tasks wait at this barrier until all processors arrive.

who0(*numproc, *me, *host): Return the number of allocated processors, the ID number of the processor calling who0(), and the ID number of the host processor.

These low-level routines are illustrated in a simple producer-consumer pair of tasks shown below.

```
host()              /* producer */
{int nprocs, me, host, bytes, msgtype, node;
   double time[2], result, data[128], clock0();
   time[0] = clock0();      /*start time */
```

```
        nprocs=32;
        open0(&nprocs, &me, &host);    /* allocate 32 processors */
        load0("node tasks", -1);    /* load all 32 processors with task code */
        bytes = sizeof(data);
        msgtype = 1;
        node = 0;
        send0(data, bytes, msgtype, node);        /* send to node 0 */
        bytes = sizeof(result);
        msgtype = 2;
        recv0(&result, bytes, msgtype);         /* receive from a node */
        time[1] = clock();
        printf("host tool %f seconds to send & receive", time[1]-time[0]);
        close0(1);        /* release all allocated processors */
}
node()                    /* consumer */
{int nprocs, me, bytes, msgtype, node;
        double time, result, data[128], clock0();
        open0(&nprocs, &me, &host);
        bytes = sizeof(data);
        msgtype = 1;
        /* receive data from host and distribute to other processors */
        recv0(data, bytes, msgtype);
        close0();
}
```

High-level routines permit more elaborate communication patterns. These routines use nprocs (number of processors allocated), top (topology—either a hypercube, fully connected, or ring), ord (numbering of processors—integers in gray code or natural sequence), and dir (direction of broadcast in the case of a ring).

barrier0(): Wait for barrier synchronization as specified by setarc0().

bcast0(*buf, bytes, root): Broadcast a message to all processors.

gand0(*buf, items, datatype, msgtype, root): Compute AND of set of vectors.

gcomb0(*buf, items, datatype, msgtype, root, void (*comb)())): Compute a user defined combination of vectors.

getarcs0(*nprocs, *top, *ord, *dir): Return number of processors and architectural parameters set by most recent setarc0() call.

ginv0(i): Return inverse binary gray code of i.

gmax0(*buf, items, datatype, msgtype, root): Compute maximum of vectors.

gmin0(*buf, items, datatype, msgtype, root): Compute minimum of vectors.

gor0(*buf, items, datatype, msgtype, root): Compute OR of vectors.

gprod0(*buf, items, datatype, msgtype, root): Compute componentwise product of vectors.

gray0(i): Return binary reflected gray code of i.

gsum0(*buf, items, datatype, msgtype, root): Compute sum of vectors.

gxor0(*buf, items, datatype, msgtype, root): Compute exclusive OR of vectors.

setarc0(*nprocs, *top, *ord, *dir): Set the number of processors and the interconnection topology to be used by all routines.

Again, we illustrate the use of these routines with a simple supervisor-worker program that broadcasts to the workers and then collects their results. The following uses both high- and low-level routines.

```
host()        /* Master */
{int n, nprocs, me, host, bytes, datatype, msgtype, node;
   float results[128];
nprocs = 32;
open0(&nprocs, &me, &host);
load0("node programs," -1);   /* allocate processors and load code */
top =1;   /* topology = hypercube */
ord = 1;  /* processors are numbered as in binary gray code */
dir = 1;  /* ring direction is forward */
setarc0(&nprocs, &top, &ord, &dir);
/* Broadcast problem size.... */
n = 128;
bytes = sizeof(n);
msgtype = 0;
bcast0(&n, bytes, msgtype, host);
/* Collect sum of all processor's results */
datatype = 4;  /* 4=float */
msgtype = 10;
gsum0(results, n, datatype, msgtype, host);
close0(1);
}
node()        /* Workers */
{int n, nprocs, me, host, bytes, datatype, msgtype, vec[128];
   float results[128];
   open0(&nprocs, &me, &host);
   setarc0(&nprocs, &top, &ord, &dir);
   /* Receive and Propagate Broadcast of n */
   bytes = sizeof(n);
   msgtype = 0;
   bcast0(&n, bytes, msgtype, host);
   /* Collect Maximum of Vector and Broadcast to all nodes */
   datatype = 2;   /* 2=integer */
   msgtype = datatype;
   root = 0;
```

```
gmax0(vec, n, datatype, msgtype, root);
bytes = n*sizeof(float);
bcast0(vec, bytes, msgtype, root);
/* Participate in Global Sum. Send Result to Host */
datatype = 4;    /* 4=float */
msgtype = 10;
gsum0(results, n, datatype, msgtype, host);
close0();
}
```

To operate correctly, all high-level routines such as bcast0() must be called by all processors that are participating in the action. The root parameter is a kind of anchor that tells all other processors who is to collect the result.

PICL also employs a collection of trace routines that are not listed here. For more details, consult the report by Heath et al. Source code and documentation for PICL is available from netlib@ornl.gov. An index to all documentation and code can be obtained by sending the message: "send index from picl." Similarly, ParaGraph index can be obtained by sending the e-mail message: "send index from paragraph."

12.2.3   Portable Programming in LINDA

Given that software development is an extremely expensive undertaking, it is distressing to realize that most of the implementation work will have to be repeated on a new machine. Gelernter proposed a universal paradigm for shared-memory access called LINDA. *LINDA* is a toolbox which provides hidden mechanisms to protect shared data. The LINDA primitives are deceptively simple and few in number.

LINDA is actually a toolbox of routines that can be used in place of message-passing or locking mechanisms to "cover up" the underlying machine. If the LINDA routines are used instead of locks and messages, there is no need for explicit synchronization or message passing. Thus, LINDA is a high-level toolbox for parallel programming. LINDA routines are imbedded in traditional languages such as Fortran and C. The programming style is altered, but only marginally.

Only four toolbox routines are needed to write a LINDA program:

out: place a value in shared memory

in: remove a value from shared memory, e.g., destructive read

rd: copy a value found in memory, e.g., nondestructive read

eval: create a task

These toolbox routines have been implemented as functions in C, leading to C-LINDA. How might they be used?

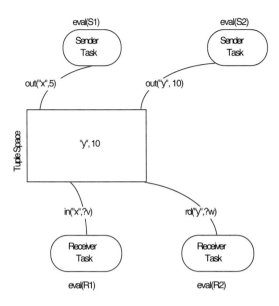

Figure 12.6   A LINDA tuple space and the operations allowed on them

LINDA Tuple Space

Figure 12.6 illustrates the concept of a tuple space. A *tuple space* is simply a collection of shared values, e.g., an idealized shared memory. They possess a structure called a tuple, which is simply an ordered set of types.

The eval() operations in Figure 12.6 create and start all of the tasks. Tasks communicate by way of the tuple space as shown. Data are copied from a sending task to the tuple space using out(), and moved from the tuple space to a receiving task using either rd() or in(). Variables that are to receive a value from tuple space are prefixed with a question mark. Thus, ?v and ?w indicate that variables v and w are to receive a value from tuple space.

Suppose all four tasks start at the same time. Figure 12.6 shows the end result of the following sequence of operations:

S2: out("y",10); S2 places ("y", 10) in the tuple space

R1: in("x",?v); R1 blocks until ("x",5) is available

R2: rd("y",?w); R2 reads ("y", 10) from the tuple space, leaving a copy behind, assigning 10 to w

S1: out("x",5); S1 places ("x",5) in the tuple space

R1: in("x",?v); R1 resumes and removes ("x",5), assigning 5 to v

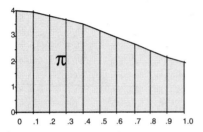

Figure 12.7 π equals the area under the curve 4/(1 + X²)

The rd() operation might be used to broadcast a value to many other tasks. That is, a master task can send a value to many worker tasks by placing a single value in the tuple space, where many workers can simultaneously rd() it.

The destructive read operation in() is used to prevent race conditions in the shared data, because tasks cannot access what is not in the tuple space. For example, suppose task R1 intends to increment x and place it back into the tuple space. The following code implements a critical section without explicit locks:

```
in("x", ?xvalue);                    /* remove xvalue from tuple    */
out("x", xvalue+1);                  /* put xvalue+1 back in tuple   */
```

The eval() function is much like an out() coupled with an m_fork() function to create a parallel task. The eval() function takes the name of a function to be executed in parallel as its argument.

12.2.4 Parallel Pie in LINDA

We illustrate the practical application of LINDA tuple space with a simple numerical analysis application. The value of π can be computed by numerically calculating the area under the curve of Figure 12.7. That is, we want to compute the integral:

$$\int_0^1 \frac{4}{(1 + x^2)} \, dx = \text{atan}(1) = \pi$$

We can do this by summing up the areas under the vertical strips, as indicated in Figure 12.7. Actually, a numerical approximation is obtained by estimating the areas under each of thousands of very narrow strips.

This is another trivially parallel problem that can be solved by a supervisor-worker paradigm. We give each worker task a segment of the area to compute in parallel. Upon completing each segment, tasks return their portions of the area which are tallied to obtain (approx.) π.

The C code for a typical worker might look like the following:

```
void pie_worker(start, stop, interval, area)
{
  int i ;
```

```
    double x, interval, area=0.0;
    for (i=start; i<=stop; i++)
    {x=(i-0.5)*interval;
        area += 4.0/(1.0+x*x);
    }
  return(area);
}
```

To make the C-LINDA illustration explicit and easy to follow, suppose we assume the x-coordinate of Figure 12.7 is divided into 90,000 strips. For simplicity, assume 4 tasks; one supervisor, and 3 workers working on 30,000 strips each. Furthermore, we illustrate the use of tuple space by passing all pertinent values through one tuple space, as illustrated in the following C-LINDA program.

```
#include <linda.h>
#include <stdio.h>
main()
{
int pie1; pie2, pie3;
int i;double area1, area2, area3, area;
double interval = 1.0/90000;
eval(pie1);
eval(pie2);
eval(pie3); /* all start, but block until first tuple is available */
out("start1", 1, 30000, interval); /* pie1 runs from 1-30000 */
out("start2", 30001, 60000, interval); /* pie2 ... */
out("start3", 60001, 90000, interval); /* ....pie3 */
in("pie1", area1);
in("pie2", area2);
in("pie3", area3); /* get results, when ready */
area = (pie1+pie2+pie3) * interval;
printf("Approx pie %20.15lf\n", area);
}
void pie1()
{
  int start,stop, i;
  double interval, x, area ;
  /* wait for a tuple to process... */
  in("start1", ?start, ?stop, ?interval) ; /* get a tuple from master task */
  /* compute local area */
  for(i=start; i<=stop; i++)
   {x=(i-0.5)*interval; area+=4.0/(1.0+x*x)}
  /* return via tuple space */
  out("pie1", area); /* send it to master task */
}

void pie2()
{
```

```
  int start,stop, i;
  double interval, x, area ;
  /* wait for a tuple to process... */
  in("start2", ?start, ?stop, ?interval) ; /* get a tuple from master task */
  /* compute local area */
  for(i=start; i<=stop; i++)
   {x=(i-0.5)*interval; area+=4.0/(1.0+x*x)}
  /* return via tuple space */
  out("pie2", area); /* send it to master task */
}
void pie3()
{
  int start,stop, i;
  double interval, x, area ;
  /* wait for a tuple to process... */
  in("start3", ?start, ?stop, ?interval) ; /* get a tuple from master task */
  /* compute local area */
  for(i=start; i<=stop; i++)
   {x=(i-0.5)*interval; area+=4.0/(1.0+x*x)}
  /* return via tuple space */
  out("pie3", area); /* send it to master task */
}
```

Why did we solve this problem in three parts? Theoretically, we could have dedicated one task to each of the 90,000 strips, giving a theoretical speedup of 90,000! The problem with such a fine-grained solution is that the task creation time is much higher than the time to compute the area under a single strip. Instead, it seems best to increase the grain size to balance the task creation overhead. On the Sequent Symmetry computer, grain sizes greater than about 5 seconds give linear speedups for the pie problem.

LINDA was designed to solve the problems of portability among parallel programmers. Unfortunately, there are a number of LINDA implementations that are not compatible with one another. Therefore, writing your application in LINDA does not guarantee it will run on another parallel computer with LINDA toolbox routines. For example, Kernel LINDA for the Cogent XTM is not compatible with C-LINDA. In addition, C-LINDA routines for distributed memory machines such as the iPSC/2 do not always work the way they do on shared-memory machines such as the Sequent Symmetry.

12.3 CODE/ROPE

CODE (Computation Oriented Display Environment) and POKER were the first attempts to apply graphical design techniques to parallel programming. Using two fundamental symbol types and hierarchy, a parallel program can be described in

CODE by drawing "bubbles" for various kinds of processes, and arcs for data dependencies. Hierarchical decomposition is used to hide unnecessary detail, and to facilitate decomposition.

CODE computational units (bubbles) carry a semantics very similar to functional/dataflow semantics. A unit is allowed to *fire* when its inputs are available and the guards are TRUE.

Arcs carry data dependencies: demand, mutual exclusion, and control signals are considered data, and computational units are connected to one another by these arcs to form a computation. Figure 12.5 shows a simple CODE diagram for the supervisor/workers paradigm. The double circle "bubble" is a replicated computational unit. It represents N workers all working in parallel to produce a result which flows out to the terminal bubble.

The specification of a computation is not complete without textual constraints. For example, Figure 12.5 must be annotated with text to define how many workers, the source code of each unit represented by a bubble, and the firing rules as predicates.

ROPE (Reusability Oriented Programming Environment) is a library of CODE components (simple bubbles or entire subgraphs) that can be inserted into a CODE design.

CODE/ROPE works with a series of translators called TOAD, to generate Ada, Fortran, and C source code for a specific parallel computer. TOAD_Fortran, for example, generates Fortran for Cray/COS. A TOAD tool exists to generate Fortran calls to SCHEDULE described in the previous section. This feature relieves the programmer of details concerning each parallel computer system, and allows him or her to concentrate on the problem at hand.

12.3.1 Calculation of π

We illustrate the calculation of π as defined above using CODE/ROPE as both design and implementation mechanism. We can do this by summing up the areas under the vertical strips, as indicated in Figure 12.7.

The estimation of π is essentially a summation problem. We can do summation by two data-parallel methods: (1) subdivision, or (2) divide-and-conquer. The subdivision method simply divides the interval of summation into roughly equal subintervals, and then performs parallel summations on them. The divide-and-conquer method recursively divides the interval into two, each of these are in turn divided into two, and so on until the smallest interval is found. The summations are performed in pairs, and the partial sums passed up a merge tree until the final total emerges from the root task.

We present a solution with elements of both methods, simply to show that both can be represented in CODE/ROPE. In our simplified solution, we divide the initial interval into two equal-length subintervals, and then we divide each subinterval into 3 equal-length sub-sub-intervals. That is, we use divide-and-conquer at the first level, and subdivision at the second level.

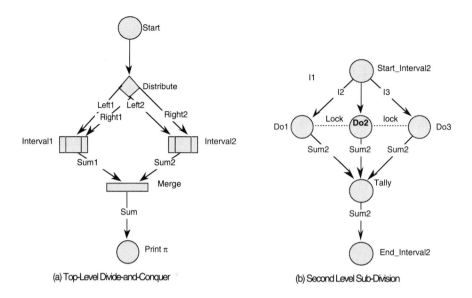

Figure 12.8 CODE/ROPE design of calculation of π (a) top-level design uses divide-and-conquer parallelism; (b) uses subdivision method of parallelism

Figure 12.8(a) shows the top-level design using divide-and-conquer, and Figure 12.8(b) shows the second-level design using subdivision. The bubbles of Figure 12.8 have been shaded for a visual effect, and are not part of the drawing capabilities of CODE/ROPE.

The diamond bubble in Figure 12.8(a) contains instructions to distribute the two subintervals to two decomposable tasks designated by a double rectangle and labeled Interval1 and Interval2. The sums produced by parallel tasks Interval1 and Interval2 are sent to the Merge bubble where a firing rule is used to decide what to do with the two inputs, Sum1 and Sum2. In this case, the rule specifies an "and" merge, where both Sum1 and Sum2 are obtained before the Merge task fires. The value of Sum = Sum1 + Sum2 is then printed by task Print π.

The parallel tasks Interval1 and Interval2 are each decomposed into subtasks. Figure 12.8(b) shows this decomposition for Interval2. The interval that was bracketed between Left2..Right2 is subdivided into three parts bracketed by I1, I2, and I3. Start_Interval2 then passes these on to three parallel tasks Do1, Do2, and Do3. Each Do task simultaneously updates Sum2, which is passed back to the top level by Tally. The simultaneous update of Sum2 in this manner creates a potential race condition which is removed by a Lock as shown by the dotted arc connecting Do1, Do2, and Do3. This inhibitor arc prevents Do tasks from executing at the same time.

The full specification of a CODE/ROPE design is given by text where source code for each task and switch settings for distribution and locking are found.

12.4 FULL LIFE CYCLE ENVIRONMENTS

A full life cycle environment contains tools for the entire life cycle of parallel programming. This typically encompasses the following phases:

1 Source code conversion tool for parallelizing existing serial programs

2 Design tool for viewing an exiting program or entering a new one

3 Scheduling tool for optimal placement of parallel tasks

4 Optimizing compiler

5 Parallel program debugger

6 Performance analysis tool

7 Database for coordinating tools operating on source and binary components

These tools work off of the database which typically holds everything needed during design and coding. For example, the FAUST system by Guarna and others at the University of Illinois runs off a database with the following 8 file types:

1 Binary executable program

2 Fortran or C source program

3 Assembler version of program produced by the compilers

4 Dependency graph produced during compilation

5 Static call graph produced by the compilers

6 Execution trace produced by a run of the program

7 Annotations, e.g., documentation about traces, etc.

8 Intermediate files produced by the compilers

This database supports a variety of tools which yield static and dynamic views of the program:

1 Data dependency graph showing the dependence among variables

2 Control flow graph

3 Animation of call-graph display

The conversion tools of FAUST are minimal, essentially pointing out places in the source code that might be manually parallelized by the programmer. FAUST might be combined with Start/Pat or R^n/PTOOL, for example, which are tools for conversion of serial loops into parallel loops.

FAUST also does not provide high-level design tools such as found in CODE/ROPE. Nor does it provide scheduling tools such as found in Wu's HYPERTOOL and Lewis' PPSE.

12.4.1 PPSE

At the time of this writing, the only parallel program support environment that attempts to provide full life cycle support of parallel programming is the PPSE system under development at Oregon Advanced Computing Institute, OACIS. PPSE consists of the techniques and tools shown in Figure 12.9. Each tool of Figure 12.9 is briefly described below.

1 pRETS: Parallel Reverse Engineering Tool System for converting an existing serial Fortran program into a database and then restructuring the database into a parallel Fortran program. Parallelism is at the subroutine level as in BUILD/SCHEDULE.

2 Parallax: A graphical design editor for viewing pRETS databases or entering new designs into the database. This system is similar to the CODE/ROPE environment and has many of the same limitations.

3 Task Grapher: A graphical design editor and static scheduling tool that permits task graphs from Parallax to be analyzed and scheduled onto an arbitrary target machine. Parallax designs can be flattened and entered into Task Grapher. This system was described in Chapter 9, and operates much like BUILD/SCHEDULE at one level, and HYPERTOOL at another level.

4 SuperGlue: A code generator like TOAD, which takes the optimal schedules produced by Task Grapher, and the code routines produced by Parallax, and generates a compilable source code application. C-LINDA and Strand are two of the languages supported by SuperGlue. Machine independence is a goal of SuperGlue, but this is achieved by constructing new code synthesizers for each target machine.

5 EPA: Execution Performance Analyzer, similar to the PM tools found in FAUST and SCHEDULE/Trace. This tool analyzes traces produced by the running application, and updates the program's design, based on the trace.

6 OREGAMI: A technique for designing regular communication structures. An OREGAMI design, along with the target machine interconnection network topology, can be used to arrive at an optimal mapping of tasks onto processors. Currently, OREGAMI is not integrated into PPSE, and so we show it as a separate tool within PPSE.

7 Debugger: At the time of this writing, no debugger exists for PPSE. Future plans call for using target machine specific debuggers provided by each manufacturer.

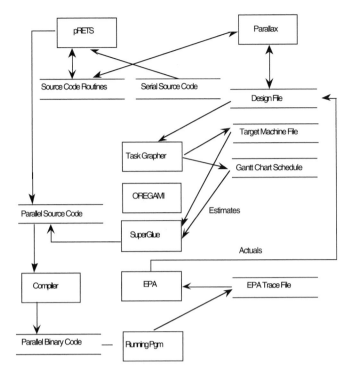

Figure 12.9   PPSE system flow diagram showing feedback via EPA

A feedback loop exists in Figure 12.9 whereby the actual timing values obtained by running the parallel program are fed back into the design. Each task in the design has an estimated execution time, and each dataflow has an estimated communication time associated with it. These times may be wrong, initially, and only through running the program can they be obtained. Once obtained from EPA, these values are used to correct the values in the design file. A second iteration of the tools produces an improved version of the parallel program.

PPSE produces code for any parallel computer that supports target languages C-LINDA, Strand, and Fortran. However, the system has only been used routinely on Sequent shared memory, and Intel and nCUBE distributed memory machines. An option of SuperGlue permits generation of stubs—undefined subroutines that do nothing. This facility is used to obtain communication delay estimates.

12.4.2   π Program in Parallax

As an illustration of Parallax, so the reader can compare it with its nearest competitor, we have provided yet another solution to the π calculation program solved earlier with CODE/ROPE. The design is shown in two levels in Figure 12.10. The top-level design shows inputs and outputs, and a replicated component. The second level shows the

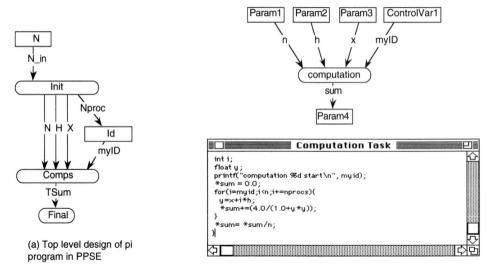

(a) Top level design of pi program in PPSE

```
int i;
float y;
printf("computation %d start\n", myid);
*sum = 0.0;
for(i=myid;i<n;i+=nprocs){
    y=x+i*h;
    *sum+=(4.0/(1.0+y*y));
}
*sum= *sum/n;
}
```

(b) Level 2 design and code fragment for pi design in PPSE

Figure 12.10   PPSE parallax design of pi problem

decomposition of the replicated component plus the C source code for each parallel task.

Replicated tasks designated by "comps" in Figure 12.10(a) are controlled by "myID," which is 0,1,2,3,... for each duplicate task. In short, the replication is enumerated to force many tasks to be created.

The source code in Figure 12.10(b) defines the actions of each task, but there are no explicit controls, synchronization, or target machine dependencies in the design. This is as it should be. The purpose of Parallax design is to capture the essence of the parallel program without allowing parallel computer architectural considerations affect the design. Instead, PPSE must provide the machine specifics.

PPSE performs a series of mappings from the Parallax design down to running code. The mappings are as follows:

1   Transformation of a hierarchical PPSE design into a flattened task graph.

2   Transformation of the flattened task graph into an execution schedule that defines not only which task is to run on what processor, but also when each task is to be activated. Scheduling is more than mapping. It includes the optimal ordering of tasks so that the overall execution time is minimized (see Chapter 9 for more on scheduling).

3   Transformation of a schedule, and its source code fragments (procedures) into a compilable parallel program. This step depends on an appropriate high-level language compiler such as C-LINDA, Strand, or Fortran, on each target parallel computer. PPSE does not include compilers, linkers, or debuggers.

4 Monitoring of the running program by EPA, and then revising the program's design based on feedback from the EPA reports.

12.4.3 Task Grapher and π

Figure 12.11(a) shows the first transformation performed automatically by PPSE. The hierarchical design of Parallax is flattened into a task graph. The replicated "comps" node of Figure 12.10(a) is flattened into six identical tasks which can be run in parallel.

This example illustrates one of the shortcomings of PPSE. Because PPSE uses static scheduling of parallel tasks, it is not possible to schedule the replicated tasks until the number of replications is known. In Figure 12.11(a) we arbitrarily used six duplicates. In general, we might not know how many duplicates to use before the program executes.

A second problem with this approach is the need to label the task graph with execution time estimates. We have estimated these to be 500 units for each duplicate, and 100 units each for the start and stop tasks. But how do we know this? These are guesses at best, and we will not know the exact time estimates until after EPA reports actual execution times.

Similarly, we must estimate the time to communicate, start a task, and coordinate dataflow between pairs of tasks. The estimates in Figure 12.11(a) are once again guesses that will be changed after EPA results are known.

The need to guess the execution and communication delay times leads to the feedback loop shown in Figure 12.9, and labeled "actuals." Even though the information comes too late for the initial design, it can be used to further tune the application.

Figure 12.11(b) shows one of many possible schedules of minimum execution time for the π problem. Many factors go into scheduling as described in Chapter 9. For example, we could have ignored intertask communication time or not; included interconnection topology or not; included link contention or not; and traded memory for communication time by duplication of identical tasks across the entire set of parallel processors. Task Grapher consists of nine different scheduling heuristics, one for each case of potential interest.

12.4.4 SuperGlue for π

The code fragments for the entire π problem design are listed below:

```
void init(n_in, n, id1, id2, id3, id4, id5, id6, h, x)
    int n_in, *n, *id1, *id2, *id3, *id4, *id5, *id6;
    double *h, *x;
{
  printf ("computation of PI Start\n");
  *n = n_in;
  *h = 1.0 / *n;
  *x = 0.5 * *h;
  *id1 = 1;
  *id2 = 2;
```

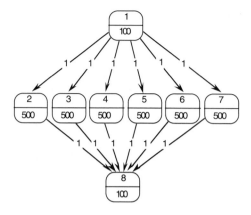

(a) Task graph of pi design created by ppse

Task Graph : Task Graph 1
Topology : Fully Connected, 4 Processors
Heuristic : El-Rewini's Mapping Heuristic - MH

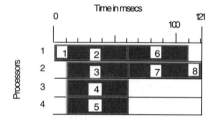

(b) Shortest elapsed time schedule of pi design

Figure 12.11   Task graph and schedule for Pi problem

```
    *id3 = 3;
    *id4 = 4;
    *id5 = 5;
    *id6 = 6;
}
```

(a) source code fragment for INIT node

```
void computation(myid, n, h, x, sum)
      int myid, n;
      float h, x, *sum;
{
    int i, nprocs=6;
    float y;
    printf("computation %d start\n,"myid);
    *sum = 0;
    for (i=myid; i<n; i+=nprocs) {
```

```
      y = x + i * h;
      *sum = *sum + (4.0 / (1.0 + y * y));
   }
      *sum = *sum / n;
}
```

(b) source code fragment for COMPUTATION node

```
void final(sum1, sum2, sum3, sum4, sum5, sum6, tsum)
   int sum1, sum2, sum3, sum4, sum5, sum6;
   float *tsum;
{
   *tsum = sum1 + sum2 + sum3 + sum4 + sum5 + sum6;
   printf ("The result: %f\n," *tsum);
}
```

(c) source code for FINAL node

The necessary glue code for coordination of tasks on some parallel computer is added to these fragments to obtain the final program. Appendix C lists the entire code generated for both C_LINDA and Strand. Brevity dictates that we list only to top level of the Strand version below. Time() is the EPA timing probe routine for capturing execution performance data to be used later for tuning.

```
-compile(free).
-exports([pi/5]).
% ******** main **********
pi(ID2,N,H,X,S):-
     time(0,Y),
     main(ID2,N,H,X,S,Y).
time(X,Y):-
     start_clock(X,Y).
main(START,FINISH,Y):-
     computation:computation(ID2,N,H,X,S2)@1,
     computation:computation(ID3,N,H,X,S3)@2,
     computation:computation(ID4,N,H,X,S4)@2,
     computation:computation(ID5,N,H,X,S5)@3,
     computation:computation(ID1,N,H,X,S1)@1,
     final:final(S1,S2,S3,S4,S5,S6,S)@2,
     init:init(N,ID1,N,H,X,ID2,ID3,ID4,ID5,ID6,)@1,
     computation:computation(ID6,N,H,X,S6)@4.
```

Notice the placement of tasks on the four processors according to the schedule computed by Task Grapher. The lower level details are given in Appendix C. The lowest level implementation is in C and consists of the routines listed above. In this way, Strand handles the communication and synchronization and C handles the actual calculations on each processor.

We did not have to be aware of the target machine other than to tell Task Grapher what its interconnection topology looked like. The details of communication and synchronization have been automated by PPSE's SuperGlue code generator.

12.4.5 EPA

PPSE's EPA (Execution Profile Analyzer) is a small software toolbox similar to the trace routines of PICL. Once installed on the target machine, these routines are called by the application to produce a timing trace of the running program. (The probes are intrusive, hence they may perturb the true timing data.)

SuperGlue automatically inserts the following routines in the appropriate place to collect start and stop times. The full program for π calculation is shown in Appendix C, and contains numerous instances of calls to these routines. The EPA routines are very simple, as listed below:

initialize_clock(): Set the clock to zero, prior to calling all other routines.

get_grain_start_time(processor_id, task_id): Write the start time, processor ID, and task ID to the trace file.

get_grain_stop_time(processor_id, task_id): Write the stop time, procesor ID, and task ID to the trace file.

get_send_begin_time(task_id, name): Write the time at which a message send is initiated to the trace file along with the sending task ID and its name.

get_send_end_time(task_id, name): Write the time at which a message send command is finished to the trace file along with the sending task ID and its name.

get_recv_begin_time(task_id, name): Write the time at which a message is requested by a waiting task to the trace file along with the task ID and its name.

get_recv_end_time(task_id, name): Write the time at which a message is received by a waiting task to the trace file along with the task ID and its name.

The processor_id is an integer identifier unique for each processor. The task_id is an integer identifier that is unique for each task. The name parameter is a string that is used to identify the message that is passed.

Communication time is a mere approximation because it does not account for all delays introduced by the operating system and blocking by other tasks. EPA uses the following formula to approximate communication delay times:

Communication Delay = (SendEndTime - SendBeginTime)
                    + (ReceiveEndTime - ReceiveBeginTime)

An example of the trace file produced by EPA is shown in the table on the next page. EPA reads the trace file information and converts it into an actual schedule showing the actual execution and communication delay times. The actuals are used to draw a speedup graph as shown in Figure 12.12.

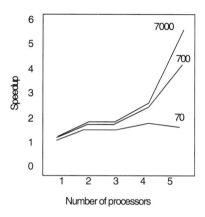

Figure 12.12 Speedup graph for calculation of π on the sequent balance computer using C-LINDA generated from PPSE SuperGlue. Grain sizes are measured in milliseconds

Figure 12.12 illustrates the influence of grain size on speedup. Grain size is measured by the time to compute each parallel task or grain. A large grain size, relative to overhead, produces a near-linear speedup. A small grain size as compared to the overhead of starting a task and communicating data results in a modest speedup.

Figure 12.12 was obtained by PPSE SuperGlue routines that used C-LINDA on the Sequent Balance 21000. As the size of the grain increases on each processor, the effects of task initiation and bus contention are mitigated. The proper balance between task initiation time and grain execution time is needed to realize a significant speedup. Note that speedup is not the same as speed.

Identifier	ProcessorID	TaskID	Clock Value
RecvBegin	1	1	520
RecvEnd	1	1	540
Start	2	1	540
Stop	2	1	2,350
SendBegin	16	1	2,350
SendEnd	16	1	2,360
RecvBegin	5	5	2,360
RecvEnd	5	5	2,360
Start	2	5	2,370
Stop	2	5	4,170
...	...	...	...
Stop	15	9	10,170

Grain size is adjusted in the π calculation problem by increasing the number of iterations performed by each parallel summation. The increase also adds to the accuracy of the estimate, assuming no roundoff errors. For the purposes of this example, we have increased the number of iterations merely to obtain the results shown in Figure 12.12.

The speedup for 70 ms grains is far from linear and in fact shows a decline in performance when 5 processors are used. The improvement peaks at 7,000 ms grains where the speedup is nearly linear.

12.4.6 pRETS

Like most other restructuring tools, the purpose of pRETS is to automatically convert serial Fortran source code into parallel Fortran source code. Unlike other tools, pRETS constructs a new version of the Fortran source in the form of an executable database. The database is actually a Prolog program which can be queried during conversion. In this section we give a brief description of pRETS. For more details, the reader should consult the papers by Harrison et al.

pRETS consists of a FORTRAN analyzer called fa which generates a Prolog knowledge base representing the abstract parse tree of the program. All other pRETS tools work on this knowledge base. The advantage of this approach is that the basic parsing and analysis of the program need only be done once, with a variety of additional tools available that work on the knowledge base. In addition, since the knowledge base is a program, users can easily extend the functionality of the pRETS system by adding their own queries.

fa has the following functionality:

Pretty Print—generate a FORTRAN program from the knowledge base.

Unroll—generate a FORTRAN program from the knowledge base in which all constant bound DO loops have been unrolled, and index constants propagated.

Data Flow—generate another knowledge base representing dataflow among subroutines in the knowledge base created by fa.

Split Subroutines—generate a separate file for each subroutine or function in the FORTRAN program. Later, when using the PPSE Parallax editor, the user can load the text of these files into nodes representing subprograms on the screen.

Build PP File—generate a file that can be imported into the PPSE Parallax Graphical Editor. This allows the user to visually see the relationships among the subprograms and functions in the FORTRAN program.

Browse—load a test file into a window and browse its contents. This is useful for seeing the pretty printed or unrolled version of the original program.

Examples of pRETS/fa

pRETS works off of a Prolog representation of the original Fortran source code. For example, the following Fortran IF statement is converted into Prolog facts as shown below.

Fortran:

```
IF(X .GT.0) THEN
    X = 1
ELSE
    X = 0
ENDIF
```

Prolog:

```
process(3,prog('',2)).
process(2,bif(op('.GT.',var(0),val('0')),0,1)).
process(0,ass(var(0),val('1'))).
process(1,ass(var(0),val('0'))).
store(0,0,'X','variable','REAL').
```

We will not give a complete listing of the conversion, but simply list a few interesting examples here.

Fortran:

```
CALL F()
CALL G(1,2)
```

Prolog:

```
process(47,call('F',[])).
process(48,call('G',[val('1'),val('2')])).
```

Fortran:

```
      GOTO (100,200,300) I
100   X = 10.
200   X = 20.
300   X = 30.
```

Prolog:

```
process(0,cgoto([5,4,3],var(0))).
process(1,ass(var(0),val('10.'))).
process(2,ass(var(0),val('20.'))).
process(3,ass(var(0),val('30.'))).
process(6,comp(0,5)).
process(5,comp(1,4)).
process(4,comp(2,3)).
store(0,0,'I','variable','INTEGER').
```

Fortran:

```
COMMON /DATA/ ARRAY(360000)
INTEGER A,B,C
```

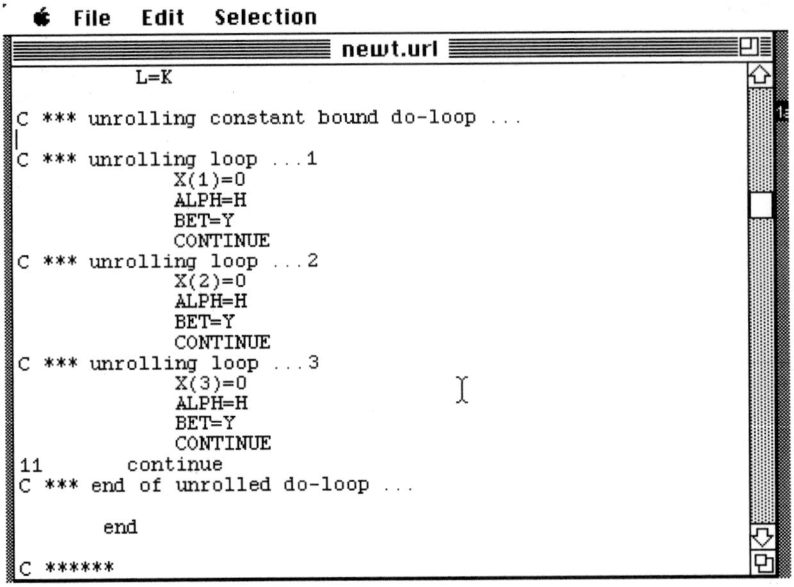

```
                          newt.url
              L=K

C *** unrolling constant bound do-loop ...

C *** unrolling loop ...1
              X(1)=0
              ALPH=H
              BET=Y
              CONTINUE
C *** unrolling loop ...2
              X(2)=0
              ALPH=H
              BET=Y
              CONTINUE
C *** unrolling loop ...3
              X(3)=0
              ALPH=H
              BET=Y
              CONTINUE
11        continue
C *** end of unrolled do-loop ...

          end

C ******
```

Figure 12.13 Loop unrolling by pRETS. Three iterations of the loop are converted into straight-line code which might be executed in parallel

Prolog:

```
process(1,decl('COMMON', '/DATA/ ARRAY(3600000)')
process(2,decl('INTEGER', 'A,B,C')).
```

Fortran:

```
    DO 10 I = 1, 1, 10
    Y = Y + X
10  CONTINUE
    END
```

Prolog:

```
process(3,ass(var(0),val('1'))).
process(0,ass(var(1), op('+', var(1), var(2)))).
process(1,generic('CONTINUE')).
process(4,do(0,3,val('1'),val('10'),2)).
process(2,comp(0,1)).
label(0,1,'10').
store(2,2,'X','variable','REAL').
store(1,1,'Y','variable','REAL').
store(0,0,'I',variable,INTEGER).
```

Using pRETS— pRETS integrates into the PPSE visual interface as illustrated by the next two examples. Loop unrolling and design visualization are two important functions performed by pRETS which aid in semi-automatic conversion.

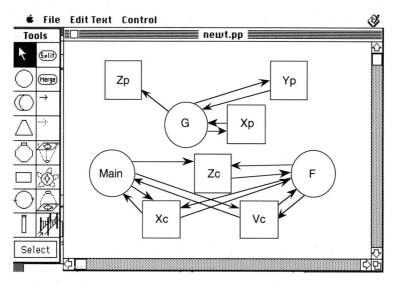

Figure 12.14 Viewing a pRETS knowledge base from within PPSE parallax—only data dependencies are shown

Identifying loop dependencies is helpful for loop unrolling. In loop unrolling, an iteration is physically replicated to avoid the actual loop. Figure 12.13 illustrates an unrolled program segment displayed in a pRETS window:

The original loop (which was DO 11 I=1,3) has been unrolled into three occurrences of the loop, with the index I replaced with its value at each "iteration" through the loop.

Perhaps the most useful capability possessed by the pRETS tool is the capability to export high-level program representations into the PPSE Parallax Graphical Editor. This gives the programmer full access to all of the forward engineering tools provided by PPSE.

An example of the export capability can be seen in Figure 12.14. (The graphical nodes are initially loaded on top of one another and must be arranged by the programmer.) From the diagram in Figure 12.14, we can locate the COMMON variables (Xc, Yc and Zc) shared among subroutines and identify dependencies.

PROBLEMS FOR DISCUSSION AND SOLUTION

1 Modify the summation program written in EXPRESS C to print out the summation of nprocs numbers. Use fsingl(), fmulti(), or fasync() in your solution.

2 Modify the summation program written in EXPRESS C to sum 32 numbers on 5 processors, using a binary tree of partial sums. That is, each processor adds together the partial sums of two subtasks.

3 Parallelize the following C source code for solving a banded matrix system of linear equations using the conjugate gradient method. For the solution in ASPAR, read the paper by Ikudome et al.

```
/* Solve ar[][] * x[] = bb[] by Conjugate gradient
method                       */
/* where ar[][] is a banded matrix with zeros every-
where                        */
/* except along a diagonal band of size
BWidth                                   */
/* Written by K. Ikudome, G. C. Fox, A. Kolawa, and J. Flower    */
/*  Modified by T. Lewis Nov
1990.                                          */
#include "stdio"
#define size 400
#define BWidth 100
#define ep 1.0e-6
float eps;
float ar[size][BWidth], bb[size], xx[size], p[size], x[size];
float r[size], newR[size], newP[size], kP[size], newX[size];
void band(A, x, b, elm, hBWidth)
{
 int elm, hBWidth;
 float A[size][BWidth], x[], b[];
{
  int i, j, band;
  float sum;
  band = hBWidth*2-1;
  for(i=0; i<elm; i++){
    sum = 0.0;
    if(i<hBWidth)
        for(j=0;j<band;j++) sum+=A[i][j]*x[j];
    else
         for(j=0;j<band;j++) sum+=A[i][j]*x[(j+1+(i-hBWidth))];
    b[i] = sum;
  }
}
main()
{
  int i,j,k,elm,hBWidth;
  float sum1,sum2,rd,alpha,beta;
  read_data(ar,xx,bb,elm,hBWidth);
  for(i=0;i<elm;i++){
    X[i] = 0.0;
    P[i] = bb[i];
    R[i] = bb[i];
  }
```

```
 sum1 = 0.0;
for(i=0;i<elm;i++) sum1+=bb[i]*bb[i];
eps=ep*sum1;                    /* RMS error bound   */
k=1;
rd = 100000.0;
while(rd>eps) {                  /* reduce error to limit */
  band(ar, P, kP, elm, hBWidth);
  sum1=sum2=0.0;
  for(i=0;i<elm;i++) sum1+=R[i]*R[i];
  for(i=0;i<elm;i++) sum1+=P[i]*kP[i];
  alpha=sum1/sum2;
  for(i=0;i<elm;i++) newX[i]=X[i]+alpha*P[i];
  for(i=0;i<elm;i++) newR[i]=R[i]*kP[i];
  sum2=0.0;
  for(i=0;i<elm;i++) sum2+=newR[i]*newR[i];
  beta=sum2/sum1;
  for(i=0;i<elm;i++) newP[i]=newR[i]+beta*P[i];
  rd=sum1;
  for(i=0;i<elm;i++){
    P[i]=newP[i];
    R[i]=newR[i];
    X[i]=newX[i];
}
 k++;
}
printresults(X);
}
```

4 Redesign the program in Problem 3 in CODE/ROPE. Do it in PPSE. Break the program into one function per task in your designs.

5 Redesign the π calculation given in Figures 12.10 and 12.11 to run on 6 processors. Compare your solution with the solutions in Appendix C.

6 Assuming speedup is computed from the ratio $T(1)/T(n)$, derive a formula that explains the speedup of Figure 12.12. Let T_0 be the (constant) time for initiating a task.

7 Give a pRETS Prolog equivalent of the following Fortran source code segments:

(a) Fortran:
```
    IF(D .GT.0.0) THEN
        X = SQRT(D)
    ELSE
        X = SQRT(-D)
    ENDIF
```

(b) Fortran:

```
CALL DATAIN(A)
```

(c) Fortran:

```
COMMON /DATA/ A(1000)
INTEGER X,Y
```

(d) Fortran:

```
      DO 10 I = 1, 1, 2
      S = S + I
10    CONTINUE
      END
```

8 Modify the C-LINDA pi program. Run it with 5, then 10 workers. How does the speedup compare?

9 Can the C-LINDA program produced by PPSE be generalized to reduce the redundant pie functions?

References

Ahuja, S., Carriero, N., and Gelernter, D., "Linda and Friends," *Computer,* 19, 8, pp. 26 – 34, August 1986.

Allan, R., Baumgartner, D., Kennedy, K., and Porterfield, A., "PTOOL: A Semi-Automatic Parallel Programming Assistant," *Proceedings International Conference on Parallel Processing,* pp. 164 – 170, August 1986.

Applelbe, W., Smith, K., and McDowell, C., "Start/Pat: A Parallel Programming Toolkit," *IEEE Software,* 6, 4, pp. 29-40, July 1989.

Babb, R. G., "Parallel Processing with Large Grain Data Flow Techniques," *IEEE Computer,* 17(7), pp. 55 – 61, July 1984.

Bates, P., "Distributed Debugging Tools for Heterogeneous Distributed Systems," *Proceedings 8th International Conference on Distributed Computer Systems,* San Jose, pp. 308 – 315, June 1988.

Browne, J. C., Azam, M., and Sobek, S., "CODE: A Unified Approach to Parallel Programming," *IEEE Software,* 6(4), pp. 10 – 17, July 1989.

Carle, A., Cooper, K. D., Hood, R. T., Kennedy, K., Torczon, L., and Warren, S. K., "A Practical Environment for Scientific Programming," *Computer,* 20(11), pp. 75 – 89, November 1987.

Dongarra, J. J., and Sorensen D. C., "SCHEDULE: Tools for Developing and Analyzing Parallel Fortran Programs," *The Characterstics of Parallel Algorithms,* L. H. Jamieson, D. B. Gannon, and R. J. Douglass, eds., The MIT Press, Cambridge, Mass., 1987.

Gelernter, D., "Generative Communication in LINDA," *ACM Trans. Prog. Lang. Systems,* 7, 1, pp. 80 – 112, 1985.

Glinert, E. P., Kopache, M. E., and McIntyre D. W., "Exploring the General-Purpose Visual Alternative," *Journal of Visual Languages and Computing*, **1,** pp. 3 – 39, March 1990.

Harrison, W., Gifford, B., and Gens, C., "pRETS: The Parallel Reverse Engineering Tool Set," *Department of Computer Science,* Portland State University, Portland, Oregon 97207-0751.

Callahan, D., and Kennedy, K., "Compiling Programs for Distributed Memory Multiprocessors," *Journal of Supercomputing*, **2,** No. 2, pp. 171 – 207, 1988.

Francioni, J. M., and Gach, M., *Design of a Communication Modeling Tool for Debugging Parallel Programs (DMCC5),* Charleston, South Carolina, pp. 1201 – 1211, April 1990.

Guarna, V. A., Gannon, D., Jablonowski, D., Maloney, A., D., and Gaur, Y., "Faust: An Integrated Environment for Parallel Programming," *IEEE Software*, 6, 4, pp. 20-28, July 1989.

Harrison, W., "Tools for Multiple CPU Environments," *IEEE Software*, 7, 3, pp. 45-51, May 1990.

Heath, M. T., Geist, G. A., Peyton, B. W., and Worley, P. H., *A User's Guide to PICL (ORNL/TM-11616),* Oak Ridge National Lab., Oak Ridge, TN 37831, October 1990.

Hough, A., and Cuny, J., Belvedere, "Prototype of a Pattern-Oriented Debugger for Highly Parallel Computation," *Proceedings 1987 International Conference Parallel Processing*, pp. 735 – 738, August 1987.

Ikudome, K., Fox, G. C., Kolawa, A., and Flower, J. W., "An Automatic and Symbolic Parallelization System for Distributed Memory Parallel Computers," *Proc. DMCC5,* (Distributed Memory Computing Conference), Charleston, SC. pp. 1105-1114, April 1990.

Kennedy, K., Cooper, K. D., and Torczon, L., "Editing and Compiling Whole Programs," *Proc. ACM SIGSoft/SIGPlan Software Engineering Symp. on Practical Software Development Environments,* ACM, New York, NY., pp. 92-101, 1986.

Meyer, D. E., Wilkerson, R. W., "HIGHLAND: A Graph-Based Parallel Processing Environment for Heterogeneous Local Area Networks," *Proc. DMCC5,* (Distributed Memory Computing Conference), Charleston, SC. pp. 742-749, April 1990.

Muhlenbein, H., Kramer, O., Limburger, F., Mevenkamp, M., and Streitz, S., "MUPPET: A Programming Environment for Message-Based Multiprocessors," *Parallel Computing,* Volume 8, pp. 201 – 221, 1988.

Pancake, C. M., and Utter, S., "Models for Visualization in Parallel Debuggers," *Supercomputing 1989*, Reno, Nevada, pp. 627 – 636, November 1989.

Peir, J. K., Gajski, D. D., and Wu, M. Y., "Programming Environments for Multiprocessors," *Supercomputing*, North-Holland, pp. 73 – 93, 1987.

Snyder, L., "Parallel Programming and the POKER Programming Environment," *IEEE Computer,* pp. 27 – 36, July 1984.

Stotts, P. D., "The PFG Environment: Parallel Programming with Petri Net Semantics," *Proceedings 21st Hawaii International Conference on System Science (HICSS-21),* Kailua, Lona, Volume 2, Software Track, pp. 630 – 638, January 5 – 8, 1988.

Thakkar, S., "Parallel Programming: Harnessing the Hardware," *IEEE Software,* 6(4), special issue on parallel programming, July 1989.

Wu, M. Y., and Gajski, D. D., "Computer-aided Programming for Message-Passing Systems: Problems and a Solution," *IEEE Proceedings,* 77(12): 1983 – 1991, December 1989.

Wu, M. Y., and Gajski, D. D., "Hypertool: A Programming Aid for Message-Passing Systems," *IEEE Trans. Parallel and Distributed Systems,* Volume 1, No. 3, pp. 101 – 119, July 1990.

Zima, H. P., Bast, H. J., and Gerndt, M., "Superb: A Tool for Semi-Automatic MIMD/SIMD Parallelization," *Parallel Computing,* 6(1):1 – 18, January 1988.

SLALOM Benchmark

/

****

S L A L O M

Scalable Language-independent Ames Laboratory One-minute Measurement

The following program is the first benchmark based on fixed time rather
than fixed problem comparison. Not only is fixed time more representative
of the way people use computers, it also greatly increases the scope and
longevity of the benchmark. SLALOM is very scalable, and can be used to
compare computers as slow as 126 floating-point operations per second
(FLOPS) to computers running a trillion times faster. The scalability can
be used to compare single processors to massively parallel collections
of processors, and to study the space of problem size vs. ensemble size
in fine detail. It resembles the LINPACK benchmark since it involves
factoring and backsolving a (nearly) dense matrix, but incorporates a
number of improvements to that benchmark that we hope will make SLALOM
a better reflection of general system performance.

The SLALOM benchmark solves a complete, real problem (optical radiosity
on the interior of a box), not a contrived kernel or a synthetic mixture of
sample operations. SLALOM is unusual since it times input, problem setup,
solution, and output, not just the solution. For slower computers, the
problem setup will take the majority of the time; it grows as the square of
the problem size. The solver grows as the cube of the problem size, and
dominates the time for large values of n.

While the following is C, you are free to translate it into any
language you like, including assembly language specific to one computer.
You may use compiler directives, hand-tuned library calls, loop unrolling,
and even change the algorithm, if you can provide a convincing argument
that the program still works for the full range of possible inputs. For
example, if you replace the direct solver with an iterative one, you must
make sure your method is correct even when the geometry is quite eccentric
and the box faces are highly reflective. (rho = .999)

The main() driver should be used with the value of 60 seconds for the SLALOM benchmark. The work done for a particular problem size is figured after timing has ceased, so there is no overhead for work assessment. The residual check $||Ax - b||$ is also done after timing has ceased. Two computers may be compared either by their problem size n, or by their MFLOPS rate, never by the ratio of execution times. Times will always be near one minute in SLALOM. We have used the following weights for floating-point operation counting, based on the weights used by Lawrence Livermore National Laboratory:

OPERATION	WEIGHT
a=b, a=(constant)	0
a<0, a<=0, a==0, a!=0, a>0, a>=0	0
-a, fabs(a), fsgn(a, b)	0
a+b, a-b, a*b, a^2	1
a<b, a<=b, a==b, a!=b, a>b, a>=b	1
(int) a, (double)b	1
1/a, -1/a	3
a/b	4
sqrt(a)	4
Format to or from ASCII string	6
sin(a), cos(a), tan(a), log(a), atan(a), exp(a)	8

We invite you to share with us the results of any measurements that you make with SLALOM. We do NOT accept anonymous data; machine timings will be referenced and dated.

The least you need to do to adapt SLALOM to your computer is:

1. In the "Measure" routine, set NMAX to a value large enough to keep the computer working for a minute. Vary it slightly if it helps (for reasons of cache size, interleaving, etc.)

2. Replace the timer call in "When" with the most accurate wall-clock timer at your disposal. If only CPU time is available, try to run the job standalone or at high priority, since we are ultimately interested in the top of the statistical range of performance.

3. Edit in the information specific to your test in the "What" routine, so that final output will be automatically annotated.

4. Compile, link, and run the program, interacting to select values of n that bracket a time of one minute. Once everything is running, run it as a batch job so as to record the session.

Examples of ways you may optimize performance:

1. Unroll the loops in SetUp1 and SetUp2; it is possible to vectorize both SetUp1 and SetUp2 at the cost of some extra operations, program complexity, and storage.

2. Replace the innermost loops of Solver with calls to well-tuned libraries of linear algebra routines, such as DDOT from the Basic Linear Algebra Subroutines (level 1 BLAS). Better still, use a tuned library routine for all of Solver; the sparsity exploited in Solver is only a few percent, so you will usually gain more than you lose by applying a dense symmetric solver.

3. Parallelize the SetUp and Solver routines; all are highly parallel. Each element of the matrix can be constructed independently, once each processor knows the geometry and part of the partitioning into regions. A substantial body of literature now exists for performing the types of operations in Solver in parallel.

4. Overlap computation with output. Once the Region routine is done, the first part of the output file (patch geometry) can be written while the radiosities are being calculated.

Examples of what you may NOT do:

1. The tuning must not be made specific to the particular input provided. For example, you may not eliminate IF tests simply because they always come out the same way for this input; you may not use precomputed answers or table look-up unless those answers and tables cover the full range of possible inputs; and you may not exploit symmetry for even values of the problem size.

2. You may not disable the self-consistency tests in SetUp3 and Verify, nor alter their tolerance constants.

3. You may not change the input or output files to unformatted binary or other format that would render them difficult to create or read for humans.

4. You may not eliminate the reading of the "geom" file by putting its data directly into the compiled program.

5. You may not change any of the work assessments in Meter. If you use more floating-point operations than indicated, you must still use the assessments provided. If you find a way to use fewer operations and still get the job done for arbitrary input parameters, please tell us!

                              -John Gustafson, Diane Rover, Michael Carter,
                              and Stephen Elbert
                              Ames Laboratory, Ames, Iowa 50011
                              4/11/91
****
/

/
***/
/* The following program finds a value n such that a problem of size n   */
/* takes just under "goal" seconds to execute.   */
/*   */
/* Calls: Meter   Measures execution time for some application.   */
/*   What   Prints work-timing statistics and system information.   */
/
***/


```c
#include                <stdio.h>
#include                <math.h>
#include                <sys/time.h>

/* NMAX = Largest npatch for your computer; adjust as needed. */
#define     NMAX        2048
#define     EPS         (0.5e-8)
#define     FALSE       (1==0)
#define     TRUE        (!FALSE)
#define     MAX(a,b)    (((a) > (b)) ? (a) : (b))


/* Global variables and function return types: */
double  goal,       /* User input, fixed-time benchmark goal, in seconds. */
        timing,     /* Elapsed time returned by Meter routine, in seconds.*/
        work,       /* In this case, number of FLOPs performed.           */
        When(),     /* Wall clock in seconds.                             */
        Ddot();     /* Double dot product.                                */
int     mean,       /* Avg between upper and lower bounds for bisection   */
                    /* method.                                            */
        n,          /* The problem size.                                  */
        nupper,     /* Upper bound on problem size, used in iterating     */
                    /* toward goal.                                       */
        Meter(),    /* Driver for following benchmark functions.          */
        Reader (),  /* Reads problem description from 'geom' file.        */
        Region (),  /* Subdivides box faces into patches.                 */
        SetUp3 (),  /* Set up matrix to solve.                            */
        Storer (),  /* Write result to 'answer' file.                     */
        Verify ();  /* Verify the radiosity solution from solver.         */
void    SetUp1 (),  /* Set up matrix to solve.                            */
        SetUp2 (),  /* Set up matrix to solve.                            */
```

```
        Solver ();   /* Solve the radiosity matrix.                    */

main ()
{
    int     ok;           /* Return code temporary storage.      */

    /* Get desired number of seconds: */
    printf ("Enter the number of seconds that is the goal: ");
    scanf ("%lg", &goal);

    /* Get lower and upper bounds for n from the standard input device: */
    do {
        printf ("Enter a lower bound for n: ");
        scanf ("%d", &n);
        if (n <= 0)
            exit(0);
        ok = Meter (n, &timing, &work);
        if (timing >= goal)
            printf ("Must take less than %g seconds.  Took %g.\n",
                goal, timing);
    } while (!ok || timing >= goal);

    do {
        printf ("Enter an upper bound for n: ");
        scanf ("%d", &nupper);
        if (nupper <= 0)
            exit(0);
        ok = Meter (nupper, &timing, &work);
        if (timing < goal) {
            printf ("Must take at least %g seconds.  Took %g.\n",
                goal, timing);
            n = MAX(nupper, n);
        }
    } while (!ok || timing < goal);

    /*
     * While the [n, nupper] interval is larger than 1, bisect it and
     * pick a half:
     */
    while (nupper - n > 1) {
        mean = (n + nupper) / 2;
        ok = Meter (mean, &timing, &work);
        if (timing < goal)
            n = mean;
        else
            nupper = mean;
        printf ("New interval: [%d,%d]\n", n, nupper);
```

```
        }

        /* Ensure that most recent run was for n, not nupper. */
        ok = Meter (n, &timing, &work);

        /* Print out final statistics. */
        What (n, timing, work);
}



/
*******************************************************************************/
/* This routine should be edited to contain information for your system.     */
/
*******************************************************************************/
What (n, timing, work)
int n;
double timing, work;
{
        int         i;
        static char *info[] = {
            "Machine:    SUN 4/370GX",
            "Processor:  SPARC + FPU",
            "Memory:     32 MB",
            "# of procs: 1",
            "# used:     1",
            "Cache:      128 KB",
            "NMAX:       512",
            "Clock:      25 MHz",
            "Disk:       .3GB SCSI+.7GB SMD",
            "Node name:  tantalus@al.iastate.edu",
            "OS:         UNIX, SUNOS 4.0.3",
            "Timer:      Wall, gettimeofday()",
            "Alone:      yes",
            "Language:   C",
            "Compiler:   cc",
            "Options:    -dalign -fast -libmil -cg89",
            "Run by:     J. Gustafson, Ames Laboratory",
            "Date:       9 Apr 1991",
            NULL
        };

        printf ("\n");
        for (i = 0 ; info[i] ; i++)
            puts (info[i]);
        printf ("M ops:      %-13lg\n", work * 1e-6);
        printf ("Time:       %-.3lf seconds\n", timing);
```

```
    printf ("n:        %-6d\n", n);
    printf ("MFLOPS:     %-.5lg\n", (work / timing) * 1e-6);
    printf ("Approximate data memory use: %d bytes.\n",
      8 * n * n + 120 * n + 800);
}




/
*****************************************************************************/
/*  This routine measures time required on a revised LINPACK-type benchmark, */
/*  including input, matrix generation, solution, and output.               */
/*                                                                         */
/*  Calls: Reader  Reads the problem description from secondary storage.    */
/*         Region  Partitions box surface into rectangular regions (patches).*/
/*         SetUp1  Sets up equations from patch geometries-parallel faces.  */
/*         SetUp2  Sets up equations from patch geometries-orthogonal faces. */
/*         SetUp3  Sets up equations-row normalization and radiant props.   */
/*         Solver  Solves the equations by LDL factorization.              */
/*         Storer  Stores solution (patch radiosities) on secondary storage. */
/*         When    Returns wall-clock time, in seconds.                    */
/
*****************************************************************************/


Meter (npatch, timing, work)
int     npatch;      /* In, problem size, here the number of equations. */
double  *timing,     /* Out, number of seconds measured.               */
        *work;       /* Out, work done, here the number of FLOPs.      */
{
    static
    double  area[NMAX],       /* Areas of patches * 8 * pi.             */
            box[7],           /* Dimensions of box in x, y, z directions. */
            coeff[NMAX][NMAX], /* The coefficients of the eqns to solve. */
            diag[3][NMAX],    /* Diag terms of the eqns to solve. (RGB) */
            emiss[6][3],      /* (RGB) emissivities of patches.         */
            place[3][NMAX],   /* Width-height-depth position of patches. */
            result[3][NMAX],  /* Answer radiosities (RGB).              */
            rho[6][3],        /* (RGB) Reflectivities of patches.       */
            rhs[3][NMAX],     /* Right-hand sides of eqns to solve (RGB). */
            size[2][NMAX];    /* Width-height sizes of patches.         */
    double  ops[8],           /* Floating-point operation counts.       */
            p[6],             /* Number of patches in faces.            */
            sec[8],           /* Times for routines, in seconds.        */
            tmp1, tmp2;       /* Double temporary variables.            */
    int     i,                /* Loop counter.                          */
            itmp1,            /* Integer temporary variable.            */
            non0;             /* Index of first nonzero off-diagonal elem. */
    static
```

```c
int     loop[6][2];          /* Patch number ranges for faces.          */
static char *tasks[] = {      /* Names of all the functions in benchmark.   */
    "Reader", "Region", "SetUp1", "SetUp2", "SetUp3", "Solver", "Storer"
};
static char *format =         /* Output line format.                     */
    "%6.6s%8.3f%17.0f%14.6f%10.1f %%\n";


/* First check that npatch lies between 6 and NMAX: */
if (npatch < 6) {
    printf ("Must be at least 6, the number of faces.\n");
    return (FALSE);
}
else if (npatch > NMAX) {
    printf ("Exceeds %d = maximum for this system.\n", NMAX);
    return (FALSE);
}


/* Ensure that previous 'answer' file is deleted: */
unlink ("answer");


/* Time the tasks, individually and collectively.   */
sec[0] = When();
if (!Reader (box, rho, emiss))
    return (FALSE);
sec[1] = When();
if (!Region (npatch, loop, box, place, size, area))
    return (FALSE);
sec[2] = When();
SetUp1 (npatch, loop, coeff, place, size);
sec[3] = When();
SetUp2 (npatch, loop, coeff, place, size);
sec[4] = When();
if (!SetUp3 (npatch, loop, area, rho, emiss, coeff, diag, rhs))
    return (FALSE);
sec[5] = When();
non0 = loop[1][0];
Solver (npatch, non0, coeff, diag, rhs, result);
sec[6] = When();
Storer (npatch, loop, place, size, result);
sec[7] = When();
*timing = sec[7] - sec[0];
for (i = 0 ; i < 7 ; i++)
    sec[i] = sec[i+1] - sec[i];


/* Assess floating-point work done by each routine called, and total: */
/* Note the ops counts are talleyed into a double array, and there     */
/* some strange casts to double in some equations.  This is to         */
```

```
    /* prevent integer overflow.                                        */
    itmp1 = 0;
    tmp1 = 0.0;
    for (i = 0 ; i < 6 ; i++) {
        p[i] = loop[i][1] - loop[i][0] + 1;
        tmp1 += p[i] * p[i];
        itmp1 += sqrt(p[i] * box[i] / box[i + 1]) + 0.5;
    }
    tmp2 = p[0] * p[3] + p[1] * p[4] + p[2] * p[5];
    ops[0] = 258;
    ops[1] = 154 + (double) 8 * itmp1 + npatch;
    ops[2] = 6 + 532 * tmp2;
    ops[3] = 8 * npatch
            + 370 * ((double) npatch * npatch - tmp1 - 2 * tmp2) / 2.0;
    ops[4] = 72 + (double) 9 * npatch + (double) npatch * npatch - tmp1;
    ops[5] = npatch * (npatch * ((double) npatch + 7.5) - 2.5) - 21
            + (non0+1) * ((non0+1) * (2 * ((double) non0+1) - 16.5) + 35.5)
            + (non0+1) * npatch * (9 - 3 * ((double) non0+1)));
    ops[6] = 48 * npatch;
    *work = ops[0] + ops[1] + ops[2] + ops[3] + ops[4] + ops[5] + ops[6];

    /* Display timing-work-speed breakdown by routine. */
    printf ("%d patches:\n", npatch);
    printf (" Task  Seconds        Operations      MFLOPS    %% of Time\n");
    for (i = 0 ; i < 7 ; i++) {
        if (sec[i] == 0.0)
            sec[i] = 0.001;
        printf (format, tasks[i], sec[i], ops[i], (ops[i] / sec[i]) * 1e-6,
            100.0 * sec[i] / *timing);
    }
    printf (format, "TOTALS", *timing, *work, (*work / *timing) * 1e-6, 100.0);
    Verify (npatch, coeff, diag, rhs, result);

    return (TRUE);
}


/
*********************************************************************************/
/*  This function should return the actual, wall clock time (not CPU time)   */
/*  in seconds as accurately as possible.  Change it to your system timer.   */
/
*********************************************************************************/
double
When()
{
    struct timeval tp;
    struct timezone tzp;
```

```
        gettimeofday (&tp, &tzp);
        return ((double) tp.tv_sec + (double) tp.tv_usec * 1e-6);
}




/
******************************************************************************/
/* The following routine reads in the problem description from secondary     */
/* storage, and checks that numbers are in reasonable ranges.                */
/
******************************************************************************/
Reader (box, rho, emiss)
double  box[],          /* Out: Dimensions of box in x, y, z directions.   */
        rho[][3],       /* Out: (RGB) Reflectivities of patches.           */
        emiss[][3];     /* Out: (RGB) emissivities of patches.             */
{
    /*
     * Local variables:
     *   infile  Device number for input file.
     *   i, j    Loop counters.
     *   tmp1    Maximum emissivity, to check that emissivities are not all 0.
     */
    int     i, j,       /* Loop counters.                            */
            n;          /* Number of args fscanf()'ed from file.     */
    double  tmp1;       /* Maximum emissivity.                       */
    FILE    *infile;    /* Input file pointer.                       */
    char    buff[81];   /* Buffer used to eat a line of input.       */

    /* Open the input file and read in the data. */
    if ((infile = fopen ("geom", "r")) == NULL) {
        printf ("slalom:  'geom' geometry file not found.\n");
        exit (1);
    }

    /* Read the box coordinates and error check. */
    n = 0;
    for (i = 0 ; i < 3 ; i++) {
        n += fscanf (infile, "%lg", &box[i]);
    }
    fgets (buff, 80, infile);       /* Eat the rest of the line. */
    if (n != 3) {
        printf ("Must specify exactly 3 box coordinates.\n");
        exit(1);
    }

    /* Read the reflectivities and error check. */
```

```
        n = 0;
        for (j = 0 ; j < 3 ; j++) {
            for (i = 0 ; i < 6 ; i++) {
                n += fscanf (infile, "%lg", &rho[i][j]);
            }
        }
        fgets (buff, 80, infile);        /* Eat the rest of the line. */
        if (n != 18) {
            printf ("Must specify exactly 18 box coordinates.\n");
            exit(1);
        }


        /* Read the emissivities and error check. */
        n = 0;
        for (j = 0 ; j < 3 ; j++) {
            for (i = 0 ; i < 6 ; i++) {
                n += fscanf (infile, "%lg", &emiss[i][j]);
            }
        }
        fgets (buff, 80, infile);        /* Eat the rest of the line. */
        if (n != 18) {
            printf ("Must specify exactly 18 box coordinates.\n");
            exit(1);
        }
        fclose (infile);


        /* Now sanity-check the values that were just read. */
        for (j = 0 ; j < 3 ; j++) {
            if (box[j] < 1.0 || box[j] >= 100.0) {
                printf ("Box dimensions must be between 1 and 100.\n");
                return (FALSE);
            }
            box[j+3] = box[j];

            tmp1 = 0.0;
            for (i = 0 ; i < 6 ; i++) {
                if (rho[i][j] < 0.000 || rho[i][j] > 0.999) {
                    printf ("Reflectivities must be between .000 and .999.\n");
                    return (FALSE);
                }
                if (emiss[i][j] < 0.0) {
                    printf ("Emissivity cannot be negative.\n");
                    return (FALSE);
                }
                if (tmp1 < emiss[i][j])
                    tmp1 = emiss[i][j];
            }
```

```
            if (tmp1 == 0.0) {
                printf ("Emissivities are zero.  Problem is trivial.\n");
                return (FALSE);
            }
        }
    box[6] = box[3];
    return (TRUE);
}



/
*****************************************************************************/
/* The following routine decomposes the surface of a variable-sized box      */
/* into patches that are as nearly equal in size and square as possible.     */
/
*****************************************************************************/
Region (npatch, loop, box, place, size, area)

int     npatch,         /* In: Problem size.                          */
        loop[][2];      /* Out: Patch number ranges for faces.        */
double  area[],         /* Out: 8pi * areas of the patches.           */
        box[],          /* In: Dimensions of box in x, y, z directions. */
        place[][NMAX],  /* Out: Width-height-depth positions of patches. */
        size[][NMAX];   /* Out: Width-height sizes of patches.        */

{

    int     icol,   /* Loop counter over the number of columns. */
            ipatch, /* Loop counter over the number of patches. */
            iface,  /* Loop counter over the number of faces.   */
            itmp1,  /* Integer temporary variables.             */
            itmp2,  /* Integer temporary variables.             */
            last,   /* Inner loop ending value.                 */
            lead,   /* Inner loop starting value.               */
            numcol, /* Number of columns on faces.              */
            numpat, /* Number of patches on a face.             */
            numrow; /* Number of rows of patches in a column.   */
    double  height, /* Height of a patch within a column.       */
            tmp1,   /* double temporary variables.              */
            tmp2,   /* double temporary variables.              */
            tmp3,   /* double temporary variables.              */
            tmp4,   /* double temporary variables.              */
            width;  /* Width of a column of patches.            */

    /* Allocate patches to each face, proportionate to area of each face. */
    tmp1 = 2.0 * (box[0] * box[1] + box[1] * box[2] + box[2] * box[0]);
    tmp2 = 0.0;
```

```
tmp3 = npatch;
loop[0][0] = 0;
for (iface = 0 ; iface < 5 ; iface++) {
    tmp2 = tmp2 + box[iface] * box[iface + 1];
    loop[iface][1] = (int) (tmp3 * tmp2 / tmp1 + 0.5) - 1;
    loop[iface + 1][0] = loop[iface][1] + 1;
}
loop[5][1] = npatch - 1;

/* Subdivide each face into numpat patches. */
for (iface = 0 ; iface < 6 ; iface++) {
    numpat = loop[iface][1] - loop[iface][0] + 1;
    tmp3 = 0.0;
    if (iface >= 3)
        tmp3 = box[iface-1];
    numcol = (int) (sqrt(numpat * box[iface] / box[iface + 1]) + 0.5);
    if (numcol > numpat)
        numcol = numpat;
    if (numcol == 0)
        numcol = 1;
    width = box[iface] / numcol;
    itmp1 = numcol - 1;
    tmp1 = 0.0;
    for (icol = 0 ; icol < numcol ; icol++) {
        itmp2 = itmp1 / numcol;
        numrow = (itmp1 + numpat) / numcol - itmp2;
        if (numrow == 0) {
            printf ("Eccentric box requires more patches.\n");
            return (FALSE);
        }
        height = box[iface + 1] / numrow;
        tmp2 = 0.0;
        tmp4 = width * height * (8.0 * M_PI);
        lead = loop[iface][0] + itmp2;
        last = lead + numrow;
        for (ipatch = lead ; ipatch < last ; ipatch++) {
            size[0][ipatch] = width;
            size[1][ipatch] = height;
            place[0][ipatch] = tmp1;
            place[1][ipatch] = tmp2;
            place[2][ipatch] = tmp3;
            area[ipatch] = tmp4;
            tmp2 = tmp2 + height;
        }
        tmp1 = tmp1 + width;
        itmp1 = itmp1 + numpat;
    }
```

```
            }

        return (TRUE);
}



/
*******************************************************************************/
/* This routine sets up the radiosity matrix for parallel patches.           */
/
*******************************************************************************/
void
SetUp1 (npatch, loop, coeff, place, size)
int     npatch,        /* In: Problem size.                                  */
        loop[][2];     /* In: Patch number ranges for faces.                 */
double  coeff[][NMAX], /* Out: The coefficients of the eqns to solve.        */
        place[][NMAX], /* In: Width-height-depth positions of patches.       */
        size[][NMAX];  /* In: Width-height sizes of patches.                 */
{
    int     i, j, k,   /* General loop counters.                             */
            m, n,      /* General loop counters.                             */
            iface,     /* Loop counter over the number of faces.             */
            ipatch,    /* Loop counter over the number of patches.           */
            jface,     /* Face coupled to iface when computing mat. elems.   */
            jpatch;    /* Patch coupled to ipatch when computing mat. elems. */
    double  d[2][2][2],  /* Point-to-point couplings between patch corners.  */
            d2[2][2][2], /* Squares of d values, to save recomputation.      */
            tmp1, tmp2,  /* Double temporary variables.                      */
            tmp3, tmp4,  /* Double temporary variables.                      */
            tmp5, tmp6,  /* Double temporary variables.                      */
            tmp7, tmp8;  /* Double temporary variables.                      */

        for (iface = 0 ; iface < 3 ; iface++) {
            jface = iface + 3;
            tmp1 = place[2][loop[jface][0]] * place[2][loop[jface][0]];
            tmp6 = tmp1 + tmp1;
            for (ipatch = loop[iface][0] ; ipatch <= loop[iface][1] ; ipatch++) {
                for (jpatch=loop[jface][0] ; jpatch <= loop[jface][1] ; jpatch++) {
                    for (j = 0 ; j < 2 ; j++) {
                        d [0][0][j] = place[j][jpatch] - place[j][ipatch];
                        d [1][0][j] = d[0][0][j] + size[j][jpatch];
                        d [0][1][j] = d[0][0][j] - size[j][ipatch];
                        d [1][1][j] = d[1][0][j] - size[j][ipatch];
                        d2[0][0][j] = d[0][0][j] * d[0][0][j];
                        d2[1][0][j] = d[1][0][j] * d[1][0][j];
                        d2[0][1][j] = d[0][1][j] * d[0][1][j];
                        d2[1][1][j] = d[1][1][j] * d[1][1][j];
```

```
            }


        tmp2 = 0.0;
          for (m = 0 ; m < 2 ; m++) {
              for (i = 0 ; i < 2 ; i++) {
                  tmp3 = d2[m][i][1] + tmp1;
                  tmp4 = sqrt(tmp3);
                  tmp5 = 1.0 / tmp4;
                  tmp8 = 0.0;
                  for (k = 0 ; k < 2 ; k++) {
                      for (n = 0 ; n < 2 ; n++) {
                          tmp7 = d[k][n][0];
                          tmp8 = -tmp7 * atan(tmp7 * tmp5) - tmp8;
                      }
                      tmp8 = -tmp8;
                  }
                  tmp2 = -4.0 * tmp4 * tmp8 - tmp2 - tmp6 *
                    log(((d2[1][0][0] + tmp3) * (d2[0][1][0] + tmp3)) /
                       ((d2[0][0][0] + tmp3) * (d2[1][1][0] + tmp3)));
              }
              tmp2 = -tmp2;
          }
          for (m = 0 ; m < 2 ; m++) {
              for (i = 0 ; i < 2 ; i++) {
                  tmp4 = sqrt(d2[m][i][0] + tmp1);
                  tmp5 = 1.0 / tmp4;
                  tmp8 = 0.0;
                  for (k = 0 ; k < 2 ; k++) {
                      for (n = 0 ; n < 2 ; n++) {
                          tmp7 = d[k][n][1];
                          tmp8 = -tmp7 * atan(tmp7 * tmp5) - tmp8;
                      }
                      tmp8 = -tmp8;
                  }
                  tmp2 = -4.0 * tmp4 * tmp8 - tmp2;
              }
              tmp2 = -tmp2;
          }
          coeff[ipatch][jpatch] = tmp2;
          coeff[jpatch][ipatch] = tmp2;
      }
    }
   }
  }
```

```
/
************************************************************************/
/* This routine sets up the radiosity matrix for orthogonal patches.    */
/
************************************************************************/
void
SetUp2 (npatch, loop, coeff, place, size)
int     npatch,         /* In: Problem size.                      */
        loop[][2];      /* In: Patch number ranges for faces.     */
double  coeff[][NMAX],  /* Out: The coefficients of the eqns to solve. */
        place[][NMAX],  /* In: Width-height-depth positions of patches. */
        size[][NMAX];   /* In: Width-height sizes of patches.     */
{
    int     m,          /* General loop counters.                 */
            iface,      /* Loop counter over the number of faces. */
            ipatch,     /* Loop counter over the number of patches. */
            jface,      /* Face coupled to iface when computing mat. elems. */
            jpatch;     /* Patch coupled to ipatch when computing mat. elems.*/

    double  tmpb, tmpa,
            c11d, c12d, c21d, c22d, c11s, c12s, c21s, c22s,
            d11d, d12d, d21d, d22d, d11s, d12s, d21s, d22s,
            d11i, d12i, d21i, d22i, a10s, a20s, b01s, b02s,
            e1111, e1211, e2111, e2211, e1112, e1212, e2112, e2212,
            e1121, e1221, e2121, e2221, e1122, e1222, e2122, e2222;

    for (iface = 0 ; iface < 6 ; iface++) {
        for (m = 0 ; m < 2 ; m++) {
            jface = (iface + m + 1) % 6;
            for (ipatch=loop[iface][0] ; ipatch <= loop[iface][1] ; ipatch++) {
                a10s = place[m][ipatch] - place[2][loop[jface][0]];
                a20s = a10s + size[m][ipatch];
                a10s = a10s * a10s;
                a20s = a20s * a20s;
                for (jpatch=loop[jface][0] ; jpatch<=loop[jface][1];jpatch++) {
                    c11d = place[m][jpatch] - place[1-m][ipatch];
                    c12d = c11d + size[m][jpatch];
                    c21d = c11d - size[1-m][ipatch];
                    c22d = c12d - size[1-m][ipatch];
                    c11s = c11d * c11d;
                    c12s = c12d * c12d;
                    c21s = c21d * c21d;
                    c22s = c22d * c22d;
                    b01s = place[1 - m][jpatch] - place[2][ipatch];
                    b02s = b01s + size[1 - m][jpatch];

                    /* Bump the term by a small real to avoid
```

```
/* singularities in coupling function:
b01s = b01s * b01s + 1e-35;
b02s = b02s * b02s + 1e-35;
d11s = a10s + b01s;
d12s = a10s + b02s;
d21s = a20s + b01s;
d22s = a20s + b02s;
d11d = sqrt(d11s);
d12d = sqrt(d12s);
d21d = sqrt(d21s);
d22d = sqrt(d22s);
d11i = 1.0 / d11d;
d12i = 1.0 / d12d;
d21i = 1.0 / d21d;
d22i = 1.0 / d22d;

tmpa =    d11d * ( c11d * atan (c11d * d11i)
                 - c12d * atan (c12d * d11i)
                 - c21d * atan (c21d * d11i)
                 + c22d * atan (c22d * d11i))
        + d12d * (-c11d * atan (c11d * d12i)
                 + c12d * atan (c12d * d12i)
                 + c21d * atan (c21d * d12i)
                 - c22d * atan (c22d * d12i))
        + d21d * (-c11d * atan (c11d * d21i)
                 + c12d * atan (c12d * d21i)
                 + c21d * atan (c21d * d21i)
                 - c22d * atan (c22d * d21i))
        + d22d * ( c11d * atan (c11d * d22i)
                 - c12d * atan (c12d * d22i)
                 - c21d * atan (c21d * d22i)
                 + c22d * atan (c22d * d22i));

e1111 = c11s + d11s;
e1211 = c12s + d11s;
e2111 = c21s + d11s;
e2211 = c22s + d11s;
e1112 = c11s + d12s;
e1212 = c12s + d12s;
e2112 = c21s + d12s;
e2212 = c22s + d12s;
e1121 = c11s + d21s;
e1221 = c12s + d21s;
e2121 = c21s + d21s;
e2221 = c22s + d21s;
e1122 = c11s + d22s;
e1222 = c12s + d22s;
```

```
                    e2122 = c21s + d22s;
                    e2222 = c22s + d22s;

                    tmpb =     c11s * log( e1111 * e1122 / (e1112 * e1121))
                             - c12s * log( e1211 * e1222 / (e1212 * e1221))
                             - c21s * log( e2111 * e2122 / (e2112 * e2121))
                             + c22s * log( e2211 * e2222 / (e2212 * e2221))
                             - d11s * log( e1111 * e2211 / (e1211 * e2111))
                             + d12s * log( e1112 * e2212 / (e1212 * e2112))
                             + d21s * log( e1121 * e2221 / (e1221 * e2121))
                             - d22s * log( e1122 * e2222 / (e1222 * e2122));

                    coeff[ipatch][jpatch] = fabs(4.0 * tmpa + tmpb);
                    coeff[jpatch][ipatch] = coeff[ipatch][jpatch];
                }
            }
        }
    }
}


/
***************************************************************************/
/* This routine sets up the radiosity matrix... normalizes row sums to 1,  */
/* and includes terms derived from reflectivites and emissivities of faces. */
/
***************************************************************************/
SetUp3 (npatch, loop, area, rho, emiss, coeff, diag, rhs)
int     npatch,          /* In: Problem size.                              */
        loop[][2];       /* In: Patch number ranges for faces.             */
double  area[],          /* In: 8 * pi * areas of the patches.             */
        rho[][3],        /* In: (RGB) Reflectivities of the face interiors.  */
        emiss[][3],      /* In: (RGB) Emissivities of the face interiors.   */
        coeff[][NMAX],   /* Out: The coefficients of the eqns to solve.    */
        diag[][NMAX],    /* Out: (RGB) Diagonal terms of the system.        */
        rhs[][NMAX];     /* Out: (RGB) Right-hand sides of system to solve. */
{

    /*
     * Local variables:
     *    iface    Loop counter over the number of faces.
     *    ipatch   Outer loop counter over the number of patches.
     *    j        Loop counter over each color (R-G-B).
     *    jpatch   Inner loop counter over the number of patches.
     *    tmp1     double temporary variable.
     *    vtmp1-2  double vector temporary variables.
     */
```

```
    int     j,          /* (RGB) Loop counter over each color.          */
            iface,      /* Loop counter over the number of faces.       */
            ipatch,     /* Outer loop counter over the number of patches. */
            jpatch;     /* Inner loop counter over the number of patches. */
    double  tmp1,       /* Double temporary variable.                   */
            vtmp1[3],   /* Double vector temporary variables.           */
            vtmp2[3];   /* Double vector temporary variables.           */

    /* Ensure that row sums to 1, and put in reflectivities (rho) and   */
    /* emissivities.                                                    */
    for (iface = 0 ; iface < 6 ; iface++) {
        for (j = 0 ; j < 3 ; j++) {
            vtmp1[j] = 1.0 / rho[iface][j];
            vtmp2[j] = emiss[iface][j] * vtmp1[j];
        }
        for (ipatch = loop[iface][0] ; ipatch <= loop[iface][1] ; ipatch++) {
            tmp1 = 0.0;
            for (jpatch = 0 ; jpatch < loop[iface][0] ; jpatch++) {
                tmp1 += coeff[ipatch][jpatch];
            }
            for (jpatch = loop[iface][1]+1 ; jpatch < npatch ; jpatch++) {
                tmp1 += coeff[ipatch][jpatch];
            }
            /* Make sure row sum (total form factor) is close to 1: */
            if (fabs(tmp1 - area[ipatch]) > (0.5e-9 * tmp1)) {
                printf ("Total form factor is too far from unity.\n");
                return (FALSE);
            }
            tmp1 = -tmp1;
            /* Set coplanar patch interactions to zero. */
            for (jpatch=loop[iface][0] ; jpatch <= loop[iface][1] ; jpatch++) {
                coeff[ipatch][jpatch] = 0.0;
            }
            /* Assign diagonal entries and right-hand sides. */
            for (j = 0 ; j < 3 ; j++) {
                diag[j][ipatch] = vtmp1[j] * tmp1;
                rhs[j][ipatch] = vtmp2[j] * tmp1;
            }
        }
    }
    return (TRUE);
}



/
**************************************************************************/
/* This routine factors and backsolves a real, symmetric, near-dense matrix */
```

```
/* by LDL factorization.  No pivoting; the matrix is diagonally dominant.    */
/
************************************************************************************/
void
Solver (npatch, non0, coeff, diag, rhs, result)
int     npatch,        /* In: Problem size.                                   */
        non0;          /* In: Index of first nonzero off-diagonal mat. elem.*/
double  coeff[][NMAX], /* In/Out: The coefficients of the eqns to solve.     */
        diag[][NMAX],  /* Out: (RGB) Diagonal terms of the system.           */
        rhs[][NMAX],   /* In: (RGB) Right-hand sides of system to solve.     */
        result[][NMAX]; /* Out: (RGB) solution radiosities.                  */
{
    int    i, j,       /* General loop counters.       */
           k, m;       /* General loop counters.       */
    double tmp1;       /* Double temporary variable. */

    /* Load lower triangle of coefficients, diagonal, and solution vector. */
    for (m = 0 ; m < 3 ; m++) {
        for (i = non0 ; i < npatch ; i++) {
            coeff[i][i] = diag[m][i];
            result[m][i] = rhs[m][i];
            for (j = 0 ; j < i ; j++) {
                coeff[i][j] = coeff[j][i];
            }
        }

        /* Factor matrix, writing factors on top of original matrix. */
        for (j = 0 ; j < non0 ; j++) {
            coeff[j][j] = 1.0 / diag[m][j];
            result[m][j] = rhs[m][j];
        }

        for (j = non0 ; j < npatch ; j++) {
            for (k = non0 ; k < j ; k++) {
                coeff[j][k] -= Ddot (k, &coeff[k][0], 1, &coeff[j][0], 1);
            }
            for (k = 0 ; k < j ; k++) {
                tmp1 = coeff[j][k];
                coeff[j][k] = tmp1 * coeff[k][k];
                coeff[j][j] -= tmp1 * coeff[j][k];
            }
            coeff[j][j] = 1.0 / coeff[j][j];
        }

        /* Backsolve, in three stages (for L, D, and L transpose). */
        for (k = non0 ; k < npatch ; k++) {
            result[m][k] -= Ddot (k, &result[m][0], 1, &coeff[k][0], 1);
```

```
        }

        for (k = 0 ; k < npatch ; k++) {
            result[m][k] *= coeff[k][k];
        }

        for (k = npatch - 2 ; k >= non0 ; k--) {
            result[m][k] -= Ddot (npatch-(k+1), &result[m][k+1], 1,
                                  &coeff[k+1][k], NMAX);
        }

        for (k = non0 - 1 ; k >= 0 ; k--) {
            result[m][k] -= Ddot (npatch-non0, &result[m][non0], 1,
                                  &coeff[non0][k], NMAX);
        }

    }
}


/
***************************************************************************/
/* The following routine writes the answer to secondary storage.          */
/
***************************************************************************/
Storer (npatch, loop, place, size, result)
int      npatch,          /* In: Problem size.                            */
         loop[][2];        /* In: Patch number ranges for faces.           */
double   result[][NMAX],  /* In: (RGB) Radiosity solutions.               */
         place[][NMAX],   /* In: Width-height-depth positions of patches. */
         size[][NMAX];    /* In: Width-height sizes of patches.           */
{
    int    i,             /* General loop counter.                        */
           iface,          /* Loop counter over number of faces.           */
           ipatch;         /* Loop counter of number of patches within a face. */
    FILE   *outfile;      /* Output file pointer.                         */

    /* Write patch geometry to 'answer' file. */
    if ((outfile = fopen("answer", "w")) == NULL) {
        printf ("Unable to open 'answer' file.\n");
        exit (1);
    }
    fprintf (outfile, "%d patches:\n", npatch);
    fprintf (outfile,
      " Patch  Face       Position in w, h, d            Width    Height\n");
    for (iface = 0 ; iface < 6 ; iface++) {
        for (ipatch = loop[iface][0] ; ipatch <= loop[iface][1] ; ipatch++) {
            fprintf (outfile,
```

```
                        "%5d   %4d%11.51f%11.51f%11.51f   %11.51f%11.51f\n",
                    ipatch+1, iface+1,
                    place[0][ipatch],
                    place[1][ipatch],
                    place[2][ipatch],
                    size[0][ipatch],
                    size[1][ipatch]);
        }
    }

    /* Write patch radiosities to 'answer' file. */
    fprintf (outfile, "\n Patch  Face  Radiosities\n");
    for (iface = 0 ; iface < 6 ; iface++) {
        for (ipatch = loop[iface][0] ; ipatch <= loop[iface][1] ; ipatch++) {
            fprintf (outfile, "%5d   %4d%12.81f%12.81f%12.81f\n",
                    ipatch+1, iface+1,
                    result[0][ipatch],
                    result[1][ipatch],
                    result[2][ipatch]);
        }
    }
    fclose(outfile);
}



/
******************************************************************************/
/* This routine verifies that the computed radiosities satisfy the equations.*/
/*                                                                            */
/*  John Gustafson, Diane Rover, Michael Carter, and Stephen Elbert           */
/*  Ames Laboratory, 3/18/91                                                  */
/
******************************************************************************/
Verify (npatch, coeff, diag, rhs, result)
int     npatch;         /* In: Problem size.                               */
double  coeff[][NMAX],  /* In: The coefficients of the eqns to solve.      */
        diag[][NMAX],   /* In: (RGB) Diagonal terms of the system.         */
        rhs[][NMAX],    /* In: (RGB) Right-hand sides of system to solve.  */
        result[][NMAX]; /* In: (RGB) Radiosity solutions.                  */
{
    double  tmp1, tmp2; /* Double temporary variables. */
    double  anorm,      /* Norm accumulation variable. */
            xnorm;      /* Norm accumulation variable. */
    int     i, j, m;    /* General loop counters.      */

    tmp1 = 0.0;
    for (m = 0 ; m < 3 ; m++) {
```

```
        /* Copy lower triangle of coefficients to upper triangle, */
        /* and load diagonal.                                    */
        for (i = 0 ; i < npatch ; i++) {
            coeff[i][i] = diag[m][i];
            for (j = 0 ; j < i ; j++) {
                coeff[i][j] = coeff[j][i];
            }
        }
        /* Multiply matrix by solution vector, and accum. norm of residual. */
        anorm = xnorm = 0.0;
        for (j = 0 ; j < npatch ; j++) {
            tmp2 = rhs[m][j];
            for (i = 0 ; i < npatch ; i++) {
                tmp2 -= (coeff[j][i] * result[m][i]);
                anorm = MAX(anorm, fabs(coeff[j][i]));
            }
            xnorm = MAX(xnorm, fabs(result[m][j]));
            tmp1 += fabs(tmp2);
        }
    }
    /* printf ("anorm = %g  xnorm = %g\n", anorm, xnorm); */
    tmp1 /= (anorm * xnorm);
    if (tmp1 > 3 * EPS) {
        printf ("Residual is too large: %1g\n", tmp1);
        return (FALSE);
    }
    return (TRUE);
}


#ifdef     SUN4



/
***********************************************************************/
/* Double precision dot product specifically written for Sun 4/370.   */
/* By Michael Carter and John Gustafson, May 30, 1990                  */
/* This code unrolls the dot product four ways since that's how many   */
/* registers are available on the SPARC.  Other RISC system will require */
/* something very similar.  Also, unit stride is take advantage of in the */
/* form of special cases.                                              */
/
***********************************************************************/
double
Ddot (n, a, ia, b, ib)
register
int    n,      /* Number of elements in vectors.  */
       ia,     /* Stride of a vector in ELEMENTS. */
```

```
        ib;      /* Stride of b vector in ELEMENTS. */
register
double  *a,     /* Pointer to first vector.        */
        *b;     /* Pointer to second vector.       */
{
    register double sum0 = 0.0,
                    sum1 = 0.0,
                    sum2 = 0.0,
                    sum3 = 0.0;
    register int    m = n & 3;
    int             t;

    /* The ragged cleanup part. */
    while (m--) {
        sum0 += *a * *b;
        a += ia;
        b += ib;
    }


    /* The fast pipelined part */
    n >>= 2;
    if (ib == 1 && ia != 1) {
        t = ia;
        ia = ib;
        ib = t;
        t = (int) a;
        b = a;
        a = (double *) t;
    }

    /* We can optimize if one or more strides are equal to 1. */
    if (ia == 1) {
        /* This runs if both strides are 1. */
        if (ib == 1) {
            ia <<= 2;
            ib <<= 2;
            while (n--) {
                sum0 += a[0] * b[0];
                sum1 += a[1] * b[1];
                sum2 += a[2] * b[2];
                sum3 += a[3] * b[3];
                a += ia;
                b += ib;
            }
        }
        /* This runs if stride of a only is equal to 1. */
        else {
```

```
            ia <<= 2;
            while (n--) {
                sum0 += a[0] * *b;
                b += ib;
                sum1 += a[1] * *b;
                b += ib;
                sum2 += a[2] * *b;
                b += ib;
                sum3 += a[3] * *b;
                a += ia;
                b += ib;
            }
        }
    }
    /* This runs for the more general case.        */
    /* This is about .5 MFLOPS slower on Sun 4/370 */
    else {
        while (n--) {
            sum0 += *a * *b;
            a += ia;
            b += ib;
            sum1 += *a * *b;
            a += ia;
            b += ib;
            sum2 += *a * *b;
            a += ia;
            b += ib;
            sum3 += *a * *b;
            a += ia;
            b += ib;
        }
    }


    return (sum0 + sum1 + sum2 + sum3);
}


#else


/
*******************************************************************************/
/* Generic double-precision dot product.  Unrolling will help pipelined      */
/* computers.  Modify accordingly.                                           */
/
*******************************************************************************/
double
Ddot (n, a, ia, b, ib)
```

```
register
int      n,        /* Number of elements in vectors.   */
         ia,       /* Stride of a vector in ELEMENTS.  */
         ib;       /* Stride of b vector in ELEMENTS.  */
register
double  *a,        /* Pointer to first vector.         */
        *b;        /* Pointer to second vector.        */
{
    register double sum = 0.0;

    while (n--) {
        sum += *a * *b;
        a += ia;
        b += ib;
    }
    return (sum);
}


#endif
```

DataParallel C Implementation of Gaussian Ellimination

```
/* This program completely solves a system of linear equations using
   (1) gaussian elimination with partial pivoting and (2) back substitution.
   Contributed by Mike Quinn 1990. */

#define N        128
#define EPSILON  1.0e-08
#define FALSE    0
#define TRUE     1
#define ID       (this-r)

domain system { double a[N+1]; int pivot; int marked;
                void back_substitution();
                void initialize_system();
                int gaussian_elmination(); } r[N];

main()
{
   double coeff;
   int    picked;
   void   print_results();
   int    solution;

   initialize_system();
   solution = gaussian_elimination();
   if (solution) {
      back_substitution();
      print_results();
   } else printf ("No solution\n");
}

void system::initialize_system()
{
   int j, seed;
   float random();
```

```
      marked[i] = 0;
      seed = ID * ID;
      a[N] = 0.0;
      for (j = 0; j < N; j++) {
         a[j] = random(&seed);
         a[N] += j * a[j];
      }
   }


int system::gaussian_elimination()
{
   int i, k;

   for (i = 0; i < N - 1 ; i++) {
      if (!marked) {
         double tmp;
         tmp = fabs(a[i]);
         if (tmp == (>?= tmp)) picked = ID;
         if (ID == picked) {
            marked = 1;    /* Mark pivot row */
            pivot = i;     /* Remember permuted position */
         }
      }
      double row[N+1];
      row = r[picked].a;
      if (fabs(row[i]) < EPSILON) return (FALSE);

      if (!marked) {
         tmp = a[i] / row[i];
         for (k = i; k < N+1; k++)
            a[k] = a[k] - row[k] * tmp;
      }
   }
   if (!marked) pivot = N-1;
   return (TRUE);
}


void system::back_substitution()
{
   int i;

   for (i = N-1; i >= 0; i--) {
      if (pivot == i)
         picked = ID;
      coeff = r[picked].a[N] / r[picked].a[i];
      if (pivot < i)
```

```
            a[N] -= coeff * a[i];
    }
}


void print_results()
{
    int i;

    for (i = 0; i < N; i++)
        printf ("x[%d] = %10.6f\n", pivot[i], a[i][N]/a[i][pivot[i]]);
}


/* C routines to generate random numbers (90.08.27) */
/*      Adapted from "Algorithms," Robert Sedgewick */

#define random_b  31415821
#define random_m  100000000
#define random_m1 10000


int mult(p,q)
    int p, q;
{
    int p1, p0, q1, q0;
    p1 = p / random_m1;
    p0 = p % random_m1;
    q1 = q / random_m1;
    q0 = q % random_m1;
    return ((((p0*q1+p1*q0)%random_m1)*random_m1+p0*q0)%random_m);
}


float random(random_a)
    int *random_a;
{
    *random_a = (mult(*random_a,random_b)+1)%random_m;
    return ((float)*random_a/(float)random_m);
}
```

Appendix C

PPSE Solution to π Calculation

Strand<u>88</u> Source Code Generated By PPSE

```
-compile(free).
-exports([pi/5]).

% ******** main **********
pi(ID2,N,H,X,S):-
      time(0,Y),
      main(ID2,N,H,X,S,Y).
time(X,Y):-
      start_clock(X,Y).
main(START,FINISH,Y):-
      computation:computation(ID2,N,H,X,S2)@1,
      computation:computation(ID3,N,H,X,S3)@2,
      computation:computation(ID4,N,H,X,S4)@2,
      computation:computation(ID5,N,H,X,S5)@3,
      computation:computation(ID1,N,H,X,S1)@1,
      final:final(S1,S2,S3,S4,S5,S6,S)@2,
      init:init(N,ID1,N,H,X,ID2,ID3,ID4,ID5,ID6,)@1,
      computation:computation(ID6,N,H,X,S6)@4.

init(N,ID1,N,H,X,ID2,ID3,ID4,ID5,ID6,):-
      start_time(1, 16, Z00001),
      init_time(N,ID1,N,H,X,ID2,ID3,ID4,ID5,ID6,,Z00001,Z00002),
      stop_time(1, 16, Z00002,Z0003).
start_time(X,Y,Z):-
      get_grain_start_time(X,Y,Z).
stop_time(X,Y,Z1,Z2):-
      get_send_begin_time(16, id1_n_h_x,Z000001),
      get_send_begin_time(16, id2_n_h_x,Z000002),
      get_send_begin_time(16, id3_n_h_x,Z000003),
      get_send_begin_time(16, id4_n_h_x,Z000004),
      get_send_begin_time(16, id5_n_h_x,Z000005),
      get_send_begin_time(16, id6_n_h_x,Z000006),
      get_grain_stop_time(X,Y,Z2).
```

```prolog
init_time(N,ID1,N,H,X,ID2,ID3,ID4,ID5,ID6,,Z00001,Z00002):-
        Z00002 is Z00001,
        init_f(N,ID1,N,H,X,ID2,ID3,ID4,ID5,ID6,).


computation(ID2,N,H,X,S2):-
        start_time(2, 4, Z00001),
        computation_time(ID2,N,H,X,S2,Z00001,Z00002),
        stop_time(2, 4, Z00002,Z0003).
start_time(X,Y,Z):-
        get_send_end_time(16, id2_n_h_x,Z000001),
        get_recv_begin_time(4, id2_n_h_x,Z000002),
        get_recv_end_time(4, id2_n_h_x,Z000003),
        get_grain_start_time(X,Y,Z).
stop_time(X,Y,Z1,Z2):-
        get_send_begin_time(4, s2,Z000004),
        get_grain_stop_time(X,Y,Z2).
computation_time(ID2,N,H,X,S2,Z00001,Z00002):-
        Z00002 is Z00001,
        computation_f(ID2,N,H,X,S2).


final(S1,S2,S3,S4,S5,S6,S):-
        start_time(1, 14, Z00001),
        final_time(S1,S2,S3,S4,S5,S6,S,Z00001,Z00002),
        stop_time(1, 14, Z00002,Z0003).
start_time(X,Y,Z):-
        get_send_end_time(12, s1,Z000001),
        get_send_end_time(12, s2,Z000002),
        get_send_end_time(12, s3,Z000003),
        get_send_end_time(12, s4,Z000004),
        get_send_end_time(12, s5,Z000005),
        get_send_end_time(12, s6,Z000006),
        get_recv_begin_time(14, s1,Z000007),
        get_recv_begin_time(14, s2,Z000008),
        get_recv_begin_time(14, s3,Z000009),
        get_recv_begin_time(14, s4,Z0000010),
        get_recv_begin_time(14, s5,Z0000011),
        get_recv_begin_time(14, s6,Z0000012),
        get_recv_end_time(14, s1,Z0000013),
        get_recv_end_time(14, s2,Z0000014),
        get_recv_end_time(14, s3,Z0000015),
        get_recv_end_time(14, s4,Z0000016),
        get_recv_end_time(14, s5,Z0000017),
        get_recv_end_time(14, s6,Z0000018),
        get_grain_start_time(X,Y,Z).
stop_time(X,Y,Z1,Z2):-
        get_grain_stop_time(X,Y,Z2).
final_time(S1,S2,S3,S4,S5,S6,S,Z00001,Z00002):-
```

```
        Z00002 is Z00001,
        final_f(S1,S2,S3,S4,S5,S6,S).
```

Foreign Function Interface

```
100    body start_clock start_clock (int?,int^) c
101    body get_grain_start_time get_grain_start_time (int?,int?,int^) c
102    body get_grain_stop_time get_grain_stop_time (int?,int?,int^) c
103    body get_send_begin_time get_send_begin_time (int?,char[]?,int^) c
104    body get_send_end_time get_send_end_time (int?,char[]?,int^) c
105    body get_recv_begin_time get_recv_begin_time (int?,char[]?,int^) c
106    body get_recv_end_time get_recv_end_time (int?,char[]?,int^) c
107    body computation_f computation (int?,int?,chars?,chars?,chars^) c
108    body final_f final (chars?,chars?,chars?,chars?,chars?,chars?,chars^) c
109    body init_f init (int?,int^,int^,chars^,chars^,int^,int^,char-
s^,chars^,int^,int^,chars^,chars^,int^,int^,chars^,chars^,int^,int^,chars^,cha
rs^,int^,int^,chars^,chars^) c
```

MAKE File for Building π Application

```
#    Default makefile for building Strand Abstract Machine
#    Version 1.1
#    (See usermake.template)

CFLAGS    = -O
LINKFLAGS = -Z800000
THISFILE  = PI.make
USIFS     = PI.sif
UOBJECTS  = time_strand.o computation.o final.o init.o
LIBS      = -lpps -lm

strand:& st.o samlib.o libuser.a $(UOBJECTS)
cc $(LINKFLAGS) -o strand st.o samlib.o $(UOBJECTS) libuser.a $(LIBS)

safe:
 rm -f samlib.h
chmod u+w user.h
ln -s user.h samlib.h
 touch samlib.h
make $(MFLAGS) -f $(THISFILE)

fast:
```

```
 rm -f samlib.h
chmod u+w userfast.h
ln -s userfast.h samlib.h
 touch samlib.h
make $(MFLAGS) -f $(THISFILE)


samlib.o $(UOBJECTS):samlib.h


samlib.c:$(USIFS)
 malis $(USIFS)


samlib.h:
chmod u+w user.h
ln -s user.h samlib.h
 touch samlib.h
```

C-LINDA Source Code for π Calculation Generated By PPSE

```
#include <stdio.h>
#include "time_linda_c.h"
#include "computation.c"
#include "final.c"
#include "init.c"

/* window start : PI */

int computation_4(id2,n,h,x,s2)
int *id2;
int *n;
chars *h;
chars *x;
chars *s2;
{
    get_grain_start_time(2, 4);
    computation(id2,n,h,x,s2);
    get_grain_stop_time(2, 4);
}


int computation_6(id3,n,h,x,s3)
int *id3;
int *n;
chars *h;
chars *x;
chars *s3;
```

```
{
     get_grain_start_time(1, 6);
     computation(id3,n,h,x,s3);
     get_grain_stop_time(1, 6);
}


int computation_8(id4,n,h,x,s4)
int *id4;
int *n;
chars *h;
chars *x;
chars *s4;
{
     get_grain_start_time(1, 8);
     computation(id4,n,h,x,s4);
     get_grain_stop_time(1, 8);
}


int computation_10(id5,n,h,x,s5)
int *id5;
int *n;
chars *h;
chars *x;
chars *s5;
{
     get_grain_start_time(1, 10);
     computation(id5,n,h,x,s5);
     get_grain_stop_time(1, 10);
}


int computation_12(id1,n,h,x,s1)
int *id1;
int *n;
chars *h;
chars *x;
chars *s1;
{
     get_grain_start_time(4, 12);
     computation(id1,n,h,x,s1);
     get_grain_stop_time(4, 12);
}


int final_14(s1,s2,s3,s4,s5,s6,s)
```

```
chars *s1;
chars *s2;
chars *s3;
chars *s4;
chars *s5;
chars *s6;
chars *s;
{
    get_grain_start_time(1, 14);
    final(s1,s2,s3,s4,s5,s6,s);
    get_grain_stop_time(1, 14);
}


int init_16(n,id1,n,h,x,id2,n,h,x,id3,n,h,x,id4,n,h,x,id5,n,h,x,id6,n,h,x)
int *n;
int *id1;
int *n;
chars *h;
chars *x;
int *id2;
int *n;
chars *h;
chars *x;
int *id3;
int *n;
chars *h;
chars *x;
int *id4;
int *n;
chars *h;
chars *x;
int *id5;
int *n;
chars *h;
chars *x;
int *id6;
int *n;
chars *h;
chars *x;
{
    get_grain_start_time(1, 16);
    init(n,id1,n,h,x,id2,n,h,x,id3,n,h,x,id4,n,h,x,id5,n,h,x,id6,n,h,x);
    get_grain_stop_time(1, 16);
}
```

```
int computation_18(id6,n,h,x,s6)
int *id6;
int *n;
chars *h;
chars *x;
chars *s6;
{
     get_grain_start_time(3, 18);
     computation(id6,n,h,x,s6);
     get_grain_stop_time(3, 18);
}


/*    scheduling   */

int processor1()
{
     int *n;
     int *id1;
     int *n;
     chars *h;
     chars *x;
     int *id2;
     int *n;
     chars *h;
     chars *x;
     int *id3;
     int *n;
     chars *h;
     chars *x;
     int *id4;
     int *n;
     chars *h;
     chars *x;
     int *id5;
     int *n;
     chars *h;
     chars *x;
     int *id6;
     int *n;
     chars *h;
     chars *x;
     chars *s3;
     chars *s5;
     chars *s4;
     chars *s1;
     chars *s2;
```

```
chars *s6;
chars *s;

get_recv_begin_time (16, "init_13_n");
in ("init_13_n", ?n);
get_recv_end_time ("16, "init_13_n");
init_16 (n,id1,n,h,x,id2,n,h,x,id3,n,h,x,id4,n,h,x,id5,n,h,x,id6,n,h,x);
get_send_begin_time (16, "computation_1_id1");
out ("computation_1_id1", *id1);
get_send_end_time (16, "computation_1_id1");
get_send_begin_time (16, "computation_1_n");
out ("computation_1_n", *n);
get_send_end_time (16, "computation_1_n");
get_send_begin_time (16, "computation_1_h");
out ("computation_1_h", *h);
get_send_end_time (16, "computation_1_h");
get_send_begin_time (16, "computation_1_x");
out ("computation_1_x", *x);
get_send_end_time (16, "computation_1_x");
get_send_begin_time (16, "computation_2_id2");
out ("computation_2_id2", *id2);
get_send_end_time (16, "computation_2_id2");
get_send_begin_time (16, "computation_2_n");
out ("computation_2_n", *n);
get_send_end_time (16, "computation_2_n");
get_send_begin_time (16, "computation_2_h");
out ("computation_2_h", *h);
get_send_end_time (16, "computation_2_h");
get_send_begin_time (16, "computation_2_x");
out ("computation_2_x", *x);
get_send_end_time (16, "computation_2_x");
get_send_begin_time (16, "computation_3_id3");
out ("computation_3_id3", *id3);
get_send_end_time (16, "computation_3_id3");
get_send_begin_time (16, "computation_3_n");
out ("computation_3_n", *n);
get_send_end_time (16, "computation_3_n");
get_send_begin_time (16, "computation_3_h");
out ("computation_3_h", *h);
get_send_end_time (16, "computation_3_h");
get_send_begin_time (16, "computation_3_x");
out ("computation_3_x", *x);
get_send_end_time (16, "computation_3_x");
get_send_begin_time (16, "computation_4_id4");
out ("computation_4_id4", *id4);
get_send_end_time (16, "computation_4_id4");
get_send_begin_time (16, "computation_4_n");
```

```
out ("computation_4_n", *n);
get_send_end_time (16, "computation_4_n");
get_send_begin_time (16, "computation_4_h");
out ("computation_4_h", *h);
get_send_end_time (16, "computation_4_h");
get_send_begin_time (16, "computation_4_x");
out ("computation_4_x", *x);
get_send_end_time (16, "computation_4_x");
get_send_begin_time (16, "computation_5_id5");
out ("computation_5_id5", *id5);
get_send_end_time (16, "computation_5_id5");
get_send_begin_time (16, "computation_5_n");
out ("computation_5_n", *n);
get_send_end_time (16, "computation_5_n");
get_send_begin_time (16, "computation_5_h");
out ("computation_5_h", *h);
get_send_end_time (16, "computation_5_h");
get_send_begin_time (16, "computation_5_x");
out ("computation_5_x", *x);
get_send_end_time (16, "computation_5_x");
get_send_begin_time (16, "computation_6_id6");
out ("computation_6_id6", *id6);
get_send_end_time (16, "computation_6_id6");
get_send_begin_time (16, "computation_6_n");
out ("computation_6_n", *n);
get_send_end_time (16, "computation_6_n");
get_send_begin_time (16, "computation_6_h");
out ("computation_6_h", *h);
get_send_end_time (16, "computation_6_h");
get_send_begin_time (16, "computation_6_x");
out ("computation_6_x", *x);
get_send_end_time (16, "computation_6_x");


get_recv_begin_time (6, "computation_3_id3");
in ("computation_3_id3", ?id3);
get_recv_end_time ("6, "computation_3_id3");
get_recv_begin_time (6, "computation_3_n");
in ("computation_3_n", ?n);
get_recv_end_time ("6, "computation_3_n");
get_recv_begin_time (6, "computation_3_h");
in ("computation_3_h", ?h);
get_recv_end_time ("6, "computation_3_h");
get_recv_begin_time (6, "computation_3_x");
in ("computation_3_x", ?x);
get_recv_end_time ("6, "computation_3_x");
computation_6 (id3,n,h,x,s3);
get_send_begin_time (6, "final_9_s3");
```

```
out ("final_9_s3", *s3);
get_send_end_time (6, "final_9_s3");


get_recv_begin_time (10, "computation_5_id5");
in ("computation_5_id5", ?id5);
get_recv_end_time ("10, "computation_5_id5");
get_recv_begin_time (10, "computation_5_n");
in ("computation_5_n", ?n);
get_recv_end_time ("10, "computation_5_n");
get_recv_begin_time (10, "computation_5_h");
in ("computation_5_h", ?h);
get_recv_end_time ("10, "computation_5_h");
get_recv_begin_time (10, "computation_5_x");
in ("computation_5_x", ?x);
get_recv_end_time ("10, "computation_5_x");
computation_10 (id5,n,h,x,s5);
get_send_begin_time (10, "final_11_s5");
out ("final_11_s5", *s5);
get_send_end_time (10, "final_11_s5");


get_recv_begin_time (8, "computation_4_id4");
in ("computation_4_id4", ?id4);
get_recv_end_time ("8, "computation_4_id4");
get_recv_begin_time (8, "computation_4_n");
in ("computation_4_n", ?n);
get_recv_end_time ("8, "computation_4_n");
get_recv_begin_time (8, "computation_4_h");
in ("computation_4_h", ?h);
get_recv_end_time ("8, "computation_4_h");
get_recv_begin_time (8, "computation_4_x");
in ("computation_4_x", ?x);
get_recv_end_time ("8, "computation_4_x");
computation_8 (id4,n,h,x,s4);
get_send_begin_time (8, "final_10_s4");
out ("final_10_s4", *s4);
get_send_end_time (8, "final_10_s4");


get_recv_begin_time (14, "final_7_s1");
in ("final_7_s1", ?s1);
get_recv_end_time ("14, "final_7_s1");
get_recv_begin_time (14, "final_8_s2");
in ("final_8_s2", ?s2);
get_recv_end_time ("14, "final_8_s2");
get_recv_begin_time (14, "final_9_s3");
in ("final_9_s3", ?s3);
get_recv_end_time ("14, "final_9_s3");
get_recv_begin_time (14, "final_10_s4");
```

```
          in ("final_10_s4", ?s4);
          get_recv_end_time ("14, "final_10_s4");
          get_recv_begin_time (14, "final_11_s5");
          in ("final_11_s5", ?s5);
          get_recv_end_time ("14, "final_11_s5");
          get_recv_begin_time (14, "final_12_s6");
          in ("final_12_s6", ?s6);
          get_recv_end_time ("14, "final_12_s6");
          final_14 (s1,s2,s3,s4,s5,s6,s);
          get_send_begin_time (14, "EXTERNAL_s");
          out ("EXTERNAL_s", *s);
          get_send_end_time (14, "EXTERNAL_s");
}


int processor2()
{
          int *id2;
          int *n;
          chars *h;
          chars *x;
          chars *s2;

          get_recv_begin_time (4, "computation_2_id2");
          in ("computation_2_id2", ?id2);
          get_recv_end_time ("4, "computation_2_id2");
          get_recv_begin_time (4, "computation_2_n");
          in ("computation_2_n", ?n);
          get_recv_end_time ("4, "computation_2_n");
          get_recv_begin_time (4, "computation_2_h");
          in ("computation_2_h", ?h);
          get_recv_end_time ("4, "computation_2_h");
          get_recv_begin_time (4, "computation_2_x");
          in ("computation_2_x", ?x);
          get_recv_end_time ("4, "computation_2_x");
          computation_4 (id2,n,h,x,s2);
          get_send_begin_time (4, "final_8_s2");
          out ("final_8_s2", *s2);
          get_send_end_time (4, "final_8_s2");
}

int processor3()
{
          int *id6;
          int *n;
          chars *h;
          chars *x;
          chars *s6;
```

```
        get_recv_begin_time (18, "computation_6_id6");
        in ("computation_6_id6", ?id6);
        get_recv_end_time ("18, "computation_6_id6");
        get_recv_begin_time (18, "computation_6_n");
        in ("computation_6_n", ?n);
        get_recv_end_time ("18, "computation_6_n");
        get_recv_begin_time (18, "computation_6_h");
        in ("computation_6_h", ?h);
        get_recv_end_time ("18, "computation_6_h");
        get_recv_begin_time (18, "computation_6_x");
        in ("computation_6_x", ?x);
        get_recv_end_time ("18, "computation_6_x");
        computation_18 (id6,n,h,x,s6);
        get_send_begin_time (18, "final_12_s6");
        out ("final_12_s6", *s6);
        get_send_end_time (18, "final_12_s6");
}


int processor4()
{
        int *id1;
        int *n;
        chars *h;
        chars *x;
        chars *s1;

        get_recv_begin_time (12, "computation_1_id1");
        in ("computation_1_id1", ?id1);
        get_recv_end_time ("12, "computation_1_id1");
        get_recv_begin_time (12, "computation_1_n");
        in ("computation_1_n", ?n);
        get_recv_end_time ("12, "computation_1_n");
        get_recv_begin_time (12, "computation_1_h");
        in ("computation_1_h", ?h);
        get_recv_end_time ("12, "computation_1_h");
        get_recv_begin_time (12, "computation_1_x");
        in ("computation_1_x", ?x);
        get_recv_end_time ("12, "computation_1_x");
        computation_12 (id1,n,h,x,s1);
        get_send_begin_time (12, "final_7_s1");
        out ("final_7_s1", *s1);
        get_send_end_time (12, "final_7_s1");
}


/*   main program   */
real_main()
```

```
{
    eval (processor1());
    eval (processor2());
    eval (processor3());
    eval (processor4());
}
```

Index